HOSTELS GERMANY

HELP US KEEP THIS GUIDE UP TO DATE

Every effort has been made by the authors and editors to make this guide as accurate and useful as possible. However, many things can change after a guide is published—establishments close, phone numbers change, facilities come under new management, etc.

We would love to hear from you concerning your experiences with this guide and how you feel it could be improved and be kept up to date. While we may not be able to respond to all comments and suggestions, we'll take them to heart and we'll also make certain to share them with the authors. Please send your comments and suggestions to the following address:

The Globe Pequot Press
Reader Response/Editorial Department
P.O. Box 480
Guilford, CT 06437

Or you may e-mail us at:

editorial@globe-pequot.com

Thanks for your input, and happy travels!

HOSTELS SERIES

HOSTELS GERMANY

The Only Comprehensive,

Unofficial,

Opinionated

Guide

Paul Karr
and Martha Coombs

Guilford, Connecticut

Cover, text, and map design: M. A. Dubé
Contributing freelancers: Klaus Heindl and Michael Roth
Other assistance: Evan Halper

Library of Congress Cataloging-in-Publication Data
  Karr, Paul.
    Hostels Germany : the only comprehensive, unofficial, opinionated guide / by Paul Karr and Martha Coombs. — 1st ed.
        p.   cm. — (Hostels series)
      ISBN 0-7627-0919-7
    1. Tourist camps, hostels, etc.—Germany—Guidebooks. I. Coombs, Martha. II. Title. III. Series.

TX907.5.G5 K35 2001
647.9443'06—dc21   2001023231

Manufactured in the United States of America
First Edition/First Printing

CONTENTS

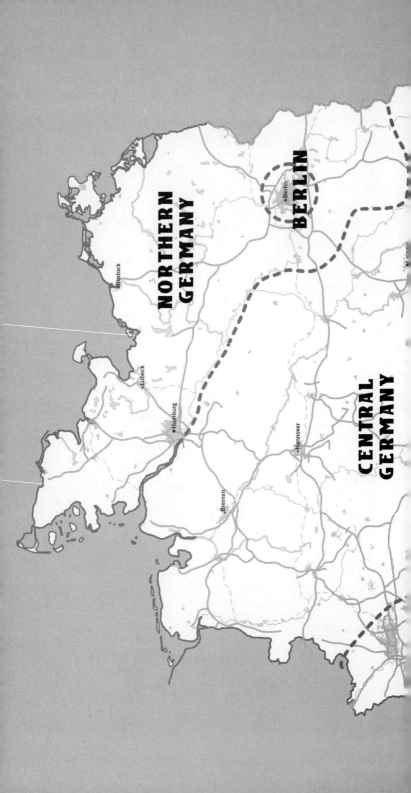

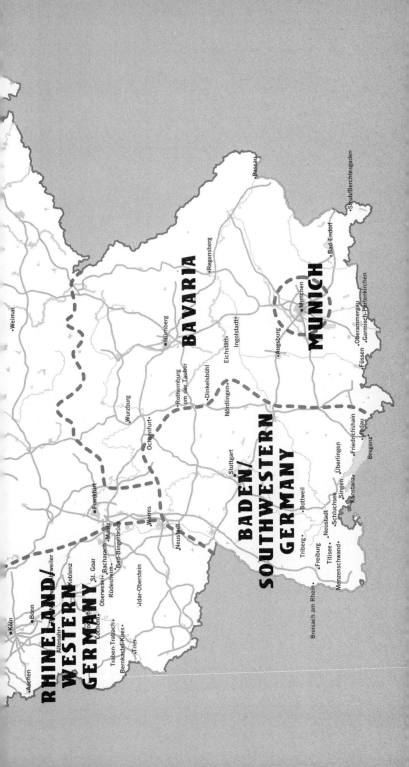

RHINELAND/
WESTERN
GERMANY

BAVARIA

BADEN/
SOUTHWESTERN
GERMANY

MUNICH

Aachen

Köln
Bonn

Altenahr
Ahrweiler
Koblenz

Cochem

Traben-Trabach
Bernkastel-Kues

Trier

Oberwesel
Rüdesheim
Mainz

St. Goar
Bacharach
Bad-Bingerbrüs

Idar-Oberstein

Worms

Frankfurt

Neustadt

Weimar

Würzburg

Ochsenfurt

Rothemburg
om der Tauber

Dinkelsbühl

Nördlingen

Nürnberg

Regensberg

Eichstätt

Ingolstadt

Passau

Bad Endorf

Schtb/Berchtesgaden

München

Augsburg

Oberammergau
Garmisch-Partenkirchen

Füssen

Stuttgart

Bottweil

Triberg
Freiburg

Titisee
Neustadt

Menzenschwand

Schluchsee
Singen

Konstanz
Lindau

Überlingen

Friedrichshain

Bregenz

Breisach am Rhein

ACKNOWLEDGMENTS

Paul Karr thanks Martha once again for companionship and editorial assistance. She is simply stunning. Martha thanks her friends, family, and teachers—especially language teachers—as well as the music of Fred J Eaglesmith. And Paul. Very special thanks from us both to Hammy for inspiration and song.

From both of us, thanks to the following, who went beyond the call of duty: Knut Dinter of the DJH for photos; Hedda Manhardt of the Munich Tourism Office and Ingrid Scherer-Mohr of the German National Tourist office for giving patient answers to our frequent questions; and Toby Pyle of American Youth Hostels for a world of help as well as continuous encouragement and assistance.

Thanks again to our friends in New England, Europe, Georgia, Canada, and Japan. Special thanks to the Karr, Coombs, Couture, and Bottinger families for bringing light and joy to our travels, for being our homes away from home.

Thanks to the good folks at TravelGuard for attending to our travel insurance needs; CellHire for handling all our communication needs; and to efficient and pleasant Kemwel for assisting with auto rental arrangements. DER Travel of Chicago, a topflight tour company, gets our hearty thanks for lots of information and assistance and for making rail travel throughout Germany and Europe a real pleasure. They are true professionals. And thanks to gonzo freelancers Klaus Heindl and Michael Roth in Germany for deciphering the German hostel system and contributing some wickedly funny write-ups.

And thanks, finally, to a world (literally) of new friends met or made on the road. So many of you have taught us about your corner of the world or otherwise made this work enjoyable and useful.

Thank you all.

The prices and rates listed in this guidebook were confirmed at press time. We recommend, however, that you call establishments before traveling to obtain current information.

HOW TO USE THIS BOOK

What you're holding in your hands is the first-ever attempt of its kind: a fairly complete listing and rating of the most popular hostels in Germany. Dozens of hostellers from countries all over the globe were interviewed in the course of putting this guide together, and their comments and thoughts run throughout its pages. Who knows? You, yourself, might be quoted somewhere inside.

We wrote this guide for two pretty simple reasons: First, we wanted to bring hostelling to a wider audience. Hostels continue to grow in popularity, but many North American travelers still don't think of them as options when planning a trip. We wanted to encourage that because—at its best—the hostelling experience brings people of greatly differing origins, faiths, and points of view together in a convivial setting. You learn about these people, and also about the place in which the hostel is situated, in a very personal way that no textbook could ever provide.

Second, we wanted very much to give people our honest opinions of the hostels. You wouldn't send your best friend to a fleabag, and we don't want readers traveling great distances only to be confronted with filthy kitchens, nasty managers, or dangerous neighborhoods. At least, we thought, we could warn them about unsafe or unpleasant situations ahead of time.

Of course we would also tip our friends off to the truly wonderful hostels—the ones with treehouses, cafes, free breakfasts, and real family spirit. So that's what we've done. Time after time on the road, we have heard fellow travelers complaining that the guidebooks they bought simply listed places to stay but didn't rate them. Well, now we've done it—and we haven't pulled a single punch or held back a bit of praise.

How We Wrote This Book

The authors, along with a cadre of assistants, fanned out across Germany with notebooks and laptops in hand during the summer of 2000. Sometimes we identified ourselves in advance as authors; sometimes we just popped in for surprise visits. We counted rooms, turned taps, tested beds. And then we talked with managers and staff.

Before we left we also took the time to interview plenty of hostellers in private and get their honest opinions about the places they were staying or had already stayed.

The results are contained within this book: actual hosteller quotes, opinions, ratings and more.

What Is a Hostel?

If you've picked up this book, you probably know what a hostel is. A surprising number of people interviewed for this book, however, weren't sure at all what it means.

So let's check your knowledge with a little pop quiz. Sharpen up your pencils, put on your thinking caps, then dive in.

1. A hostel is:

    A. a hospital.

    B. a hospice.

    C. a hotel.

    D. a drunk tank.

    E. none of the above.

        (correct answer worth 20 points)

2. A hostel is:

    A. a place where international travelers bunk up.

    B. a cheap sleep.

    C. a place primarily dedicated to bunks.

    D. all of the above.

        (correct answer worth 20 points)

3. You just turned 30. Word on the street has it that you'll get turned away for being that age. Do you tell the person at the hostel desk the grim news?

    A. No, because a hostel is restricted to students under twenty-seven.

    B. No, because a hostel is restricted to elderly folks over sixty-five.

    C. No, because they don't care about your midlife crisis.

    D. Yes.

        (correct answer worth 10 points)

4. You spy a shelf labeled FREE FOOD! in the hostel kitchen. What do you do?

    A. begin stuffing pomegranates in your pockets.

    B. ask the manager how Food ended up in jail.

    C. run for your life.

        (correct answer worth 5 points)

5. Essay question. Why do you want to stay in a hostel?
(extra credit; worth up to 45 points)

Done? Great! And the envelope, please. . .

1. **E.** None of the above. The word *hostel* is German, and it means "country inn for youngsters" or something like that.
2. **D.** All of the above. You got that one, right?
3. **D.** Normally, there are no age limits or restrictions at a hostel. However, in Bavaria—the south of Germany—there *is* an age limit; if you're twenty-seven or older, you can stay only under special conditions. Some hostels in Berlin also enforce this unfair restriction. (see chapters 6 and 7 for details.)
4. **A.** Free means free.
5. Give yourself 15 points for every use of the word "friends," "international," or "cool," okay? But don't give yourself more than 45. Yes, we mean it. Don't make us turn this car around right now. We will. We mean it.

What? All you wrote was "It's cheap"? Okay, okay, give yourself 20 points.

So how did you do?

100 points:	Born to be wild
80–100:	Get your motor runnin'
40–80:	Head out on the highway
20–40:	Lookin' for adventure
0–20:	Hope you don't come my way

Don't be embarrassed if you flunked this little quiz, though. Hostel operators get confused and blur the lines, too. You'll sometimes find a campground or retreat center or college setting aside a couple bunks—and calling itself a hostel anyway. In those cases we've used our best judgment about whether a place is or isn't a hostel.

Also, we excluded some joints—no matter how well-meaning—if they (a) exclude men or women, (b) serve primarily as a university residence hall (with a very few special exceptions), or (c) serve you a heavy side of religious doctrine with the eggs in the morning.

In a few cases our visits didn't satisfy us either way; those places were either left out, set aside for a future edition, or briefly described here but not rated.

The bottom line? If it's in this book, it probably is a hostel. If it isn't, it's not, and don't let anyone tell you otherwise. There. 'Nuff said.

Understanding the Ratings

All the listings information in this book was current as of press time. Here's the beginning of an entry in the book, from a hostel in the Rhine Valley.

JUGENDBURG STAHLECK

(Bacharach Hostel)

55422 Bacharach

Phone: 06743–1266

Fax: 06743–2684
E-mail: jh-bacharach@djh-info.de
Web site: www.djh-info.de
Rates: 25,20 DM–31,20 DM per Hostelling International member (about $13–$16 US); doubles 73 DM (about $37 US)
Beds: 166
Private/family rooms: Yes
Kitchen available: No
Credit cards: No
Season: Closed December 24 to December 26
Affiliation: Hostelling International-DJH
Regional hostel office: Rheinland-Pfalz/Saarland
Extras: Table tennis, piano, cafeteria ($), patio

First things first. See those little pictures? Those are icons, and they signify something important we wanted you to know about the hostel. We've printed a key to these icons on page 6.

The overall hostel rating consists of those hip-looking thumbs sitting atop each entry. It's pretty simple: Thumbs up means good. Thumbs down means bad.

We've used these thumbs to compare the hostels to one another; only a select number of hostels earned the top rating of two thumbs up, and a few were considered unpleasant enough to merit a thumb down. You can use this rating as a general assessment of a hostel.

Often we didn't give any thumbs at all to a hostel that was a mixed-bag experience. Or maybe, for one reason or another—bad weather, bad luck, bad timing, remoteness, an inability to get ahold of the staff, or our own confusion about the place—we just didn't feel we collected enough information to properly rate that hostel for you.

That said, here's a key to what these ratings mean:

Cream of the crop; recommended

Pretty good

No thumbs   OK; average; jury's still out

So-so

Only if you're desperate

The rest of the information is pretty much self-explanatory:

Address is usually the hostel's street address; occasionally we add the mailing address if that's where the hostel gets mail.

Phone number is the primary phone number.

Fax number is the primary fax number.

E-mail is the staff's e-mail address, for those who want to get free information or (sometimes) book a room by computer.

Web site indicates a hostel's World Wide Web page address.

Rates are the cost per person to stay at the hostel—when all the currency converting's said and done, expect to pay somewhere around $15 US per person, more (sometimes considerably more) in cities or popular tourist areas. For private or family rooms, we've listed the total price for two people to stay in the room; usually it's higher than the cost of two singles, sometimes considerably so. Single or triple room rates will vary; ask ahead if you're unsure what you'll pay.

Note that these rates sometimes vary by season, or by membership in a hostelling group such as Hostelling International (HI); we have tried to include a range of prices where applicable. Most HI member hostels, for instance, charge $2.00 to $4.00 extra per day if you don't belong to one of Hostelling International's worldwide affiliates.

Also, a few hostels might charge you about $1.00 to supply sheets or towels if you haven't brought your own. (Sleeping bags, no matter how clean you think they are, are often frowned upon.) Finally, various local, municipal, or other taxes might add slightly to the rates quoted here.

Credit cards can be a good way to pay for a bed in a foreign country (you get the fairest exchange rates on your home currency); here, we have mentioned whether cards are accepted by the hostels. More and more hostels are taking them, and even if we haven't listed a hostel as accepting credit cards things may have changed. When in doubt, call ahead and ask.

Beds indicates the number of beds available at the hostel.

Private/family rooms are rooms for a couple, a family with children, or (sometimes) a single traveler. Sometimes it's nice to have your own room on the road: It's more private, more secure, and your snoring won't bother anyone. They're becoming more common in Europe but are still hard to snag during the busy season.

KEY TO ICONS

 Attractive natural setting

 Ecologically aware hostel

 Superior kitchen facilities or great cafe/restaurant

 Offbeat or eccentric place

 Superior bathroom facilities

 Romantic private rooms

 Comfortable beds

 A particularly good value

 Wheelchair accessible

 Good for business travelers

 Especially well suited for families

 Good for active travelers

 Visual arts at hostel or nearby

 Music at hostel or nearby

 Great hostel for skiers

 Bar or pub at hostel or nearby

 Editors' choice: among our very favorite hostels

So book months ahead for one if you're going to a popular place like Berlin or Munich. Really.

Kitchen available simply indicates whether the hostel allows hostellers to cook in a kitchen or not. In North America and the UK, almost every hostel has a kitchen—but the situation changes in Germany. Very few of these hostels have a kitchen setup. Almost all, however, with very few exceptions, serve a delicious meal instead, so take advantage and fill 'er up. Breakfast is often included with the price of your bed, and if it is we have noted this under "Extras" (see below).

Office hours indicates the hours when staff are at the front desk and answer the phones, or at least would consider answering the phones. Although European custom is to use military time (23:30 for 11:30 P.M.), we've used "American" time throughout this book.

Keep in mind that nothing is fixed in stone, however; some hostel staffs will happily field calls in the middle of the night if you're reasonable, while others can't stand it. Try to call within the listed hours if possible.

A good rule to follow: The smaller a place, the harder it is for the owner/manager to drag him/herself out of bed at four in the morning just because you lost your way. Big-city hostels, however, frequently operate just like hotels—somebody's always on duty, or at least on call.

Do keep in mind that Germans are notorious for their strict attitudes toward time and punctuality. Don't expect the front desk to stay open a few minutes late or end the lockout ten minutes early. Don't knock it; adapt and deal. It's just their way.

Season indicates what part of the year a hostel is open—if it's closed part of the year. We've made our best effort at listing the seasons of each hostel, but schedules sometimes change according to weather or a manager's vacation plans. Call if you're unsure whether a hostel will be open when you want to stay there.

Lockout and **Curfew.** Some hostels have hours during which you are locked out of the place (in other words, you're not permitted on the premises). Some also have a curfew; be back inside before this time, or you'll be locked out for the night.

Affiliation indicates whether a hostel is affiliated with Hostelling International. For more information about what these organizations do, see "About Affiliation" (page 11).

Extras lists some of the other amenities that come with a stay at the hostel. Some—but not all—will be free; there's an amazing variety of services, and almost as big a variety in managers' willingness to do nice things for free. Laundries, for instance, are never free, and there's almost always a charge for meals, lockers, bicycle or other equipment rentals, and other odds and ends. On the other hand, some hostels maintain free information desks, and a few will pick you up at rail stations and the like.

With each entry, we've also given you a little more information about the hostel, to make your stay a little more informed—and

8   HOSTELS GERMANY

fun. The sidebar to the left is part of the hostel entry that began above.

What does all that stuff mean?

Best bet for a bite tells you where to find food in the area; usually, we'll direct you to the cheapest and closest supermarket. But sometimes, in the interest of variety—and good eatin'—we'll point you toward a surprising health food store, a farmers' market or place rich with local color, or even a fancy place well worth the splurge.

Insiders' tip is a juicy secret about the area, something we didn't know until we got to the hostel ourselves.

What hostellers say relates what hostellers told us about a hostel—or what we imagine they would say.

Gestalt is the general feeling of a place, our (sometimes humorous) way of describing what it's about.

Best bet for a bite:
Hotel Kranenturm

Insiders' tip:
Fritz's wine bar
(Weingut)

What hostellers say:
"The best I've ever seen!"

Gestalt:
Bacharach on track

Hospitality:

Cleanliness:

Party index:

Safety rates urban hostels only, so this hostel didn't include this rating. This grade is normally based on both the quality of the neighborhood and the security precautions taken by the hostel staff.

 No worries

 Dial 911

Hospitality rates the hostel staff's friendliness toward hostellers (and travel writers).

 Smile city

 Very hostile hostel

Cleanliness rates, what else, the general cleanliness of a place. Bear in mind that this can change—rapidly—depending on the time of year, turnover in staff, and so forth. Use it only as a general guide.

 Spic-and-span

 Don't let the bedbugs bite

The **party index** is our way of tipping you off about the general scene at the hostel:

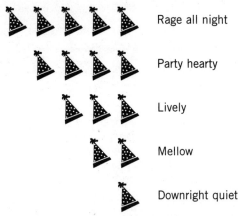

Rage all night

Party hearty

Lively

Mellow

Downright quiet

Finally, **How to get there** includes directions to many hostels—by car, bus, train, plane or even ferry, in some cases. Subway directions are given in big cities if applicable. Often these directions are complicated, however. In those cases, managers have asked (or we recommend) that you call the hostel itself for more precise directions.

At the end of each chapter, you'll notice dozens and dozens of hostels listed. These listings are shorter than our usual reviews, and they were compiled from the archives of the "official" German hostel association. It's the first time we've ever included such brief information on hostels in one of our books, so let us tell you why we did it.

First, you're unlikely to stay in one of these places. Nearly all of these hostels are located in parts of Germany where Americans don't usually visit; they're almost exclusively filled with school groups; and, to be honest, they're mostly deadly dull. We wanted to focus our research on the places you'll probably wind up staying. Second, many of the managers at these hostels do not speak English—any English. This is not good, for us or for you. Third, and perhaps most importantly, a reality check: This book would have ended up running, like, a thousand pages longer if we had included all 600-plus hostels found in Germany. And the thought of toting a book that heavy around the country for eight weeks frankly scared the heck out of us.

Some of the hostels in these listings, however, were indeed visited during the course of working on this book, and we've saved all those tasty review tidbits on our laptops in case we ever do decide to make a bigger book that includes full reviews of all those other hostels.

A SHORT HISTORY OF HOSTELLING

Hostelling as we know it started around 1907 right here in Germany, when Richard Schirmann, an assistant schoolteacher in the hill town of Altena, Germany, decided to make one of the empty classrooms a space for visiting students to sleep. That was not a completely unique idea, as Austrian inns and taverns had been offering reduced rates and bunk space to students since 1885. But Schirmann would develop much grander plans. He was about to start a movement.

His idea was to get students out of the industrial cities and into the countryside. Schirmann was a strong believer that walking and bicycling tours in the fresh air were essential to adolescent development and learning. But such excursions were impossible without a place to spend the night. His logic was simple: Since rural school-houses were deserted during weekends and holidays, why not make use of those spaces?

The caretakers of the school he chose agreed to serve as house-parents, and some fast ground rules were established. Students were responsible for piling up the tables and benches in the classroom and laying out thin straw sacks on the floor. At some ungodly early-morning hour, the students were to stack the straw mats back up and organize the classroom back as they found it. Boys and girls slept in separate rooms but were treated as equals. Detractors cried scandal, wondering aloud what was going on in these schoolrooms after dark.

The experiment worked, sort of. Altena became a haven for student excursions into the countryside, but finding shelter in other communities proved difficult. Sometimes the situation would become dire. Late one night in the summer of 1909, Schirmann decided it was time to expand his movement beyond Altena. His goal was to establish a network of hostels in walking distance from one another; beginning in a schoolhouse with straw mats, Schirmann eventually acquired the use of a castle. It still stands—the Ur-hostel, if you will—in Altena, and it's still used as a hostel.

After World War I the movement really began to spread. By 1928 there were more than 2,000 hostels worldwide. Today tens of thousands of hostellers stay at HI-affiliated hostels each year, hailing from everywhere from Alaska to Zaire. Thousands more stay at independent hostels. The goal of a single association of hostels located within a day's walk of one another will probably never be realized in the United States. But in Germany—with more than 600 hostels—it *is* reality.

You may never get to all 600; we certainly didn't. But wherever you do end up, you're likely to find a promising brew of cultural exchange and friendship over pots of ramen noodles and instant coffee almost anywhere you go.

In that sense, perhaps, Richard Schirmann's dream has been realized after all.

A Word about Affiliations

A majority of hostels in this book are affiliated with Hostelling International (HI); the rest, we've labeled independent hostels.

Deutsches Jugenderherbergswerk (DJH) is Germany's Hostelling International affiliate. The organization is part of the International Youth Hostel Federation, which has 5,000 member hostels in seventy countries worldwide. Member hostels are held to a number of regulations, such as maximum number of beds per shower, even a minimum amount of space that must exist between top bunks and the ceiling. To get into an HI hostel you must sometimes have an HI membership card (see below).

These hostels are kind of strict with rules (what did you expect?), and some big-city joints (in huge concrete tenement-like blocks) seem to thrive on packing in busloads of schoolkids or tourists. That said, they also are uniformly clean, safe, informative—and a little blah. Small-town hostels in Germany are different—a lot of them are in castles! (Yes, real castles.) The atmosphere ranges from funky to fun to grimly institutional, depending on the management. English isn't always spoken well, but it is usually spoken by at least one staff member. Also take note that virtually every one of these hostels kicks you out very early for the entire day, and they're strict about it. (There are some exceptions for couples paying more for a double room.) At least a breakfast is often included in the rate, and the dinner (which you pay for) is almost always good and filling.

Independents (no affiliation) are what we call all the rest. In Germany nearly all of these are in the big cities—Munich, Berlin, and Hamburg. Some of these independent owners have opted not to join DJH and Hostelling International because membership costs are high and the rules are strict. Such a decision—in and of itself—does not reflect on the quality of the hostel. It would be foolish to write a hostel off simply because it is not affiliated.

However, you need to know that things in an independent hostel are more laid-back—and that's not always a good thing. Some of them are just Party Central twenty-four hours a day—and night. Liquor isn't always officially off-limits at these places. (In HI joints, you usually must either buy it at the hostel bar or restaurant or forget about it.) Some independent hostels do the lockout thing, but it's not as common or long-lasting as the one at HI hostels. Rooms are probably homier, but they're also more crowded and smoky. There's no guarantee of quality, and the standards, upkeep, noise level, and beer flow tend to vary wildly from place to place. Some are outstandingly fun; some are grungy beyond belief.

A few independent hostels in Germany are run by church organizations such as convents. These obviously have stricter lockouts, curfews, and alcohol rules than anyone else in this book. Some also ban unmarried couples from sharing a bed. If they do, we have banned THEM from this book.

HOW TO HOSTEL

Hostelling is, generally speaking, easy as pie. Plan ahead a bit and use a little common sense, and you'll find check-in goes pretty smoothly.

Reserving a Bed

Getting a good bunk will often be your first and biggest challenge, especially if it's high season. Summer is usually high season, but in many areas—such as the Bavarian Alps—winter is the toughest time to get a bed. Popular cities like Berlin and Munich seem to be busy almost year-round. And to hit Oktoberfest, well, you might have to book a *year* in advance. No kidding. Hostellers often have an amazingly laissez-faire attitude about reservations; many simply waltz in at midnight expecting a bed will be available.

Sometimes it is. Sometimes it isn't.

Almost every Hostelling International abode takes advance reservations of some form or another, so if you know where you're going to be, use this service. Be aware that you might need a credit card number to hold a bed, and other hostels require you to send a deposit check in the mail. You might also need to show up by a certain hour like 6:00 P.M. to get in.

The larger and busier HI hostels in Germany are also affiliated with the worldwide International Booking Network (IBN, for short), whereby you can buy a bunk at your next HI stop while sleeping in another one. The Germans also run something called the German Fax Reservation System and the Fax-System-Austria-Germany, two other ways to book a night in advance of arrival while you're tooling around Europe. Contact DJH or the individual hostels to find out if you can use this option on the road.

Independent hostels are sometimes stricter and sometimes more lax about taking solid reservations. Note that they're often much faster to fill up than HI joints because of the wild popularity of no-rules places, so check into their policies. A growing number of these independent joints now take on-line reservations via the Internet.

If you can't or won't reserve, the best thing to do is get there super-early. Office opens at 8:00 A.M.? Get there at 7:00. No room, but checkout ends at 11:00? Be back at 11:05 in case of cancellations or unexpected checkouts. The doors are closed again till 4:30 in the afternoon? No problem. Come back around 4:00 with a paperback and camp out on the porch. That's your only shot if you couldn't or wouldn't reserve ahead, and hostellers are somewhat respectful of the pecking order: It really is first come, first served. So come first.

Paying the Piper

Once you're in, be prepared to pay for your night's stay immediately—before you're even assigned a bunk. Take note ahead of time which hostels take credit cards, checks, and so forth. Learn the local currency, and don't expect every little hostel to change your big bill for a couple bucks' worth of laundry.

You will almost always be required to give up your passport and (if you have one) Hostelling International card for the night. Don't sweat it; it's just the way it's done over there, and in fact they have good reasons. Sometimes it's a police requirement. Also, if an emergency happens (nah, no chance), the passport might help hostel staff locate your significant others.

Remember to pay ahead if you want a weekly stay. Often you can get deep discounts, though the downside is that you'll almost never get even a partial refund if you decide you can't stand it and leave before the week is up.

If you're paying by the day, rebook promptly each morning; hostel managers are very busy during the morning hours, keeping track of check-ins, checkouts, cleaning duties, and cash. You'll make a friend if you're early about notifying them of your plans for the next day. Managers hate bugging guests all morning or all day about whether they'll be staying on. Don't put the staff through this.

All right, so you've secured a bed and paid up. Now you have to get to it. This may be no easy task at some hostels, where staff and customers look and act like one and the same. A kindly manager will probably notice you bumbling around and take pity. As you're being shown to your room, you're also likely get a short tour of the facilities and a briefing on the ground rules.

On checkout you'll get your card and passport back. You might need to pay a small amount if you lose your room key—usually about $5.00, but sometimes as much as $25.00 US.

Knowing the Ground Rules

There's one universal ground rule at every hostel: You are responsible for serving and cleaning up after yourself. And there's a corollary rule: be courteous. So while you're welcome to use the kitchen facilities (if a kitchen's available), share the space with your fellow guests—don't spread your five-course meal all over the counter space and rangetop burners if other hungry folks are waiting. And never, ever, leave a sink full of dirty pots and pans behind. That's bad form.

Hostel guests are almost always asked to mark their name and check-in date on all the food they put in the refrigerator. Only a shelf marked FREE FOOD is truly up for grabs; everything else belongs to other hostellers, so don't touch it. (Hostellers get very touchy about people stealing their grub.) Some of the better-run hostels have a spice rack and other kitchen essentials on hand. If you're not sure whether something is communal, ask. Don't assume anything is up for grabs unless it is clearly marked as such.

Then there's the lockout, a source of bitter frustration among non-European hostellers. Many hostels in Germany kick everybody out in the morning and don't let them back in until the afternoon or early evening; big-city joints are sometimes but not always immune to this rule. Lockouts tend to run from around 9:30 A.M. (which is ungodly, we say, but pretty typical) to 5:00 or 6:00 P.M., during which time your bags might be inside your room—but you won't be. A few places let you back in around 2:00 or 3:00 P.M. Oooooooh, the generosity.

The practice has its pros and cons; managers usually justify a lockout by noting that it forces travelers to interact with the locals, and also allows their staff to "meticulously clean" the rooms. The real reason is usually that the hostel can't or won't pay staff to hang around and baby-sit you all day. On the other hand, these hostels never become semiresidential situations stuffed with couch potatoes, like many U.S. hostels do, so maybe the lockouts do solve that problem.

Curfews are also very common; usually the front doors lock between 11:00 P.M. and midnight, and they won't give you a key. Big-city joints generally have some system in place to let you get in twenty-four hours: a guard, a numbered keypad, or a room key that also opens the main door. But check first.

In the reviews we've tried to identify those hostels that enforce lockouts. Usually you wouldn't want to be hanging out in the hostel in the middle of the day anyway, but after several sleepless nights of travel—or when you're under the weather—daytime downtime sure is appreciated. So beware. Note that even if we haven't listed a lockout or a curfew, it might exist. These things change. Assume that you WILL get kicked out at 9:00 A.M. for the day, and—except in big cities—will need to be back by midnight.

Finally, some hostels also enforce a limit on your stay—anywhere from three days, if the hostel is really popular, to about two weeks.

Savvy budget travelers have learned how to get around this unfortunate situation, of course: They simply suck it up and spend a night at the "Y" or a convenient motel—then check back into the cheaper hostel first thing in the morning. But we didn't tell you to do that. Uh-uh.

Etiquette and Smarts

Again, to put it simply, use common sense. Hostellers are a refreshingly flexible bunch. All these people are able to make this system work by looking after one another; remember, in a hostel you're a community member first and a consumer second. With that in mind, here are some guidelines for how to act:

- The first thing you should do after check-in is get your bed made. When you're assigned a bed, stick to it. Don't spread your stuff out on nearby bunks, even if they are empty. Someone's going to be coming in late-night for one of them, you can bet the backpack on it.

- Be sure to lock your valuables in a locker or safe if they've got one or in the trunk of your car. Good hostels offer lockers as a service; it might cost a little, but it's worth it. Bring a padlock in case the hostel has run out or charges an arm and a leg.

- Set toiletries and anything else you need in a place where they are easily accessible. This avoids your having to paw through your bag late at night, potentially disturbing other guests from their slumber. The same goes for early-morning departures: If you're taking off at the crack of dawn, take precautions not to wake the whole place.

- If you're leaving early in the morning, try to make all arrangements with the manager before going to bed the night before. Managers are usually accommodating and pleasant folks, but guests are expected to respect their privacy and peace of mind by not pushing things too far. Dragging a manager out of bed at four in the morning to check out—or for some other trivial matter—is really pushing it.

- Be sure to mind the bathroom. A quick wiping of the shower floor with a towel after you use it is common courtesy.

- Finally, be sure to mind the quiet hours. Some hostels have curfews, but very few force lights-out. If you are up after hours, be respectful. Don't crank the television or radio too loud; don't scream in the hallways late at night. (Save that for the beach—and for annoying people staying in much nicer digs.)

Packing

Those dainty hand towels and dapper shaving kits and free soaps you get at a hotel won't be anywhere in sight at the hostel. In fact, even some of the base essentials may not be available—kitchens are NOT a given in Germany, for instance. You're on your own, so bring everything you need to be comfortable.

There are only a few things you can expect the hostel to supply:

- a bed frame with a mattress and pillow
- shower and toilet facilities
- a common room with some spartan furniture
- maybe a few heavy blankets.

Some of the more chic hostels we've identified in this guide may be full-service. But they are the exception to the rule.

Bring stuff this to keep your journey through hostel territory comfortable:

- If you're traveling abroad from the United States, you obviously need a passport. Unlike U.S. hostels, a German hostel will often take your passport as collateral when you check in. Don't get nervous; this is extremely common. It's the equivalent, over there, of taking down your driver's license number when you write a check. However, in the unlikely event that someone loses your passport, make sure you've got backup copies of the issuing office, date, and passport number in your luggage and also back home.

- Hostelling International membership cards are a good thing to have on hand—most of the official German hostels require one even to stay. They can be purchased at many foreign HI hostels for about $25 annually per person, or $35 for a family membership. You can also buy cards at U.S. hostels ahead of time, or from the American Youth Hostels headquarters in Washington, D.C. If you can't get one before you arrive in Germany and you'll be there at least a week, don't panic: You can buy an HI "guest stamp" for 6 DM (about $3.00 US), and when you collect six of those, you get a free card.

This card identifies you as a certified superhosteller and gets you the very cheapest rate for your bed in all HI (and also some unaffiliated) hostels. At $2.00 to $4.00 per night, the savings can add up fast.

Sometimes that membership card also gets you deals at local restaurants, bike shops, and tours. Again, it will be easier to deal with the front desk at some of the more cautious hostels (even non-member ones) if you can flash one of these cards.

- Red Alert! Do not plan on using a sleeping bag in every hostel. A good number of places simply won't allow it—problems with ticks and other creatures dragged in from the great outdoors have propelled this prohibition. The alternative is a sleepsack, which is basically two sheets sewn together with a makeshift pillowcase.

You can find them at most budget travel stores, or make your own. Personally we hate these confining wraps, and we rarely get through the night in one without having it twist around our bodies so tight that we wake up wanting to charge it with attempted manslaughter. Our preferred method is to bring our own set of sheets, though that might be too much extra stuff to carry if you're backpacking.

Some hostels give you free linen; most that don't will rent sheets for about $1.00 to $3.00 US per night. You don't get charged for use of the standard army surplus blankets or the musty charm that comes with them.

- Some people bring their own pillows, as those supplied tend to be on the frumpy side. This is a good idea if you're traveling by car and can afford the space. Small pillows are also useful for sleeping on trains and buses.

- We definitely suggest earplugs for light sleepers, especially for urban hostels—but also in case you get caught in a room with a heavy snorer.

- A small flashlight is a must—not only for late-night reading but also to find your bed without waking up the entire dorm.

- A little bit of spice is always nice, especially when you have had one too many plates of pasta. You'll find the cost of basil, oregano, and the like in convenience stores way too high to stomach once you're on the road. Buy it cheap before you leave and pack it in jars or small plastic bags.

- Check which hostels have laundry facilities. Most won't, and you'll need to schlep your stuff to the local laundromat. It'll be expensive, so bring lotsa money.

- Wearing flip-flops or other plastic sandals in the shower might help you avoid a case of athlete's foot.

- Be sure your towel is a quick-drying type. Otherwise you'll wind up with mildew in your pack—and your food.

TRAVELING IN GERMANY

GETTING THERE

Take a careful look at your transportation options when planning a hostel journey. You should be able to hop from city to city by bus or train without a problem, but you could have trouble getting to rural hostels without a car.

From North America by Plane

The airline business is crazy: Great deals and rip-off fares come and go with a regularity that is frightening to behold—supply, demand, season, the stock market, and random acts of cruelty or kindness all appear to contribute to the quixotic nature of fares.

As a result, there is no one simple piece of advice we can give you, other than this one: Find a darned good travel agent who cares about budget travelers, and trust him/her with all the planning. You can cruise the Internet if you like, and you might find an occasional great deal your agent doesn't know about. Just make sure the sellers are reputable before giving out that credit-card number.

A couple tips:

• **Charters** are the cheapest way to go, though it's no-frills all the way.

From the United States, most direct routes are run by the big airlines. Lately, USAirways has run big off-season specials from American gateway cities like Atlanta to places like Frankfurt, Munich, and Stuttgart. You might be able to get a good deal on Germany's Lufthansa (800–645–3880), with its periodic Internet specials, or the ultracheap LTU (800–888–0200), which flies to Düsseldorf, Frankfurt, and Munich from New York, Orlando, and Miami. British Airways and Northwest also fly to Germany regularly. From Canada you can sometimes get very cheap flights on Air Canada (800–776–3000). There are more flights in summer, but they're superpopular and more expensive as you approach lift-off date, so book as early as possible.

• **Cheap-ticket brokers** (also called consolidators or bucket shops) are a great bet for saving money, but you have to be fast on your feet to keep up, as the deals appear and disappear literally daily. London and New York are major centers for bucket shops. The introduction to *Europe: The Rough Guide* is a good source of quickie material on hubs, connections, and consolidators to Europe from just about anywhere in the world.

• **Flying as a courier** comes highly recommended by some folks who've tried it. Others are nervous about it. It works this way: You agree to carry luggage for a company in exchange for a very cheap round-trip ticket abroad. You must be flexible about your departure and return dates, you can't change those dates once assigned to you—and you usually can bring only carry-on luggage.

There isn't nearly as much demand for couriers from smaller destinations to Europe as there is from places like New York or Los Angeles; but it's still worth a shot. Check out guidebooks and Web sites on the subject.

From Europe by Plane

Flights within Europe used to be fantastically expensive. However, times are changing: A raft of cut-rate short-hop airlines have sprung up, such as Go!, Easyjet, British Midland, and Virgin Express. Check out the papers and travel agents for the latest-breaking deals, and be prepared to sometimes fly into or out of a weird airport to save the dough.

From Europe by Train

Most folks travel by train around Europe, and it's a sensible choice. Services and connections are generally good, so getting to Germany by rail is normally a straightforward matter of booking and then taking a long-distance journey, possibly with a change or two en route. You've got two choices: (1) buy point-to-point tickets for every leg of the journey or (2) buy a Europe-wide pass.

If you're math-and-map friendly, definitely buy a copy of the *Thomas Cook European Rail Timetable* before you go—or in an English-language bookstore in London, Paris, or elsewhere in Europe after you arrive. It's an invaluable reference to the changing train schedules of Great Britain and Eastern and Western Europe.

From England by Train

(Air routes within Europe are covered in the previous section.)

There's only one way to get to Germany from England by train: Begin with **Eurostar.** They've got a monopoly on the sub-Chunnel service that takes you from England to Brussels or Paris in under three hours, but they run it well: You'll never get onto a faster or more efficiently run train. You can have breakfast in SoHo and lunch in Paris—without the delays of airport check-in and checkout and with pretty minimal customs and immigration formalities. From either Paris or Brussels, you can take a daytime or overnight train directly to Munich or Berlin.

Of course you pay extra for the privilege. Tickets run from as little as 99 pounds (about $175 US) off-season, booking in advance, up to much more if you book on short notice or travel during a summer weekend. And—bummer—buying a single one-way ticket isn't much cheaper than purchasing a round-tripper. So you might as well go whole hog.

At least there are discounts for Eurail and BritRail pass holders and for young travelers.

Always check ahead for price information. Book ahead by fifteen days and you might save as much as 50 percent! It's easiest to book ahead through your travel agent at home, but Eurostar also has offices in London's Waterloo Station, Paris's Gare du Nord, and Brussels's Gare du Midi.

The Eurostar runs from London to Paris about twenty times a day and to Brussels about ten times a day—both less frequently on weekends—and you must have a reservation ahead of time. One additional plus with Eurostar: If you somehow manage to miss your train (you oaf), they will let you reschedule your ride for another convenient and available time—within certain limits—at no extra penalty! Wouldn't it be nice if the airlines worked that way? Yep. It sure would.

From Continental Europe by Train

From elsewhere in Europe, getting to Germany by rail is an absolute snap. You've got three choices: (1) buy point-to-point tickets for every leg of the journey, (2) get a regional pass, or (3) buy a Europe-wide pass.

• **Eurail passes** can be key if you're touring Germany en route to someplace else in Europe. Here's the rule: If you're seeing Germany as part of a long trip, get the Eurail. In our experience these passes are a great deal for covering big distances. DER Travel (800–782–2424), a German company with offices in Chicago, sells Eurail passes and really impresses us as experts on travel in their homeland. You can also buy a Eurail pass from the equally knowledgeable folks at Rail Europe (800–438–7245 in the United States; 800–361–7245 in Canada).

Sure, they're not cheap, but they're superconvenient and cover almost everything. If you do get the Eurail pass, you've gotta play by the rules: Wait until the first day you're going to use it, then go to the station early and have the pass validated (stamped) by a ticket agent. Write the current date into the first square (it should have a "1" beneath it)—and remember to put the day first (on top), European-style.

Now it gets easier. Just show your pass to ticket agents when you want to reserve a seat on a train (which is crucial in summer season, on weekends, and during rush hours); that smiling person will print you out a seat reservation, which you show to the conductor. You must reserve seats before the train arrives, and since you'll have no idea where or when that is, it's best to reserve a day or two ahead as you're getting off the train.

If you can't or won't get a reservation, just show your pass to the conductor. Sometimes he'll let you get on anyway.

Finally, don't fold, bend, or otherwise mangle the long cardboard pass (and that can be difficult to achieve while fumbling for your money belt at the station as the train whips in). For some reason, that might invalidate the whole thing.

The cost of these passes depends on a few things: how long you're traveling and how much comfort you want. First-class passes, which few hostellers buy, cost 50 percent more and give you a little more legroom. Call one of the railpass vendors listed above for the very latest pricing information.

And new for 2000, Eurail has introduced a shorter, more flexible option called the Eurail Selectpass. It's good for first class train (and ferry) travel in any three bordering countries for five, six, eight, or ten days in a two-month period. Prices range from $328 a person for five days, to $476 for ten days—the days do not have to be consecutive. For those persons age twenty-five and under, the pass is an even better deal at $230 to $334.

- **Point-to-Point Tickets** might be the best route to go if you're just blowing through Germany in a hurry. Get them at stations at ticket windows or—if you have cash, coins, or credit cards—automatic machines.

A few more tips on cross-European train travel:

- If you're just buying point-to-point tickets, go for second-class.
- From long distances away, like Denmark or Spain, you can sometimes take a sleeper car (also known as a couchette). At less than $20 US per person (quite a bit more for a double), it saves you a night in a hotel or hostel and gets you closer to where you want to go. The drawback is that you sleep four or, more likely, six to a room.
- Remember that trains don't run as frequently on weekends; Saturday is usually the worst day to travel. International trains and sleeper cars usually run seven days a week, and Fridays and Sundays are feast or famine; check schedules and think like a local.

From Europe by Bus

Eurolines is a Europe-wide company running comfortable long-distance buses around Europe for very competitive rates, certainly cheaper than trains and cheaper than planes if you're booking on short notice. They serve quite a network of cities.

GETTING AROUND

By Train

Trains are still king in Europe. Sure, the car dominates everyday life for locals, but when you're a tourist you just can't beat the iron horse.

Deutsche Bahn (DB), the national train company, is incredibly efficient; their trains are usually fast (sometimes very fast), clean, comfortable and—obviously—quite punctual. Ticket agents all speak English and have access to DB's lightning-fast trip-planning software, which can get you where you want to go faster than you can.

While these rail systems cross an incredible variety of landscape, even the iron horse can't get everywhere. It's likely, at some point, that you might need to supplement your train travel with some form of gondola, lift, bus, cog railway, or steam train. All part of the fun.

A few other things to keep in mind:

- The EurAide offices in the Munich and Berlin train stations are an absolute godsend for trip planning. They'll set up your train reservations, reserve sleeper-train beds, give tours, whatever you need—usually at little cost, and always in perfect English.

- Germany is a big country. Going from Berlin to anywhere else is gonna take you half a day, at least, maybe all day. The super-fast InterCity Express (ICE) trains blast along at 80 or more miles an hour, and they can save you time, but they also cost a little extra—reservations are required, too. Definitely go for second-class tickets on these babies unless you're loaded.

- One final note: Big-city German train stations and their neighborhoods can get a little rough late at night. Ever heard of skinheads? Germany invented them, and they're still actively circulating the streets and stations of Hamburg and East Berlin, among other locales. Stay away from the guys with the jackets and white-laced boots. You don't need the trouble.

Tickets and Passes

What to buy? If you're going to be doing lots of short city-to-city hops, just buy tickets each day; it's cheaper. If you'll be in the area for a week or two, get a pass.

The **German Railpass** gets you four days of rail travel in one month. It costs about $250 US for first-class seating ($380 for two people traveling together in first class); about $175 for second-class seating (about $260 for two people traveling together in second class); and about $140 per person for travelers under twenty-seven years old. You can tack extra days of travel onto the pass for anywhere from $6.00 to $32.00, depending on your age.

Remember that a German pass or Eurail pass saves you 75 percent on Romantic Road and Castle Road bus tours and gets you a free *ride* on most Rhine and Moselle River ferries.

If you're gonna be around for a *really* long time, you can buy a **BahnCard** in German train stations for 130 to 260 DM (about $65 to $130 US), depending on your age. That gets you a half-price discount on second-class tickets for a whole year, and the savings can really add up.

Contact the tourism offices or travel offices listed in this book for the latest pricing info, or just stand in line at any German train station ticket office. The staff are exceptionally knowledgeable about this stuff.

Always remember to punch your train ticket before you get on the train; there will be a machine in every station that stamps the current date and time on the ticket, showing the conductor that it has been "used up."

By Bus

Buses can be a cheaper ride than the train, or more expensive, depending on local whims. They're extremely useful in places where trains simply don't go—reasonably on time, scenic, and with lots of locals riding alongside you happy to give advice or opinions or soccer scores.

It might take you all day to make connections, but most bus drivers are helpful and knowledgeable. As a bonus, they'll sometimes let you off where you want to go even if there isn't an actual scheduled bus stop there. They are also quite accustomed to hostellers asking "where's my stop??" and handle the situation calmly and professionally. Usually. (In small towns, though, anything goes.)

In German cities, you often buy tickets in transit stations, at newsstands, or right on the bus—it's more expensive to buy 'em from the driver, however.

Always remember to punch your ticket for local bus rides; there will be a machine either at the bus stop or on the bus. Most single tickets are good for one hour; most passes are good for a day or more.

By Boat

On a few occasions you might be cruising lakes or rivers; your Eurail pass covers some (though not all) of these journeys.

For instance, Donaudampfschiffarhtsgesellschaft (DDSG), the tongue-twisting transport organization, runs cruises up and down the scenic Rhine River, including a bunch of pokey regular boats, a fast hydrofoil (which is more expensive, of course), and even the occasional steamer. The best part? All rides on this line are free with a Eurail pass.

Other ferries run around Lake Konstanz (also known as Lake Constance or the Bodensee) between Switzerland, Austria, and Germany.

By Car

Renting a car is definitely the most expensive way to see Europe, and yet it has advantages: You can cover the hamlets a whole lot quicker, you have complete freedom of movement, and you get that cool feeling of the wind and rain rushing past your ears.

And Germany is by far the cheapest country in Europe in which to rent a car, with plenty of opportunities to rent in one city and drop off—with no penalty—in another. The country's high-speed Autobahns are free, too, unlike the highways in most other European countries. (The gas isn't cheap, but at least the tiny Euro-cars get terrific gas mileage.) Watch out for traffic jams, though. Even on the high-speed roads, weekends, holidays, and rush-hours can bring horrific gridlock. Our tip? Try driving during lunch or on a Sunday.

By all means try to book your rental ahead from your home country. It's cheaper. We don't know why. It just is. Rentals will set you back $40 to $70 US a day for a small car, and that might or might not include heavy taxes and insurance tacked onto the price. An automatic-drive car will be more expensive.

If you can, rent or lease long-term through a company such as Kemwel (800–678–0678), a good firm that books long-term rentals for a fraction of the daily rate if you book ahead from your home country. They do short-term rentals as well. The other usual American companies also rent in Germany.

Speeds and distance in continental Europe are always measured in kilometers. Just to remind you, 1 kilometer is a little less than 0.6 mile, and 100 miles equal roughly 160 kilometers. Here are some common speed limits you might see on road signs, with their U.S. equivalents:

40 kph	=	25 miles per hour
100 kph	=	62 miles per hour
50 kilometers away	=	31 miles away

Gas is measured in liters, and there are roughly four liters to the U.S. gallon. Gas prices are listed per liter, so multiply by four and then convert into home currency to estimate the price per gallon you'd pay back home—you'll be shocked. Want a bike yet?

What else? Well, you drive on the right, just as you do in the rest of continental Europe. However, also like the rest of Europe, drivers tend to be rather aggressive, especially in open-highway situations—that supercharged car in your rear-view might have just been doing 100 miles an hour. Pull over and let him go. And no giving the finger back to the guy. You can get tossed in the pokey or fined heavily for it—yes, really.

PHONES

Two words: phone card.

Dealing with pay phones can be frustrating, so don't bother pumping change unless you're truly desperate. Instead, buy phone cards at tobacco shops, train station windows, or small markets and stick 'em into the slots in the phones.

Don't bother trying to call Mom and Dad back home with these cards. Instead, get a phone card from the United States or your home country before you arrive. It'll be cheaper and easier, though a few phones might block your phone card.

You dial differently depending on whether you are in the country or not. Inside the countries, dial the numbers as shown.

To call Germany from North America or anywhere else, dial 0049 and *drop the first zero* from the numbers printed in this book *or the call won't go through.*

To call the United States, Canada, or wherever else you might hail from, dial 001 and then the number you are calling.

Remember that it's cheaper to make coin calls at night, and that directory assistance (dial 11833) can get expensive.

There are cheaper alternatives for calling home. Right now, all three giant communications corporations have seemingly monopolized the way you call home. Many of the larger hostels in Europe have special phones that have been installed by companies like AT&T, MCI, and Sprint. The calls come with a weighty per-call charge that can add up real fast, in addition to the exorbitant rates they charge per minute. What's more, you can use these phones only if you have an existing account with the carrier. The situation is made more frustrating because these companies sometimes won't accept a credit card.

MONEY

You'll need it, that's for sure, although Germany isn't the most expensive place in Europe. With the recently strong dollar, it's even something of a deal right now.

Germany's unit of currency is the Deutsche Mark, also spelled Deutschmark and abbreviated DM. Two Deutsche Marks equal almost exactly one U.S. dollar. So if you want to do a rough conversion, just divide the German price by two and voila!—you've got your approximate U.S. equivalent.

The main bills you'll use while in Germany are these:

> **10 DM bill = about $5 U.S.**
> **20 DM bill = about $10 U.S.**
> **50 DM bill = about $25 U.S.**
> **100 DM bill = about $50 U.S.**

There are bigger bills worth 200 DM (about $100 U.S.), 500 DM (about $250 U.S.) and 1,000 DM (about $500 U.S.), too, though you're unlikely to get your mitts on one of those babies at an ATM.

Each Deutsche Mark is divided into 100 pfennings (abbreviated Pf), which are a lot like pennies (where do ya think we got the word from, anyway?). Anyway, the German coins include:

> **50 Pf coin = about 25 cents**
> **10 Pf coin = about 5 cents**
> **5 Pf coin = about 2½ cents**
> **2 Pf coin = about 1 cent**
> **1 Pf coin = about ½ cent**

Like most European countries, the Germans also use a couple bigger, heavier coins that are worth more than most U.S. coins. They include:

> **1 DM coin = about 50 cents U.S.**
> **2 DM coin = about $1 U.S.**
> **5 DM coin = about $2.50 U.S.**

To get money remember this: Always get it from an ATM if possible. If you must change money, use a big bank instead of a tourist office, train station, bureau de change, or small bank; their rates are all terrible, and they figure you won't know the difference. Try to spend all your change before you leave one country for another unless you're coming back, since you can't change these suckers into any other currency after you leave the country. It's a use-it-or-lose-it situation, basically.

No sweat, right? The real challenge, as we've said, it to keep your balance with all that really heavy change rattling around in your pockets.

TRAVEL INSURANCE

Travel Insurance might seem like a useless expenditure, but it might come in handy, too. This insurance typically covers everything from baggage loss and injuries in an air travel accident (nah, that won't happen, don't even think about it) to medical expenses incurred while you're traveling. It's also helpful if someone puts a dent in that rental car and you have waived the necessary coverage to save bucks.

We'd recommend buying some sort of travel insurance. The best we've found so far for European traveling is one in Wisconsin called Travel Guard (800–826–1300).

SPEAKING GERMAN

English will get you by in touristed areas of Germany, which probably covers most of the places you're going. However, occasionally you'll want to get way off the beaten track, where you might have a little more trouble. Just think: This might be your only chance to forge a meaningful bond while getting the right bus tickets, too.

In the small German towns, English is well understood by some folks, poorly understood by other folks, and not understood at all by still others. Don't assume that just because someone happens to work in, oh, say, a train ticket office that he/she will know your language. Learn a little German before you go, and don't despair. You'll be OK with a bit of brushing up and a little sign or body language where necessary. Hereforth, a short primer.

GERMAN (DEUTSCH)

WHAT THEY SAY	HOW THEY SAY IT (approximately)	WHAT THEY MEAN
Gutten tag	Goo ten tag	hello, good day
bitte	beetah	please; excuse me; may I help you?
danke	Don K	thanks
danke shane	Don KeShane	thank you very much
ein	ine	one
zwei	dzvye	two
drei	dry	three
zug	zoog	train
U-Bahn	oo baan	subway
S-Bahn	S baan	commuter/suburban train
Bahnof	baa-noff	train station
Hauptbahnhof	how baa-noff	main train station
Bus	boose	bus
Ich möhte . . .	Eek mookta	I'd like . . .
ein Fahrkarte	ine far carta	a ticket
Jugendherberge	you get her burger	hostel
Doppelzimmer	dopple zimmer	double room
platz	plats	square
sprechen	spricken	speak
Sie Englisch	zee English	English

OTHER RESOURCES

There's surprisingly little out there about hostelling and hostels—
that's why you're reading this, right?—but we did find a few sources.
Most simply list phone numbers and addresses.

Remember that hostels are constantly opening, closing, renovating, being sold, and changing their policies. So not everything written in a guidebook will still be true by the time you read it. Be smart
and call ahead to confirm prices, availability, and directions, rather
than rolling into town depending on a bed—and getting a nasty surprise like a vacant lot instead. We know; it has happened to us.

HOSTEL ASSOCIATION HEADQUARTERS

Germany's hostel association headquarters are located in the far
north of the country, so it's unlikely you'll drop by. Still, they're a
wellspring of info if you need it.

Deutsches Jugendherbergswerk (DJH)

Headquarters office:
Bad Meinberger Strasse 1
D-32760 Detmold
Telephone: 49–5231–9936–0
Fax: 49–5231–9936–66 or 49–5231–9995–90
Office hours: 8:00 A.M.–4:30 P.M. (until 2:30 P.M. Friday)

Travel office:
Telephone: 49–5231–7401–0
Fax: 49–5231–7401–49
Office hours: 8:00 A.M.–4:30 P.M., (until 2:30 P.M. Friday)

REGIONAL OFFICES

These regional DJH offices might be able to help you with queries
in a pinch while you're in Germany. English should be spoken by all.

Baden-Württemberg Region (Southwestern Germany)

Karlsruhe office:
Weinweg 43
76137 Karlsruhe
Telephone: 0721–96210–0
Fax: 0721–613470
E-mail: djh-bad-wuert@t-online.de

Stuttgart office:
Schwieberdinger Strasse 62
70435 Stuttgart
Telephone: 0711–16686–0
Fax: 0711–16686–30
E-mail: djh-bad-wuert@t-online.de

Berlin-Brandenburg (Berlin / Northern Germany)
DJH Landesverband Berlin-Brandenburg e.V.
Tempelhofer Ufer 32
D-10963 Berlin
Telephone: 030–264952–0
Fax: 030–2620437
E-mail: DJH-Berlin-Brandenburg@jugendherberge.de

Hannover Region (Central Germany)
DJH-Landesverband Hannover e.V.
Ferd.-Wilh.-Fricke-Weg 1
30169 Hannover
Telephone: 0511–16402–22–37
Fax: 0511–16402–32
E-mail: djh-lvb-hannover@t-online.de

Mecklenburg-Vorpommern (Northern Germany)
JH Landesverband Mecklenburg-Vorpommern e.V.
Erich-Schesinger-Strasse 41
18059 Rostock
Telephone: 0381–776670
Fax: 0381–7698682
E-mail: DJH-MV@t-online.de
Web: www.djh-mv.de

Rhineland (Western Germany)
Mainz office:
DJH Landesverband Rheinland-Pfalz/Saarland e.V.
In der Meielache 1
D-55122 Mainz
Telephone: 06131–37446–0
Fax: 06131–37446–22
E-mail: djh-mainz@t-online.de

Düsseldorf office:
DJH Landesverband Rheinland e.V.
Düsseldorferstrasse 1
40545 Düsseldorf
Telephone: 0211–5770320–4957
Fax: 0211–57703–50
E-mail: service-center@djh-rheinland.de

Sachsen (Central Germany)

DJH-Landesverband Sachsen e.V.
Zschopauer Strasse 216
D-09126 Chemnitz
Telephone: 0371–56153–0
Fax: 0371–56153–99
E-mail: service@djh-sachsen.de
Web: www.djh-sachsen.de

Sachsen-Anhalt (Central Germany)

DJH Landesverband Sachsen-Anhalt
Bleckenburgstrasse 12
39104 Magdeburg
Telephone: 0391–40196–35
Fax: 0391–40196–38

Thüringen (Central Germany)

DJH Landesverband Thüringen e.V.
Servicebüro
Carl-August-Allee 13
D-99423 Weimar
Telephone: 03643–8500–00
Fax: 03643–8500–02
E-mail: djhthue@aol.com
Web: www.djh-thueringen.de

Unterweser-Ems (Central Germany)

DJH Landesverband Unterweser-Ems e.V.
Woltmershauser Allee 8
28199 Bremen
Telephone: 0421–59830–10/11
Fax: 0421–59830–55
E-mail: service@djh-unterweser-ems.de

Westfalen (Western Germany)

Deutsches Jugendherbergswerk
Landesverband Westfalen-Lippe e.V.
Eppenhauser Strasse 65
58093 Hagen
Telephone: 02331–9514–0
Fax: 02331–9514–10
E-mail: info@djh-wl.de

TOURISM OFFICES

In the USA:
German National Tourist Office
122 East Forty-second Street
Fifty-second Floor
New York, NY 10168
Telephone: 212–661–7200
Fax: 212–661–7174
E-mail: gntony@aol.com

In England:
German National Tourist Office
P.O. Box 2695
London W1A 3NT
Telephone: 020–7317–0908
Fax: 020–7495–6129

WEB SITES

There are, alas, very few Web sites worth checking out. Don't bother twirling your browser to these coordinates:

www.djh.de

This is the home site of the "official" German hostel association. It only works with a Java-enabled browser, and—what's worse—is completely in German. Not really helpful.

The Hostels

BERLIN

Page numbers follow hostel names

BERLIN

Population 3.5 million and growing, Berlin's one crazy place these days. Newly flush with its position as capital of a reunified Germany (let's face it, you never realized Bonn was the old capital anyway), construction projects are sprouting like mad. There's a palpable energy as entrepreneurs, artists, clubbers, and just about everyone else tries to carve out an exciting new direction. It might be the most exciting city in the world right now—no kidding.

That's not to say it's a physically attractive place, though. Years of Iron Curtain life have turned chunks of the city into run-down

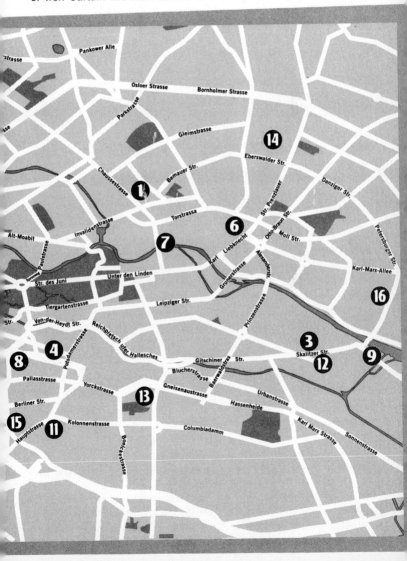

quarters and fascist-architecture hotels and housing projects. You come here for the culture and the fascinating history, not pretty buildings and quaint alleyways. Fortunately, some parks provide a bit of green relief from the concrete, and some are quite close to the central sightseeing districts.

GETTING ORIENTED

Zoologischer Garten Station—almost always called Zoo Station or Bahnof Zoo—is big and confusing, but it will probably be your introduction to Berlin and it's the best place to orient yourself and get ready for the party. Want a big hint? *The* place to get all your local tourist tips—not to mention make onward train reservations—is the American-run EurAide office at Zoo Station. Also at the train station you'll find tour companies such as Berlin Walks, a very good one (try the Third Reich tour).

For purposes of organizing your visit to this sprawling city, we've divided Berlin into a few areas. Going from west to east, the huge downtown area is composed of the western districts known as Charlottenberg, Tiergarten, and Schöneberg; two central areas near the old Berlin wall, Mitte ("middle") and Kreuzberg; and two eastern neighborhoods, Prenzlauer Berg and Friedrichshain. Each of these areas has its own individual character, and collectively they are chock-full of hostels. Any hostel that's outside these five areas is probably gonna take some time to get to.

In each write-up we've indicated in which of the these areas a hostel is located. If a hostel's not in one of these areas, we've labeled it as being in the Outer Districts.

GETTING AROUND

Berlin's so big that it had to gradually build a tremendous transport network to get everyone around—and it did. What's amazing is that when East and West Berlin joined hands in 1989, the two networks were seamlessly joined. Today, tons of buses, streetcars, subways, and commuter trains ensure that things keep moving.

Subways (the **U-Bahn**) are marked by a "U." Aboveground trains (the **S-Bahn,** free with Eurail passes) are marked by an "S." **Bus** and **streetcar** stops are marked with an "H" by the side of the road, and **night buses** (those with an "N" in the number) run all night long, though less frequently than day buses do.

Figuring out where the rides go shouldn't be too hard—maps are everywhere. But figuring out the complicated ticket system *could* be a little difficult without some help; there are three zones, each costing a different price, and there are hostels located in all three. Here's what we'd do: Buy a transit pass each day (or every couple days), then use it—a lot—to sightsee and get around. You might pay a little bit extra, but if you're gonna be hopping around a lot, it works out as a better deal than individual tickets. And it's *really* worth the time you'll save not having to stand in line or trying to decipher ticket machines.

Transit passes come in several levels. The **Tageskarte,** the daily transit pass, costs 7.80 to 8.50 DM per day (about $4.00 US);

three or more people doing all their traveling together can save by buying a **Gruppentageskarte** for 20.00 to 22.50 DM (about $10 to $11 US) per day. There's also a three-day **Welcome Card** (72 DM; about $36 US) and a **7-Tage-Karte-Card** (40 to 48 DM; about $20 to $24 US) for those staying a little longer. Do the math and you'll see why they save you money over the long run.

WHAT TO SEE

You could spend days and days in Berlin, alternating between Cold War sight-seeing and bar-hopping among the city's hundreds of enjoyable Kneipen (pubs).

To see the sights, we'd possibly begin with a quick walk or ride. From Zoo Station, you might take a public transit ride over to Charlottenburg Palace. It's every bit as impressive as you'd expect; there are spacious grounds, plus museum after museum filled with regal items. A closer sight to the station would be the Kaiser-Wilhelm-Gedächtniskirche memorial church, about a block away.

In the other direction, toward the Wall, you might try a get-acquainted stroll along famous Kurfurstendamm boulevard (but Berliners-in-the-know just call it Ku-damm), a long, wide and drab—but oh-so-Berlin—collection of department stores, restaurants, and bars.

After getting that first taste of the city, we'd hop a bus for the Mitte district, where the sights come fast and furious near the former border checkpoint that divided East and West known as the Checkpoint Charlie House.

The Brandenburg Gate, built in the late 1700s, is the usual starting point on a walking tour from west to east and a point of pride for Berliners, who now consider it the heart of their city. The huge radio tower—with its 1,200 feet of steel and antenna right in the center of town—is the next obvious point on a tour. You can ascend to a platform halfway up and check out the new German capital from high up in the air. From there, head east along wide Unter den Linden ("Under the Lime Trees") boulevard for a really grand look at Berlin's pre-Nazi glories.

Or make a short hop over to Museumsinsel, a small island in the Spree River stocked with enormous and impressive museums; look for such landmarks as the huge cupola of the Berliner Dom (cathedral). Some of the offerings include the Altes Museum (Old Museum), Alte Nationalgalerie (Old National Gallery), Bode Museum, and Pergamon Museum.

Nearby you'll find a number of churches that testify to the atrocities of the last world war including the Nikolaikirche (first begun in the thirteenth century). Also close by, the Nikolaiviertel section is the city's most ancient. Begin at the Nikolai church and filter through alleys and squares, stopping for a bite or a beer when you get the urge.

Most of the same key sights, in roughly the same order, can be seen by jumping onto the city's #100 bus at Zoo Station and riding from west to east. That's the cheap way. For a more romantic look at things, find out about one of the city boat tours running along the Spree River.

THE HOSTEL SCENE

The hostels in Berlin, predictably enough, range from near-dumps to boring warehouse-style places to near-pristine palaces. (We did note that an amazing number of the places here, no matter what they're like, charge you extra dough just to get sheets. Boo to that!)

We've found that the backpacker-style joints here are about as groovy as any in Europe—there's a very laid-back feel to them, which is at odds with the normal hostels-in-Germany way of doing things. In other words, the difference between an "official" hostel and an "independent" one in this city is huge in terms of atmosphere.

BERLIN HOSTELS at a glance

	RATING	COST	IN A WORD	PAGE
Circus Hostel	👍👍	25–45 DM	cool	46
The Guest House Hostel	👍👍	27.50–40.00 DM	historic	54
Hotel Transit Hostel	👍	33–90 DM	great	55
Die Fabrik Hostel	👍	30–66 DM	fun	50
Nordufer Hostel	👍	38–40 DM	okay	57
Odyssee Globetrotter Hostel	👍	24–32 DM	rockin'	58
Backpacker Mitte Hostel	👍	25–30 DM	American	39
Lette 'm Sleep Hostel	👍	25–35 DM	relaxed	56
Clubhouse Hostel	👍	25–30 DM	clubby	47
Ernst Reuter Hostel	👍	28–35 DM	quiet	51
Berlin Guest House Hostel	👍	34–50 DM	blah	43
Wannsee Hostel	👍	34–42 DM	distant	61
CVJM Haus	👍👎	40–42 DM	Christian	49
Tegel Hostel	👍👎	38 DM	German	60
Berlin Youth Hotel	👍👎	45–180 DM	boring	45
Backpacker's Paradise	👍👎	10–13 DM	campy	41

BERLIN HOSTELS at a glance (continued)

	RATING	COST	IN A WORD	PAGE
Jugendgästehaus am Zoo	👍👎	35–52 DM	worn	62
Feurigstrasse Guest House	👎	38–55 DM	drab	52
BaxPax Hostel		18–22 DM	new	42
Hubertusallee Student Hotel		30–80 DM	adequate	59

BACKPACKER MITTE HOSTEL

Chausseestrasse 102,
10115 Berlin
Phone: 030–262–5140 or 030–2839–0965
Fax: 030–2839–0935
E-mail: backpacker@snafu.de
Rates: 25–30 DM per person (about $13–$15 US); doubles 76 DM (about $38 US)
Credit cards: No
Private/family rooms: Yes
Kitchen available: Yes
Beds: 60
Season: Open year-round
Office hours: 7:00 A.M.–10:00 P.M.
Affiliation: None
Extras: Bike rentals, laundry, tours

Located in Mitte

This super-friendly place gets big points for being a hoppin' hang-out in the heart of the Mitte neighborhood and all its pleasures. The character isn't so much Berlin, however, as a get-together of dudes and dudettes from California and Jersey and Australia, places like that. You'll hear lots of sentences beginning with grating constructions like "Like, you know, it was, like, so, like cool, when we, like, threw up on the bartender."

If that sets your heart racing with joy, by all means head for this place. If it doesn't, enjoy the rooms at night, but spare yourself the lame conversations.

Okay, okay, we'll talk about the hostel instead of the hostellers. We noted several different kinds of decor in the rooms, which are surprisingly fancy and decorated in a typical Mitte-90s design (you'll have to see it to see what we mean). Other rooms are a little more sedate, with finny or flowery motifs, but all are a welcome change from the depressing or institutional walls of your usual hostel. This one almost feels homey. The dorms contain two to six beds each. Sheets do cost extra, but there's a laundry on the premises. They offer all the usual services, too, renting bicycles and even giving advice on work and work visas and stuff like that. All in all, this is a very hosteller-friendly sort of place—and staff is fluently English-speaking and friendly, too, which really helps.

The self-serve kitchen, unusual for a Berlin hostel, is handy and extremely well equipped—especially since there's a market just around the corner for groceries in case you want to whip up a creative feast. If you abhor the thought of cooking, though, the hostel has an arrangement with a Turkish/Italian restaurant downstairs that offers significant discounts on meals to its guests. The restaurant also serves breakfast for a few bucks.

Wanna see the city with a bunch of other hostellers? No problem. The hostel has also made an arrangement with a tour company, Berlin Walks; you can meet tour guides at the reception desk for a walk around town. (Yes, it costs money.) Ask at reception for more details. Future plans include a cool backyard where you can chill and grill to your heart's content. And if you're tripping through Berlin during November through February, you'll be rewarded with an ample 7.00 DM discount off the cost of your bed. If you're part of a foursome or more, one of you will receive a free night. Unfortunately, those discounts don't carry over into the peak season.

Best bet for a bite:
Humboldt University
Mensa

Insiders' tip:
Georgbrau bar brews
own beer

What hostellers say:
"Like, you know . . ."

Gestalt:
Mitte you there

Safety:

Hospitality:

Cleanliness:

Party index:

As we've said, there is really nothing special about the atmosphere here; you'll likely spend a lot of your free time hanging around drinking beer with Australians. Fun, we suppose, but you're here to see Berlin—and this place is very near the center of Berlin's active, almost crazed nightlife. The nighttime action in Mitte is intense, as it has been since the days of playwright Bertolt Brecht and the cabaret scene of the 1920s. Think Liza Minelli belting "Life is a cabah-ray, old chum" in pseudo-S&M gear—except with more piercings, tattoos, and multicolored hair—and you've more or less got the picture.

How to get there:

By bus: Contact hostel for transit details.
By car: Contact hostel for directions.
By train: From Zoo Station, take U-Bahn line U6 to Zinnowitzer Strasse stop; walk to hostel.

BACKPACKER'S PARADISE

Ziekowstrasse 161,

Berlin

Phone: 030–433–8640

Rates: 10–13 DM (about $5.00–$7.00 US) per person
Credit cards: No
Beds: Number varies
Private/family rooms: No
Kitchen available: No
Season: June 15–August 31
Office hours: Open twenty-four hours
Affiliation: None
Extras: Laundry, breakfast ($), bonfires

Located in the Outer Districts

Note: Must be under age twenty-seven to stay (flexible)

This is incredibly far from the interesting parts of Berlin you've come to see—it's more than an hour by public transportation from the city center. And get one thing straight: The place consists mainly of a tent. Yeah, a tent. Germany's so nutty these days that it's not even the only tent in the country, either—there's a tent hostel in Munich, too, more famous and probably a better overall place. But we digress.

Before you show up salivating, get another thing straight. You don't come here for great beds, not at all. In fact, a "bed" here could mean anything from a pad under the tent to a cot—but it will be extremely simple, no matter what. How do you think they manage to charge so little? (This is by *far* the cheapest place in town.) They manage because you're not getting much.

If you can get past that flaw and sleep twisted like a pretzel, however, the laid-back staffers do offer two key services in the morning: They lay out a breakfast buffet that's dirt cheap, and they also run a laundry. The age limit mentioned above probably will be waived if you try to get in. Does that give you some idea of what this place is about? It's about the vibe, daddy-o, and restrictions just get in the way. So away with 'em.

Best bet for a bite:
Penny Markt

Insiders' tip:
Zitty for entertainment info

What hostellers say:
"Duuuuude, got a light?"

Gestalt:
Tent pole

Safety:

Hospitality:

Cleanliness:

Party index:
🎉🎉🎉

If you're short on cash and show up in summer, this is easily your best bed—er, tent—in town. Just remember that, as we've warned you previously, it's quite a ways from the action; a lengthy train ride, and *then* a bus ride, is required just to get here. (Note that it's right beside the Tegel Guest House Hostel, described below).

How to get there:

By bus/train: From train station take S-Bahn line S25 or U-Bahn line U6 to Alt-Tegel Station, then change to #222 or N22 bus and continue to Titusweg stop; walk to hostel.

By car: Contact hostel for directions.

BAXPAX HOSTEL

Skalitzer Strasse 104,

10997 Berlin-Kreuzberg

Phone: 030–695–18322

Fax: 030–695–18372
E-mail: info@baxpax.de
Web site: www.baxpax.de
Rates: 18–22 DM per person (about $9.00–$11.00 US)
Credit cards: No
Beds: 65
Private/family rooms: None
Kitchen available: Yes
Season: Open year-round
Office hours: Open twenty-four hours
Affiliation: None
Extras: Bike rentals, tours, Internet, pool table, movie theater, sheets ($)

Located in Friedrichshain/Kreuzberg

BaxPax just opened as we were wrapping up this first edition of *Hostels Germany*, by the very same folks who brought you the Backpacker Mitte (see page 39). The jury's still out, but we did get a sneak peek.

Best bet for a bite:
Kaiser's Markt

Insiders' tip:
See last paragraph

What hostellers say:
"Good new place."

Gestalt:
Pax a punch

Hospitality:

Party index:

The building is an old factory that once produced men's bowler hats. Keying into the hip Oranienstrasse neighborhood, it caters to hostellers who need little privacy; there are no private rooms here at all. Rooms contain between four and ten beds—*real* beds, not bunks. Bathroom facilities are shared and rooms are coed, although there is also one dorm just for women.

Although it's located in a highly trafficked area, the sleeping rooms face the back of the building, providing some quiet. The hostel sets aside a place behind the desk for backpacks and other luggage—we'd rather see lockers—and there's a safety box for smaller valuables like passports and nose rings. You'll have to shell out extra dough for sheets and towels, though. The public phone here only takes change, no phone cards. Sheesh! Staff will sell you various transport tickets, including long-distance bus tickets for one of the new intra-Europe coach companies.

The place is quite roomy—it was a factory, after all—and has plenty of common areas. Management claims you can drive a car (maybe a Trabi) through the extra-wide hallways, though we're not saying you should actually try. Plans are in motion for a movie room, with seats from an old theater being installed to render the experience more authentic.

For food, the Kottbusser Tor area is just a subway stop away. This neighborhood is populated by Turkish immigrants, and there are good and cheap markets supplying fresh fruits and veggies, which is great since there is a well-equipped kitchen to play chef in. German supermarkets also abound. If you're into other people's unwanted junk, flea markets here should keep you occupied. During the summer there's a pool at Görlitzer park to dunk your toes in.

How to get there:

By bus: Contact hostel for transit details.

By car: Contact hostel for directions.

By train: From Zoo Station, take U-Bahn line U2 one stop to Wittenberg Platz, then change to U1 and continue to Görlitzer Bahnhof. Hostel is 10 yards from station.

JUGENDGÄSTEHAUS BERLIN (BERLIN GUEST HOUSE HOSTEL)

Kluckstrasse 3,

10785 Berlin

Phone: 030–26110–97 or 030–26110–98

Fax: 030–26503–83
E-mail: jh-berlin@jugendherberge.de
Web site: www.jugendherberge.de/jghb/jghb0.htm
Rates: 34–50 DM per Hostelling International member (about $17–$25 US)
Credit cards: No
Beds: 350
Private/family rooms: Yes
Kitchen available: No
Season: Open year-round
Office hours: Open twenty-four hours
Curfew: 3:00 A.M.
Affiliation: Hostelling International-DJH
Regional office: Berlin-Brandenburg
Extras: Cafeteria ($), Internet access, computer room, table tennis, VCR, TV room, parking, breakfast, information desk, meeting rooms, garden, luggage storage

Located in Schöneberg

Huge, German, and perfect in every way—except in terms of being interesting fun or humorous—this place is the DJH's showpiece, a contemporary design that warehouses you without making you feel that way. Too much.

Best bet for a bite:
Merz Schöneberger

Insiders' tip:
Market on Wednesday to Saturday mornings

What hostellers say:
"Kinda sterile."

Gestalt:
Warehouse district

Safety:

Hospitality:

Cleanliness:

Party index:

It's a big bland building with a somewhat interesting postmodern sculpture on the front lawn. Inside, they've got more than 300 beds, in a tremendous variety of shapes and sizes. Breakfast is included in the price, no matter what sort of room you get, and the auxiliary services they offer are incredible. Try Internet access, a computer work room, a game room with table tennis, meeting rooms, and meals, for starters. Three lounges—including one with a television—provide areas for hanging out.

But the draw here is that it's in the Schöneberg neighborhood, known as Berlin's quiet place to hang in a cafe without the crush of city noise and traffic. (It's also the center of gay Berlin, but that's another story.) This hostel is very central, close to both the Potsdamer Platz and the world-famous Brandenburg Gate, where Berliners celebrated—and continue to celebrate—the smashing of the Wall.

While in the area, you might head over to the Topographie des Terrors museum for a brutal history lesson of war-crimes exhibits. Appropriately (and chillingly) enough, it's on the same spot where the Gestapo and SS ran their operations for a dozen years, up to and through World War II. Find it by walking over (or taking the S-Bahn) to Anhalter Bahnof Station.

How to get there:

By car: Take Autobahn to Berlin, exiting at signs for Innsbrucker Platz; turn left at Hauptstrasse and continue to Potsdamer Strasse.

KEY TO ICONS

Attractive natural setting

Ecologically aware hostel

Superior kitchen facilities or cafe

Offbeat or eccentric place

Superior bathroom facilities

Romantic private rooms

Comfortable beds

Editors' choice: among our very favorite hostels

A particularly good value

Wheelchair accessible

Good for business travelers

Especially well suited for families

Good for active travelers

Visual arts at hostel or nearby

Music at hostel or nearby

Great hostel for skiers

Bar or pub at hostel or nearby

Make a left onto Lützowstrasse, then make a right onto Kluckstrasse and continue to hostel.

By bus: Take #129 bus to Gedenkstätte.

By train: From Zoo Station, take U-Bahn line U2 toward Vinetastrasse to Wittenbergplatz stop, then take U-Bahn line U1 or U15 to Kurfürstenstrasse Station. Walk ¼ mile up Potsdamer Strasse; make a left onto Lützowstrasse, then make a right onto Kluckstrasse and continue to hostel.

JUGENDHOTEL BERLIN (BERLIN YOUTH HOTEL HOSTEL)

Kaiserdamm 3,

14057 Berlin

Phone: 030–322–1011

Fax: 030–322–1012
Rates: 45–180 DM per person (about $23–$90 US); doubles 98–280 DM (about $50–$140 US)
Beds: 117
Private/family rooms: Yes
Kitchen available: No
Season: Open year-round
Office hours: Open twenty-four hours
Affiliation: None
Extras: Breakfast

Located in Charlottenburg

Breakfast is included at this hostel, which is located in Charlottenburg (west of Zoo Station) not very close to the main sights. It's an old-fashioned, unexciting, typically German place inside and out. The blah dorms range in size from singles to doubles to triples, and every room has its own bathroom.

This is really not a place where you'll be able to socialize, at least not in English. Most guests here are German sports groups—so you can count on a lot of soccer (only they call it football) played in the halls and wet towel snapping. However, if you can stand this jock-ular atmo, you'll be relieved to know that the hostel does provide something of a safe on-site for small valuables. Backpacks can be held at the desk.

If you're older than twenty-six, heads up: You can stay if there's room at the inn, but you'll pay double. They also charge for the linens here—and

Best bet for a bite:
Store House Grill
(Cajun!)

Insiders' tip:
Beers at Ax Bax

What hostellers say:
"Gotta train to catch!"

Gestalt:
Double or nothing

Safety:

Hospitality:

charge wayyyyy too much per bed if you ask us. This is supposed to be a cheapish hotel with dorm rooms and a few extras. But they forgot to make it cheap.

Cleanliness:

Party index:

How to get there:

By bus: Contact hostel for transit details.

By car: Contact hostel for directions.

By train: Take U-Bahn line U2 to Sophie-Charlotte-Platz, then walk along Kaiserdamm to hostel.

CIRCUS HOSTEL

Am Zirkus

Rosa-Luxemburgstrasse 39–41,

1933 Berlin

Phone: 030–2839–1433

Fax: 030–2839–1484

E-mail: circus@mind.de

Rates: 25–45 DM per person (about $13–$23 US); doubles 70 DM (about $35 US)

Credit cards: No

Beds: 90

Private/family rooms: Yes

Kitchen available: No

Season: Open year-round

Office hours: Open twenty-four hours

Affiliation: None

Extras: Internet access, bar, travel office, breakfast, restaurants ($), TV room, laundry, museum tickets, city tours

Located in Mitte

Close to the action in the historic center of Berlin, this hostel (which was formerly a trading house) serves up decent rooms at surprisingly low prices. There's a laid-back atmosphere, happy and flexible staff, lack of rules, even Internet access. Not bad, not bad at all.

The hostel's located in a stone building constructed in 1914 and 1915, then renovated just a couple of years ago in accordance with local historical ordinances. All the sanitary, electric, and heating systems were replaced, though the original stone staircases remain.

Dorms consist of single, double, triple, quad, five-bedded and six-bedded rooms. Of the seven double rooms, four have a standard double bed and three have two single beds, which can be pushed together to simulate a double. Duvets cover the beds. Only the few apartments—doubles and quads—have their own kitchens and bathrooms; other showers and bathrooms are located in hallways, and there are no communal kitchens besides those in the apartments. Luckily, supermarkets and cheap, good restaurants abound in the surrounding area—if you don't feel like dining at one of the hostel's two in-house restaurants, that is.

The services here are fantastic, all administered by cool staff. They include three Internet terminals; a bar; a booking service selling cut-rate train, bus, and museum tickets; and free breakfast (provided by one of the restaurants) with your bunk—it includes rolls, salami, croissants, and hot beverages. Two in-house restaurants dole out meals: One is a fancy French-German place; the other is an Italian trattoria. Both give great discounts to guests. They've also got bicycles for rent and washers and dryers for the grungy hosteller. The television lounge gets international satellite TV, and they lay out newspapers for you to read as well. You can even book an onward bed at certain other European hostels.

Like we said, not bad at all. Put this one on your short list of places to stay.

How to get there:

By bus: Contact hostel for transit details.
By car: Contact hostel for directions.
By train: From Zoo Station, take U-Bahn line U2 to Rosa-Luxembourg-Platz stop; walk to hostel. Or take U-Bahn line U6 or S-Bahn to Friedrichstrasse stop; walk to hostel.

Best bet for a bite:
Trattoria
Insiders' tip:
Oranienburger Strasse for Indian
What hostellers say:
"I like it!"
Gestalt:
Big top
Safety:
Hospitality:
Cleanliness:
Party index:

CLUBHOUSE HOSTEL

Johannisstrasse 2,
10117 Berlin
Phone: 030–2809–7979

Web site: www.clubhouse-berlin.de
Rates: 25–30 DM (about $13–$15 US) per person; doubles 80 DM (about $40 US)
Credit cards: No
Beds: 58
Private/family rooms: Yes
Kitchen available: No
Season: Open year-round
Office hours: Open twenty-four hours
Affiliation: None
Extras: Breakfast, Internet access, bar

Located in Mitte

This place is fairly standard, but the superior location—it's close to a hopping area with a serious nightlife factor—and friendly staff (some of them Aussies when we stopped by) push it into the "thumbs-up" category. What's even better, school groups are *not* accepted here.

Best bet for a bite:
Brooklyn (American food)

Insiders' tip:
Cafe Silberstein bar

What hostellers say:
"Pretty rad."

Gestalt:
Club bed

Safety: 👍

Hospitality: 👍

Cleanliness: 👍👎

Party index:
🎉🎉🎉🎉

The dorms are boring but clean, with an IKEA feeling. (That's a Swedish design firm heavy on blond woods and minimalist, black and steel-gray fixtures.) These rooms are divided into triples, doubles, and singles with no bunks. Sleep sacks are not allowed, so you'll have to fork over about two bucks for sheets; at least this is a fee you only have to pay once during the course of your stay. They have no kitchen and don't offer the services of some of the city's other backpacker-style joints. But there is something like a lounge, where you can hang around on fluffy sofas and drink beer, coffee, tea, or juices. Internet access is available; and late sleepers will rejoice over the gracious noon check-out time.

Remember that this place books up very early, however. Staff advises making a firm booking two to three *weeks* in advance between April and October if you want a double room, a week in advance during that time for dorms.

Why so popular? It's near one of the best parts of Mitte, that's why—right in the heart of Berlin's nightly party. There are so many sights, bars, and restaurants here you're going to be tripping over yourself. Staff told us that the hottest techno club in Berlin is steps away from the hostel and that Oranienburger Strasse and Tor are notorious for their shiny, happy club scene. Guests come from every corner of the globe to be part of it; during high season you'll encounter Americans, Brits, Japanese, Koreans, and, of course, Europeans. (In January and February, for some reason, the hostel is inundated with folks from South America living it up during their school breaks.) Staff is multilingual, obviously.

This hostel goes out of its way to provide local tours given by the owner, who worked in Berlin for the British Embassy when the city was still divided and can give hostellers an in-depth overview of the city's complicated political history. He illuminates even the drabbest, most insignificant-looking building (which other people would simply ignore). The tour lasts five hours, so wear those comfy walking shoes. If you'd rather see the city on your own schedule, the hostel staff sells transit passes. They can also make reservations and book round-Europe bus tickets for you.

How to get there:

By bus: Contact hostel for transit details.

By car: Contact hostel for directions.

By train: Take S-Bahn lines #1 or #25 to Oranienburger Strasse stop or U-Bahn line U6 to the Oranienburger Tor stop; walk to hostel.

CVJM HAUS

Einemstrasse 10,
10787 Berlin
Phone: 030–264–9100

Fax: 030–261–4308
Rates: 40–42 DM (about $20–$21 US) per person; doubles 78–84 DM (about $39–$42 US)
Credit cards: No
Beds: 80
Private/family rooms: Yes
Kitchen available: No
Season: Open year-round
Office hours: 8:00 A.M.–5:00 P.M.
Affiliation: None
Extras: Breakfast

Located in Schöneberg

This place is very popular, despite the specter of sleeping under the watchful eye of Bible-thumping ownership. They do manage to keep the message from overwhelming the goal of providing cheap and decent beds, and these *are* decent beds—in single, double, and quad rooms that are institutional but adequate. The sky-blue paint job doesn't hurt, either. Still, all in all it's a pretty boring place, frequented mostly by field-tripping German school groups. So it's not full of partying animals, obviously.

The one advantage to this place is that it's pretty close to the western center of Berlin, with all the nightlife—such as the clubs and pubs on Winterfeldplatz and along Goltzstrasse—that this location brings. In fact, the joint's located smack in the middle of one of the city's gayest (and we don't mean happiest) neighborhoods. If you're into that, fine: Stay here and make a beeline for the area around Motzstrasse. If you're not, you might think about staying elsewhere.

For some more recent and sobering history, visit the Rathaus Schöneberg, where JFK delivered his famous speech promising American support of Berlin residents (and accidentally referred to himself as a "jelly

Best bet for a bite:
Goltzstrasse for cheap eats

Insiders' tip:
Try "Berlin White" beer

What hostellers say:
"Somewhere over the rainbow . . ."

Gestalt:
Schöne-ing star

Safety:

Hospitality:

Cleanliness:

Party index:

doughnut" in German!). You could also check out the plaque at the Nollendorfplatz U-Bahn station eulogizing gay prisoners killed in Nazi concentration camps.

But the Schöneberg area really is more lighthearted than this, more conducive to freewheeling social pursuits than history lessons. There are scads of bars, cafes, clubs, and restaurants catering mostly to the gay lifestyle.

Good location, sure, but this place is simply too dull (they do supply breakfast with your bunk, though). Stay one night to check out the area if you must, but as soon as you can find a better place to stay, book it.

How to get there:

By bus: Contact hostel for transit details.

By car: Contact hostel for directions.

By train: From Zoo Station, take U-Bahn lines U2 or U15 to Nollendorfplatz stop; walk to hostel.

DIE FABRIK

Schlesische Strasse 18,
10997 Berlin
Phone: 030–611–7116

Fax: 030–617–1504
E-mail: info@diefabrik.com
Web site: www.diefabrik.com
Rates: 30–66 DM (about $15–$33 US) per person; doubles 94 DM (about $47 US)
Credit cards: No
Beds: 120
Private/family rooms: Yes
Kitchen available: No
Season: Open year-round
Office hours: Open twenty-four hours
Affiliation: None
Extras: Bike rentals, breakfast ($), meals ($)

Located in Kreuzberg

Once an industrial building, this hostel has been well renovated into a very good hostel-cum-bed-and-breakfast near the river that divides Berlin in half.

Best bet for a bite:
Kleine Markthalle for chicken

Insiders' tip:
Exercise caution after dark

What hostellers say:
"Lotsa fun."

It's cheapest in the cavernous fifteen-bed bunkroom at the bottom, also known in Europe as a "sleep-in," but it's actually not too bad. You'll get more exercise and pay more for the privacy of smaller quad, triple, double, and single rooms as you ascend. All rooms are roomy and airy with plenty of windows. They rent bicycles, offer breakfast—though you've gotta pay extra for that—and serve meals in a cafe.

The location, in too-hip-to-be-true Kreuzberg, is ideal. This is the neighborhood to hit for the best Turkish food, not to mention oodles of punkers, longhairs and other not-conforming-to-society folks.

How to get there:

By bus: Take bus #265 or N65 to Taborstrasse stop; walk to hostel.

By car: Contact hostel for directions.

By train: From Zoo Station, take U-Bahn line U1 or U15 to Schlesisches Tor stop; walk to hostel.

Gestalt: Fabrik of society
Safety:
Hospitality:
Cleanliness:
Party index:

JUGENDHERBERGE BERLIN "ERNST REUTER"

(Ernst Reuter Berlin Hostel)

Hermsdorfer Damm 48-50,

13467 Berlin

Phone: 030–404–1610

Fax: 030–404–5972
E-mail: jh-ernst-reuter@jugendherberge.de
Web site: www.jugendherberge.de/ernst/ernst0.htm
Rates: 28–35 DM per HI member (about $14–$18 US)
Credit cards: No
Beds: 111
Private/family rooms: Yes
Kitchen available: No
Season: Closed December 6–January 6
Office hours: Open twenty-four hours
Curfew: 1:00 A.M.
Affiliation: Hostelling International-DJH
Regional office: Berlin-Brandenburg
Extras: TV, table tennis, foosball, breakfast, meals ($), laundry, lockers, luggage storage, information desk

Located in Outer Districts

This hostel is located in the suburbs of Berlin, with excellent connections into the city center by public transport (night and day), despite the long haul out here. If everything else is full, it's not a bad choice.

The series of connected buildings here are made of stone, around forty years old, and nicely decorated and painted. A great green lawn, lush overhanging trees, and picnic tables out front dress up the outside, sure, but it's also some 9 miles out of town.

Some rooms and sections are newer and better lit than others. The dorms inside are mostly five- or six-bedded affairs (sixteen of those); there are four family rooms as well. Bathrooms and showers are in the hallways; in some cases you have to walk downstairs a floor to use 'em. Ugh!

Anyway, they have plenty of hosteller services to distract you, including Internet access, a guest laundry, a television lounge for couch potatoes, a game room with two table tennis tables, and an information desk dispensing crucial info about the city. They serve a big breakfast buffet throughout the day, then at night often serve a hot dinner for about four bucks. (There's no kitchen for hostellers to cook in.)

Jogging trails and woods surround the hostel, yet you can buy food just a couple hundred yards away when hunger pangs strike. You can also hit the nearby Alt-Tegel subway station's shops for other vital goods, often at lower prices than in the city. And here's one final tip: Rather than enduring the complicated transit route to get into town, inquire about taking the local sightseeing boat from here into central Berlin; it leaves from the Tegel Greenwichpromenade. Neat.

Best bet for a bite:
U-Bahn for grub

Insiders' tip:
Tip magazine for listings

What hostellers say:
"Okay."

Gestalt:
Mellow yellow

Safety:

Hospitality:

Cleanliness:

Party index:

How to get there:

By bus: From Zoo Station, take U-Bahn line U9 to Leopoldplatz stop, then change to U-Bahn line U6 and continue to Alt-Tegel stop; change to #125 bus and continue to Jugendherberge (hostel) stop.

By car: From the north take Highway 111 to Berliner Ring, exiting at signs for Hermsdorfer Damm. From the south take Highway 115 and Highway 111 to Stadtring Nord, exiting at signs for Hermsdorfer Damm.

By train: See "By bus" directions or if you're leaving from Ost Station, take S-Bahn train to Friedrichstrasse stop, then change to U-Bahn line U6 or S-Bahn line S25 and continue to Tegel station.

JUGENDGÄSTEHAUS FEURIGSTRASSE
(FEURIGSTRASSE GUEST HOUSE HOSTEL)

Feurigstrasse 63,
Berlin
Phone: 030–781–5211

Fax: 030–788–3051
Rates: 38–55 DM (about $14–$20 US) per person; doubles 90 DM (about $45 US)
Credit cards: No
Beds: 200
Private/family rooms: Yes
Kitchen available: No
Season: Open year-round
Office hours: Open twenty-four hours
Affiliation: None
Extras: Breakfast

Located in Schöneberg

This boring-looking structure is located in a very cool area, and there's no denying the superior drinking, eating, and shopping opportunities that abound at every turn. However, it's hard to ignore the drab hostel interior and focus on what's outside. And they don't speak any English—at *all*. At one point our German reviewer sent us this telegraphic dispatch, which sounded a lot like an SOS signal:

". . . this is a terrible place . . . it is expensive, old and odd . . . you feel like you're in barracks . . . only school-classes visit this place . . . STOP."

That was enough to keep us from staying. But we threw him a flotation device, and he kept at it until he got the full story. Here's what else he found out: The rooms are four- or six-bedded dormitories, and breakfast is included with a night's stay. However, it's more expensive to stay here in high summer season than it is during the rest of the year. They also charge for sheets, as do many other places in the city.

The surrounding area is a haven for book junkies, he added, so if you're actu-

Best bet for a bite:
Thai place on Vorbergstrasse

Insiders' tip:
Metropolis (in English) for events listings

What hostellers say:
"Reading is fundamental."

Gestalt:
Book nook

Safety: 👍

Hospitality: 👍👎

Cleanliness: 👍👎

Party index:

ally thinking of staying (and we can't imagine that you still are), bring a few extra deutsche marks and stock up on your reading material.

How to get there:

By bus: Take #204 or #348 bus to Kaiser-Wilhelm-Platz stop; walk to hostel.
By car: Contact hostel for directions.
By train: From Zoo Station take U-Bahn line U7 to Kleistpark station; walk to hostel.

GÄSTEHAUS (GUEST HOUSE HOSTEL)

Wiener Strasse 14,

10999 Berlin

Phone: 030–618–2008

Fax: 030–618–2006
E-mail: info@freiraum-berlin.com
Web site: www.freiraum-berlin.com
Rates: 27.50–40.00 DM (about $14–$20 US) per person; doubles 70 DM (about $35 US)
Credit cards: Yes
Beds: 35
Private/family rooms: Yes
Kitchen available: No
Season: Open year-round
Office hours: Open twenty-four hours
Affiliation: None
Extras: Apartments, pool access nearby

Located in Kreuzberg

This small guest house attracts travelers of all stripes, but its lack of a common room/hangout area deters backpacker types from flocking here to meet like-minded others. It's a fairly quiet hostel that draws an older crowd who like to blend with locals, soak up the sights on their own terms—and save money in the process.

Best bet for a bite: Cafe Jolesch

Insiders' tip: Viktoriapark for peace and quiet

What hostellers say: "Hip 'n' happening"

Gestalt: Best guest house

Safety:

Hospitality:

Cleanliness:

Party index:

The joint started out as a mere bed-without-the-breakfast agency matching people in need of accommodations with beds. After operating the agency for seven years, the manager/owner decided that he'd rather establish an actual hostel. (He still sets folks up with beds through his agency if the guest house is full.)

Rooms come in combinations of singles, doubles, triples, and one six-bedded dorm room. There are also three apartments that each have a small kitchen and its own bathroom. All other hostelers must share bathrooms with their fellow guests.

You're close to green and leafy Görlitzer Park, which has an indoor pool for splashing in, as well as Spreewald Platz—always good for a cheap nosh. Oranienstrasse is a stone's throw away, too, and that's where you want to go to check out the techno clubs. Night buses (those with an "N" in the number) whisk you to and from the hostel all night long, as there's no curfew to worry about.

Ivos, the friendly manager, also runs a helpful Web page (www.net4berlin.com) with English links to help you figure out the complicated and trendy Berlin*szene*. He's from East Berlin and can educate you on how the city has changed, then direct you to cafes and bars. One of his faves is the Anker Klause, just a few minutes' walk from the hostel.

How to get there:

By bus: Contact hostel for transit details.

By car: Contact hostel for directions.

By train: From Zoo Station, take U-Bahn lines U1, U12, or U15 to Görlitzer Bahnof stop; walk to hostel.

HOTEL TRANSIT HOSTEL

Hagelberger Strasse 53-54,

10965 Berlin

Phone: 030–789–0470 or 030–785–5051

Fax: 030–7890–4777

E-mail: welcome@hotel-transit.de

Web site: www.hotel-transit.de

Rates: 33–90 DM (about $17–$45 US) per person; doubles 105 DM (about $53 US)

Credit cards: Yes

Beds: 150

Private/family rooms: Yes

Kitchen available: No

Season: Open year-round

Office hours: Open twenty-four hours

Affiliation: None

Extras: TV room, bar, breakfast, courtyard

Located in Kreuzberg

This hotel doubles as a hostel, and it offers considerable goodies—a nice courtyard, roomy dorms, a good location, and friendly, English-speaking staff.

The cool, cool furnishings in the dorms and doubles give you a happy feeling right away. Attempt to watch television in the room shared with the hoppin' bar, or hang in the courtyard; we don't care. Sleep in if you want, 'cause there's no lockout and a free breakfast is included with your bunk. Be warned, though, that this place attacts plenty of school groups. When we checked the place out on a Monday night (a night not known for being raucous), the bar was teeming with garrulous kids, making it apparent that the hostel succeeds at bringing folks together. Staff assures us that was a fluke . . . but you'll have to go yourself to find out for sure.

The rooms have no more than six beds each, assuring a (relative) modicum of privacy—much appreciated when you've done time in the notorious *mehrbettzimmer* (dormitories, literally "many-bedded room") in lots of other hostels. If you and your traveling companion require even more privacy, there are doubles at a slight extra cost, still well within price reach for the budget hosteller.

Best bet for a bite:
Chandra Kumari (Sri Lankan)

Insiders' tip:
Bike rentals nearby

What hostellers say:
"More fun than I thought possible."

Gestalt:
Transition abroad

Safety:

Hospitality:

Cleanliness:

Party index:

Breakfast is offered at no extra cost—a buffet that includes cheese, sausage, bread, cereal, and choice of coffee, tea, or hot chocolate. You can eat as much as you want, so you might make it through till dinner if you're lucky. As an additional service, the hostel works with two local tour companies to help you understand the intricate political and cultural history of this sprawling metropolis. Note that these tours do cost extra.

This a great neighborhood, as we've said before, and—as befits it—there's a great travel store called Outdoor on Bergmannstrasse. Head there to stock up on guidebooks and maps, some of them actually in English. For some nice green space in which to toss around a Frisbee, head to nearby Viktoria Park.

How to get there:

By bus: Contact hostel for transit details.

By car: Contact hostel for directions.

By train: From train station take U-Bahn line U6 or U7 to Mehringdamm stop; walk to hostel.

LETTE 'M SLEEP HOSTEL

Lettestrasse 7,
10437 Berlin
Phone: 030–4473–3623

Fax: 030–4473–3625
E-mail: info@backpackers.de
Rates: 25–35 DM (about $13–$18 US) per person; doubles 90 DM (about $45 US)
Credit cards: No
Beds: 45
Private/family rooms: Yes
Kitchen available: Yes
Season: Open year-round
Office hours: Open twenty-four hours
Affiliation: None

Extras: Internet access, TV, information desk, garden, snacks

Located in Prenzlauer Berg

The only hostel in Prenzlauer Berg, this newish place is pretty good for the money.

The clean-enough dorms are three- to six-bedded. Each room has only a sink, not a bathroom, but there are plenty of other extras—a television lounge, Internet access for checking that e-mail, a hosteller kitchen, and a beer-gardeny backyard. Some of the double rooms have kitchens, a great bonus, but there's also a main kitchen for everybody to use. Staff are very helpful and friendly, speak multiple languages, and will point you toward the best sights, bars, and discount transit deals.

There are tons of rockin' clubs, pubs, and cafes nearby, so you can't possibly get bored here. Ignore the post-industrial look of the area and the half-finished buildings, and head out for a beer or a coffee. There's also a convenient Spar market close at hand. Note that although it's usually a quiet, safe neighborhood, a staffer confided a recent theft of the hostel TV. That incident appears to have been just an isolated blip on an otherwise calm radar screen, but keep an eye on your stuff anyway. By the way, if you want to be hip and with it, refer to the 'hood as "Prenzle Berg" just like the locals do.

This hostel is extremely popular in July and August, so much so that reservations are not accepted. Staff advise that you either call and be placed on a rather lengthy waiting list or just stay the night elsewhere and show up at the hostel around midday after most folks have checked out.

Best bet for a bite:
Offenbach Stuben

Insiders' tip:
Nosthalgia bar for good vodka

What hostellers say:
"But I don't *wanna* sleep."

Gestalt:
Prenz charming

Safety:

Hospitality:

Cleanliness:

Party index:

How to get there:

By bus: Contact hostel for transit details.

By car: Contact hostel for directions.

By train: Take U-Bahn line U2 to Eberswalder Strasse stop, then walk down Danziger Strasse 1 block to Lychener Strasse. Turn left and continue to Lettestrasse, then turn right and walk to hostel.

JUGENDGÄSTEHAUS NORDUFER (NORDUFER GUEST HOUSE HOSTEL)

Nordufer Strasse 28,
13351 Berlin
Phone: 030–4519–9112

Fax: 030–452–4100
Rates: 38–40 DM (about $19–$20 US) per person
Credit cards: No
Beds: 130
Private/family rooms: Yes
Kitchen available: No
Season: Open year-round
Office hours: 7:00 A.M.–5:00 P.M. (sometimes later)
Affiliation: None
Extras: Pool access ($), breakfast

Best bet for a bite:
Schleusenkrug Müller
(by the canal)

Insiders' tip:
#100 bus for cheap
sight-seeing

What hostellers say:
"I feel so relaxed!"

Gestalt:
Pool party

Safety:

Hospitality:

Cleanliness:

Party index:

Located in Outer Districts

This place is definitely off the beaten track, outside the city central sight-seeing zone—though actually very well equipped if you don't mind the commute.

They've got everything from single to doubles to larger dormitories. It's all quiet enough and well managed, and staff are relaxed enough to lay back on what rules there are here. Breakfast is included with your bed, by the way, and it's very good and plentiful. You can also pay a bit extra for access to a swimming pool next door, or head for the lake instead.

Of all the "Outer-District" hostels in town, this one is the closest; it's just across the canal from Tiergarten. You won't find tons and tons of nightlife around here, but strap on your walking shoes and you'll find parks aplenty.

How to get there:

By bus: From Zoo Station, take U-Bahn line U9 to Leopoldplatz stop; change to line U6 and continue to Seestrasse stop, then take #126 bus to hostel.

By car: Contact hostel for directions.

By train: From Zoo Station take U-Bahn line U9 to Westhafen stop, then cross bridge and continue to Nordufer Strasse. Or take U-Bahn line U9 to Leopoldplatz stop; change to U6 and continue to Seestrasse stop, then take #126 bus to hostel.

ODYSSEE GLOBETROTTER HOSTEL

Grünberger Strasse 23,
10243 Berlin
Phone: 030–2900–0081

Fax: 030–2900–0081
Rates: 24–36 DM (about $12–$18 US); doubles 50–72 DM (about $25–$36 US)

Credit cards: No
Beds: 82
Private/family rooms: Yes
Kitchen available: No
Season: Open year-round
Office hours: Open twenty-four hours
Affiliation: None
Extras: Bar, lockers, breakfast ($), pool table, Internet access

$ 🍺

Located in Friedrichshain

This is it: Berlin's most party-hearty hostel (and that's saying something in a town where almost every hostel *must* have a bar to survive). Even when you're not partying, you'll be socializing. It's fun, fun, fun.

The rooms? They've got doubles, quads, six-bedded dorms, and eight-bedded ones too; per usual, the cost of your bunk drops with each incremental drop in privacy. They've got lockers, a pool table, e-mail access, and the bar's open till *dawn*. (No, silly, there's no curfew here.) In fact, someone at the hostel told us that it never closes!

You can shoot some stick in the pool room and store stuff in lockers. Even the absence of a laundry is somewhat mitigated by the fact that there's one right around the corner—ask the staff for details.

The place is located in Friedrichshain, Berlin's drab-looking yet quickly developing nightspot-of-the-moment. It is actually starting to get a little expensive to live around here, which must seem incredible to the old-timers in the neighborhood.

Best bet for a bite:
Dachkamer

Insiders' tip:
Pentascop's a freaky bar

What hostellers say:
"Wild."

Gestalt:
Space Odyssee

Safety:

Hospitality:

Cleanliness:

Party index:

How to get there:

By bus: From Ost Station take #147 or #250 bus to hostel.
By car: Contact hostel for directions.
By train: From Zoo Station take any S-Bahn train east to Warschauer Strasse stop, then walk north up Warschauer Strasse; turn left at Grünberger Strasse. Hostel is on right.

STUDENTHOTEL HUBERTUSALLEE (HUBERTUSALLEE STUDENT HOTEL)

Delbrückstrasse 24,
Berlin
Phone: 030–891–9718

Fax: 030–892–8698
Rates: 30–80 DM (about $15–$40 US); doubles 70–110 DM
(about $35–$55 US)
Credit cards: No
Beds: Number varies
Private/family rooms: Yes
Kitchen available: No
Season: Open March 1–October 31
Office hours: Open twenty-four hours
Affiliation: None
Extras: Breakfast

Located in Outer Districts

Best bet for a bite:
U-Bahn stop

Insiders' tip:
Buy a transit pass

What hostellers say:
"Nice bathrooms."

Gestalt:
Shower power

Cleanliness:

Party index:

Situated a couple miles southwest of the city center, near a small lake, this place is hardly worth mentioning—it's neither easy to get to nor superattractive. And they charge you for sheets, besides.

On the other hand, let's give them credit for this: Every room in the joint has a bathroom and shower in it, and that's saying something. Consider it a good desperation pick if you happen to have a car (yeah, right). Otherwise it's probably best to cross it off your list.

How to get there:
By bus: Take #119 bus or #129 bus to hostel, or contact hostel for transit details.
By car: Contact hostel for directions.
By train: Contact hostel for transit details.

JUGENDGÄSTEHAUS TEGEL
(TEGEL GUEST HOUSE HOSTEL)
Ziekowstrasse 161,
Berlin
Phone: 030–433–3046
Fax: 030–434–5063
Rates: 38 DM per person (about $19 US)
Credit cards: No
Beds: 220
Private/family rooms: Sometimes
Kitchen available: No
Season: Open year-round
Office hours: 7:30 A.M.–11:00 P.M.
Affiliation: None
Extras: Breakfast

Located in Outer Districts

This place is somewhat remote and extremely German—to the point that we couldn't make our English (or our schoolbook German) understood at all—consequently, it's not our first pick in town.

Dorms are equipped with a variety of setups, anywhere from three to eight beds to a dormitory; private-room space is often available. These rooms are adequate—nothing special, but certainly fresh and clean. Management does include breakfast with the price of your bed, however. The place is very busy and popular with German groups, so check in advance before showing up expecting a bunk.

How to get there:

By bus/train: From train station take S-Bahn line S25 or U-Bahn line U6 to Alt-Tegel Station, then change to #222 or N22 bus and continue to Tituweg stop; walk to hostel.

By car: Contact hostel for directions.

Best bet for a bite:
Stock up at breakfast

Insiders' tip:
Phone ahead for booking

What hostellers say:
"Bitte."

Gestalt:
Group dynamics

Safety:

Hospitality:

Cleanliness:

Party index:

JUGENDGÄSTEHAUS BERLIN "AM WANNSEE" (BERLIN-WANNSEE GUEST HOUSE HOSTEL)

Badeweg 1,
14129 Berlin
Phone: 030–803–2035

Fax: 030–803–5908
E-mail: jh-wannsee@jugendherberge.de
Web site: www.jugendherberge.de/jghw/jghw0.htm
Rates: 34–42 DM per HI member (about $17–$21 US)
Credit cards: No
Beds: 288
Private/family rooms: Yes
Kitchen available: No
Season: Open year-round
Office hours: Open twenty-four hours
Curfew: 1:00 A.M.
Affiliation: Hostelling International-DJH
Regional office: Berlin-Brandenburg
Extras: Lake, disco, garden, table tennis, parking, laundry, TV room, luggage storage

Located in Outer Districts

To get here you make a very long trip out to what turns out to be a peaceful, sleepy neighborhood that comes with its own lake. That's correct: It's set right on Berlin's biggest lake.

It's a depressing building once you arrive, however, with an exceptionally plain post-industrial design even for a German hostel. Think a concrete structure with multicolored flags. On second thought, think "bomb shelter." A few bright splotches of paint here and there do help a bit. All seventy-two rooms here are four-bedded rooms, and they've decked the place out with everything modern you'd need. There's a disco of sorts, a game room containing a table tennis table, a television lounge, a luggage room, and a guest laundry. It's all adequate if a bit boring. Caution, however, before booking your bunk: Schoolkids often book this big place absolutely full, meaning this peaceful quiet neighborhood is occasionally overrun with the pitter-patter of restless German youths.

To escape you might head for the lake and walk, swim, or boat. There's also the depressing Wannsee museum, commemorating (if that's the word) the place where the Nazis met in 1938 and decided to proceed with the mass extermination of Jews.

Best bet for a bite:
Better eat here

Insiders' tip:
Peacocks on Pfaueninsel

What hostellers say:
"Nice lake!"

Gestalt:
See side

Safety:

Hospitality:

Cleanliness:

Party index:

How to get there:

By bus: Take #118 bus to Badewag stop and walk 30 yards to hostel.

By car: From Berliner Ring take Highway A115, following signs toward Mitte to exit for Spanische Allee; make a left onto Kronprinzessinnenweg and another left onto Badeweg.

By train: From Zoo Station take S-Bahn line S1 or S7 to Nikolassee Station. Exit station at Strandbad sign and make a left onto Fussgängerbrücke; cross bridge and make a left onto Kronprinzessinnenweg. The hostel will be on the right.

JUGENDGÄSTEHAUS AM ZOO (ZOO GUEST HOUSE HOSTEL)

Hardenbergstrasse 9a,
10623 Berlin

Phone: 030–312–9410

Fax: 030–312–550–330
Rates: 35–52 DM (about $18–$26 US); doubles 85–95 DM (about $43–$48 US)
Credit cards: No
Beds: Number varies
Private/family rooms: Yes
Kitchen available: No

Season: Open year-round
Office hours: 9:00 A.M.–midnight
Lockout: 10:00 A.M.–2:00 P.M.
Affiliation: None
Extras: Breakfast (groups only)

Located in Charlottenburg

As you can tell from the name of this hostel, it's the closest one to the city zoo—and, by extension, huge Zoo Station.

However, the hostel frankly leaves some things to be desired. In fact, speaking of negative first impressions, the first time we dropped by the place, nobody opened the door as we rang and pounded on it—despite the long hours that reception claims the place is open. Imagine if it had been the freezing cold and dark of winter, we had just stumbled off a late-arriving train, and the door refused to open!

Anyway, *somebody* must be opening that door, because the place has been very popular in recent years due to its prime location near the station—maybe too popular for its own good. The bunks are beat up; breakfast is served to groups only, not individual saps like yourself. At least it's very close to a number of bars and clubs.

Yeah, there's a lot to do in the surrounding areas. The Erotic Museum, right near the main train station, isn't the best in Europe, but it's fine as a quick stop if you've really got sex on the brain. One of our favorite discoveries in the neighborhood, though, is Savignyplatz, a square just a block or two away from the train station (going west). Its jazz bars, clubs, and pubs are among the city's classiest and most atmospheric, and they're not too expensive, either.

That city zoo is actually pretty decent as such things go. And don't forget to take a minute and drop by the giant KaDeWe department store, Europe's most humongous department store and a famous relic of the former GDR. Our hot tip is that you can check your e-mail cheaply on the fly inside the store. Head for the electronics section and flag down a clerk.

Best bet for a bite:
Mövenpick Marché on Ku'dammom

Insiders' tip:
Ewige Lampe for jazz

What hostellers say:
"Couldn't be any closer to the station."

Gestalt:
Zoo Station

Safety: 👍👍

Hospitality: 👍

Cleanliness: 👍👍

Party index:

How to get there:

By bus: Take #145 bus to Steinplatz stop; walk to hostel.

By car: Contact hostel for directions.

By train: From Zoo Station exit back of train station; walk down Hardenbergstrasse to hostel. From Ost Station take U-Bahn line U2 or U9 or S-Bahn to Zoologischer Garten (Zoo Station). Exit back of Zoo Station; walk down Hardenbergstrasse to hostel.

NORTHERN GERMANY

3 Rostock

2 Lübeck

1 Hamburg

NORTHERN GERMANY

Northern Germany might not seem, at first glance, to be the most interesting area: It's darned flat, for one thing, and the weather—influenced by the ocean—can get pretty blah. But look again. There's a ton of history, dating back to the Vikings. Later, as capital of the Hanseatic League, the region ruled the European roost for a time. And the local beer is pretty good. So's the coffee.

Big cities are few and far between up here, so if you're touring the area you're probably going to hotfoot it straight to Hamburg. That's a good plan if you feel like diving into a hectic city with tons of culture. If it's summertime, though, and you wanna kick back a little, you couldn't do much better than to head for one of the many German islands fringing the North and Baltic Seas. Up toward the Danish border, the northern coast is chock-full of old towns and cities and great beaches. Handsome Lübeck and Rostock are two other cities you should work into your itinerary—and bring that beach towel. Swimsuits are usually optional. Or, beginning in Berlin, you could explore the surprisingly pretty countryside of Brandenburg province.

Getting to northern Germany isn't too hard, even if the airport here is relatively insignificant. That's because semiregular trains roll into Hamburg from Berlin, Frankfurt, Munich, Copenhagen, Köln, Amsterdam, and other points. From here you can fan out into the countryside using the efficient German train system. Or try taking a ferry from Sweden or Denmark to the northern tip of the country, from where you'll connect soon enough to one of these three cities.

HAMBURG

Hamburg has got so much stuff going on at once it's futile to try to savor all of it. What an interesting mixture: young and old, gay and straight, punk and straitlaced, seedy and respectable, German and Asian—all salted by the brine of the ocean that originally gave the place life. (And don't forget that this was the first place in the world to properly appreciate the Beatles.)

Yes, there's water, water everywhere here—more than 2,000 bridges over the Alser and Elbe Rivers and their various canals, more than there are in Venice even. The North Sea is actually more than 50 miles away from Hamburg, but that hasn't slowed down activity at one of the world's busiest ports or its 18 miles of docks.

German-descended hostellers might drop by the Emigration Office and Museum to find out if their ancestors once sailed from here. Non-German but culinary-minded hotshots would probably hit the Hot Spice Gewerzmuseum instead, with a pile of hot-t-t-t-t spices—some said to be aphrodisiacs—to check out. Just remember that all the museums in the city are closed on Monday; that might be a good time to hit Harry's Harbour Bazaar, an exceedingly kitschy flea market–type place in the racy Reeperbahn red-light district.

Use the good U-Bahn and S-Bahn networks to get around town; it's a quick hop from the main train station, where you'll likely arrive, to three of these four hostels. If you're gonna try to see some museums or move around a lot on the subway exploring, the one-day Hamburg Card is a good deal; it gives you free public transit and museum entry for about $8.00 US per day. And remember to take a bit of caution, especially in rough-and-tumble or seedy areas.

HAMBURG HOSTELS at a glance

	RATING	COST	IN A WORD	PAGE
Schanzenstern	👍	33–60 DM	happenin'	70
Instant Sleep Backpacker	👍	30–60 DM	good	66
Auf dem Stintfang	👍	27.00–42.50 DM	central	67
Horner Rennbahn	👍	30.00–35.50 DM	distant	69

INSTANT SLEEP BACKPACKER HOSTEL

277 Max-Brauer-Allée,
22796 Hamburg
Phone: 040–4318–2310

Fax: 040–4318–2311
E-mail: backpackerhostel@instantsleep.de
Rates: 29–45 DM (about $15–$23 US); doubles 76 DM (about $38 US)
Credit cards: No
Beds: Number varies
Private/family rooms: Yes
Kitchen available: Yes
Season: Open year-round
Office hours: 9:00 A.M.–2:00 P.M.
Affiliation: None
Extras: Laundry, TV, VCR, Internet access, fax service, balcony, travel information, lockers

We can't guarantee that you'll fall asleep instantly, but this new place seems like a winner, though it's still too early in the game to say for sure.

A backpacker-style hostel on the first floor of a second-floor building redone after the war, it's got more modern comforts than you might expect—Internet access, a laundry setup, a communal kitchen— plus a range of bedding options. You could go for a double (there are three), triple (choose from five), the quad, or five-bedded dorms, or to save a few more bucks try out the larger eight- or ten-bedded ones. Each room is painted in a different color or theme, with different wallpapers; each has lockers and curtains, too. Alas, the bathrooms and showers are located off the hallways.

The surrounding area is chock-full of bars, alternative-lifestyle hangouts, and good ethnic food, so dive in without predetermined ideas. You might convert to Communism by the time you're through, sure, but you'll have a good time in the process. Really. Go ahead. If you don't have the energy to walk far, as close as right across the street you'll find tons of cheap ethnic food stalls, pubs, clubs, markets, coffee shops, pastry shops—anything you'd need—and all the locals hang out here, not the tourists.

Also make sure to get to the old center and check out all the neat churches here in Hamburg. You've got the St. Michaelis church for fans of Baroque (you can climb to the top or take an elevator); the St. Jacobi church (with a beautiful old altar, bombed-out tower, and really old organ); and the fourteenth-century St. Katharinen church, which you can't miss because a statue of the aforementioned saint tops the 350-foot spire.

Best bet for a bite:
Gorki Park

Insiders' tip:
Transmontana coffee shop nearby

What hostellers say:
"Cool."

Gestalt:
Sleeper

Safety:

Hospitality:

Cleanliness:

Party index:

How to get there:

By bus: Contact hostel for transit details.
By car: Contact hostel for directions.
By train: From station take U-Bahn line U3 or S-Bahn lines S3 or S21 to Sternschanze stop; walk ¼ mile to hostel.

JUGENDHERBERGE "AUF DEM STINTFANG" (HAMBURG STINTFANG HOSTEL)

Alfred Wegener Weg 5,

20459 Hamburg

Phone: 040–313–488

Fax: 040–315–407
E-mail: jh-stintfang@t-online.de
Rates: 27.00–42.50 DM per HI member (about $14–$21 US)

Credit cards: No
Web site: www.schoelzel.com/Jugendherberge-hamburg
Beds: 332
Private/family rooms: Yes
Kitchen available: Yes
Season: Closed January 1–31 and December 24–26
Office hours: 6:00 A.M.–9:30 A.M.; 11:30–1:00 A.M.
Lockout: 9:30 A.M.–11:30 A.M.
Curfew: 1:00 A.M.
Affiliation: Hostelling International-DJH
Regional office: Nordmark
Extras: Breakfast, meals ($), table tennis, tour discounts, Internet access, fax service, computer room, TV room, laundry, luggage storage, meeting room

You couldn't be more centrally located than in this huge hostel, which has scored unbelievable position right along the harbor just a mile from Hamburg's main train station. The sleaze, sex trade, boat traffic, and boisterous fish markets—among other fun stuff—of St. Pauli and the Reeperbahn are practically at your, um, fingertips.

You ascend stone steps between actual trees— a nice touch—and enter through big glass doors. (But the upstairs windows are so small that, at first glance, you can't help but think you're walking straight into the world's best-kept chicken-breeding barn.) Inside, bunks come in two- to eight-bedded rooms—twenty-three with two to four beds, thirteen with five or six beds, and twenty-three bigger than that—and everything's pretty modern. How many hostels have you slept in that had fax, computer *and* e-mail services on-site? And the meals here are very, very good for a hostel at a low cost. If you don't like 'em, or wanna save money, they also have a kitchen on premises; that's quite a rarity in German hostels, we'll tell you that. There's a television room, game room, and a lounge, too.

Great, right? Not so fast—it's all just a little too Germanly run for our taste. Lockout? Curfew? Segregated dorms? A three-night maximum stay rule that's usually enforced? Chill out, man; Hamburg is supposed to be Boho.

Best bet for a bite:
Sagres

Insiders' tip:
Erotica museum nearby

What hostellers say:
"Whoa!"

Gestalt:
St. Pauli girl

Safety:

Hospitality:

Cleanliness:

Party index:

For fun, blow the hostel and hit one of the quadruple-threat of nearby attractions. First and foremost, a must-see if you're here on the weekend, is the Fischmarkt: yes, a fish market—just what it sounds like—with a bizarre twist. Sunday morning, from around 5:00 to 10:00 A.M., you mingle with the masses and check out the catch of the day to cool music and loads of strong drink (only the Germans could've come up with *this*). Other produce, meats, and knickknacks are also available, and prices soften toward ten o'clock. It's absolutely nuts, and you've gotta see it to believe it. Afterward, brunch is served in the auction hall with (what else?) schnapps.

The rest of the week, the St. Pauli neighborhood just to the west is quite hip and active day or night, with an incredible number of restaurants, bars, and other diversions in which to blow your hard-earned wad. The Reeperbahn just north of the hostel is a naughty (although legal) red-light district; it's really only a "sight" if you're a desperate guy on the make. Finally, harbor tours by boat are a good bet to kill an afternoon; the hostel sometimes can get you a serious discount.

How to get there:

By bus: Take #112 bus and walk 200 yards to hostel.

By car: Take Ludwig-Erhard-Strasse (B4) to Zeughausmarkt and continue to Neumayerstrasse.

By train: From train station take S-Bahn line S1, S2, or S3 or U-Bahn line U3 to Landungsbrücken stop. Walk 200 yards uphill to hostel.

JUGENDGÄSTEHAUS "HORNER RENNBAHN" (HAMBURG-HORNER RENNBAHN GUEST HOUSE HOSTEL)

Rennbahnstrasse 100,

22111 Hamburg

Phone: 040–651–1671

Fax: 040–655–6516

E-mail: jgh-hamburg@t-online.de

Rates: 30.00–35.50 DM per HI member (about $15–$18 US)

Credit cards: No

Beds: 267

Private/family rooms: Yes

Kitchen available: Yes

Season: Closed February 1–28 and December 23–31

Office hours: 7:00–9:30 A.M.; 12:30 P.M.–1:00 A.M.

Curfew: 1:00 A.M.

Affiliation: Hostelling International-DJH

Regional office: Nordmark

Extras: Patio, grill, pool table, table tennis, grounds, breakfast, foosball, fireplace, stage, piano, parking, meals ($)

This is probably the least convenient of Hamburg's four hostels, set 4 or 5 miles out in the hinterlands east of the city center. Your fellow hostellers will also likely be school groups, schoolkids, and school bus drivers—all speaking German, of course—so prepare the earplugs. (Ironically, the place is four stories of brick and looks a lot like those

70s-architecture high schools we all attended.)

So face it—you're probably not going to be hanging out downtown if you're booked here. At least the place is very nicely furnished, with good new two- to six-bedded rooms—eighteen with two to four beds each and the lion's share (thirty-eight) containing five or six beds. It's very much a place of such kid- and adult-friendly services as table tennis and a grill on a terrace. They've also got two fireplaces, a foosball table, and a small practice room with stage for that choral group or rock band you're touring Europe with. Needless to say, there's a grand piano in there. Wanna make like Liberace? This is the place.

Our advice? If you're stuck out here, battle for position at the games tables and *use* them. Also note that the included breakfast is pretty filling, so stock up.

How to get there:

By bus: From Berliner Tor downtown take #160 bus to Horner Rennbahn Station; walk ½ mile along Tribünenweg to hostel.

By car: Take Autobahn to Ring 2, exiting in the direction of Wandsbek; continue 4 miles to hostel.

By train: From train station take U-Bahn line U3 to Horner Rennbahn Station; walk ½ mile along Tribünenweg to hostel.

Best bet for a bite:
Good luck

Insiders' tip:
Buskers congregate outside City Hall

What hostellers say:
"Too far out."

Gestalt:
Far and away

Safety:

Hospitality:

Cleanliness:

Party index:

SCHANZENSTERN HOSTEL

Bartelsstrasse 12,
20357 Hamburg
Phone: 040–439–8441

Fax: 040–439–3413
Web site: www.schanzenstern.de
Rates: 33–60 DM per person (about $17–$30 US); doubles 90 DM (about $45 US)
Credit cards: No
Season: Open year-round
Office hours: 6:30–2:00 A.M.
Affiliation: None
Extras: Restaurant ($), breakfast ($), garden

A converted factory or warehouse of some sort, this place makes up for location (in an interesting neighborhood) what it might lack in first-glance ambience.

The rooms inside are neat and clean, and the double rooms are a bargain: They're private and furnished, if a bit spartan—think spindly folding metal chairs, standard-issue bunks, tiny arty writing tables, and a dresser. The rest of the dorms here mostly contain from three to five beds (you pay less for a bunk in the bigger ones, of course), and there are some singles as well at a premium price, which is still fairly cheap. There aren't any bathrooms in the rooms, although you can shower in some dorms. Breakfast is served each morning, for about $5.00 US extra, and a nice garden cafe serves other meals during the day and night.

As we've noted above, the Schanzenviertel district is best for people-gawking: Gays, lesbians, Turks, Asians—you'll see 'em all here. A place for lefties, not righties. (Let's just say that the hammer and sickle haven't exactly gone out of style in this neighborhood.)

You might also head for some other parts of town and check out both the interesting ship museum and the St. Pauli-Museum—especially neat for music fans, 'cause it documents the Beatles' mop-top days in grungy Hamburg clubs just before they became famous.

Best bet for a bite:
'bok Imbiss

Insiders' tip:
Internet place a few blocks east of main station

What hostellers say:
"Not bad"

Gestalt:
Hamburg helper

Safety: 👍

Hospitality: 👍

Cleanliness: 👍

Party index: 🎉🎉🎉

How to get there:

By bus: From bus terminal walk to train station and follow the directions given "By train."

By car: Take Highway A7 to Bahrenfeld exit or Highway A24 to Horn exit, continuing north up Schanzensternstrasse to Susannenstrasse; make two lefts to Bartelsstrasse. Or contact hostel for directions.

By train: From station take U-Bahn line U3 or S-Bahn line S3 or S21 to Sternschanze stop, then walk ¼ mile south down Schanzensternstrasse to corner of Bartelstrasse. Hostel is on right, at corner.

KEY TO ICONS

- Attractive natural setting
- Ecologically aware hostel
- Superior kitchen facilities or cafe
- Offbeat or eccentric place
- Superior bathroom facilities
- Romantic private rooms
- Comfortable beds
- Editors' choice: among our very favorite hostels
- A particularly good value
- Wheelchair accessible
- Good for business travelers
- Especially well suited for families
- Good for active travelers
- Visual arts at hostel or nearby
- Music at hostel or nearby
- Great hostel for skiers
- Bar or pub at hostel or nearby

LÜBECK

It's not often that you're going to check into a town that was built around 1100. But Lübeck was. And check this out—the downtown area, where most of the hostels are, is actually on an island. Pretty unusual (though it used to be more common in medieval times).

The city's main attraction is its old-world ambience: This was once one of the command posts for that big bad Hanseatic League you're always reading about in your history books. Most of the impressive gates, fortifications, and cathedrals built with that cash still stand tall today. Also of note, Thomas Mann's novel *Buddenbrooks* was written about the city, though we've absolutely no idea why you should care about that fact when picking a hostel.

If you're planning on museum hopping, invest in the Lübeck Card to get all the bus rides you want, train rides to Travemünde, and significant discounts on museum fees. If you can't or won't get one of those, at least remember that every Friday museums in the city are free—except for the Holstentor, that is.

JUGENDHERBERGE LÜBECK (LÜBECK HOSTEL)

Am Gertrudenkirchhof 4,
23568 Lübeck

Phone: 0451–33433, 0451–388–2208, or 0451–388–5981

Fax: 0451–34540
E-mail: jhluebeck@dJugendherberge-nordmark.de
Rates: 28–33 DM per HI member (about $14–$17 US)
Credit cards: No
Beds: 218
Season: Open year-round
Office hours: 7:30 A.M.–midnight
Affiliation: Hostelling International-DJH
Regional office: Nordmark
Extras: Breakfast, grill, table tennis, cafeteria ($), parking, disco, luggage storage, laundry, meeting room, garden

This hostel's not right in the center of town, unlike the other two mentioned here, but it's still a very reasonable option—and much closer than many big-city "official" hostels tend to be, just a mile or so from the main train station as the crow flies. (If the crow carries a backpack and has sore feet, who knows?) The bottom line is this: You'll still be able to get to all the sights, bars, and other stuff with your own two feet.

The place is made up of a series of white-washed buildings. Inside, beds are in two- to six-bedded rooms with sinks—more specifically, there are twenty-five rooms with two to four beds apiece, then twenty-six more with five or six beds apiece—and they've set up a good array of amenities. Try the outdoor grill, meal service, free breakfast included with your stay, and a games area with table tennis. There's a small "disco" for practicing your night moves, a garden for hanging out in during good weather, and a very useful laundry room, too.

The other advantage to this hostel's position is its proximity to the watery suburb of Travemünde, whence regular ferries head up to Scandinavian lands.

How to get there:

By bus/train: From station take 1, 3, 11, 12, or 31 bus to Gustav-Radbruch-Platz stop; walk 200 yards to hostel.

By car: Take Highway A1 to Lübeck-Zentrum, then follow signs in the direction of Innenstadt to Holstentor, Untertrave, and Jugendherberge.

Best bet for a bite:
Hostel cafeteria

Insiders' tip:
Great jazz club nearby

What hostellers say:
"Decent."

Gestalt:
Lübeck job

Safety:

Hospitality:

Cleanliness:

Party index:

JUGENDGÄSTEHAUS LÜBECK (LÜBECK GUEST HOUSE HOSTEL)

Mengstrasse 33,
23552 Lübeck
Phone: 0451–702–0399

Fax: 0451–77012
E-mail: Jugendgastehausluebeck@dJugendherberge-nordmark.de
Rates: 28.50–37.00 DM per HI member (about $15–$19 US)
Credit cards: No
Beds: 73
Private/family rooms: Yes
Kitchen available: No
Season: Closed December 23–January 5
Office hours: Open twenty-four hours
Affiliation: Hostelling International-DJH
Regional office: Nordmark
Extras: Breakfast, meals ($)

Smack in the middle of town, you'll fall over backward (well, maybe not; depends on how many beers you've had) when you realize how central this place is. Too bad the feel is incredibly institutional:

Don't expect to joke around a lot with the staff, don't expect cookies in a jar at the reception desk, and don't expect mints on the pillows.

Every room has four or fewer beds, at least, and all have their own sinks. A breakfast is also included in the price of your bunk. They serve meals here, too—a welcome bonus if you don't feel like scouting out cheap grub in the downtown area. Strap on the feed bag and head for the assembly-line meals in the dining room if you're so inclined.

How to get there:

By bus/train: From station take #1 bus, or walk ½ mile to hostel.

By car: Take Autobahn to Lübeck-Zentrum exit.

RUCKSACKHOTEL HOSTEL

Kanalstrasse 70,
23552 Lübeck

Phone: 0451–706–892

Fax: 0451–707–3429
Rates: 21–26 DM per person (about $11–$13 US);
doubles 75 DM (about $38 US)
Credit cards: No
Beds: 30
Private/family rooms: Yes
Kitchen available: Yes
Season: Open year-round
Affiliation: None
Extras: Meals ($), concerts

A pretty small independent entry, this one gets points not only for location—it's on one edge of the moatlike river that encircles the island of central Lübeck—but also its philosophy: It's run communally and puts a strong emphasis on the arts, the environment, and human rights. If you're not a Republican, you'll fit right in.

The place features good doubles with private bathrooms, four- to eight-bedded dorms that are also decent, a lounge, a kitchen, and a vegetarian snack bar. As a super-big bonus, one of the city's coolest music clubs is *right on premises!* If you dig music, put down this book right now and make a reservation.

How to get there:

By bus/train: From Lübeck Station, take #8 bus to Falkenstrasse stop; cross bridge to hostel.

By car: Contact hostel for directions.

Hospitality:

Party index:

ROSTOCK

Yet another interesting (and very old) northern German town, Rostock's day has long since come and gone. There's a surprising spirit in the nightlife, though, so dig in for a night if you want. Just ignore the occasional blocks of fascist-style buildings (this was East Germany once, remember), and concentrate on such treats as gabled homes. among the other highlights: pieces of the former city walls, a high church steeple, and the very attractive (and very pink) city hall near the Steintor gate. It's not hard to reach the place—regular trains come through from Berlin or, if you've taken a ferry to Germany, nearby Straslund.

Don't miss the summertime fun during the annual July regatta: The preceding festivities include an anything-goes race.

JUGENDGÄSTESCHIFF "TRADITIONSSCHIFF" (ROSTOCK TRADITIONSSCHIFF HOSTEL)

Postfach 48,

18106 Rostock-Schmarl

Phone: 0381–716–224

Fax: 0381–714–014

Web site: www.djh-mv.de

Rates: 27.50–40.00 DM per Hostelling International member (about $14–$20 US)

Credit cards: No

Beds: 85

Private/family rooms: Yes

Kitchen available: No

Season: Closed December 21–28

Office hours: 3:00–6:00 P.M.

Affiliation: Hostelling International-DJH

Regional office: Mecklenburg-Vorpommerm
Extras: Bar, meals ($), parking

This place isn't nearly central enough, given what an interesting city Rostock is. From the main station you have to take a connecting city train to another station—okay—and then, get this, hoof it an additional mile or more past hideous-looking apartment blocks and even beyond a *lighthouse*, for gosh sakes, before you're here. Needless to say, if you're sleeping here, you're not gonna be partying late-night in town, or you'll never make it back.

Best bet for a bite:
Beer garden on Kröpeliner-Strasse

Insiders' tip:
Lollipop disco nearby

What hostellers say:
"Where the hell *is* it?!"

Gestalt:
Ship ahoy

Safety:

Hospitality:

Cleanliness:

Party index:

But take heart, 'cause there is just one little cool thing about it—it's a *boat!* Yeah, that's right, a boat, as befits this very maritime area where the fish is king and water is life. Okay, it's a *big* boat (a freighter weighing 10,000 tons, no longer seaworthy, and now a museum). Don't let that stop you, though—if you're ticking off the wildest hostels in Europe, you just gotta visit this one.

The hostel consists almost solely of triples and doubles. Things are fairly simple here, though meals and a small bar also add interest. Besides the tiny nearby beach, there's a small (obviously) ship museum onboard if you're into the history of seafaring.

How to get there:

By bus: Contact hostel for transit route.

By car: Take Route B103 to Rostock-Schmarl or E55 to Warnow-Fähre.

By train: From train station take S-Bahn to Lütten-Klein Station, then walk east 1 mile and make a left. Continue past parking lots to hostel.

JUGENDHERBERGE WARNEMÜNDE (ROSTOCK WARNEMÜNDE HOSTEL)

Parkstrasse 46,

18119 Rostock OT Warnemünde

Phone: 0381–548–170

Fax: 0381–548–1723
E-mail: jh.warne@t-online.de
Web site: www.djh-mv.de

Rates: 25.50–30.50 DM per HI member (about $13–$16 US)
Credit cards: No
Beds: 184
Private/family rooms: Yes
Kitchen available: No
Season: Closed December 10–27
Office hours: 10:00 A.M.–7:30 P.M.
Affiliation: Hostelling International-DJH
Regional office: Mecklenburg-Vorpommern
Extras: Grounds, beach access, parking, meals ($)

It's cheap and it's just a hundred yards from the nice beach. That's about all there is to say about this alternative Rostock choice, a non-descript four-story slab that is even farther from downtown than the other hostel.

It's actually located in a suburb that turns beach town in summer. If it's really hot out, this is a much better choice than the Rostock hostel because you can quickly reach the city by S-Bahn. The appealing grounds include a nice green lawn—totally at odds with the bunkerlike gray thing hanging over it.

Anyhow, good staffing keeps everything moving smoothly—must be all that salt air. All sixty-two rooms here are pretty small—either doubles, triples, or quads. Otherwise it's unexceptional and efficient. The only real service they offer is the serving of meals.

Don't have time to ride all the way into town for the sights? No problem. Warnemünde is a resort on the Baltic Sea, so you just might decide not to take that transit ride into town if the sun's shining and the clothes are coming off—this is potential nude beach territo-

Best bet for a bite:
Fish off the boats

Insiders' tip:
Beach ferry from Stadthafen downtown

What hostellers say:
"Get my towel."

Gestalt:
Beachy keen

Safety: 👍

Hospitality: 👍

Cleanliness: 👍

Party index:

ry, after all. Grab a towel and hit the sand, or just wander around looking at the cutesy cottages of the fisherfolk, who once outnumbered the tourists here. One of 'em even has a regional museum inside, just south of the main plaza.

Adequate hostel, nice beach, nice spot to get away from cities for awhile.

How to get there:

By bus/train: From Rostock Station take the S-Bahn to Lichtenhagen Station, then take #36 bus to Strand (beach) stop.

By car: Take Highway A19, exiting for Rostock, then continue on the B103 in the direction of Warnemünde.

JUGENDHERBERGE ALBERSDORF

(Albersdorf Hostel)

Bahnhofsstrasse 19,

25767 Albersdorf

Phone: 04835–642

Fax: 04835–8462
Rates: 22–27 DM per HI member
(about $11–$14 US)
Beds: 114
Private/family rooms: Yes
Kitchen available: No
Season: Closed December 23–
January 5
Affiliation: HI-DJH
Regional office: Nordmark
Extras: Basketball court, volley-
ball net, table tennis, pool
table, laundry, meals ($), park-
ing, wheelchair access

How to get there:
By bus: Contact hostel for transit
details.
By car: Take Highway A23 to
B203.
By train: From Hamburg station
take S-Bahn to Bahnstrecke
Hamburg-Heide; then walk ¼
mile to hostel.

JUGENDHERBERGE ASCHBERGHAUS

(Ascheffel Hostel)

24358 Ascheffel

Phone: 04353–307

Fax: 04353–815
Rates: 20–25 DM per HI member
(about $10–$13 US)
Beds: 36

Private/family rooms: Yes
Kitchen available: Yes
Season: Closed November 1 to
Easter
Affiliation: HI-DJH
Regional office: Nordmark
Extras: Soccer field, meals ($),
parking

How to get there:
By bus/train: From Owschlag or
Eckernförde Station take bus to
Ascheffel (Baumgarten stop),
then walk 1 mile to hostel.
By car: Exit for Owschlag, then
drive 4 miles toward
Eckernförde.

JUGENDHERBERGE BAD DOBERAN

(Bad Doberan Hostel)

Tempelberg,

18209 Bad Doberan

Phone: 038203–62439

Fax: 038203–62228
E-mail: jugendherberge-
tempelberg@t-online.de
Web site: www.djh-mv.de
Rates: 23–28 DM per HI member
(about $12–$14 US)
Beds:124
Private/family rooms: No
Kitchen available: No
Season: Closed November 1–
January 31
Affiliation: HI-DJH
Regional office: Mecklenburg-
Vorpommerm
Extras: Volleyball, meals ($)
How to get there:
By bus: Contact hostel for

transit route.

By car: Take Highway B105 for ¼ mile to Dr.-Leber-Strasse and Lindenstrasse.

By train: From Bad Doberan Station walk ½ mile to hostel.

JUGENDHERBERGE BAD FREIENWALDE

(Bad Freienwalde Hostel)

Hammerthal 3,

16259 Bad Freienwalde

Phone: 03344–3875

Fax: 03344–31598

E-mail: Jugendherberge-bad-freienwalde@jugendherberge.de

Web site: www.jugendherberge.de/badfr/badfr0.htm

Rates: 21–26 DM per HI member (about $10–$13 US)

Beds: 48

Private/family rooms: Yes

Kitchen available: No

Season: Closed November 1–March 1

Affiliation: HI-DJH

Regional office: Berlin-Brandenburg

Extras: Meals ($)

How to get there:

By bus/train: From Bad Freienwalde Station contact hostel for transit route.

By car: From Berliner Ring, exit for Hohenschönhausen; take Highway B158 to Bad Freienwalde and then a little farther on the B167 in the directions of Eberswalde-Finow

"SPORTABZEICHEN-JUGENDHERBERGE"

(Bad Oldesloe Hostel)

Konrad-Adenauer-Ring 2,

23843 Bad Oldesloe

Phone: 04531–5945

Fax: 04531–67574

E-mail: Jugendherbergeoldesloe@dJugendherberge-nordmark.de

Rates: 25–27 DM per HI member (about $13–$14 US)

Beds: 125

Private/family rooms: Yes

Kitchen available: Yes

Season: Closed December 5–January 5

Affiliation: HI-DJH

Regional office: Nordmark

Extras: Grill, sports facilities, meals ($), parking, wheelchair access

How to get there:

By bus: Contact hostel for transit details.

By car: Exit for Bad Oldesloe off Highway B75 to Konrad-Adenauer-Ring, watching for signs for Schwimmhalle.

By train: Trains run to Bad Oldesloe Station from Hamburg and Lübeck. Contact hostel for further transit details.

JUGENDHERBERGE BAD SAAROW

(Bad Saarow Hostel)

Dorfstrasse 20,

15526 Bad Saarow

Phone: 033631–2664

Fax: 033631–59023

E-mail: Jugendherberge-Bad-Saarow@jugendherberge.de

Web site: www.jugendherberge.de

Rates: 21–26 DM per HI member (about $11–$13 US)

Beds: 92

Private/family rooms: Yes

Kitchen available: No
Season: Contact hostel for current season
Affiliation: HI-DJH
Regional office: Berlin-Brandenburg
Extras: Tennis, disco, volleyball, music practice rooms

How to get there:

By bus:/train From Berlin take train to Fürstenwalde, then take Zubringerbus to Bad Saarow. Contact hostel for details on express bus.

By car: Take Highway 12 to Fürstenwalde exit, then take Landstrasseto Bad Saarow-Pieskow.

KARL-MAY-JUGENDHERBERGE
(Bad Segeberg Hostel)
Kastanienweg 1,
23795 Bad Segebcrg
Phone: 04551-2531

Fax: 04551-4518
Rates: 22–27 DM per HI member (about $11–$14 US)
Beds: 152
Private/family rooms: Yes
Kitchen available: No
Season: Closed December 23–January 5
Affiliation: HI-DJH
Regional office: Nordmark
Extras: Disco, grill, table tennis, volleyball, piano, fireplace, boat rentals, parking, meals ($), wheelchair access

How to get there:

By bus/train: Contact hostel for transit details.

By car: From Hamburg, Lübeck, or Kiel take Highways B432, 205, and 206.

JUGENDHERBERGE BARTH (Barth Hostel)
Donnerberg,
18356 Barth
Phone: 038231-2843

Fax: 038231-2090
Web site: www.djh-mv.de
Rates: 22–32 DM per HI member (about $11–$16 US)
Beds: 155
Private/family rooms: Yes
Kitchen available: No
Season: Closed November 1–March 31
Affiliation: HI-DJH
Regional office: Mecklenburg-Vorpommerm
Extras: Horse-riding nearby, meals ($), wheelchair access, parking

How to get there:

By bus/train From Stralsund take train to Barth, or take bus from Ribnitz or Damgarten to Barth.

By car: From Rostock or Stralsund take Highway B105 to Kreuz Löbnitz.

JUGENDHERBERGE UECKERMÜNDE-BELLIN
(Bellin Hostel)
Dorfstrasse,
17375 Bellin
Phone: 039771-22411

Fax: 039771-22554
Web site: www.djh-mv.de
Rates: 25–30 DM per HI member (about $13–$15 US)
Beds: 80
Private/family rooms: Yes
Kitchen available: No
Season: Closed December1–January 31
Affiliation: HI-DJH

Regional office: Mecklenburg-
Vorpommerm
Extras: Meals ($), parking, wheel-
chair access
How to get there:
By bus/train: Take train to
Ueckermünde Station, then take
bus in the direction of Altwarp-
Luckow to Dorfmitte stop.
By car: Take Highway A11 to
Prenzlau, then take Highway
B109 to hinter Jatznik and con-
tinue in the direction of
Torgelow to Bellin. Or contact
hostel for directions·

FAMILIENHERBERGE PRORA

(Binz-Prora Family Hostel)
Strandstrasse 12,
18609 Binz
Phone: 038393–32844

Fax: 038393–32845
E-mail: jh-prora@t-online.de
Web site: www.prora.city-map.de
Rates: 27–42 DM per HI member
(about $14–$21 US)
Beds: 150
Private/family rooms: Yes
Kitchen available: No
Season: Closed December 19–27
Affiliation: HI-DJH
Regional office: Mecklenburg-
Vorpommerm
Extras: Meeting room, video room,
parking, meals ($)
How to get there:
By bus/train: Take D-Zug train or
Intercity train to Binz, then take
bus to Prora-Ost and walk ¼
mile to hostel.
By car: Take Highway B96 to
Kreuzung Karow, then take
Highway 196A following signs
to Prora-Ost.

JUGENDHERBERGE BINZ/RÜGEN

(Binz/Rügen Hostel)
Strandpromenade 35,
18609 Binz
Phone: 038393–32597

Fax: 038393–32596
E-mail: jugendherberge-binz
@t-online.de
Web site: www.jugendherberge-
binz.de
Rates: 36.00–41.50 DM per HI
member (about $18–$21 US)
Beds: 143
Private/family rooms: Yes
Kitchen available: Yes
Season: Closed December 13–28
Affiliation: HI-DJH
Regional office: Mecklenburg-
Vorpommerm
How to get there:
By bus: Contact hostel for transit
details.
By car: Contact hostel for direc-
tions.
By train: Take direct train to Binz
Station from Berlin or Köln.
Contact hostel for further transit
details.

JUGENDHERBERGE BORGWEDEL

Kreisstrasse 17,
24857 Borgwedel
Phone: 04354–219

Fax: 04354–1305
Rates: 22–27 DM per HI member
(about $11–$14 US)
Beds: 282
Private/family rooms: Yes
Kitchen available: No
Season: Closed December 23–
January 5

Affiliation: HI-DJH
Regional office: Nordmark
Extras: Table tennis, volleyball, boats, meals ($)

How to get there:
By bus/train: Take train to Schleswig Station, then take bus to Borgwedel. Contact hostel for transit details.
By car: Contact hostel for directions.

JUGENDHERBERGE BORN-IBENHORST
(Born-Ibenhorst Hostel)
Umweltstudienplatz,
Im Darsser Wald,
18375 Born-Ibenhorst
Phone: 038234–229

Fax: 038234–231
Web site: www.djh-mv.de
Rates: 23–34 DM per HI member (about $12–$17 US)
Beds: 180
Private/family rooms: Yes
Kitchen available: No
Season: Closed November 1– February 28
Affiliation: HI-DJH
Regional office: Mecklenburg-Vorpommerm
Extras: Grounds, cafeteria ($), laundry, wheelchair access, parking

How to get there:
By bus/train: Take train from Ribnitz to Damgarten (West) or Barth, then take bus in the direction of Born to Jugendherberge Ibenhorst stop and walk to hostel.
By car: Contact hostel for directions.

JUGENDHERBERGE BRAUNSDORF
(Braunsdorf Hostel)
Dorfstrasse 17,
15518 Braunsdorf
Phone: 033633–635

Fax: 033633–65630
Rates: 19–24 DM per HI member (about $10–$12 US)
Beds: 54
Private/family rooms: Yes
Kitchen available: No
Season: Contact hostel for current season
Affiliation: HI-DJH
Regional office: Berlin-Brandenburg

How to get there:
By bus/train: Take S-Bahn train to Erkner or Fürstenwalde, then take bus to Braunsdorf (several per day) and walk 250 yards to hostel.
By car: Take Autobahn Route 12, exiting at signs for Storkow, then follow Landstrasse to Markgrafpieske-Braunsdorf.

JUGENDHERBERGE BREMSDORFER MÜHLE
15890 Bremsdorf
Phone: 033654–272

Fax: 033654–49044
E-mail: Jugendherberge-bremsdorfer-muehle@jugendherberge.de
Web site: www.jugendherberge.de/brm/brm0.htm
Rates: 19–24 DM per HI member (about $10–$12 US)
Beds: 140
Private/family rooms: Yes
Kitchen available: No
Season: Open year-round
Affiliation: HI-DJH

Regional office: Berlin-
Brandenburg
Extras: Volleyball, basketball,
pool, meals ($)

How to get there:
By bus:/train Take train to
Eisenhüttenstadt or Beeskow
and then take bus. Contact hos-
tel for transit details.
By car: Take Berliner Ring and
Autobahn Route 12 to exit for
Storkow, then follow
Landstrasse to Storkow, taking
Highway B246 through Beeskow
to Jugendherberge.

JUGENDHERBERGE BUCKOW
(Buckow Hostel)
Berliner Strasse 36,
15377 Buckow
Phone: 033433–286

Fax: 033433–56274
E-mail: Jugendherberge-
Buckow@jugendherberge.de
Web site: www.jugendherberge.de
Rates: 21–26 DM per HI member
(about $11–$13 US)
Beds: 106
Private/family rooms: Yes
Kitchen available: No
Season: Open year-round
Affiliation: HI-DJH
Regional office: Berlin-
Brandenburg
Extras: Grill, volleyball, play-
ground, meals ($)

How to get there:
By bus/train: From Berlin's Zoo
Station or Lichtenberg Station,
take S-Bahn line S5 to
Strausberg, then take bus to
Buckow.
By car: Take Berliner Ring to
Lichtenberg exit, then take
Highway B1 to Müncheberg,
and follow Landstrasse 6 miles

to Buckow/Waldsieversdorf.

JUGENDHERBERGE BURG/SPREEWALD
(Burg/Spreewald Hostel)
Jugendherbergsweg 8,
03096 Burg/Spreewald
Phone: 035603–225

Fax: 035603–13248
E-mail: Jugendherberge-
Burg@jugendherberge.de
Web site: www.jugendherberge.de
Rates: 21–26 DM per HI member
(about $11–$13 US)
Beds: 202
Private/family rooms: Yes
Kitchen available: No
Season: Open year-round
Affiliation: HI-DJH
Regional office: Berlin-
Brandenburg
Extras: Volleyball, basketball,
meals ($)

How to get there:
By bus/train: Take train to Cottbus
Station. From station take #44,
#46, or #47 bus to Burg/Bleske
stop and walk ¾ mile to hostel.
By car: Take Autobahn Route 13
from Berlin or Dresden to
Dreieck Spreewald, then take
Autobahn Route 15 in the direc-
tion of Cottbus/Forst to exit for
Vetschau. Follow Landstrasse
into city.

JUGENDHERBERGE BÜSUM
(Büsum Hostel)
Dr.-Martin-Bahr-Strasse 1,
25761 Büsum
Phone: 04834–93371

Fax: 04834–93376
Rates: 22–27 DM per HI member

(about $11–$14 US)
Beds: 206
Private/family rooms: Yes
Kitchen available: No
Season: Closed December 23–
January 31
Affiliation: HI-DJH
Regional office: Nordmark
Extras: Volleyball, parking, wheel-
chair access, meals ($)

How to get there:
By bus: Contact hostel for transit
details.
By car: Take Highway A23 to
Heide, then merge onto
Highway B203 and continue to
Büsum.
By train: Take train to Heide
Station, then change trains to
Büsum. From Büsum Station
walk ½ mile or take taxi to hostel.

JUGENDHERBERGE
BURG AUF FEHMARN
(Burg auf Fehmarn Hostel)
Mathildenstrasse 34,

23769 Burg auf Fehmarn
Phone: 04371–2150

Fax: 04371–6680
Rates: 22–27 DM per HI member
(about $11–$14 US)
Beds: 188
Private/family rooms: No
Kitchen available: No
Season: Closed December 23–
January 5
Affiliation: HI-DJH
Regional office: Nordmark
Extras: Piano, playground, grill,
table tennis, foosball, volleyball,
meals ($), parking, laundry,
wheelchair access

How to get there:
By bus/train: Take train to
Puttgarden Station then take

bus to Burg. Contact hostel for
further transit details.
By car: Contact hostel for directions.

JUGENDHERBERGE
BURG STARGARD
(Burg Stargard Hostel)
Dewitzer Chaussee 07,

17094 Burg Stargard
Phone: 039603–20207

Fax: 039603–20207
Web site: www.djh-mv.de
Rates: 25–30 DM per HI member
(about $13–$15 US)
Beds: 126
Private/family rooms: Yes
Kitchen available: No
Season: Closed January 3–31
Affiliation: HI-DJH
Regional office: Mecklenburg-
Vorpommerm
Extras: Grounds, parking, meals
($)

How to get there:
By bus: Contact hostel for transit
details.
By car: Take Highway B96 to exit
for Neustrelitz-Greifwald, then
continue to Neubrandenburg.
By train: Take train from
Neubrandenburg Station or
Neustrelitz Station to Burg
Stargard. Then walk 1 mile to
hostel.

JUGENDHERBERGE
CHOSSEWITZ
(Chossewitz Hostel)
Weichensdorfer Strasse 3,

15848 Chossewitz
Phone: 033673–5757
Fax: 033673–55100

E-mail: Jugendherberge-
Chossewitz@jugendherberge.de
Web site: www.jugendherberge.de
Rates: 21–26 DM per HI member
(about $11–$13 US)
Beds: 58
Private/family rooms: Yes
Kitchen available: No
Season: Open year-round
Affiliation: HI-DJH
Regional office: Berlin-
Brandenburg
Extras: Volleyball, basketball, pro-
grams, meals ($)

How to get there:
By bus/train: Contact hostel for
transit details.
By car: Take Autobahn Route 12 to
exit for Fürstenwalde-Ost, then
follow Landstrasse to Beeskow
and take Highway B168 to
Friedland; continue in direction
of Weichensdorf and then
Chossewitz.

JUGENDHERBERGE COTTBUS

(Cottbus Hostel)
Klosterplatz 2–3,
03046 Cottbus
Phone: 0355–22558

Fax: 0355–23798
Rates: 21–26 DM per HI member
(about $11–$13 US)
Beds: 43
Private/family rooms: Yes
Kitchen available: Yes
Season: Contact hostel for current
season
Affiliation: HI-DJH
Regional office: Berlin-
Brandenburg
Extras: Meals ($)

How to get there:
By bus: Contact hostel for transit
details.

By car: From the north take
Autobahn Route 13 from Berlin
or Dresden to Dreieck
Spreewald, then follow
Autobahn Route 15 to exit for
Cottbus-West. From the south
take Autobahn Route 13 to exit
for Ruhland, then take Highway
B 169 to Cottbus.
By train: From Cottbus Station
walk 2 miles to hostel, or con-
tact hostel for transit details.

JUGENDHERBERGE CUXHAVEN-DUHNEN

(Cuxhaven Hostel)
Schlensenweg 2,
27476 Cuxhaven
Phone: 04721–48552

Fax: 04721–45794
E-mail: Jugendherberge cuxhaven
@dJugendherbergenordmark.de
Rates: 24–29 DM per HI member
(about $12–$15 US)
Beds: 277
Private/family rooms: Yes
Kitchen available: No
Season: Closed December 15–
January 5
Affiliation: HI-DJH
Regional office: Nordmark
Extras: Grill, beach, playground,
basketball, piano, meals ($),
parking, wheelchair access

How to get there:
By bus/train: Take train to
Cuxhaven Station. From station
take #1 or #21 bus in the
direction of Döse/Duhnen to
Seelust stop, or walk 1 mile to
hostel.
By car: Take Highway A27 from
Bremen to Cuxhaven, or take
Highway B73 from Hamburg to
Cuxhaven.

JUGENDHERBERGE DAHMEN
(Dahmen Hostel)
Dorfstrasse 14,

17166 Dahmen

Phone: 039933–70552

Fax: 039933–70650
Web site: www.djh-mv.de
Rates: 25–32 DM per HI member
(about $13–$16 US)
Beds: 130
Private/family rooms: Yes
Kitchen available: No
Season: Closed December 1–
January 15
Affiliation: HI-DJH
Regional office: Mecklenburg-
Vorpommerm
Extras: Grounds, laundry, parking
How to get there:
By bus: Take bus from Teteow to
Malchin. Or contact hostel for
transit details.
By car: Take Highway A24 to exit
for Linstow. Head in direction of
Malchin.
By train: Take train to Waren.
Contact hostel for further transit
details.

JUGENDHERBERGE DASSOW-HOLM
(Dassow Hostel)
An der B 105,

23942 Dassow

Phone: 038826–80614

Fax: 038826–80614
Web site: www.djh-mv.de
Rates: 24.50–29.50 DM per HI
member (about $13–$15 US)
Beds: 122
Private/family rooms: Yes
Kitchen available: No

Season: Closed October 1–April
30
Affiliation: HI-DJH
Regional office: Mecklenburg-
Vorpommerm
Extras: Grounds, meals ($), park-
ing, wheelchair access

How to get there:
By bus:/train Take train to
Grevesmühlen Station, then
take bus in the direction of
Dassow to Holm stop.
By car: Take Highway B105 from
Lübeck or Rostock through
Dassow. Hostel is located in
woods on main road.

JUGENDHERBERGE DEMMIN
(Demmin Hostel)
**Rudolf-Breitscheid-Strasse,
Postfach 1201,**

17102 Demmin

Phone: 03998–223–388

Fax: 03998–223–388
Web site: www.djh-mv.de
Rates: 21–26 DM per HI member
(about $11–$13 US)
Beds: 32
Private/family rooms: No
Kitchen available: No
Season: November 1–March 31
Affiliation: HI-DJH
Regional office: Mecklenburg-
Vorpommerm
Extras: Bike rentals, meals ($)
How to get there:
By bus: Contact hostel for transit
details.
By car: Contact hostel for direc-
tions.
By train: Take train to Demmin
Station, then walk ¾ mile to
hostel.

JUGENDHERBERGE ECKERNFÖRDE
(Eckernförde Hostel)
Sehestedter Strasse 27,
24340 Eckernförde
Phone: 04351-2154

Fax: 04351-3604
Rates: 22-27 DM per HI member (about $11-$14 US)
Beds: 164
Private/family rooms: Yes
Kitchen available: No
Season: Closed December 23-January 5
Affiliation: HI-DJH
Regional office: Nordmark
Extras: Grill, table tennis, basketball, volleyball, piano, meals ($), parking, laundry

How to get there:
By bus: Contact hostel for transit details.
By car: Take Highway A7 in the direction of Flensburg, then exit for Rendsburg-Büdelsdorf, and continue to Eckenförde.
By train: Take train from Kiel to Eckernförde. From Eckernförde Station walk ¾ mile toward Rendsburg to hostel.

JUGENDHERBERGE EUTIN
(Eutin Hostel)
Jahnhöhe 6,
23701 Eutin
Phone: 04521-2109

Fax: 04521-74602
Rates: 22-27 DM per HI member (about $11-$14 US)
Beds: 172
Private/family rooms: Yes
Kitchen available: No
Season: Closed December 23-January 5
Affiliation: HI-DJH
Regional office: Nordmark
Extras: Table tennis, meals ($), parking, laundry

How to get there:
By bus: Contact hostel for transit details.
By car: Contact hostel for directions.
By train: Take train from Lübeck or Kiel to Eutin; from Eutin Station walk ¾ mile to hostel.

JUGENDHERBERGE FELDBERG
(Feldberg Hostel)
Klinkecken 6,
17258 Feldberg
Phone: 039831-20520

Fax: 039831-20520
Web site: www.djh-mv.de
Rates: 23.50-28.50 DM per HI member (about $12-$15 US)
Beds: 75
Private/family rooms: Yes
Kitchen available: No
Season: Closed November 1-February 28
Affiliation: HI-DJH
Regional office: Mecklenburg-Vorpommerm
Extras: Parking, meals ($)

How to get there:
By bus/train: Take train or bus from Neustrelitz to Feldberg.
By car: Take Highway B104 from Neubrandenburg or Prenzlau to Woldegk or Highway B96 to Neustrelitz and then Highway B198 in the direction of Woldegk to Möllenbeck.

"SPORTABZEICHEN-JUGENDHERBERGE"

(Flensburg Hostel)

Fichtestrasse 16,

24943 Flensburg

Phone: 0461–37742

Fax: 0461–312952
Rates: 22–27 DM per HI member (about $11–$14 US)
Beds: 198
Private/family rooms: Yes
Kitchen available: No
Season: Closed December 23–January 28
Affiliation: HI-DJH
Regional office: Nordmark
Extras: Table tennis, volleyball, parking, meals ($)

How to get there:
By bus: From ZOB bus station, take #3, #5, or #7 bus to Stadion (stadium) stop. Or walk 2 miles to hostel.
By car: Contact hostel for directions.
By train: From Flensburg Station take #1 bus to ZOB bus station, then take #3, #5, or #7 bus to Stadion (stadium) stop. Or walk 2 miles to hostel.

JUGENDHERBERGE FRIEDRICHSTADT

(Friedrichstadt Hostel)

Ostdeutsche Strasse 1,

25840 Friedrichstadt

Phone: 04881–7984

Fax: 04881–7984
Rates: 20–25 DM per HI member (about $10–$13 US)
Beds: 65
Private/family rooms: Yes
Kitchen available: No

Season: Closed December 1–January 15
Affiliation: HI-DJH
Regional office: Nordmark
Extras: Grill, piano, meals ($), parking

How to get there:
By bus: Contact hostel for transit details.
By car: Take Highway B5 to Friedrichstadt.
By train: From Hamburg or Husum take train to Friedrichstadt. From Friedrichstadt Station walk ½ mile to hostel or take taxi.

JUGENDHERBERGE GEESTHACHT

(Geesthacht Hostel)

Berliner Strasse 117,

21502 Geesthacht

Phone: 04152–2356

Fax: 04152–77918
E-mail: Jugendherbergegeesthacht@dJugendherbergenordmark.de
Rates: 22–27 DM per HI member (about $11–$14 US)
Beds: 123
Private/family rooms: Yes
Kitchen available: No
Season: Closed December 23–January 5
Affiliation: HI-DJH
Regional office: Nordmark
Extras: Grill, basketball, table tennis, parking, wheelchair access, meals ($)

How to get there:
By bus/train: From Hamburg Hauptbahnof take S-Bahn line S2 or S 21 to Hamburg-Bergedorf Station, then change

to #131 bus to Ziegenkrug stop
or #231 bus to Höchelsberg
stop and walk 200 yards to
hostel.

By car: Take Autobahn A1 in the
direction of Lübeck, through
Elbbrücken to Highway A25,
then continue to Geesthachts.

JUGENDHERBERGE GLÜCKSTADT

(Glückstadt Hostel)

Pentzstrasse 12,

25348 Glückstadt

Phone: 04124–2259

Fax: 04124–2259
Rates: 20–25 DM per HI member
(about $10–$13 US)
Beds: 45
Private/family rooms: Yes
Kitchens available: No
Season: Closed October 1–April 1
Affiliation: HI-DJH
Regional office: Nordmark
Extras: Table tennis, parking,
meals ($)

How to get there:

By bus: Contact hostel for transit
details.
By car: Take Highways A23 and
then B431 to Glückstadt.
By train: From Hamburg or Heide
take train to Glückstadt. From
Glückstadt Station walk ½ mile
to hostel.

JUGENDHERBERGE GRAAL-MÜRITZ

(Graal-Müritz Hostel)

An der Jugendherberge 32,

18181 Seeheilbad (Graal-Müritz)

Phone: 038206–520

Fax: 038206–204
E-mail: jh-graal-mueritz@sund
data.de
Web site: www.djh-mv.de
Rates: 23–28 DM per HI member
(about $12–$14 US)
Beds: 80
Private/family rooms: Yes
Kitchen available: No
Season: Closed November 1–
January 31
Affiliation: HI-DJH
Regional office: Mecklenburg-
Vorpommerm
Extras: Parking, meals ($)

How to get there:

By bus:/train From Rostock or
Stralsund Station, take train to
Rövershagen Station. Or take
train from Rostock or Ribnitz-
Damgarten Station to Graal.
By car: Contact hostel for direc-
tions.

JUGENDHERBERGE GRABOW

(Grabow Hostel)

Jugendherberge 1,

19300 Grabow

**Phone: 0172–389–6097 or
038756–27954**

Fax: 038756–27954
Web site: www.djh-mv.de
Rates: 18.00–21.50 DM (about
$9.00–$11.00 US)
Beds: 46
Private/family rooms: Yes
Kitchen available: No
Season: Closed December 19–
January 31
Affiliation: HI-DJH
Regional office: Mecklenburg-
Vorpommerm
Extras: Meeting room, meals ($)

How to get there:

By bus: Contact hostel for transit details.
By car: Take Highway A24 to Neustadt-Glewe.
By train: Take train to Grabow. From Grabow Station walk 1 mile to hostel.

JUGENDHERBERGE BECKERWITZ

(Gramkow OT Beckerwitz Hostel)

Haus Nr. 21,

23968 Gramkow OT Beckerwitz

Phone: 038428–60362

Fax: 038428–60362
Web site: www.djh-mv.de
Rates: 26–34 DM per HI member (about $13–$17 US)
Beds: 106
Private/family rooms: Yes
Kitchen available: No
Season: Closed October 1–March 31
Affiliation: HI-DJH
Regional office: Mecklenburg-Vorpommerm
Extras: Meals ($), parking
How to get there:
By bus/train: From Wismar Station take bus to Beckerwitz, or travel from Wismar via Boltenhagen and Tarnewitz. Contact hostel for further transit details.
By car: Take Highway B105 to Grevesmühlen and then Gägelow.

JUGENDHERBERGE KÖRISER SEE

(Gross Köris Hostel)

Am See 5,

15746 Gross Köris

Phone: 033766–62730

Fax: 033766–62734
E-mail: www.jugendherberge.de
Web site: www.jugendherberge.de/ koeri/koeri0.htm
Rates: 21–26 DM per HI member (about $11–$13 US)
Beds: 78
Private/family rooms: Yes
Kitchen available: No
Season: Open year-round
Affiliation: HI-DJH
Regional office: Berlin-Brandenburg
Extras: Grill, volleyball, meals ($)
How to get there:
By bus/train: From Berlin or Königs Wusterhausen take S-Bahn train to Gross Köris and walk 1 mile to hostel, or take bus to Klein Köris Schmiede stop.
By car: Take Berliner Ring to Schönefelder Kreuz to Autobahn Route 13, exiting at signs for Gross Köris-Landstrasee. Turn after 1 mile and continue 1 mile to Klein Köris.

JUGENDHERBERGE GÜSTROW-SCHABERNACK

(Güstrow Hostel)

Heidberg 33,

18273 Güstrow

Phone: 03843–840–044

Fax: 03843–840–045
E-mail: jh-guestrow@t-online.de
Web site: home.t-online.de/home/ jh-guestrow
Rates: 29–37 DM per HI member (about $15–$19 US)
Beds: 110
Private/family rooms: Yes
Kitchen available: No
Season: Closed December 17–January 9

Jugendherberge Güstrow-Schabernack
Güstrow Hostel • Güstrow

(photo courtesy of Deutsches Jugendherbergswerk)

Affiliation: HI-DJH
Regional office: Mecklenburg-Vorpommerm
Extras: Grounds, parking, laundry, bar/cafeteria, meals ($)

How to get there:
By bus/train: From Berlin or Rostock take train to Güstrow. Then walk to bus stop and take #4 bus to Schabernack/Inselsee stop.
By car: Contact hostel for directions.

JUGENDHERBERGE HEIDE
(Heide Hostel)
Poststrasse 4,
25746 Heide
Phone: 0481–71575

Fax: 0481–72901
Rates: 22–27 DM per HI member (about $11–$14 US)
Beds: 82
Private/family rooms: Yes
Kitchen available: No
Season: Closed December 23–January 31
Affiliation: HI-DJH
Regional office: Nordmark
Extras: Grill, piano, pool table, table tennis, wheelchair access, parking, meals ($)

How to get there:
By bus: Contact hostel for transit details.
By car: Take A23 to Heide-West, exiting at signs for Marktplatz.
By train: Take train from Hamburg or Westerland to Heide. Contact hostel for additional transit details.

HAUS DER JUGEND HELGOLAND

(Helgoland Hostel)

Postfach 580,

27487 Helgoland

Phone: 04725–341

Fax: 04725–7467
E-mail: haus-der-jugend-helgoland
@t-online.de
Rates: 25–30 DM per HI member
(about $13–$15 US)
Beds: 146
Private/family rooms: Yes
Kitchen available: No
Season: Closed November 1–
March 31
Affiliation: HI-DJH
Regional office: Nordmark
Extras: Table tennis, grill, pool,
piano, meals ($)
How to get there:
By bus/train: Contact hostel for
transit details.
By car: From Cuxhaven,
Brunsbüttel, Büsum, Hörnum,
Bremerhaven, or
Wilhelmshaven, contact hostel
for directions.

JUGENDHERBERGE SEEBAD-HERINGSDORF

(Seebad-Heringsdorf Hostel)

Puschkinstrasse 7–9,

17424 Seebad Heringsdorf

Phone: 038378–22325

Fax: 038378–32301
E-mail: jh_heringsdorf@t-
online.de
Web site: home.t-online.de/home/
jh_heringsdorf
Rates: 31–40 DM per HI member
(about $16–$20 US)

Beds: 167
Private/family rooms: Yes
Kitchen available: No
Season: Closed December 1–
January 31
Affiliation: HI-DJH
Regional office: Mecklenburg-
Vorpommerm
Extras: Parking, meals ($), wheel-
chair access
How to get there:
By bus: Contact hostel for transit
details.
By car: Take Highway B111 from
Wolgast to Heringsdorf, or take
Highway B110 from Anklam to
Heringsdorf.
By train: Take train from Wolgast
to Heringsdorf, then walk ½
mile to hostel.

JUGENDHERBERGE HÖRNUM

(Hörnum/Sylt Hostel)

Friesenplatz 2,

25997 Hörnum/Sylt

Phone: 04651–880–294

Fax: 04651–881–392
E-mail: Jugendherbergehoernum
@dJugendherberge-nordmark.de
Rates: 24–29 DM per HI member
(about $12–$15 US)
Beds: 168
Private/family rooms: Yes
Kitchen available: No
Season: Closed December 1–
January 15
Affiliation: HI-DJH
Regional office: Nordmark
Extras: Table tennis, grill, park-
ing, meals ($)
How to get there:
By bus/train: From Westerland
Station walk to ZOB bus station
and take bus to Hörnum-Nord

stop, then walk ⅓ mile to hostel.

By car: Contact hostel for directions.

JUGENDHERBERGE HUSUM

(Husum Hostel)

Schobüller Strasse 34,

25813 Husum

Phone: 04841–2714

Fax: 04841–81568
Rates: 24–29 DM per HI member (about $12–$15 US)
Beds: 181
Private/family rooms: Yes
Kitchen available: No
Season: Closed December 23– January 31
Affiliation: HI-DJH
Regional office: Nordmark
Extras: Table tennis, grill, meals ($), laundry, parking, wheelchair access

How to get there:

By bus/train: Take train to Husum, then take bus to Westerkampweg.

By car: Take Highway A7 to Schuby or Highway A23 to Heide, then continue to Husum.

JUGENDHERBERGE INZMÜHLEN

(Inzmühlen Hostel)

Umweltstudienplatz

Wehlener Weg 10,

21256 Inzmühlen

Phone: 04188–342

Fax: 04188–7858
Rates: 22–27 DM per HI member (about $11–$14 US)
Beds: 164

Private/family rooms: Yes
Kitchen available: No
Season: Closed December 23– January 31
Affiliation: HI-DJH
Regional office: Nordmark
Extras: Grounds, playground, table tennis, badminton, volleyball, grill, parking, meals ($), wheelchair access

How to get there:

By bus: Contact hostel for transit details.

By car: Take Autobahn from Bremen to Hamburg, exiting at signs for Rade-Welle-Handeloh. Then continue on Highway A7, exiting at signs for Egestorf and continuing through Undeloh and Wesel.

By train: From Hannover, Soltan, or Hamburg take train to Handeloh. From Handeloh Station walk 1 mile to hostel.

JUGENDHERBERGE ITZEHOE

(Itzehoe Hostel)

Juliengardeweg 13,

25524 Itzehoe

Phone: 04821–62270

Fax: 04821–5710
Rates: 22–27 DM per HI member (about $11–$14 US)
Beds: 75
Private/family rooms: Yes
Kitchen available: No
Season: Closed December 15– January 15
Affiliation: HI-DJH
Regional office: Nordmark
Extras: Table tennis, grill, programs, parking, meals ($)

How to get there:

By bus: Contact hostel for transit details.

By car: Contact hostel for directions.

By train: Take train to Itzehoe. From Itzehoe Station walk ¾ mile to hostel.

JUGENDHERBERGE KAPPELN

(Kappeln Hostel)

Eckernförder Strasse 2,

24376 Kappeln

Phone: 04642–8550

Fax: 04642–81086
E-mail: Jugendherberge kappeln@dJugendherberge-nordmark.de
Rates: 22–27 DM per HI member (about $11–$14 US)
Beds: 170
Private/family rooms: Yes
Kitchen available: No
Season: Closed December 23–January 5
Affiliation: HI-DJH
Regional office: Nordmark
Extras: Piano, table tennis, beach volleyball, grill, fireplace, parking, meals ($), laundry, wheelchair access

How to get there:
By bus/train: Contact hostel for transit route.
By car: Take Autobahn Highway 7, exiting for Rendsburg-Büdelsdorf, then continue on Highway B203 to Kappeln.

JUGENDHERBERGE KIEL

(Kiel Hostel)

Johannesstrasse 1,

24143 Kiel

Phone: 0431–731488

Fax: 0431–735723
E-mail: Jugendherberge kiel@dJugendherberge-nordmark.de
Rates: 28–33 DM per HI member (about $15–$17 US)
Beds: 265
Private/family rooms: Yes
Kitchen available: No
Season: Closed December 24–26
Affiliation: HI-DJH
Regional office: Nordmark
Extras: Table tennis, piano, pool, performance stage, parking, meals ($), wheelchair access

How to get there:
By bus/train: Take train or ferry to Kiel. From Kiel Station take #11 or #12 bus to stop D, or contact hostel for transit details.
By car: Follow signs via Ostufer und Norwegenkai to Jugendherberge (hostel). Or contact hostel for directions.

JUGENDHERBERGE KÜHLUNGSBORN

(Kühlungsborn Hostel)

Dünenstrasse 4,

18225 Ostseebad Kühlungsborn

Phone: 038293–17270

Fax: 038293–17279
Web site: www.djh-mv.de
E-mail: Jugendherberge-kuehlungsborn@t-online.de
Rates: 25.50–30.16 DM per HI member (about $13–$15 US)
Beds: 124
Private/family rooms: Yes
Kitchen available: No
Season: Closed November 1–March 31
Affiliation: HI-DJH
Regional office: Mecklenburg-Vorpommerm

Extras: Parking, meals ($), wheelchair access

How to get there:

By bus: From Rostock take bus to Kühlungsborn and walk 200 yards to hostel.

By car: Take Highway B105 to Bad Doberan or Neubukow, then continue to Kröpelin.

By train: Take train from Bad Doberach to Kühlungsborn Ost Station and take bus to Kühlungsborn; from Kühlungsborn Station, walk 200 yards to hostel.

JUGENDHERBERGE LIEPNITZSEE

(Lanke/Ützdorf Hostel)

Wandlitzer Strasse 6,

16359 Lanke/Ützdorf

Phone: 033397-21659

Fax: 033397-62750

E-mail: Jugendherberge-Liepnitzsee@jugendherberge.de

Web site: www.jugendherberge.de

Rates: 21–26 DM per HI member (about $11–$13 US)

Beds: 39

Private/family rooms: Yes

Kitchen available: No

Season: Open year-round

Affiliation: HI-DJH

Regional office: Berlin-Brandenburg

Extras: Meals ($)

How to get there:

By bike: Take train to Basdorf, then bike approximately 8 miles on bike path to Ützdorf.

By bus: From Berlin, take S-Bahn to Bernau, then take bus to hostel.

By car: Take Berliner Ring to Highway A11, then continue on the A11 to Lanke exit; drive into Lanke, then turn left and continue 1 mile to Ützdorf.

By train: From Berlin take S-Bahn to Bernau, then take bus to hostel.

JUGENDHERBERGE LAUENBURG

(Lauenburg Hostel)

Am Sportplatz 7,

21481 Lauenburg

Phone: 04153-2598

Fax: 04153-2310

Rates: 22–27 DM per HI member (about $11–$14 US)

Beds: 130

Private/family rooms: Yes

Kitchen available: No

Season: Closed December 23–January 5

Affiliation: HI-DJH

Regional office: Nordmark

Extras: Piano, table tennis, pool table, disco, volleyball, grill, parking, meals ($)

How to get there:

By bus: Contact hostel for transit details.

By car: From the north take Autobahn Route 25 from Dreieck to Geesthacht, then continue along Highway B5 to Lauenburg. From the south take Highway B209 from Lüneburg or Lübeck. From the east take Highway A24 Hamburg or Berlin, exiting at signs for Hornbek, then continuing in the direction of Büchen-Lauenburg.

By train: From Lübeck or Lüneburg take train to Lauenburg. From Lauenburg Station, walk 1 mile to hostel. From Hamburg Hauptbahnhof Station take #31 bus to hostel.

JUGENDHERBERGE MÖVENBERG
(List/Sylt Hostel)
25992 List/Sylt
Phone: 04651–870–397

Fax: 04651–871–039
Rates: 24–29 DM per HI member (about $12–$15 US)
Beds: 333
Private/family rooms: Yes
Kitchen available: No
Season: Closed January 1–April; November 5–December 26
Affiliation: HI-DJH
Regional office: Nordmark
Extras: Piano, grill, table tennis, parking, laundry, meals ($)

How to get there:
By bus: From Westerland take bus to List, then walk 1½ miles to hostel. Or contact hostel for further transit details.
By car: Contact hostel for directions.
By train: Contact hostel for transit details.

JUGENDHERBERGE LÜBBEN
(Lübben Hostel)
Zum Wendenfürsten 8,
15907 Lübben
Phone: 03546–3046

Fax: 03546–182–597
E-mail: Jugendherberge-Luebben@jugendherberge.de
Web site: www.jugendherberge.de
Rates: 21–26 DM per HI member (about $11–$13 US)
Beds: 127
Private/family rooms: Yes
Kitchen available: No
Season: Open year-round

Affiliation: HI-DJH
Regional office: Berlin-Brandenburg
Extras: Basketball, volleyball, meals ($), laundry

How to get there:
By bus: Contact hostel for transit route.
By car: Take Autobahn Route 13 from Berlin or Dresden to signs exiting for Freiwalde, then take Highway B115 to Lübben and shortly make left to hostel.
By train: From Berlin or Cottbus, take train to Lübben.

JUGENDHERBERGE ZIELOW
(Ludorf OT Zielow Hostel)
Seeufer 7,
17207 Ludorf OT Zielow
Phone: 039923–2547

Fax: 039923–2547
Web site: www.djh-mv.de
Rates: 29–34 DM per HI member (about $15–$17 US)
Beds: 74
Private/family rooms: Yes
Kitchen available: No
Season: Closed December 21–28
Affiliation: HI-DJH
Regional office: Mecklenburg-Vorpommerm
Extras: sports equipment, water sports, meals ($), parking

How to get there:
By bus/train: Take train to Waren. From Waren Station take bus to Röbel, then continue by bus through Neustrelitz to Vipperow stop and walk 2 miles to hostel.
By car: Contact hostel for directions.

JUGENDHERBERGE MALCHOW

(Malchow Hostel)

Platz der Freiheit 3,

17213 Malchow

Phone: 039932–14590

Fax: 039932–14579
Rates: 22.50–27.50 DM per HI member (about $11–$14 US)
Beds: 88
Private/family rooms: No
Kitchen available: No
Season: Closed November 1– January 31
Affiliation: HI-DJH
Regional office: Mecklenburg-Vorpommerm
Extras: Parking

How to get there:

By bus:/train Contact hostel for transit route.
By car: From Berlin or Rostock take Highway A19 to Malchow.

JUGENDHERBERGE MALENTE

(Malente Hostel)

Kellerseestrasse 48,

23714 Malente

Phone: 04523–1723

Fax: 04523–2539
Rates: 22–27 DM per HI member (about $11–$14 US)
Beds: 206
Private/family rooms: Yes
Kitchen available: No
Season: December 15–January 5
Affiliation: HI-DJH
Regional office: Nordmark
Extras: Programs, piano, grill, volleyball, table tennis, meals ($), parking, wheelchair access

How to get there:

By bus: Contact hostel for transit details.
By car: Contact hostel for directions.
By train: From train station walk 2 miles to hostel via Lindenallee, Kellerseepromenade, and Kellerseestrasse.

JUGENDHERBERGE KÖTHENER SEE

(Märkisch Buchholz Hostel)

Dorfstrasse 20,

15748 Märkisch Buchholz

Phone: 033765–80555

Fax: 033765–84870
E-mail: Jugendherberge-Koethener-See@jugendher berge.de
Web site: www.jugendherberge.de
Rates: 19–26 DM per HI member (about $10–$13 US)
Beds: 110
Private/family rooms: Yes
Kitchen available: No
Season: Open year-round
Affiliation: HI-DJH
Regional office: Berlin-Brandenburg
Extras: Volleyball, laundry, meals ($)

How to get there:

By bus/train: Contact hostel for transit route.
By car: From Berlin or Dresden take Highway A13 to exit for Teupitz/Halbe, then continue through Halbe to Märkisch-Buchholz; just before bridge take highway to Köthen.

JUGENDHERBERGE MILOW

(Milow Hostel)

Friedensstrasse 21,
14715 Milow
Phone: 03386–280–361

Fax: 03386–280–369
E-mail: Jugendherberge-
Milow@jugendherberge.de
Web site: www.jugendherberge.de
Rates: 21–26 DM per HI member
(about $11–$13 US)
Beds: 96
Private/family rooms: Yes
Kitchen available: No
Season: Open year-round
Affiliation: HI-DJH
Regional office: Berlin-
Brandenburg
Extras: TV, grill, disco,
playground, fields, meals ($)

How to get there:
By bus: Contact hostel for transit
route.
By car: Take Autobahn Route 2,
exiting at signs for Brandenburg/
Havel, then Highway B102 to
Premnitz, then Landstrasse 1
mile to Milow.
By train: From Brandenburg/Havel
Station travel the direction of
Rathenow to Premnitz Station,
then walk 1½ miles to hostel.

JUGENDHERBERGE MIROW

(Mirow Hostel)
Retzower Strasse,
17252 Mirow
Phone: 039833–20726

Fax: 039833–22057
Web site: www.djh-mv.de
Rates: 29–39 DM per HI member
(about $15–$20 US)
Beds: 80
Private/family rooms: Yes
Kitchen available: No
Season: Contact hostel for current

season
Affiliation: HI-DJH
Regional office: Mecklenburg-
Vorpommerm
Extras: Meditation rooms, park-
ing, wheelchair access, meals
($)

How to get there:
By bus/train: Take train from
Neustrelitz to Mirow. From Mirow
Station take bus to Schleuse stop
and walk to hostel, or walk 2½
miles to hostel.
By car: Take Highway A19 to
Röbel, then continue on
Highway B198 in the direction
of Neustrelitz to Mirow.

JUGENDHERBERGE MÖLLN

(Mölln Hostel)
Am Ziegelsee 2,
23879 Mölln
Phone: 04542–2601

Fax: 04542–86718
Rates: 22–27 DM per HI member
(about $11–$14 US)
Beds: 162
Private/family rooms: Yes
Kitchen available: No
Season: Closed December 15–
January 28
Affiliation: HI-DJH
Regional office: Nordmark
Extras: Beach volleyball, table
tennis, photo darkroom, parking,
meals ($)

How to get there:
By bus: Take bus from Wandsbek-
Markt in Hamburg to Mölln.
By car: Take Autobahn from Hamburg
or Berlin to Talkau, Mölln, and
Ratzeburg, taking Highway B207 to
Mölln Nord via Breitenfelde.
By train: Take train from Hamburg
or Lübeck to Mölln.

JUGENDHERBERGE MÜNCHEHOFE

(Münchehofe Hostel)

Strasse der Jugend 2,

15374 Münchehofe

Phone: 033432–8734

Fax: 033432–8734
Rates: 21–26 DM per HI member
(about $11–$13 US)
Beds: 96
Private/family rooms: Yes
Kitchen available: No
Season: Open year-round
Affiliation: HI-DJH
Regional office: Berlin-
Brandenburg
Extras: Meals ($)

How to get there:
By bus: Contact hostel for transit
details.
By car: Take Berliner Ring to exit
for Lichtenberg, then follow
Highway B1 to Müncheberg; at
fork in the road take Highway
B5 to Münchehofe via
Obersdorf.
By train: Take train to
Müncheberg and walk 3 miles
through woods to hostel. Or take
train to Obersdorf and walk 2
miles to hostel.

JUGENDHERBERGE MURCHIN

(Murchin Hostel)

Jugendherberge Nr. 1,

17390 Murchin

Phone: 03971–210–732

Fax: 03971–210–732
Web site: www.djh-mv.de
Rates: 17.50–29.00 DM per HI
member (about $9.00–$15.00
US)

Beds: 50
Private/family rooms: No
Kitchen available: No
Season: Closed December 21–28
Affiliation: HI-DJH
Regional office: Mecklenburg-
Vorpommerm
Extras: Parking, grounds

How to get there:
By bus/train: Take train to
Anklam; from Anklam Station
take bus to Murchin.
By car: Take Highway B110, pass
through Anklam and continue in
the direction of Usedom.

"KIEK IN" HOSTEL

(Neumünster Hostel)

Gartenstrasse 32,

24534 Neumünster

Phone: 04321–419–960

Fax: 04321–419–9699
Rates: 28–33 DM per HI member
(about $14–$17 US)
Beds: 208
Private/family rooms: Yes
Kitchen available: No
Season: Open year-round
Affiliation: HI-DJH
Regional office: Nordmark
Extras: Cafeteria, piano, grill,
table tennis, volleyball, patio,
parking, meals ($), wheelchair
access

How to get there:
By bus/train: Take train from
Hamburg to Kiel, then take bus
#62 to Feuerwache/
Gartenstrasse stop and
walk to hostel.
By car: Take Autobahn Highway 7
to exit for Neumünster-Süd,
then follow Altonaer Strasse;
make a left at Holstenring, then
a right onto Gartenstrasse.

JUGENDHERBERGE NIEBÜLL
(Niebüll Hostel)
Deezbüll Deich 2,
25899 Niebüll
Phone: 04661–8762

Fax: 04661–20457
Rates: 22–27 DM per HI member
  (about $11–$14 US)
Beds: 38
Private/family rooms: Yes
Kitchen available: No
Season: Closed November
  1–Easter
Affiliation: HI-DJH
Regional office: Nordmark
Extras: Volleyball, basketball,
  grill, parking, meals ($)

How to get there:
By bus: Contact hostel for transit
  details.
By car: From Heide take Highway
  B5 to Niebüll; or take Highway
  A7 from Flensburg to Harrislee
  and continue to Niebüll.
By train: Take train from Hamburg
  or Westerland to Niebüll. Contact
  hostel for further transit details.

JUGENDHERBERGE OLDENBURG/ HOLSTEIN
(Oldenburg/Holstein Hostel)
Göhlerstrasse 58 a,
23758 Oldenburg/Holstein
Phone: 04361–7670

Fax: 04361–60731
Rates: 22–27 DM per HI member
  (about $11–$14 US)
Beds: 84
Private/family rooms: Yes
Kitchen available: No
Season: Closed December 23–
  January 5

Affiliation: HI-DJH
Regional office: Nordmark
Extras: Playground, grill, table tennis, volleyball, parking, laundry,
  meals ($)

How to get there:
By bus: Contact hostel for transit
  details.
By car: Take Highway A1 to
  Oldenburg-Süd, heading in the
  direction of Göhl, then make a
  right-hand exit between the
  towns of Schützenhof and
  Feuerwache; continue to
  Oldenburg/Holstein.
By train: Take train from Lübeck or
  Puttgarden to
  Oldenburg/Holstein.

JUGENDHERBERGE OTTERNDORF
(Otterndorf Hostel)
Schleusenstrasse 147,
21762 Otterndorf
Phone: 04751–3165

Fax: 04751–4577
Rates: 22–27 DM per HI member
  (about $11–$14 US)
Beds: 212
Private/family rooms: Yes
Kitchen available: No
Season: Closed December 23–
  January 5
Affiliation: HI-DJH
Regional office: Nordmark
Extras: Badminton, basketball,
  disco, meals ($), laundry,
  wheelchair access, parking

How to get there:
By bus: Contact hostel for transit
  details.
By car: Take Highway B73.
By train: Take train to Cuxhaven.
  From center of Cuxhaven, facing
  church, walk 1½ miles out on
  Schleusenstrasse to hostel.

JUGENDHERBERGE PLAU AM SEE
(Plau am See Hostel)
Meyenburger Chaussee 1 a,
19395 Plau am See
Phone: 038735–44345

Fax: 038735–44345
Web site: www.djh-mv.de
Rates: 25–30 DM per HI member
(about $13–$15 US)
Beds: 124
Private/family rooms: Yes
Kitchen available: No
Season: Closed November 1–
March 31
Affiliation: HI-DJH
Regional office: Mecklenburg-
Vorpommerm
Extras: Grounds, parking, meals
($)

How to get there:
By bus: Contact hostel for transit
details.
By car: Contact hostel for transit
details.
By train: Take train via Güstrow or
from Pritzwalk to Plau. From Plau
Station walk ½ mile to hostel.

JUGENDHERBERGE PLÖN
(Plön Hostel)
Ascheberger Strasse 67,
24306 Plön
Phone: 04522–2576

Fax: 04522–2166
Rates: 22–27 DM per HI member
(about $11–$14 US)
Beds: 221
Private/family rooms: Yes
Kitchen available: No
Season: Closed December 23–
January 5

Affiliation: HI-DJH
Regional office: Nordmark
Extras: Volleyball, basketball,
grill, table tennis, pool table,
fireplace, parking, meals ($)

How to get there:
By bus/train: Take train from Kiel
or Lübeck to Plön. From Plön
Station walk 1 mile to hostel or
take bus or taxi.
By car: Take Highway B430 or
Highway B76 to Plön.

JUGENDHERBERGE PREBELOW
(Prebelow Hostel)
Prebelow 02,
16831 Zechlinerhütte (Prebelow)
Phone: 033921–70222

Fax: 033921–70362
E-mail: Jugendherberge-prebe-
low@jugendherberge.de
Web site: www.jugendherberge.
de/prebe/prebe0.htm
Rates: 21–26 DM per HI member
(about $12–$13 US)
Beds: 85
Private/family rooms: Yes
Kitchen available: No
Season: Open year-round
Affiliation: HI-DJH
Regional office: Berlin-
Brandenburg
Extras: TV, VCR, beach volleyball,
basketball, playground, meals ($)

How to get there:
By bus:/train Take train to
Rheinsberg, then change to
Grosszerlang bus to
Jugendherberge (hostel) stop.
By car: Take Autobahn Highway 24
from Berlin or Hamburg, exiting at
signs for Neuruppin; continue on
Landstrasse through Alt-Ruppin
und Rheinsberg to Prebelow.

JUGENDHERBERGE RATZEBURG

(Ratzeburg Hostel)
Fischerstrasse 20,
23909 Ratzeburg
Phone: 04541–3707

Fax: 04541–84780
Rates: 22–27 DM per HI member (about $11–$14 US)
Beds: 135
Private/family rooms: Yes
Kitchen available: No
Season: Closed December 23–January 5
Affiliation: HI-DJH
Regional office: Nordmark
Extras: Piano, table tennis, grill, meals ($), parking, laundry

How to get there:
By bus/train: Take train to Ratzeburg. From Ratzeburg Station take bus to Marktplatz stop and walk to hostel.
By car: From the south take Highway A24 to Talkau, then Highway B207 to Ratzeburg. From the north take Highway A1 to Bad Odesloe, then Highway B208 to Ratzeburg.

JUGENDHERBERGE RENDSBURG

(Rendsburg Hostel)
Rotenhöfer Weg 48,
24768 Rendsburg
Phone: 04331–71205

Fax: 04331–75521
Rates: 22–27 DM per HI member (about $11–$14 US)
Beds: 138
Private/family rooms: Yes
Kitchen available: No
Season: Closed December 23–January 31
Affiliation: HI-DJH
Regional office: Nordmark
Extras: Disco, grill, table tennis, pool table, meals ($), laundry, parking, wheelchair access

How to get there:
By bus/train: Take train to Rendsburg. From Rendsburg Station walk 1½ mile to hostel or take #1, #2, or #3 city bus to hostel.
By car: Take Highway A7 RD/Schacht-Audorf in the direction of Rendsburg.

JUGENDHERBERGE RIBNITZ-DAMGARTEN

(Ribnitz-Damgarten Hostel)
Am Wasserwerk,
18311 Ribnitz-Damgarten
Phone: 03821–812–311

Fax: 03821–812–311
Web site: www.djh-mv.de
Rates: 20.00–31.50 DM per HI member (about $10–$16 US)
Beds: 34
Private/family rooms: No
Kitchen available: No
Season: Closed December 19–27
Affiliation: HI-DJH
Regional office: Mecklenburg-Vorpommerm
Extras: Grounds, meals ($)

How to get there:
By bus: Contact hostel for transit details.
By car: Take Highway B105 from Rostock or Stralsund to Ribnitz-Damgarten.
By train: From Rostock or Stralsund take train to Ribnitz-Damgarten. Contact hostel for further transit details.

SCHARBEUTZ

JUGENDHERBERGE FLESSENOW

(Rubow OT Flessenow Hostel)

Am Scheriner See 1b

19067 Rubow OT Flessenow

Phone: 03866–82400

Fax: 03866–82401
E-mail: jugendherberge.flessenow@t-online.de
Web site: www.schweriner-see.de/jh-flessenow.htm
Rates: 22.50–29.50 DM per HI member (about $11–$15 US)
Beds: 123
Private/family rooms: Yes
Kitchen available: No
Season: Closed October 1–April 30
Affiliation: HI-DJH
Regional office: Mecklenburg-Vorpommerm
Extras: Grounds, parking, meals ($)

How to get there:
By bus/train: Take train to Schwerin, then take #102 bus to Flessenow.
By car: Take Highway B104 from Schwerin toward Günstrow or Retgendorf toward Flessenow.

JUGENDHERBERGE ST. MICHAELISDONN

(St. Michaelisdonn Hostel)

Am Sportplatz 1,

25693 St. Michaelisdonn

Phone: 04853–923

Fax: 04853–8576
Rates: 22–27 DM per HI member (about $11–$14 US)
Beds: 70
Private/family rooms: Yes
Kitchen available: No
Season: Closed December 10–January 15
Affiliation: HI-DJH
Regional office: Nordmark
Extras: Table tennis, grill, disco, sauna, bike rentals, bike storage room, meals ($), laundry, wheelchair access

How to get there:
By bus: Contact hostel for transit details.
By car: Take Highway A23 from Hamburg or Heide to St. Michaelisdonn.
By train: From Hamburg or Westerland take train to St. Michaelisdonn. Contact hostel for further transit details.

JUGENDHERBERGE SCHARBEUTZ-KLINGBERG

(Scharbeutz Hostel)

Uhlenflucht 28–30,

23684 Scharbeutz

Phone: 04524–428

Fax: 04524–1637
Rates: 22–27 DM per HI member (about $11–$14 US)
Beds: 262
Private/family rooms: Yes
Kitchen available: No
Season: Closed December 15–January 20
Affiliation: HI-DJH
Regional office: Nordmark
Extras: Piano, grill, volleyball, meals ($), parking

How to get there:
By bus/train Contact hostel for transit details.
By car: Take Highway A1 to Pansdorf, then follow signs to Scharbeutz.
By train: Take train from Lübeck or Puttgarden to Scharbeutz or from Kiel to Pönitz. Contact hostel for further transit details.

JUGENDHERBERGE SCHLESWIG

(Schleswig Hostel)

Spielkoppel 1,

24837 Schleswig

Phone: 04621–23893

Fax: 04621–20796
Rates: 22–27 DM per HI member
(about $11–$14 US)
Beds: 120
Private/family rooms: Yes
Kitchen available: No
Season: Closed December 15–
January 15
Affiliation: HI-DJH
Regional office: Nordmark
Extras: Piano, table tennis, grill,
meals ($), parking

How to get there:

By bus/train: Take train to
Neumünster or Flensburg. From
Neumünster or Flensburg
Stations, take #1a, #1b, or #4
bus to Stadttheater stop or
Schwimmhalle stop.
By car: Exit for Schleswig-Jagel or
Schuby, using Highway B76 or
Highway B77.

JUGENDHERBERGE SCHÖNBERG

(Schönberg Hostel)

Stakendorfer Weg 1,

24217 Schönberg

Phone: 04344–2974

Fax: 04344–4484
E-mail: Jugendherberge
schoenberg@dJugend
herberge-nordmark.de
Rates: 22–27 DM per HI member
(about $11–$14 US)
Beds: 233
Private/family rooms: Yes
Kitchen available: No

Season: Closed December 23–
January 5
Affiliation: HI-DJH
Regional office: Nordmark
Extras: Piano, table tennis,
volleyball, grill, disco, parking,
wheelchair access, laundry

How to get there:

By bus: Contact hostel for transit
details.
By car: Take Highway A7 to Kiel,
then Highway B502 in the direction of Ostufer to Schönberg.
By train: Take train to Kiel, then
change to bus to Schönberg/
Ostsee. Contact hostel for further transit details.

JUGENDHERBERGE SCHÖNWALDE

(Schönwalde Hostel)

Am Ruhsal 1,

23744 Schönwalde am Bungsberg

Phone: 04528–206

Fax: 04528–9732
Rates: 20–25 DM per HI member
(about $10–$13 US)
Beds: 61
Private/family rooms: Yes
Kitchen available: No
Season: Closed November 1–
Easter
Affiliation: HI-DJH
Regional office: Nordmark
Extras: Table tennis, basketball,
meals ($)

How to get there:

By bus/train: Take train to
Neustadt or Eutin, then continue
via bus to Schönwalde am
Bungsberg.
By car: Take Highway A1 to exit
for Neustadt-Nord.

JUGENDHERBERGE SCHWERIN

(Schwerin Hostel)

Waldschulweg 3,

19061 Schwerin

Phone: 0385–326–0006

Fax: 0385–326–0303
Web site: www.djh-mv.de
Rates: 25–30 DM per HI member (about $13–$15 US)
Beds: 91
Private/family rooms: Yes
Kitchen available: No
Season: Closed December 6–27
Affiliation: HI-DJH
Regional office: Mecklenburg-Vorpommerm
Extras: Parking, meals ($)

How to get there:
By bus/train: From Schwerin Station walk 500 meters in the direction of center to Marienplatz. Or take #14 bus to last stop, Jugendherberge (hostel).
By car: Drive ⅓ mile in the direction of center to Marienplatz.

JUGENDHERBERGE STADE

(Stade Hostel)

Kehdinger Mühren 11,

21682 Stade

Phone: 04141–46368

Fax: 04141–2817
Rates: 22–27 DM per HI member (about $11–$14 US)
Beds: 139
Private/family rooms: Yes
Kitchen available: No
Season: Closed December 23–January 5
Affiliation: HI-DJH

Regional office: Nordmark
Extras: Piano, volleyball, table tennis, pool table, darts, disco, meals ($)

How to get there:
By bus: Contact hostel for transit details.
By car: From Hamburg take Highway B73; from the direction of Bremen take Highway B74. From the south take Highways B3 and B73.
By train: From Hamburg or Cuxhaven take train to Stade and walk to hostel; or from Bremervörde or Bremerhaven take train to Stade. Contact hostel for further transit details.

JUGENDHERBERGE STRALSUND

(Stralsund Hostel)

Am Kütertor 1,

18439 Stralsund

Phone: 03831–292–160

Fax: 03831–297–676
E-mail: jh-stralsund@sunddata.de
Web site: atair.sunddata.de/jh-stralsund
Rates: 25–30 DM per HI member (about $13–$15 US)
Beds: 164
Private/family rooms: Yes
Kitchen available: No
Season: Closed November 1–December 28
Affiliation: HI-DJH
Regional office: Mecklenburg-Vorpommerm
Extras: Meals ($)

How to get there:
By bus/train: From Straslund Station take #4 or #5 bus to Kütertor stop. Or walk ¾ mile to hostel.

By car: Take Highway B105, exiting in the direction of Rostock, or take Highway B96 in the direction of Greifswald.

JUGENDHERBERGE DEVIN
(Stralsund-Devin Hostel)
Strandstrasse 21,
18439 Stralsund
Phone: 03831–490–289

Fax: 03831–490–291
E-mail: jh-devin@sunddata.de
Web site: atair.sunddata.de/jh-devin
Rates: 22–33 DM per HI member (about $11–$17 US)
Beds: 166
Private/family rooms: Yes
Kitchen available: No
Season: Closed January and February
Affiliation: HI-DJH
Regional office: Mecklenburg-Vorpommerm
Extras: Parking, meals ($), wheelchair access

How to get there:
By bus/train: Take train to Stralsund. From Stralsund Station take #3 bus to Devin.
By car: Take Highway B96 in the direction of Stralsund-Greifswald to hostel.

JUGENDHERBERGE TETEROW
(Teterow Hostel)
Am Seebahnhof 7,
17166 Teterow
Phone: 03996–172–668

Fax: 03996–172–668
Web site: www.djh-mv.de

Rates: 25–30 DM per HI member (about $13–$15 US)
Beds: 100
Private/family rooms: Yes
Kitchen available: No
Season: Closed October 1– April 30
Affiliation: HI-DJH
Regional office: Mecklenburg-Vorpommerm
Extras: Grounds, parking, meals ($)

How to get there:
By bus: Contact hostel for transit details.
By car: Take Highway A19 to Teterow. Contact hostel for further directions.
By train: From Güstrow or Neubrandenurg take train to Teterow. From Teterow Station walk 1 mile to hostel.

JUGENDHERBERGE TÖNNING
(Tönning Hostel)
Umweltstudienplatz
Badallee 28,
25832 Tönning
Phone: 04861–1280

Fax: 04861–5956
Rates: 24–29 DM per HI member (about $12–$15 US)
Beds: 135
Private/family rooms: Yes
Kitchen available: No
Season: Closed December 1– January 5
Affiliation: HI-DJH
Regional office: Nordmark
Extras: Piano, table tennis, volleyball, grill, pool table, meals ($), parking, laundry, wheelchair access

How to get there:
By bus: Contact hostel for transit details.
By car: Take Highway A23 and Highway B5 to Tönning.
By train: Take train from Hamburg or Westerland to Tönning.

JUGENDHERBERGE TRAVEMÜNDE
(Travemünde Hostel)
Mecklenburger Landstrasse 69,
23570 Travemünde
Phone: 04502–2576

Fax: 04502–4620
Rates: 22–27 DM per HI member (about $11–$14 US)
Beds: 80
Private/family rooms: Yes
Kitchen available: No
Season: Closed October 15– March 1
Affiliation: HI-DJH
Regional office: Nordmark
Extras: Table tennis, volleyball, basketball, grill, meals ($), parking

How to get there:
By bus: Contact hostel for transit route.
By car: Contact hostel for transit route.
By train: Take train from Lübeck to Travemünde. From Travemünde Station, walk ½ mile to hostel.

JUGENDHERBERGE WANDLITZ
(Wandlitz Hostel)
Prenzlauer Chaussee 146,
16348 Wandlitz
Phone: 033397–22109
Fax: 033397–62735

E-mail: Jugendherberge-Wandlitz@jugendherberge.de
Web site: www.jugendherberge.de
Rates: 21–26 DM per HI member (about $11–$13 US)
Beds: 148
Private/family rooms: Yes
Kitchen available: No
Season: Closed December 18– April 30
Affiliation: HI-DJH
Regional office: Berlin-Brandenburg
Extras: Volleyball, table tenins, grill, piano, meals ($)

How to get there:
By bus: Contact hostel for transit details.
By car: Take Berliner Ring, exiting at signs for Pankow, then continue on Highway B109 to Wandlitz.
By train: Take train from Berlin or Brandenburg to Wandlitzsee. Contact hostel for further transit details.

JUGENDHERBERGE WAREN
(Waren Hostel)
Auf dem Nesselberg 2,
17192 Waren
Phone: 03991–667–606

Fax: 03991–667–606
Web site: www.djh-mv.de
Rates: 25–30 DM per HI member (about $13–$15 US)
Beds: 58
Private/family rooms: Yes
Kitchen available: Yes
Season: November 1–March 31
Affiliation: HI-DJH
Regional office: Mecklenburg-Vorpommerm
Extras: Meals ($), parking

How to get there:

By bus/train: Take train to
Waren/Müritz. From
Waren/Müritz take #1, #3, or
#5 bus to Wasserwerk stop.
By car: Take Highway A19 to
Waren, using Highway B192 to
Nesselberg.

JUGENDHERBERGE WESTENSEE

(Westensee Hostel)

Am See 24,

24259 Westensee

Phone: 04305–542

Fax: 04305–1360
E-mail: Jugendherberge
westensee@dJugendherberge-
nordmark.de
Rates: 22–27 DM per HI member
(about $11–$14 US)
Beds: 138
Private/family rooms: Yes
Kitchen available: No
Season: December 23–January 5
Affiliation: HI-DJH
Regional office: Nordmark
Extras: Piano, volleyball, table
tennis, playground, meals ($),
disco, parking, laundry, wheel-
chair access

How to get there:

By bus: Contact hostel for transit
details.
By car: Take Highway A7 from
Hamburg or Flensburg, exiting
at signs for Felde/Westensee. Or
take Highway A210 or Highway
B202 from Kiel or Rendsburg,
exiting at signs for
Felde/Westensee.
By train: Contact hostel for transit
details.

JUGENDHERBERGE WINGST

(Wingst Hostel)

Molkereistrasse 11,

21789 Wingst

Phone: 04778–262

Fax: 04778–7594
Rates: 22–27 DM per HI member
(about $12–$14 US)
Beds: 202
Private/family rooms: Yes
Kitchen available: No
Season: Closed February, also
December 23–January 5
Affiliation: HI-DJH
Regional office: Nordmark
Extras: Piano, grounds, basket-
ball, table tenins, grill, meals
($), parking, laundry, wheelchair
access

How to get there:

By bus: Contact hostel for transit
details.
By car: Take Highway B73 from
Hamburg or Cuxhaven to
Wingst.
By train: Take train from Hamburg
or Cuxhaven to Wingst. From
Wingst Station walk ¾ mile to
hostel.

JUGENDHERBERGE WITTDÜN

(Wittdün Hostel)

Mittelstrasse 1,

25946 Wittdün/Amrum

Phone: 04682–2010

Fax: 04682–1747
Rates: 24–29 DM (about
$12–$15 US)
Beds: 218
Private/family rooms: Yes
Kitchen available: No

Season: Closed December 1–
January 2
Affiliation: HI-DJH
Regional office: Nordmark
Extras: Table tennis, meals ($),
laundry, wheelchair access

How to get there:
By bus: Contact hostel for transit
details.
By car: Contact hostel for directions.
By train: Contact hostel for transit
details.

JUGENDHERBERGE WYK AUF FÖHR
(Wyk auf Föhr Hostel)
Fehrstieg 41,
25938 Wyk auf Föhr
Phone: 04681–2355

Fax: 04681–5527
Rates: 24–29 DM per HI member
(about $12–$15 US)
Beds: 168
Private/family rooms: Yes
Kitchen available: No
Season: Closed December 23–
January 31
Affiliation: HI-DJH
Regional office: Nordmark
Extras: Table tennis, volleyball,
grill, basketball, meals ($), park-
ing, laundry

How to get there:
By bus: Contact hostel for transit
details.
By car: Contact hostel for directions.
By train: Contact hostel for transit
details.

JUGENDHERBERGE ZINGST
(Zingst Hostel)
Glebbe 14,
18374 Zingst
Phone: 038232–15465

Fax: 038232–12285
Web site: www.djh-mv.de
Rates: 24–35 DM per HI member
(about $12–$18 US)
Beds: 160
Private/family rooms: Yes
Kitchen available: No
Season: Closed January 3–31
Affiliation: HI-DJH
Regional office: Mecklenburg-
Vorpommerm
Extras: Grounds, parking, meals
($)

How to get there:
By bus/train: From Ribnitz or
Damgarten (West) Station take
train to Barth Station and
change to bus to Zingst.
By car: Take Highway B105 from
Rostock or Stralsund to
Kreuzung Löbnitz and Barth.

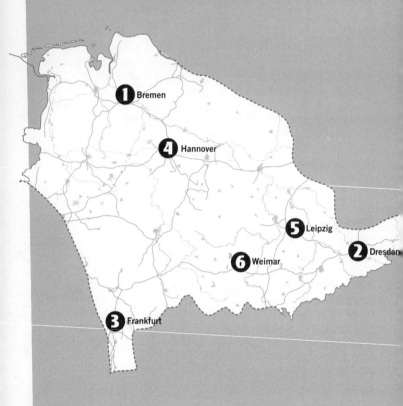

CENTRAL GERMANY

1 Bremen
4 Hannover
5 Leipzig
2 Dresden
6 Weimar
3 Frankfurt

CENTRAL GERMANY

Central Germany, as defined by this guidebook, is sweeping and huge—and amorphous. If you look at a map, you'll see very few famous cities in this gigantic area and few distinguishing physical characteristics, either, aside from the Harz Mountains, which are much better known to the Germans than to the rest of the world.

Still, the area has been the site of much history and industry. Over in former East Germany, Dresden, in the province of Saxony, was bombed to smithereens during World War II—yet it has rebounded to become one of Germany's most cultural cities, full of the arts. Nearby Leipzig is a hoppin' university town with never-ending nightlife and bustle.

The two central states of Hessen and Thüringen contain little of tourist interest, but they are home both to Frankfurt—with its high-energy economy but the agreeable country taverns of a much smaller town—and pockets of hills, such as the Odenwald (south of Frankfurt), where the Brothers Grimm did their thing and wrote fairy tales that long outlived them. Farther to the north, Bremen and Hannover recall the maritime heritage of Hamburg and northern Germany.

BREMEN

This very old Hanseatic town isn't on the usual tourist itinerary of Germany, but think about making a detour. You'll find plenty of cobbled neighborhoods from the old, old days here if you do. The so-called "Oster" neighborhood is where you wanna be: That's the diverse part of town, with plenty of nightlife and street sights to occupy you.

The casual traveler probably doesn't need to be overly concerned, but violence does periodically erupt here as locals try to assert their independence from Father Germany in much the same way as Basques do in Spain.

JUGENDGÄSTEHAUS BREMEN

Kalkstrasse 6,

28195 Bremen

Phone: 0421–171–369

Fax: 0421–171–102
Rates: 29.90–34.90 DM per Hostelling International member (about $15–$17 US)
Beds: 172

> **Private/family rooms:** Yes
> **Kitchen available:** No
> **Season:** Closed December 24–January 1
> **Office hours:** Open twenty-four hours
> **Affiliation:** Hostelling International-DJH
> **Regional office:** Unterweser-Ems
> **Extras:** Breakfast, bar, luggage storage, parking, pool table, foosball, event tickets, cafeteria ($), patio, disco, table tennis

You can sense when you're getting close to this riverside hostel, and whether you like beer or not, you'd better get used to it . . . 'cause you're gonna smell like beer no matter what.

It's not that the place is full of party animals, though—far from it. No, it's that huge Beck's brewery right across the street that's responsible for the malty-sour odor of this unremarkable brew. And you can't even escape once you're inside the hostel: The bar draws Beck's off a tap, and the occasional tipsy hosteller spills a little bit, so you get the picture.

Best bet for a bite:
Ostertor

Insiders' tip:
Kleinskeller Ratskeller bar

What hostellers say:
"Okay, not great . . ."

Gestalt:
Bar none

Safety:

Hospitality:

Cleanliness:

Party index:

All right, enough about the beer already. The place itself is hardly inspiring, your usual six stories of brick and glass; at least you can park right under the building. Bunks are stuffed into forty double or four-bedded rooms and five five- or six-bedded rooms that show a bit of wear and tear. They do include breakfast with the price, however, and will store your stuff during the day after checkout if you like. Receptionists are surprisingly friendly considering that you're in Germany. There are three common rooms for chilling out, a terrace, and a cafeteria serving meals with that beer on tap (oops, there we go again).

For fun, we'd hit the 500-year-old (that's what they say) bar, the Kleiner Ratskeller. There are also a ton of museums and sights downtown, such as the city hall, St. Peter's Cathedral, and an "Overseas" Museum describing other cultures besides almighty Germany. You're a couple miles from the central train station, so strap on walking shoes or get a transit pass. At least the hostel is also right on the Weser River, just 250 yards from the city center; snap a couple of shots of the boats and brewery while you're here.

How to get there:

By bus: From train station take #26 bus or #1 or #8 streetcar to Am Brill stop; continue right along river 200 yards to hostel.

By car: Contact hostel for directions.

By train: From train station go down Hanofstrasse to Herdentorsteinweg; hang a right on Am Wall, turn onto Bürgermeister-

Schmit-Strasse, then follow river. Or take #26 bus or #1 or #8 street-car to Am Brill stop; continue right along river 200 yards to hostel.

DRESDEN

Dresden is truly one of Europe's most cultural cities—more opera, classical music, and art museums than you can shake a stick at. If you're not into those things, check out the university-paced nightlife instead; it's pretty good. The place is enjoying something of a renaissance lately, meaning that hostels are really your only bet at getting central and inexpensive lodging; good thing there are a half-dozen to choose from, including two independent outfits and up to four "official" ones, depending on the time of year.

It's all pretty remarkable, considering the city was flattened in February 1945 by U.S. and British bombing raids, killing thousands and wiping many places right off the map in the span of just forty-eight hours.

To see the best stuff, head across the Elbe River to Neustadt—you can take the city's convenient S-Bahn train from the main station over to Neustadt Station if you wanna dive right in—and check out the nightlife. The "important sights" are back over by the station where you'll arrive: big old churches, museums, and the like. First stop should probably be the Stadtmuseum Dresden (Dresden City Museum), with its sobering exhibits on the bombing raids.

Reach Dresden by frequent InterCity trains from Berlin (about two hours), Munich, or Frankfurt.

DIE BOOFE HOSTEL

Louisen-Strasse 20,
01099 Dresden
Phone: 0351–801–3361

Fax: 0351–801–3362
E-mail: boofe@t-online.de
Rates: 27.00–49.50 DM per person (about $14–$25 US); doubles 79 DM (about $40 US)
Beds: 54
Private/family rooms: Yes
Kitchen available: Yes
Affiliation: None
Office hours: Open twenty-four hours
Extras: Bar, bike rentals, breakfast ($), TV, radio

First things first. A "boofe," in case you were wondering (and we just know you were), is a kind of cave dwelling once inhabited back in the very old days of regional history. At least that's what the management told us, and we don't *think* they were pulling our leg. Never can tell. Anyhow, this hostel is something of a cave—but much better, with welcoming staff, decent bunks, and a nice price. It's deservedly popular.

Best bet for a bite:
Ratskeller

Insiders' tip:
Pfunds Molkerei

What hostellers say:
"Loved the extra touches!"

Gestalt:
Natty Dresden

Safety:

Hospitality:

Cleanliness:

Party index:

OK, back to the hostel. This slab of architecture doesn't look like much from the outside, but within you'll find good rooms with one to five beds each. There are tons of singles and doubles, plus dorms, and many rooms come with private bathrooms for a slight extra charge. (They charge extra for sheets, too, as do many German hostels.) Some rooms on the top floor are in an interesting little garret.

The real story here, though, is the owner— this guy's nuts (good nuts, though). He's been known to rocket hostellers around the backstreets of town in his Trabant, that beloved little beat-up East German car that's no longer manufactured, barely runs, and has a cult following among people like U2 lead singer Bono.

In case you care, the kitchen is stocked with everything you could need for a meal—an electric oven, coffee machine, and refrigerator—plus a television and radio to hang with. Breakfast is served from 6:00 to 10:00 A.M. each morning, although it's a bit expensive at 8.00 DM (about $4.00 US) a throw; probably better to hit a local market and grab some fruit and yogurt or something. Far more popular than these rooms, however, is the hostel bar, serving beer and even a homemade "Boofe Brandy" (whatever the heck that is).

What to see in town? There's the Ratskeller bar if you wanna drink. Or, if you actually wanna experience some of that aforemen-

KEY TO ICONS

Attractive natural setting

Ecologically aware hostel

Superior kitchen facilities or cafe

Offbeat or eccentric place

Superior bathroom facilities

Romantic private rooms

Comfortable beds

Editors' choice: among our very favorite hostels

A particularly good value

Wheelchair accessible

Good for business travelers

Especially well suited for families

Good for active travelers

Visual arts at hostel or nearby

Music at hostel or nearby

Great hostel for skiers

Bar or pub at hostel or nearby

tioned culture, there's the Zwinger museum complex—pulverized toward the end of the war but restored in grand Baroque style. Among the five museums within, the Gallery of the Old Masters is the real granddaddy: It contains Raphael's *Sistine Madonna* plus work by Vermeer and Rembrandt.

How to get there:

By bus: From main station take #7 tram to Louisenstrasse stop and walk to hostel.

By car: Contact hostel for directions.

By train: From main station take S-Bahn to Neustadt Station. Exit station, turn left, and walk ¼ mile to Louisenstrasse; turn right and continue to hostel.

JUGENDGÄSTEHAUS DRESDEN (DRESDEN GUEST HOUSE HOSTEL)

Maternistrasse 22,

01067 Dresden

Phone: 0351–492–620

Fax: 0351–492–6299
E-mail: servicecenter@djh-sachsen.de
Rates: 33–48 DM (about $17–$24 US) per HI member, doubles 90 DM (about $45 US)
Beds: 450
Private/family rooms: Yes
Kitchen available: No
Season: Open year-round
Office hours: Open twenty-four hours
Affiliation: Hostelling International-DJH
Regional office: Sachsen
Extras: Breakfast, meals ($), TV room, meeting room, luggage storage, table tennis

What a huge edifice! We're talking nearly 500 bunk beds here, for gosh sakes, and they don't come cheaply, either. On the other hand, each and every room at this inn is a double or quad room, so families might like it more than individual backpacker-types.

The building has absolutely zero character (it used to be an office and convention space, so whaddya expect?), but once again we have to stress that sometimes it's the bed that's the main thing—and they're pretty good here. Many rooms come with private bathrooms too, so if you can ignore the lack of excitement in and around the hostel you'll be all right.

Best bet for a bite:
Meissner Weinkeller

Insiders' tip:
Good public library with cafe

What hostellers say:
"Ah, my own bathroom!"

Gestalt:
Big bunks

Safety:

Hospitality:

Cleanliness:

Party index:

They serve breakfast for free in a dining room, and the place is wheelchair accessible if you need that. There are two meeting rooms, a place to store your luggage, and a small game room with table tennis. If it's all too boring, check out Pragerstrasse, a pedestrian-only street of food and stuff to buy.

How to get there:

By bus/train: From main station take #7, #9, #10, or #26 tram to Ammon-Freibergerstrasse stop, then make a right on Freibergerstrasse and continue to Maternistrasse.

By car: Contact hostel for directions.

JUGENDHERBERGE
DRESDEN-OBERLOSCHWITZ
(DRESDEN-OBERLOSCHWITZ HOSTEL)

Sierkkstrasse 33,

01326 Dresden

Phone: 0351–268–3672

Fax: 0351–268–3672
E-mail: servicecenter@djh-sachsen.de
Rates: 33–48 DM (about $17–$24 US) per HI member; doubles 90 DM (about $45 US)
Beds: 51
Private/family rooms: No
Kitchen available: No
Season: Open year-round
Affiliation: Hostelling International-DJH
Regional office: Sachsen
Extras: Parking, meals ($), laundry

Getting to this hostel is an odyssey in and of itself, and it really isn't worth visiting without a car—you have to change buses a number of times to get there. However, if you do have wheels (or a buddy does) and you want some serious R&R, you've got to think about it.

The hostel's located on a hill outside the city, a beautiful sylvan location. Facilities are pretty unremarkable (how many times have we said that about German hostels?), but they do have a laundry and serve meals for an extra charge.

Best bet for a bite:
Breakfast and dinner served here

Insiders' tip:
City-Card saves bucks on transit and museums

What hostellers say:
"I feel so rested!"

Gestalt:
Saxon violins

Since you've made the effort to get all the way out here, you're unlikely to want to get all the way back in again to do something. But what the heck. The Albertinum gallery is a terrific place to see fine art—we're talking tons of jewels, among other stuff.

Safety: 👍

Hospitality: 👍

Cleanliness: 👍

Party index:

How to get there:

By bus/train: From train station take #93 bus to Schillerplatz, then change to #84 bus and continue to Malerstrasse. Or contact hostel for transit details.

By car: Contact hostel for directions.

JUGENDHERBERGE DRESDEN-RADEBEUL (DRESDEN-RADEBEUL HOSTEL)

Weintraubenstrasse 12,

01445 Dresden

Phone: 0351–838–2880

Fax: 0351–838–2881
E-mail: servicecenter@djh-sachsen.de
Web site: www.djh-sachsen.de
Rates: 25–30 DM per Hostelling International member (about $13–$15 US)
Beds: 82
Private/family rooms: Yes
Kitchen available: No
Season: Open year-round
Office hours: 8:00–10:00 A.M.; 4:00–6:00 P.M.
Curfew: Midnight
Lockout: 10:00 A.M.–4:00 P.M.
Affiliation: Hostelling International-DJH
Regional office: Sachsen
Extras: Parking, meals ($), breakfast

Reports indicated this hostel might be closed by press time, and we weren't able to get a gander at it while in town.

Wayyyyyyy out of town, this place is worth a look only if you enjoy being a long way from everything. The dorm rooms contain anything from one to five beds each; there's a lounge or two and a dining hall (obviously they serve the meals here). Radebeul is northwest of Dresden proper, a greenish suburb that's good for strolling.

Best bet for a bite:
Dampfschiff Bierhaus

Insiders' tip:
Regio-Card gets you to suburbs

What hostellers say:
"Too far to be useful."

Gestalt:
Long haul

Safety:

Party index:

How to get there:

By bus: Contact hostel for transit details.

By car: Take Autobahn A4 to Dresden-Neustadt exit.

By train: From main train station take S-Bahn line S1 to Radebeul-Weintraub Station; then walk along Weintraubenstrasse and walk to hostel.

JUGENDHERBERGE DRESDEN
"RUDI ARNDT"

Hübnerstrasse 11,

01069 Dresden

Phone: 0351–471–0667

Fax: 0351–472–8959

E-mail: servicecenter@djh-sachsen.de

Web site: www.djh-sachsen.de

Rates: 25–30 DM per Hostelling International member (about $13–$15 US)

Beds: 81

Private/family rooms: Yes

Season: Open year-round

Office hours: 8:00–10:00 A.M.; 3:00 P.M.–1:00 A.M.

Curfew: 1:00 A.M.

Affiliation: Hostelling International-DJH

Regional office: Sachsen

Extras: Breakfast, luggage storage, laundry, meals ($), pool table, swimming pool, patio

Surprisingly central, this place is a winner—especially considering that it's an "official" joint. You're just a ten minutes' walk from the main train station, yet the neighborhood's quiet. And the joint rocks to a slow groove as hostellers from all over the place converge and trade road-warrior stories.

Best bet for a bite:
Café aha

Insiders' tip:
City festival in late August

What hostellers say:
"Not bad!"

Gestalt:
Rudi Tuesday

The beds here are mostly divided into one- to five-bedded rooms, though you can pay a bit less and get put in the seven- or twelve-bedded room (try not to think of it as punishment—the bunks are more comfortable than you'd think). There are three common rooms, as well (though we'd prefer to hang on the terrace), and the staff miraculously doesn't enforce dumb rules with an iron hammer.

Because of the good location, this is obviously a very popular place, so book ahead instead of just showing up and expecting a bed to be waiting for you.

How to get there:

By bus: From main station take #3 or #5 tram to Nürnbergerplatz stop and walk down Nürnbergerstrasse; turn right on Hubnerstrasse. Hostel is on right.

By car: Contact hostel for directions.

By train: From main station walk south along Winckelmannstrasse, then turn onto Schnorrstrasse and bear onto Hübnerstrasse. Or take #3 or #5 tram to Nürnbergerplatz stop and walk down Nürnbergerstrasse; turn right on Hubnerstrasse. Hostel is on right.

Safety:

Hospitality:

Cleanliness:

Party index:

MONDPALAST BACKPACKER HOSTEL

Katharinenstrasse 11–13,

01069 Dresden

Phone: 0351–804–6061

Fax: 0351–804–6061
E-mail: mondpalast@t-online.de
Rates: 25–37 DM per person (about $13–$19 US); doubles 62 DM (about $31 US)
Beds: number varies
Private/family rooms: Yes
Kitchen available: Yes
Season: Open year-round
Affiliation: None
Office hours: Open twenty-four hours
Extras: Internet access, breakfast, TV, music room, bar

Okay, there are a ton of good hostels in Dresden. You're not going to have to sleep in the train station, so relax.

But this might be the best one of all—many rooms in the place are single or double rooms, so it's practically a hotel (though it used to be a factory, actually). Quads, six-bedded, and eight-bedded rooms are also available. And the prices aren't any higher than those at other hostels. In fact, they're lower than some of them. There's a common lounge with a television and music listening area. The staff is really laid-back and knowledgeable, and they'll direct you to the area bars.

Now here's the beauty part: You're smack in the heart of that hip Neustadt neighborhood we were talking about earlier. That means unlimited access to mucho bars, movies, discos, and the like. And

Best bet for a bite:
Raskolnikoff

Insiders' tip:
Bärenzwinger (club)

What hostellers say:
"Best in town."

Gestalt:
Hipper than thou

Safety:

you can crawl back in as late as ya want; the owners won't care.

Hospitality:

Cleanliness:

Party index:

How to get there:

By bus: From main station take #7 tram to Louisenstrasse.

By car: Contact hostel for directions.

By train: From main station take S-Bahn to Neustadt Station. Walk along Antonstrasse to Königbrückstrasse and turn left; make a right onto Katharinenstrasse and continue 100 yards to hostel.

FRANKFURT

Yeah, this is where the poet Goethe was born and spent his formative years. Frankfurt on the Main, as it's fully known, is really just a business center today, though—they don't call it "Mainhattan" for nothin', and this is Germany's busiest airport (and therefore one of your most likely points of entry).

Ignore the skyscrapers, though, and you will find stuff of interest to do here. There are some forty museums scattered around town, most centrally located—the Museum Row area alone has more than a dozen. There's Goethe's House and the neat Palmengarten, a set of greenhouses.

Oh, forget all that. Here's what we really wanna do—hang out in a Sachsenhausen cafe drinking fermented apple juice and waiting for the early-July street party known as Sound of Frankfurt, a techno-world music thing that's absolute fun (notice that it occurs while all those suits-and-ties are off at their summer cottages).

JUGENDHERBERGE UND JUGENDGÄSTEHAUS FRANKFURT AM MAIN (FRANKFURT GUEST HOUSE AND HOSTEL)

Deutschherrnufer 12,

60594 Frankfurt/Main

Phone: 069–610–0150

Fax: 069–610–01599

E-mail: jugendherberge_frankfurt@t-online.de

Web site: www.jugendherberge-frankfurt.de

Rates: 27–44 DM per HI member (about $14–$22 US)

Credit cards: No

Beds: 470

Private/family rooms: Yes
Kitchen available: No
Season: Closed December 23–January 2
Office hours: 6:30–2:00 A.M.
Lockout: 9:00 A.M.–1:00 P.M.
Curfew: Midnight
Affiliation: Hostelling International-DJH
Regional office: Hessen
Extras: Meals ($), luggage storage, meeting room, table tennis, TV room, bar/cafeteria

It's pretty unusual to find a big-city, Hostelling International–affiliated hostel in this central and happening location. We've seen it only a handful of times before—Geneva, yeah, Munich, OK, but most of the time you're stuck out in East Boondock wondering when the next (or last) bus is possibly gonna bring you to or from the part of the city you actually came to see.

But enough digression. Frankfurt's hostel sits smack dab in the Sachsenhausen district of the city, a cobbled and atmospheric quarter of alleyways, publike grub, and nightlife galore. (It's also a rather tolerant place: You'll find a wide variety of ethnicies, lifestyles, and sexual orientations represented.) You'll never go hungry or thirsty around here; they serve food till late, and you're sure to get an authentic taste of what real Frankfurt residents do.

The hostel lacks the character of its surroundings, however, in a biggggggg way. It's a huge snoozing warehouse, basically—a jumbled, four-story building whose main part looks kinda like it used to be a prison guardhouse. There are somewhat tight quarters as a result. The dorms here contain anywhere from one to twelve beds, and they've got five family rooms plus a handful of apartment-style rooms with in-room bathrooms. There's a meeting room, game room, cafeteria serving meals, storage for your luggage . . . blah blah blah. You probably didn't come here for the bed anyway, just the location. The midnight curfew is brutal, but staff have been known to let it slide until 1:00 or even 2:00 A.M., since that's when reception officially is supposed to close.

Take note that our snoops found the reservation system here way overbooked and overstressed. Make a booking in advance, confirm and reconfirm it before you arrive, and—we're just telling it like it is—try to arrive early enough in the day to have a Plan B in case they screw up anyway.

Now go find some apple wine.

Best bet for a bite:
Adolf Wagner

Insiders' tip:
Sound of Frankfurt festival

What hostellers say:
"Check out this neighborhood!"

Gestalt:
Frankfurter

Safety:

Hospitality:

Cleanliness:

Party index:

How to get there:

By bus/train: From train station take #16 tram to Frankensteiner Platz and walk to hostel. Or take S-Bahn lines S1, S2, or S6 to Lokalbahnof Station; walk ⅓ mile to hostel.

By car: Take Highway 661, exiting at signs for Offenbach-Kaiserlei or FFM-Sachsenhausen (Highway B3). Continue to hostel.

HANNOVER

Hannover is not as famous as Hamburg, its similar-sounding and not-too-distant cousin to the north, but it's still worth seeing on its own merits, especially if you're finding north-central Germany's vibe to your liking. Once a booming import town, today it's a little quieter.

The year 2000 wasn't a great time to book a hostel bed in Hannover; the Expo 2000 show brought a lot of high-tech jazz and tons of tourists into town, and you were lucky if you found a place to bed down. But with that done, the city can settle back to its happy mostly-locals existence. Computer-heads might come in winter for the big CeBIT technology fair; the rest of us probably would only think to visit in summer.

JUGENDHERBERGE HANNOVER (HANNOVER HOSTEL)

Ferdinand-Wilhem-Fricke-Weg 1,

30169 Hannover

Phone: 0511–131–7674

Fax: 0511–185–55
Rates: 27–34 DM per Hostelling International member (about $14–$17 US)
Credit cards: No
Beds: 300
Private/family rooms: Yes
Kitchen available: No
Season: Closed December 24–26
Office hours: Open twenty-four hours
Curfew: 11:30 P.M.
Affiliation: Hostelling International-DJH
Regional office: Hannover
Extras: Laundry, breakfast, cafeteria ($), meeting rooms, campground, TV room, table tennis, volleyball, basketball, pool table, luggage storage

This hostel building has a rather interesting architecture—you'll have to see it to understand it—but if you're a hardbody, this is definitely the place for you in Hannover.

It sits in the middle of a whole collection of sports building and facilities known as Sportpark, including tennis courts, pools, and a gym. Sure, you've gotta make a bit of an effort to get out here from downtown Hannover—really, it's probably only suitable for someone with a car, a van, a bus, or a pair of bionic legs—but it's possibly the best place in town, so strongly consider it if you want quiet and exercise and don't need to experience Hannover-after-dark. As a bonus, it's close to Maschsee lake.

This used to be a bit of a cash-cow warehouse, all huge dorm rooms. But the management listened to what the hosteller wanted, and now—newly fixed up—it's the lap of luxury for your average Joe. There are a bunch of doubles, quads, and five-bedded rooms with sinks, plus one huger dorm, too. But you really want to be in one of the thirty-six (yes, thirty-six!) double rooms with their own bathrooms and showers; recruit a sweetie or a travel partner, if need be, to get one. Then there are eighteen other quad rooms with showers only and hallway bathrooms.

Best bet for a bite:
Markthalle

Insiders' tip:
Get a Hannover Card

What hostellers say:
"Pretty and quiet."

Gestalt:
All sport

Safety:

Hospitality:

Cleanliness:

Party index:

The whole place comes with gorgeous water views, but little of the city noise you're normally forced to endure in an urban bunk bed. The seven meeting rooms should give you a tip-off to the usual clientele you'll be sharing the place with, though: school kiddies. German ones. Lots of 'em. 'Nuff said!

How to get there:

By bus/train: From train station walk 1½ miles to hostel. Or take #3 or #7 streetcar toward Mühlenberg to Fischerhof-Fachhochschule stop; cross bridge and make a right. Continue to hostel.

By car: Upon entering Hannover, follow signs toward STADION.

NATURFREUNDEHAUS IN DER EILENRIEDE (HANNOVER PARK HOSTEL)

Hermann-Bahlsen-Allee 8,

30655 Hannover

Phone: 0511–691–493

Fax: 0511–690–652
Rates: 34.80–43.80 DM per Hostelling International member
(about $18–$22 US)
Credit cards: No
Beds: 82

Private/family rooms: Yes
Kitchen available: No
Season: Closed December 24–26
Office hours: 8:00–10:00 A.M.; 3:00–10:00 P.M.
Affiliation: Hostelling International-DJH
Regional office: Hannover
Extras: Meeting room, breakfast, playground, table tennis, soccer, parking, meals ($)

Yet another Hannover hostel in a park (all three of 'em are, believe it or not), this one's the best of the lot, we think, even if it is a bit simple. The greenery and parklands surrounding sort of compensate for the not-central location.

They've got three kinds of rooms, all of them kinda small but nicely decorated nonetheless: singles, doubles, or triples. The singles are expensive, but the doubles and triples are almost reasonable. Two common rooms, a meeting room, and a game room—with table tennis, that staple of German hosteling—are about the only social action here, though outdoors you'll also find some fields, courts, and sports equipment. The big breakfast is a big reason to consider staying.

Best bet for a bite:
Nordsee

Insiders' tip:
Summer is festival time in city

What hostellers say:
"Quiet as a mouse."

Gestalt:
Green acres

Safety:

Hospitality:

Cleanliness:

Party index:

How to get there:

By bus/train: From station take #3 tram toward Lahe or #7 tram toward Fasannekrug, both to Spannhagengarten stop. Make left on Herman Bahlsen Allee and continue ½ mile to hostel.

By car: Take Highway A7, exiting for Hannover-Kirchhorst, then take A37 to Hannover-Buchholz. Or follow the A2 to the A37.

NATURFREUNDEHAUS AM BLAUEN SEE (HANNOVER-MISBURG HOSTEL)

Am Fahrhorstfelde 5,
30629 Hannover
Phone: 0511–580–537
Fax: 0511–580–537
Rates: 30 DM per HI member (about $15 US)
Credit cards: No
Beds: 32
Private/family rooms: Yes

Kitchen available: No
Season: Closed December 24–26
Office hours: 2:00–8:00 P.M. (sometimes closed Monday)
Affiliation: Hostelling International-DJH
Regional office: Hannover
Extras: Lake, ducks, breakfast ($), meals ($)

Note: Office closed Monday. Advance reservations always required.

Not much to add for this tiny and quiet place, the final entry in Hannover's hostelling sweepstakes. It's so far out of town you'd have to be pretty hard up for a bunk to come and stay, although the surroundings are especially quiet and green. (It's located in the woods and right beside a lake that's known for its constant duck traffic.)

If you're still reading, there are two common rooms, eight private rooms, and the usual dormitories of four to eight beds apiece. Staff is decently friendly, but there's no nightlife or culture to speak of anywhere around here, and the trip into Hannover on public transit is daunting at best. Know that German schools are very familiar with this place (they have buses), so if you really do want to stay, book ahead.

How to get there:

By bus/train: Take a breath. From Hannover Station, take #3 tram to end stop; change to #124 bus and keep going to Misburg-Garten stop. Get off. Change to #631 bus and continue to Waldfriedhof stop; walk to end of street, following signs down path to hostel. Collapse into bed.

By car: Contact hostel for directions.

Best bet for a bite:
Brauhaus Ernst August

Insiders' tip:
Cyberb@r for email

What hostellers say:
"Quack."

Gestalt:
Ducky

Safety:

Hospitality:

Cleanliness:

Party index:

KEY TO ICONS

Attractive natural setting	Comfortable beds	Especially well suited for families
Ecologically aware hostel	Editors' choice: among our very favorite hostels	Good for active travelers
Superior kitchen facilities or cafe	A particularly good value	Visual arts at hostel or nearby
Offbeat or eccentric place	Wheelchair accessible	Music at hostel or nearby
Superior bathroom facilities	Good for business travelers	Great hostel for skiers
Romantic private rooms		Bar or pub at hostel or nearby

LEIPZIG

Easily reached by direct train from Berlin or Dresden, Leipzig isn't much to look at, but the hordes of university students are loads of fun at showing their home off—and they like to party, too. So come here if you want an inside peek at the former East Germany, some frank talk about what reunification has and has not meant, and lots of beer and music.

JUGENDHERBERGE LEIPZIG-CENTRUM

Volksgartenstrasse 24,
04347 Leipzig
Phone: 0341–245–7011

Fax: 0341–245–7012
E-mail: servicecenter@djh-sachsen.de
Web site: www.djh-sachsen.de
Rates: 25–30 DM per Hostelling International member (about $13–$15 US)
Credit cards: No
Beds: 176
Private/family rooms: Yes
Kitchen available: No
Season: Closed December 23–27
Office hours: 7:00–9:00 A.M.; 2:30–11:00 P.M.
Curfew: 1:00 A.M.
Affiliation: Hostelling International-DJH
Regional office: Sachsen
Extras: Table tennis, game room, programs, meeting room, meals ($), parking

$

Best bet for a bite:
le bit

Insiders' tip:
Internet access at
"le bit" too

What hostellers say:
"Blah."

Gestalt:
Off-Zentrum

Any place called a "Zentrum" is automatically gonna feature bad '70s Fascist-style architecture, and this place—since it's in the former East Germany—is definitely no exception to that truism. It also features East German–style management and rules and isn't even close to the hopping downtown. Too bad it's the only hostel game in town so far, 'cause it would be our second pick in most other towns. But the cost of a hotel here in Leipzig is simply too great to justify a splurge—so it's the hostel or nothing.

Dorms contain two to six beds apiece, none of them too inspiring, and your showers and bathrooms are on the hallway, not in the privacy and closeness of your own bedroom. There's a meeting room for groups traveling together; other services include a game room (get out that table tennis paddle, kiddies). Like we said, they love driving home the importance of the rules (a curfew, a lockout, no eating in bed, no nookie . . .).

Safety:

Hospitality:

Cleanliness:

Party index:

How to get there:

By bus/train: From Leipzig Station take #17, #27, #37, or #57 tram toward Schönefeld to Löbauer Strasse stop.

By car: Take Highway A14 to Leipzig Nordost/Taucha, then head toward Stadtzentrum (City Center) on Highway B87, making a right onto Permoserstrasse.

WEIMAR

Here's another one of those cities you don't think to go to, but then you get there and—wow—it's really something. Weimar is special, but it takes a bit of traveling to find. (Of course, so does Berlin, and lots of you are headin' there . . . so why not detour here on the way?) Unbelievably, there are four hostels here, each okay in its own way.

JUGENDGÄSTEHAUS "MAXIM GORKI"

Zum Wilden Graben 12,
99425 Weimar
Phone: 03643–850–750

Fax: 03643–850–749
Rates: 26–31 DM per Hostelling International member (about $13–$16 US)
Credit cards: No
Beds: 60
Private/family rooms: Yes
Season: Closed December 22–27
Office hours: Open twenty-four hours
Affiliation: Hostelling International-DJH
Regional office: Thüringen
Extras: Table tennis, grill, disco, TV, breakfast, luggage storage, bar, meeting room, parking, garden

Jugendgästehaus "Maxim Gorki"
Weimar

(photo courtesy of Deutsches Jugendherbergswerk)

Named for the Russian writer, this hostel's definitely a cut above the other two "official" joints in town . . . but it's also a distance from the city, maybe 3 miles from the train station where you'll arrive. Once again (sigh), we have Exhibit A against relying too much on Hostelling International hostels. The good ones are always miles from the action.

Anyway, once you've found your way out to these hills—probably by the dreaded infrequent and early-quitting city bus—you'll find a complex of cool: a nice faux half-timbered building fronted by spruce trees and a boring street, with its own little disco, bar, television lounge, free breakfast, and game room. There's a garden, too.

Best bet for a bite:
Ratskeller

Insiders' tip:
Bus doesn't run past
8:00 P.M.

What hostellers say:
"Kinda fun."

Gestalt:
Gorki's park

Safety: 👍

Hospitality: 👍

Cleanliness: 👍

Party index:

How to get there:

By bus/train: From Weimar Station take #8 bus toward Merketal to Rainer-Maria-Rilke Strasse stop; walk to hostel.

By car: Take Highway A4 to Weimar; parking at the hostel.

JUGENDGÄSTEHAUS "AM ETTERSBERG" (WEIMAR GUEST HOUSE HOSTEL ON THE ETTERSBERG)

Ettersberg-Siedlung,
99427 Weimar

Phone: 03643–421–111

Fax: 03643–421–112
E-mail: jgh-weimar@gmx.de
Web site: www.jgh-gmx.de
Rates: 26–31 DM per HI member (about $13–$16 US)
Credit cards: No
Beds: 66
Private/family rooms: Yes
Kitchen available: No
Season: Closed December 21–27
Affiliation: Hostelling International-DJH
Regional office: Thüringen
Extras: Table tennis, playground, grill, sauna, volleyball, meeting room, laundry, parking, meals ($), television room

A sister hostel to the Maxim Gorki joint closer to town, this hostel is planning on adding seventy more beds, which should be ready by early 2001. The building, located in a lovely park, was at press time made up of rooms with small numbers of beds—two to six—and all have their own bathrooms as well as lockers for personal effects.

The common room, where most socializing occurs, has a TV and is the only place where smoking is allowed in the building—an unfortunate situation for nonsmokers who want to catch the international news or *Alf* episodes in German. You can also have meals here sometimes, adjusted to your palate—vegetarians have no problem remaining pork-free—although a group will have to be staying at the same time in order for meals to be served. If you're here alone and find no food, you may have to settle for the sodas and snacks sold at reception. They also sell bus tickets for the long ride back into town and stamps for postcards.

You'll find staff extremely friendly, helpful, and English-speaking (for the most part), though you may have to try Russian, Polish, or Spanish if no English speaker is working the desk. That's because Weimar was once a part of East Germany, so the educational system was geared to learning Slavic languages rather than western tongues.

Best bet for a bite:
Am Frauentor

Insiders' tip:
Library has Net access ($)

What hostellers say:
"Great city!"

Gestalt:
Goethe as gold

Safety:

Hospitality:

Cleanliness:

Party index:

The city is having no trouble bouncing back from its former existence, however. It boasts tons of culture and is a magnet for music and architecture students. This is the town that gave the world the Bauhaus style and Goethe, among others, after all. There's lots of green space to stretch out in, too.

How to get there:

By bus/train: From Weimar Station take #6 bus to Obelisk stop; walk ⅓ mile to hostel.

By car: Take Highway A4 to Weimar; continue to inner city and follow signs to Buchenwald/Ettersberg.

JUGENDHERBERGE "AM POSECKSCHEN GARTEN" (WEIMAR HOSTEL AT POSECKSCHEN GARDEN)

Humboldtstrasse 17,

99423 Weimar

Phone: 03643–850–792

Fax: 03643–850–793
Rates: 25–30 DM per Hostelling International member (about $13–$15 US)
Credit cards: Yes
Beds: 104
Private/family rooms: Yes
Kitchen available: No
Season: Closed December 21–27
Office hours: 7:00 A.M.–12:30 P.M.
Lockout: 10:00 A.M.–2:00 P.M.

KEY TO ICONS

 Attractive natural setting

 Ecologically aware hostel

 Superior kitchen facilities or cafe

 Offbeat or eccentric place

 Superior bathroom facilities

 Romantic private rooms

 Comfortable beds

 Editors' choice: among our very favorite hostels

 A particularly good value

 Wheelchair accessible

 Good for business travelers

 Especially well suited for families

 Good for active travelers

 Visual arts at hostel or nearby

 Music at hostel or nearby

 Great hostel for skiers

 Bar or pub at hostel or nearby

Curfew: 12:30 A.M.
Affiliation: Hostelling International-DJH
Regional office: Thüringen
Extras: Grill, breakfast, meals ($), luggage storage, bar/cafeteria

Best bet for a bite:
University Mensa

Insiders' tip:
Garten party

What hostellers say:
"Get the earplugs."

Gestalt:
Garten party

Safety:

Hospitality:

Cleanliness:

Party index:

This handsome building isn't anything special, but it's pretty well located with regard to the equally handsome streets of Weimar.

Rooms are mostly eight- to ten-bedded, though there are also some smaller rooms for couples and families; two common rooms provide the stretching-out space. They serve breakfast for free and meals at noon and dinnertime for a charge. Too bad there are rules like a curfew and plenty of schoolkids food-fighting their way around Germany and beating up the dorms a little.

How to get there:

By bus/train: From station take #6 bus toward Merketal to Poseckscher Garten stop, then turn right on Poseckschen Garten and continue to Humboldtstrasse; hostel is on that street.

By car: Take Highway A4 to Weimar. Or contact hostel for directions.

JUGENDHERBERGE GERMANIA (WEIMAR GERMANIA HOSTEL)

Karl-August-Allee 13,
Weimar
Phone: 03643–202–076

Fax: 03643–202–076
Rates: 25–30 DM per Hostelling International member (about $13–$15 US)
Beds: 121
Private/family rooms: Yes
Kitchen available: No
Season: Closed December 23–27
Office hours: Open twenty-four hours
Lockout: 10:00 A.M.–2:00 P.M.
Affiliation: Hostelling International-DJH
Regional office: Thüringen
Extras: Breakfast, luggage storage, meals ($), bar/cafeteria

The best thing about the Germania hostel is the location—you can jump off the train at 10 at night and be walkin' into your dorm room at, like, 10:05. It's that close, and if you need to blast out of town early the next morning, you couldn't pick a more perfect bunk.

Otherwise, it's bland but adequately enough equipped.

How to get there:

By bus: Contact hostel for transit route.

By car: Contact hostel for directions.

By train: From station walk straight down Karl-August-Allee 1 block to hostel on right.

CENTRAL GERMANY
OTHER HOSTELS

JUGENDHERBERGE AFFALTER
(Affalter Hostel)
Weg zur Jugendherberge 4,
08294 Affalter
Phone: 03771–33940
Fax: 03771–33951
E-mail: servicecenter
@djh-sachsen.de
Web site: www.djh-sachsen.de
Rates: 22–27 DM per HI member
(about $11–$14 US)
Beds: 35
Private/family room: No
Kitchen available: No
Season: Open year-round
Affiliation: HI-DJH
Regional office: Sachsen
Extras: Grill, parking meals ($)

How to get there:
By bus: Contact hostel for transit
details.
By car: Take Highway B169 from
Stollberg or Lössnitz to Affalter.
By train: Contact hostel for transit
details.

JUGENDHERBERGE ALTENAU
(Altenau Hostel)
Auf der Rose 11,
38707 Altenau
Phone: 05328–361
Fax: 05328–8276
Rates: 22–27 DM per HI member
(about $11–$14 US)

Beds: 164
Private/family rooms: Yes
Kitchen available: No
Season: Closed December 24–26
Curfew: 10:00 P.M.
Affiliation: HI-DJH
Regional office: Hannover
Extras: Volleyball, basketball, grill,
table tennis, pool table, darts,
ski rentals, parking, meals ($)

How to get there:
By bus: From Altenau bus station,
make two lefts onto Markt-
strasse; walk south ½ mile
uphill to hostel.
By car: Contact hostel for directions.
By train: Take train to Goslar,
then take bus to
Hallenwellenbad stop.

JUGENDHERBERGE ALTENBERG
(Altenberg Hostel)
Dresdner Strasse 70,
01773 Altenberg
Phone: 035056–32318
Fax: 025056–32707
E-mail: servicecente
r@djh-sachsen.de
Web site: www.djh-sachsen.de
Rates: 25–30 DM per HI member
(about $13–$15 US)
Beds: 115
Private/family rooms: Yes
Kitchen available: No
Season: Open year-round
Affiliation: HI-DJH

Regional office: Sachsen
Extras: Sauna, bike repair shop, meals ($), parking

How to get there:
By bus: Contact hostel for transit details.
By car: From Dresden take Highway E55 via Heidenau or Dippoldiswalde to Altenberg.
By train: Take train to Altenberg. From Altenberg Station walk ½ mile to hostel.

JUGENDHERBERGE ZINNWALD "JÄGERHÜTTE"

(Altenberg Jägerhütte Hostel)

Bergmannsweg 8,

01773 Altenberg

Phone: 035056–32361

Fax: 035056–32317
E-mail: servicecenter @djh-sachsen.de
Web site: www.djh-sachsen.de
Rates: 22–27 DM per HI member (about $11–$14 US)
Beds: 70
Private/family rooms: Yes
Kitchen available: No
Season: Contact hostel for current season
Affiliation: HI-DJH
Regional office: Sachsen
Extras: Meeting rooms

How to get there:
By bus/train: Take train to Altenberg, then take bus to Zinnwald-Wendeplatz. Or take bus from Dresden (Wiener Platz) to Wendeplatz stop in Zinnwald.
By car: Drive to Zinnwald; hostel is ½ mile northeast of town center, in woods.

JUGENDHERBERGE ZINNWALD "KLÜGELHÜTTE"

(Altenberg Klügelhütte Hostel)

Hochmoorweg 12,

01773 Altenberg

Phone: 035056–35882

Fax: 035056–32458
E-mail: servicecenter@djh-sachsen.de
Web site: www.djh-sachsen.de
Rates: 19–24 DM per HI member (about $10–$12 US)
Beds: 47
Private/family rooms: Yes
Kitchen available: No
Season: Contact hostel for current season
Affiliation: HI-DJH
Regional office: Sachsen
Extras: Grill

How to get there:
By bus/train: Take train to Altenberg. From Altenberg Station take bus to Zinnwald.
By car: Take Highway E55 to Zinnwald, exiting at signs for Hochmoor.

SCHLOSS AUGUSTUSBURG

(Augustusburg Castle Hostel)

09573 Augustusburg

Phone: 037291–20256

Fax: 037291–6341
E-mail: servicecenter @djh-sachsen.de
Web site: www.djh-sachsen.de
Rates: 22–27 DM per HI member (about $11–$14 US)

Beds: 114
Private/family rooms: Yes
Kitchen available: No
Season: Open year-round
Affiliation: HI-DJH
Regional office: Sachsen
Extras: Fitness room, ski rentals, sled rentals, badminton, grill, disco, parking, meals ($)
How to get there:
By bus: From Chemnitz or Flöha take bus to Augustusburg.
By car: Take Highway B180 to Flöha or Highway B173 to Oederan, then continue to Ausschilderung.
By train: Take train from Chemnitz or Flöha to Erdmannsdorf/Augustusburg. Contact hostel for further transit details.

JUGENDHERBERGE ARNSFELD
(Arnsfeld Hostel)
Jugendherbergsstrasse 1,
09477 Arnsfeld
Phone: 037343–88670

Fax: 037343–88670
E-mail: servicecenter @djh-sachsen.de
Web site: www.djh-sachsen.de
Rates: Contact hostel for current rates
Beds: 42
Private/family rooms: Yes
Kitchen available: No
Season: Open year-round
Affiliation: HI-DJH
Regional office: Sachsen
Extras: Volleyball, basketball, table tennis, grill, ski rentals, meals ($)
How to get there:
By bus/train: Take train to

Annaberg-Buchholz Station. From train station take bus in the direction of Satzungen or to Arnsfeld Gambrinus stop, then walk 1 mile to hostel.
By car: Contact hostel for directions.

JUGENDHERBERGE AURICH
(Aurich Hostel)
Am Ellernfeld,
26603 Aurich
Phone: 04941–2827

Fax: 04941–67482
Rates: 23.90–28.90 DM per HI member (about $12–$14 US)
Beds: 90
Private/family rooms: Yes
Kitchen available: No
Season: Closed November 1– February 28
Affiliation: HI-DJH
Regional office: Unterweser-Ems
Extras: Fireplace, sports facilities, parking, meals ($), wheelchair access
How to get there:
By bus: Contact hostel for transit route.
By car: Contact hostel for directions.
By train: Contact hostel for transit route.

JUGENDHERBERGE BAD BEDERKESA
(Bad Bederkesa Hostel)
Margaretenweg 2,
27624 Bad Bederkesa
Phone: 04745–406
Fax: 04745–8058

E-mail: jugendherberge-
badbederkesa@t-online.de
Web site: www.net-one.de/djh/
Rates: 21.50–26.50 DM per HI
member (about $11–$13 US)
Beds: 70
Private/family rooms: Yes
Kitchen available: No
Season: Closed November 1–
January 31
Affiliation: HI-DJH
Regional office: Unterweser-Ems
Extras: Meals ($)

How to get there:
By bus: Contact hostel for transit
route.
By car: Take Highway A27 from
Bremen to Cuxhaven, exiting
at signs for Debstedt/Bad Bederkesa.
By train: Contact hostel for transit
route.

JUGENDHERBERGE BAD BENTHEIM
(Bad Bentheim Hostel)
Am Wasserturm 34,
48455 Bad Bentheim
Phone: 05922–2480

Fax: 05922–6043
Rates: 23.90–28.90 DM per HI
member (about $12–$14 US)
Beds: 122
Private/family rooms: Yes
Kitchen available: No
Season: Open year-round
Affiliation: HI-DJH
Regional office: Unterweser-Ems
Extras: Playroom, table tennis,
meals ($), parking, wheelchair
access

How to get there:
By bus: Contact hostel for transit
route.

By car: Take Highway A30 to
Nordhorn/Bad Bentheim.
By train: Take train to Bad
Bentheim. From Bad Bentheim
Station walk 1 mile to hostel.

JUGENDHERBERGE BAD BLANKENBURG
(Bad Blankenburg Hostel)
Am Kesselberg 1,
07422 Bad Blankenburg
Phone: 036741–2528

Fax: 036741–47625
Rates: 21–26 DM per HI member
(about $11–$13 US)
Beds: 141
Private/family rooms: No
Kitchen available: No
Season: Closed December 23–27
Affiliation: HI-DJH
Regional office: Thüringen
Extras: Table tennis, grill,
grounds, meals ($), parking

How to get there:
By bus: Contact hostel for transit
route.
By car: Take highway B88 to Bad
Blankenburg.
By train: Take train to Bad
Blankenburg. From Bad
Blankenburg Station walk 1
mile to hostel.

JUGENDHERBERGE BAD BRAMBACH
(Bad Brambach Hostel)
Röthenbach 4,
08648 Bad Brambach
Phone: 037438–20541
or 037438–22920

E-mail: servicecenter@djh-sach
sen.de
Web site: www.djh-sachsen.de
Rates: 22–27 DM per HI member
(about $11–$14 US)
Beds: 42
Private/family rooms: Yes
Kitchen available: No
Season: Open year-round
Affiliation: HI-DJH
Regional office: Sachsen
Extras: Sauna, ski rentals, sports
facilities, meals ($), parking

How to get there:
By bus: Contact hostel for transit
details.
By car: Take Highway A72 to
Plauen-Süd, then continue on
Highway B92 through Oelsnitz
and Adorf to Bad Brambach.
By train: Take train from Plauen
to Bad Brambach. Contact hos-
tel for further transit details.

JUGENDHERBERGE
BAD GANDERSHEIM
(Bad Gandersheim Hostel)
Am Kantorberge 17,
37581 Bad Gandersheim
Phone: 05382–2967

Fax: 25382–8368
Rates: 22–27 DM per HI member
(about $11–$14 US)
Beds: 91
Private/family rooms: Yes
Kitchen available: No
Season: Closed December 24–26
Affiliation: HI-DJH
Regional office: Hannover
Extras: Programs, table tennis,
meals ($), parking

How to get there:
By bus: Take bus to Hildesheim,
Alfeld, Einbeck, and Seesen.
By car: Take Autobahn to Seesen
or Echte.
By train: Take train to Bad
Gandersheim. From Bad
Gandersheim walk 1 mile to
hostel.

JUGENDHERBERGE
BAD HOMBURG
(Bad Homburg Hostel)
Mühlweg 17,
61348 Bad Homburg
Phone: 06172–23950

Fax: 06172–22312
E-mail: Bad-Homburg
@djh-hessen.de
Rates: 29.50–34.50 DM per HI
member (about $15–$17 US)
Beds: 206
Private/family rooms: Yes
Kitchen available: No
Season: Closed December 24–26
Affiliation: HI-DJH
Regional office: Hessen
Extras: Cafeteria ($), meeting
room, breakfast, wheelchair
access

How to get there:
By bus/train: From Frankfurt
Station take S-line S5 to Bad
Homburg. Then take #3 bus to
Meiereiberg.
By car: Take Highway A5 from
Frankfurt or Kassel, exiting at
signs for Bad Homburger.
Continue in direction of Bad
Homburg-Stadtmitte, following
Hauptverkehrsstrasse and mak-
ing a right at Sportplatz.

JUGENDHERBERGE BAD IBURG

(Bad Iburg Hostel)

Offenes Holz,

49186 Bad Iburg/TW

Phone: 05403–74220

Fax: 05403–9770
Rates: 23.90–28.90 DM per HI member (about $12–$14 US)
Beds: 142
Private/family rooms: Yes
Kitchen available: No
Season: Closed one weekend each winter; contact hostel for current season
Affiliation: HI-DJH
Regional office: Unterweser-Ems
Extras: Fireplace, grill, programs, meals ($), parking

How to get there:
By bus: Contact hostel for transit details.
By car: Take Highway A1 to Lotter Kreuz, then take Highway A30 in the direction of Hannover to Osnabrück-Nahne. Or take Highway B51 to Bad Iburg.
By train: Contact hostel for transit details.

JUGENDHERBERGE BAD KARLSHAFEN

(Bad Karlshafen Hostel)

Winnefelderstrasse 7,

34385 Bad Karlshafen

Phone: 05672–338

Fax: 05672–8361
E-mail: Bad-Karlshafen @djh-hessen.de
Rates: 22–27 DM per HI member (about $11–$14 US)

Beds: 86
Private/family rooms: Yes
Kitchen available: No
Season: Closed December 24–26
Affiliation: HI-DJH
Regional office: Hessen
Extras: Table tennis, meals ($), parking

How to get there:
By bus: Contact hostel for transit details.
By car: From northwest take Highway B241 to Uslar. From West Warburg take Highway B241 through Beverungen. From Hannover Münden take Highway B80. Hostel is ½ mile north from city center.
By train: Take train to Bad Karlshafen. From Bad Karlshafen Station walk short distance to hostel.

JUGENDHERBERGE HELMARSHAUSEN

(Helmarshausen Hostel)

Gottsbürener Strasse 15,

34385 Bad Karlshafen-Helmarshausen

Phone: 05672–1027

Fax: 05672–2976
E-mail: Helmarshausen @djh-hessen.de
Rates: 23.50–28.50 DM per HI member (about $12–$14 US)
Beds: 178
Private/family rooms: Yes
Kitchen available: No
Season: Closed December 24–26
Affiliation: HI-DJH
Regional office: Hessen
Extras: Grounds, playground, cafeteria ($), parking

How to get there:
By bus/train: Take train to Bad
Karlshafen. From Bad Karlshafen
Station walk 2 miles to hostel or
take bus to Helmarshausen-Mitte
stop and walk ½ mile to hostel.
By car: Contact hostel for direc-
tions.

JUGENDHERBERGE BAD KÖSEN

(Bad Kösen Hostel)

Bergstrasse 3,

06628 Bad Kösen

Phone: 034463–27597

Rates: 19–24 DM per HI member
  (about $10–$12 US)
Beds: 119
Private/family rooms: Yes
Kitchen available: No
Season: Closed December 22–27
Affiliation: HI-DJH
Regional office: Sachsen-Anhalt
Extras: Table tennis, pool table,
  parking, meals ($), laundry

How to get there:
By bus: Contact hostel for transit
  details.
By car: Take Highway A4 to
  Apolda, continuing on Highway
  B87 in the direction of Naum-
  burg to Bad Kösen.
By train: Take train from Berlin,
  Erfurt, Leipzig, or Saalfeld to
  Bad Kösen. From Bad Kösen
  Station walk 1 mile to hostel.

JUGENDHERBERGE BAD LAUSICK / BUCHHEIM

(Bad Lausick Hostel)

Herbergsweg 2,

04651 Bad Lausick

Phone: 034345–7270

Fax: 034345–72723
Web site: www.djh-sachsen.de
Rates: 25–30 DM per HI member
  (about $13–$15 US)
Beds: 146
Private/family rooms: Yes
Kitchen available: No
Season: Contact hostel for current
  season
Affiliation: HI-DJH
Regional office: Sachsen
Extras: Grill, meals ($), laundry,
  wheelchair access, parking

How to get there:
By bus: Take bus from Leipzig to
  Mittweida to Buchheim stop,
  then walk ¼ mile to hostel.
By car: Contact hostel for direc-
  tions.
By train: Take train from Leipzig
  or Chemnitz to Bad Lausick.

JUGENDHERBERGE BAD LAUTERBERG

(Bad Lauterberg Hostel)

Flösswehrtal 25,

37431 Bad Lauterberg

Phone: 05524–3738

Fax: 05524–5708
Rates: 22–27 DM per HI member
  (about $11–$14 US)
Beds: 131
Private/family rooms: Yes
Kitchen available: No
Season: Closed December 24–26
Affiliation: HI-DJH
Regional office: Sachsen-Anhalt
Extras: Sports facilities nearby,
  parking, meals ($)

How to get there:
By bus/train: From Bad Lauterberg
Station walk 2 miles to hostel.
Or take bus to Meilerplatz stop.
By car: Take Autobahn to
Göttingen-Nord or Seesen.

JUGENDHERBERGE BAD SACHSA
(Bad Sachsa Hostel)
Jugendherbergsstrasse 9–11,
37441 Bad Sachsa
Phone: 05523–8800

Fax: 05523–7163
Rates: 22–27 DM per HI member
(about $11–$14 US)
Beds: 121
Private/family rooms: Yes
Kitchen available: No
Season: Closed December 24–26
Affiliation: HI-DJH
Regional office: Hannover
Extras: Meeting room, table tennis, pool table, meals ($), parking

How to get there:
By bus: Contact hostel for transit
route.
By car: Take Autobahn, exiting at
signs for Göttingen-Nord and
continuing on Highway B243.
Or exit for Seesen, continuing
through Osterode and Herzberg
to Bad Sachsa.
By train: Take train to Bad
Sachsa. From Bad Sachsa
Station walk 1 mile to hostel.

JUGENDHERBERGE BAD SCHANDAU
(Bad Schandau Hostel)

Dorfstrasse 14,
01814 Bad Schandau, OT
Ostrau
Phone: 035022–42408

Fax: 035022–42409
E-mail: servicecenter
@djh-sachsen.de
Web site: www.djh-sachsen.de
Rates: 25–30 DM per HI member
(about $13–$15 US)
Beds: 101
Private/family rooms: Yes
Kitchen available: No
Season: Open year-round
Affiliation: HI-DJH
Regional office: Sachsen
Extras: Grill, meals ($)

How to get there:
By bus/train: Take train from
Dresden to Bad Schandau.
Contact hostel for further
transit details.
By car: Take Highway B172 to
Bad Schandau, continuing in
direction of Schmilka and
through Ostrau to hostel.

JUGENDHERBERGE BAD ZWISCHENAHN
(Bad Zwischenahn Hostel)
Schirrmannweg 14,
26160 Bad Zwischenahn
Phone: 04403–2393

Fax: 04403–64588
E-mail: djh-segelschule@vbr.com
Web site: djh-segelschule.de
Rates: 21.50–26.50 DM per HI
member (about $11–$13 US)
Beds: 115
Private/family rooms: No
Kitchen available: No

Season: Closed November 1–30, also in winter; contact hostel for current season
Affiliation: HI-DJH
Regional office: Unterweser-Ems
Extras: Grill, parking, meals ($), stone oven
How to get there:
By bus: Contact hostel for transit route.
By car: Take Highway A28 from Oldenburg to Emden/Leer and then Bad Zwischenahn.
By train: Contact hostel for transit route.

JUGENDHERBERGE BAUTZEN

(Bautzen Hostel)
Am Zwinger 1,
02625 Bautzen
Phone: 03591–40347

Fax: 03591–40348
E-mail: servicecenter@djh-sachsen.de
Web site: www.djh-sachsen.de
Rates: 19–24 DM per HI member (about $10–$12 US)
Beds: 50
Private/family rooms: Yes
Kitchen available: No
Season: Open year-round
Affiliation: HI-DJH
Regional office: Sachsen
Extras: Sports facilities, tennis, programs, breakfast ($), meals ($)
How to get there:
By bus: Contact hostel for transit route.
By car: Take Highway A4 or Highway B6 to Bautzen.

By train: Take train from Dresden or Görlitz to Bautzen, then walk 1 mile past St-Petri-Dom church, turning left and passing Nikolai Turm tower. Make a right and continue to hostel.

JUGENDHERBERGE BERNBURG

(Bernburg Hostel)
Krumbholzallee 2,
06406 Bernburg
Phone: 03471–352–027

Fax: 03471–352–027
E-mail: jh_bbg@t-online.de
Rates: 24–29 DM per HI member (about $12–$15 US)
Beds: 65
Private/family rooms: Yes
Kitchen available: No
Season: Contact hostel for current season
Affiliation: HI-DJH
Regional office: Sachsen
Extras: Table tennis, volleyball, basketball, bike storage, parking, laundry, wheelchair access, meals ($)
How to get there:
By bus: Take bus to Jugendherberge (hostel) stop. Contact hostel for further transit details.
By car: Take Highway B185 and then Highway B71 from Halle or Magdebur to Bernburg.
By train: Take train from Halle, Magdeburg, Aschersleben, or Dessau to Bernburg.

JUGENDHERBERGE WALTERSDORF

(Bertsdorf Hostel)

Am Jägerwäldchen 2,

02763 Bertsdorf-Hörnitz

Phone: 035841-35099

Fax: 035841-37773
E-mail: servicecenter
@djh-sachsen.de
Web site: www.djh-sachsen.de
Rates: 22–30 DM per HI member
(about $11–$15 US)
Beds: 166
Private/family rooms: Yes
Kitchen available: No
Season: Open year-round
Affiliation: HI-DJH
Regional office: Sachsen
Extras: Fields, pool tables, disco,
sauna, meals ($), parking,
wheelchair access

How to get there:
By bus: Contact hostel for transit
route.
By car: Take Highway A4 to
Bautzen or Highway B96
through Oberoderwitz,
Grossschönau, and Jonsdorf.
By train: From Dresden take train
to Grossschönau Station, then
walk 2 miles to hostel. Or from
Berlin take train to Kleinbahn
Jonsdorf and walk 2 miles to
hostel.

JUGENDHERBERGE BIEDENKOPF

(Biedenkopf Hostel)

Am Freibad 15,

35216 Biedenkopf

Phone: 06461-5100

or 06461-6569

Fax: 06461-2425
E-mail: Biedenkopf@djh-
hessen.de
Rates: 23.50–28.50 DM per HI
member (about $12–$14 US)
Beds: 207
Private/family rooms: Yes
Kitchen available: No
Season: Closed December 24–26
Affiliation: HI-DJH
Regional office: Hessen
Extras: Basketball, cafeteria ($),
disco, sauna, grounds, play-
ground, parking

How to get there:
By bus/train: Take train to
Biedenkopf. From Biedenkopf
Station take bus to Kath. Kirche
stop.
By car: Contact hostel for direc-
tions.

JUGENDHERBERGE BISPINGEN

(Bispingen Hostel)

Töpinger Strasse 42,

29646 Bispingen

Phone: 05194-2375

Fax: 05194-7743
Rates: 22–27 DM per HI member
(about $11–$14 US)
Beds: 108
Private/family rooms: Yes
Kitchen available: No
Season: Contact hostel for current
season
Affiliation: HI-DJH
Regional office: Hessen
Extras: Table tennis, pool table,
meals, parking, climbing wall,
badminton, bike rentals

How to get there:
By bus/train: From train station in
Soltau, Schneverdingen,

Lüneburg, or Hamburg, take bus
to Bispingen. Contact hostel for
further transit details.
By car: Take Highway A7 to
Bispingen.

JUGENDHERBERGE BODENWERDER

(Bodenwerder Hostel)
Richard-Schirrmann-Weg,
37619 Bodenwerder
Phone: 05533–2685

Fax: 05533–6203
Rates: 22–27 DM per HI member
(about $11–$14 US)
Beds: 124
Private/family rooms: Yes
Kitchen available: No
Season: Contact hostel for current
season
Affiliation: HI-DJH
Regional office: Hannover
Extras: Table tennis, volleyball,
piano, TV, VCR, projector,
playground

How to get there:
By bus/train: Take train to
Hameln or Holzminden. Then
change to bus to Bodenwerder.
Contact hostel for further transit
details.
By car: Take Autobahn A2 to Bad
Eilsen from the west or from
Hannover.

JUGENDHERBERGE BÖRGER

(Börger Hostel)
Herbergsweg 2,
26904 Börger
Phone: 05953–228

Rates: 21.50–26.50 DM per HI
member (about $11–$13 US)
Beds: 62
Private/family rooms: Yes
Kitchen available: No
Season: Closed November 1–
March 31
Affiliation: HI-DJH
Regional office: Unterweser-Ems
Extras: Bike rentals, grill, meals
($), wheelchair access, parking

How to get there:
By bus/train: Take train to
Papenburg or Lathen. From
Papenburg Station take bus to
Börger.
By car: Drive from Cloppenburg
via Werlte to Börger or from
Meppen to Börger.

JUGENDHERBERGE BORKUM "AM WATTENMEER"

(Borkum Hostel)
Reedestrasse 231,
26757 Borkum
Phone: 04922–579

Fax: 04922–7124
E-mail: jh-borkum
@djh-unterweser-ems.de
Web site: www.borkum.de
Rates: 41.80–46.80 DM per HI
member (about $21–$23 US)
Beds: 530
Private/family rooms: No
Kitchen available: No
Season: Open year-round
Affiliation: HI-DJH
Regional office: Unterweser-Ems
Extras: Movie room, cafeteria ($),
bar, fireplace, grill, parking

How to get there:
By bus: Contact hostel for transit
details.

By car: Contact hostel for directions.

By train: Take train to Borkum-Hafen Station, then walk ¼ mile to hostel.

JUGENDHERBERGE BRAUNLAGE
(Braunlage Hostel)
Von-Langen-Strasse 28,
38700 Braunlage
Phone: 05520–2238

Fax: 05520–1569
Rates: 22–27 DM per HI member (about $11–$14 US)
Beds: 130
Private/family rooms: Yes
Kitchen available: No
Season: Closed December 24–26
Affiliation: HI-DJH
Regional office: Hannover
Extras: Table tennis, volleyball, ski trails nearby, parking, meals ($)

How to get there:
By bus/train: Take train to Bad Harzburg or Walkenried. From either station take bus to Braum. Contact hostel for further transit details.
By car: Contact hostel for directions.

JUGENDGÄSTEHAUS BRAUNSCHWEIG
(Braunschweig Hostel)
Salzdahlumer Strasse 170,
38126 Braunschweig
Phone: 0531–264–320

Fax: 0531–2643–270

E-mail: BMV@T_online.de
Rates: 28–32 DM per HI member (about $14–$16 US)
Beds: 160
Private/family rooms: Yes
Kitchen available: No
Season: Closed December 24–26
Affiliation: HI-DJH
Regional office: Hannover
Extras: Breakfast ($), parking, meals ($), wheelchair access

How to get there:
By bus:/train Take train to Braunschweig. From Braunschweig Station make a left on H-Bussing-Ring, and left again on Salzdahlumer Strasse and walk 1 mile to hostel. Or take #11 or #19 bus to Krankenhaus Salzdahlumer Strasse stop and walk to hostel.
By car: Contact hostel for directions.

JUGENDHERBERGE U. JUGENDGÄSTEHAUS BREMERHAVEN
(Bremerhaven Hostel)
Gaussstrasse 54–56,
27580 Bremerhaven
Phone: 0471–982–080

Fax: 0471–87426
Rates: 24–29 DM per HI member (about $12–$15 US)
Beds: 170
Private/family rooms: No
Kitchen available: No
Season: Open year-round
Affiliation: HI-DJH
Regional office: Unterweser-Ems
Extras: Bike rentals, table tennis, meeting room, fitness room, sauna, solarium, patio, grill, pizza oven, meals ($)

How to get there:

By bus/train: Take train to
Bremerhaven. From
Bremerhaven Station take
#502, #509, or City-Liner bus
in the direction of Leherheide to
Gesundheitsamt stop and walk
to hostel.

By car: Take Highway A27 to
Bremerhaven-Uberseehäfen exit,
then follow signs in the direction of the Innenstadt.

JUGENDHERBERGE BREMERVÖRDE

(Bremervörde Hostel)
Feldstrasse 9,
27432 Bremervörde
Phone: 04761–1275

Fax: 04761–70701
Rates: 21.50–26.50 DM per HI
member (about $11–$13 US)
Beds: 122
Private/family rooms: Yes
Kitchen available: No
Season: Open year-round
Affiliation: HI-DJH
Regional office: Unterweser-Ems
Extras: Grill, piano, sports facili-
ties, parking, meals ($)

How to get there:

By bus/train: Take train to
Bremervörde from Hamburg or
Bremerhaven. From
Bremervörde Station take bus to
Waldstrasse stop, or walk 1 mile
to hostel.

By car: Take Highway B74 from
Stade in the direction of
Bremervörde.

JUGENDHERBERGE BURG BREUBERG

(Breuberg Hostel)
Burg Breuberg,
64747 Breuberg im Odenwald
Phone: 06165–3403

Fax: 06165–6469
E-mail: BurgBreuberg
@djh-hessen.de
Rates: 24–29 DM per HI member
(about $12–$15 US)
Beds: 129
Private/family rooms: No
Kitchen available: No
Season: Closed December 24–26;
also closed every Sunday after-
noon
Affiliation: HI-DJH
Regional office: Hessen
Extras: Table tennis, parking

How to get there:

By bus/train: Take train to Höchst
or Aschaffenburg. From either
train station take #55 bus (weekdays only) to Breuberg. Contact
hostel for weekend transit route.

By car: Take Highway A3, exiting
at signs for Stockstadt, then
continuing on Highway B469 to
Obernburg and Highway B426
to Höchst. Or contact hostel for
directions.

JUGENDHERBERGE BROTTERODE

(Brotterode Hostel)
Am Zainhammer 4,
98599 Brotterode
Phone: 036840–32125

Fax: 036840–32125
Rates: 19–24 DM per HI member
(about $10–$12 US)

Beds: 65
Private/family rooms: Yes
Kitchen available: No
Season: Closed December 23–27
Affiliation: HI-DJH
Regional office: Thüringen
Extras: Table tennis, volleyball, grill, parking, meals ($)

How to get there:
By bus/train: Take train to Schmalkalden. From Schmalkalden Station take bus to Brotterode. Contact hostel for further transit details.
By car: Take Highway B88 to Grosser Inselsberg exit, continuing to Brotterode.

JUGENDHERBERGE BÜDINGEN
(Büdingen Hostel)
Jugendherberge 1,
63654 Büdingen
Phone: 06042–3697

Fax: 06042–68178
E-mail: Buedingen@djh-hessen.de
Rates: 23.50–28.50 DM per HI member (about $12–$14 US)
Beds: 121
Private/family rooms: Yes
Kitchen available: No
Season: Closed December 24–26
Affiliation: HI-DJH
Regional office: Hessen
Extras: Grill, table tennis, breakfast, parking, meals ($)

How to get there:
By bus/train: Take train to Büdingen. From Büdingen Station take bus to hostel. Contact hostel for further transit details.

By car: From south or west take Highway A66. From north or east take Highway A5 or Highway A45.

JUGENDHERBERGE TOSSENS
(Butjadingen Hostel)
Meidgrodenweg 1,
26969 Butjadingen
Phone: 04736–716

Fax: 04736–817
Rates: 19.40–24.40 DM per HI member (about $10–$12 US)
Beds: 123
Private/family rooms: No
Kitchen available: No
Season: Closed November 1– April 1
Affiliation: HI-DJH
Regional office: Unterweser-Ems
Extras: Grill, bike rentals, parking, meals ($)

How to get there:
By bus/train: Take train to Bremen, Hude, or Nordenham, then take bus to Tossens.
By car: Contact hostel for directions.

JUGENDHERBERGE CELLE
(Celle Hostel)
Weghausstrasse 2,
29223 Celle
Phone: 05141–53208

Fax: 05141–53005
Rates: 22–27 DM per HI member (about $11–$14 US)
Beds: 128

Private/family rooms: No
Kitchen available: No
Season: Contact hostel for current season
Affiliation: HI-DJH
Regional office: Hannover
Extras: Table tennis, television room, basketball, playground, pool table, foosball, bike trails, piano, VCR, breakfast, parking, meals ($)

How to get there:
By bus/train: Take train to Celle. From Celle Station take #3 bus to Jugendherberge (hostel) stop. Or walk 1 mile along and then across tracks, turn left on Brewerweg, and turn right at hostel sign.
By car: From north take Highway A7 to Schwarmstedt; from west or south go via Mellendorf; from east take Highway A2 to Watenbüttel.

JUGENDHERBERGE CHEMNITZ
(Chemnitz Hostel)
Augustusburger Strasse 369,
09127 Chemnitz
Phone: 0371–71331

Fax: 0371–73331
E-mail: servicecenter @djh-sachsen.de
Web site: www.djh-sachsen.de
Rates: 25–30 DM per HI member (about $13–$15 US)
Beds: 88
Private/family rooms: Yes
Kitchen available: No
Season: Closed December 19–28
Affiliation: HI-DJH
Regional office: Sachsen

Extras: Meeting room, programs, volleyball, basketball, grill, parking, meals ($)

How to get there:
By bus/train: Take train to Chemnitz. From Chemnitz Station take bus toward Augustusburg to Walter-Klippel-Strasse stop or S-Bahn line S 1 to Zentralhaltestelle or S 6 to Pappelhain.
By car: Contact hostel for directions.

JUGENDHERBERGE CLAUSTHAL-ZELLERFELD
(Clausthal-Zellerfeld Hostel)
Altenauer Strasse 55,
38678 Clausthal-Zellerfeld
Phone: 05323–84293

Fax: 05323–83827
Rates: 22–27 DM per HI member (about $11–$14 US)
Beds: 122
Private/family rooms: Yes
Kitchen available: No
Season: Closed December 24–26
Affiliation: HI-DJH
Regional office: Hannover
Extras: Programs, table tennis, volleyball, grill, meals ($), parking

How to get there:
By bus/train: Take train to Goslar. From Goslar Station take bus to Tannenhöhe o. Jugendherberge stop and walk to hostel. Or walk 1½ mile to hostel.
By car: Contact hostel for directions.

JUGENDHERBERGE DAHLEN

(Dahlen Hostel)

Belgernsche Strasse 25,

04774 Dahlen

Phone: 034361–55002

Fax: 034361–55003
E-mail: servicecenter
@djh-sachsen.de
Web site: www.djh-sachsen.de
Rates: 25–30 DM per HI member
(about $13–$15 US)
Beds: 125
Private/family rooms: Yes
Kitchen available: No
Season: Contact hostel for current
season
Affiliation: HI-DJH
Regional office: Sachsen
Extras: Sports facilities, meals
($), parking

How to get there:
By bus/train: From Dresden or
Leipzig take train to Dahlen.
From Dahlen Station walk 2
miles or take bus. Contact hos-
tel for further transit details.
By car: Take Highway B6 and
then Highway B182 to Dahlen.

JUGENDHERBERGE DAMME

(Damme Hostel)

Steinfelder Strasse 57,

49401 Damme

Phone: 05491–96720

Fax: 05491–967229
E-mail: jh-damme
@djh-unterweser-ems.de
Rates: 26–31 DM per HI member
(about $13–$16 US)

Beds: 164
Private/family rooms: Yes
Kitchen available: No
Affiliation: HI-DJH
Regional office: Unterweser-Ems
Extras: Cafeteria ($), gymnasiun,
grill, programs, sports facilities,
parking, wheelchair access

How to get there:
By bus/train: Take train to
Holdorf. From Holdorf Station
take #2744 or #2741 bus to
Damme. From Damme bus stop
take taxi to hostel, or contact
hostel for further transit details.
By car: Take Highway A1 to
Holdorf, continuing 1½ miles in
the direction of Steinfeld, then
follow signs in the direction of
Damme and continue to hostel.

JUGENDHERBERGE DARMSTADT

(Darmstadt Hostel)

Landgraf-Georg-Strasse 119,

64287 Darmstadt

Phone: 06151–45293

Fax: 06151–422–535
E-mail: Darmstadt
@djh-hessen.de
Rates: 24–29 DM per HI member
(about $12–$15 US)
Beds: 122
Private/family rooms: No
Kitchen available: No
Season: Closed December 24–26
Affiliation: HI-DJH
Regional office: Hessen
Extras: Cafeteria ($), boat rentals,
swimming pool, beach, parking

How to get there:
By bus/train: Take train to Darmstadt.
From Darmstadt Station take D bus

to Woog/Beckstrasse stop and walk to hostel.

By car: Take Autobahn to Darmstadt/Stadtmitte. Go straight to the center of town, then continue through tunnel in the direction of Aschaffenburg.

JUGENDHERBERGE DESSAU

(Dessau Hostel)

Waldkaterweg 11,

06846 Dessau

Phone: 0340–619–452

Fax: 0340–619–452
Rates: 21–26 DM per HI member (about $11–$13 US)
Beds: 63
Private/family rooms: Yes
Kitchen available: No
Season: December 24–26
Affiliation: HI-DJH
Regional office: Hessen
Extras: Table tennis, volleyball, pool table, grill, parking, meals ($)

How to get there:
By bus/train: Take train from Magdeburg or Leipzig to Dessau. Contact hostel for further transit details.
By car: Take Highway A9, exiting at signs for Dessau Süd or for Dessau Ost on Highways B184–185.

JUGENDHERBERGE EHRENFRIEDERSDORF

(Ehrenfriedersdorf Hostel)

Greifensteinstrasse 46,

09427 Ehrenfriedersdorf

Phone: 037346–1253

E-mail: servicecenter @djh-sachsen.de
Web site: www.djh-sachsen.de
Rates: 22–27 DM per HI member (about $11–$14 US)
Beds: 43
Private/family rooms: Yes
Kitchen available: No
Season: Closed November 1– December 31
Affiliation: HI-DJH
Regional office: Sachsen
Extras: Programs, parking, meals ($)

How to get there:
By bus/train: Take train to Chemnitz or to Annaberg. From either station take bus to Ehrenfriedersdorf, then walk 3 miles to hostel. Or contact hostel for further transit details.
By car: Contact hostel for directions.

JUGENDHERBERGE "ARTUR BECKER"

(Eisenach Hostel)

Mariental 24,

99817 Eisenach

Phone: 03691–743–259

Fax: 03691–743–260
Rates: 25–30 DM per HI member (about $13–$15 US)
Beds: 102
Private/family rooms: Yes
Kitchen available: No
Season: Closed December 24–27
Affiliation: HI-DJH
Regional office: Thüringen
Extras: Table tennis, grill, meeting room, luggage storage, parking, meals ($)

How to get there:
By bus/train: Take train to

Eisenach. From Eisenach Station take #3 bus to Liliengrund stop, then walk 300 yards to hostel.

By car: Take Highway A4 to Eisenach.

JUGENDHERBERGE EMDEN
(Emden Hostel)
An der Kesselschleuse 5,
26725 Emden
Phone: 04921–23797

Fax: 04921–32161
E-mail: jh-emden@t-online.de
Rates: 21.50–26.50 DM per HI member (about $11–$13 US)
Beds: 90
Private/family rooms: Yes
Kitchen available: No
Season: Closed November 1– February 1
Affiliation: HI-DJH
Regional office: Unterweser-Ems
Extras: Canoe rentals, kayaks, bike rentals, table tennis, programs, disco, grill, parking, meals ($)

How to get there:
By bus: Contact hostel for transit route.
By car: Take Highway A31 in the direction of Emden, exiting at signs for Emden-Ost.
By train: Contact hostel for transit route.

JUGENDHERBERGE ERBACH
(Erbach Hostel)

Eulbacher Strasse 33,
64711 Erbach
Phone: 06062–3515

Fax: 06062–62848
E-mail: Erbach@djh-hessen.de
Rates: 23.50–31.50 DM per HI member (about $12–$16 US)
Beds: 156
Private/family rooms: Yes
Kitchen available: No
Season: Closed December 24–26
Affiliation: HI-DJH
Regional office: Hessen
Extras: Soccer, baseball, parking, meals ($)

How to get there:
By bus/train: Take train to Erbach. From Erbach Station take #3 bus to Jugendherberge stop and walk to hostel. Or walk 1 mile to hostel from train station.
By car: Take Highway A3, exiting at signs for Wertheim-Stockstadt. Or take Highway A5, exiting at signs for Langen-Darmstadt.

JUGENDHERBERGE ERFURT
(Erfurt Hostel)
Hochheimerstrasse 12,
99094 Erfurt
Phone: 0361–562–6705

Fax: 0361–562–6706
E-mail: jugendherberge-erfurt @t-online.de
Rates: 25–30 DM per HI member (about $13–$15 US)
Beds: 201
Private/family rooms: Yes
Kitchen available: Yes

Season: Closed December 23–27
Affiliation: HI-DJH
Regional office: Thüringen
Extras: Meeting rooms, pool table, laundry, bar/cafeteria, meals ($), wheelchair access, parking

How to get there:
By bus/train: Take train to Erfurt. From Erfurt Station take S-Bahn line S 5 to final station (Steigerstrasse), then walk 200 yards to hostel.
By car: Take Highway A4 to Erfurter Kreuz, then continue to Highway A71 to Erfurt Gispersleben.

JUGENDHERBERGE ESCHWEGE
(Eschwege Hostel)
Fritz-Neuenroth-Weg 1,
37269 Eschwege
Phone: 05651–60099

Fax: 05651–70916
E-mail: Eschwege@djh-hessen.de
Rates: 23.50–31.50 DM per HI member (about $12–$16 US)
Beds: 182
Private/family rooms: Yes
Kitchen available: No
Season: Closed December 24–26
Affiliation: HI-DJH
Regional office: Hessen
Extras: Basketball, fireplace, disco, pianos, music practice room, meals ($), wheelchair access

How to get there:
By bus/train: Take train to Eschwege-West. From Eschwege-West Station take #1 bus to post stop and walk to hostel. Or take taxi to hostel.

By car: Take Autobahn to Friedland, Bad Hersfeld or Kassel-Ost. Or contact hostel for directions.

"EWALD-NEEMANN-JUGENDHERBERGE"
(Esens-Bensersiel Hostel)
Grashauser F 2,
26427 Esens-Bensersiel
Phone: 04971–3717

Fax: 04971–659
Rates: 26–31 DM per HI member (about $13–$16 US)
Beds: 146
Private/family rooms: Yes
Kitchen available: No
Season: Closed January 1– February 28
Affiliation: HI-DJH
Regional office: Unterweser-Ems
Extras: Fireplace, table tennis, basketball, volleyball, bike rentals, meals ($), parking, wheelchair access

How to get there:
By bus: Contact hostel for transit route.
By car: Take Highway A29 from Oldenburg to Kreuz Wilhelms-haven, then continue through Jever and Wittmund to Esens.
By train: Take train to Esens. From Esens Station walk 1½ miles to hostel.

JUGENDHERBERGE FALLINGBOSTEL
(Fallingbostel Hostel)
Liethweg 1,
29683 Fallingbostel
Phone: 05162–2274

Fax: 05162–5704
Rates: 22–27 DM per HI member (about $11–$14 US)
Beds: 93
Private/family rooms: Yes
Kitchen available: No
Season: Closed December 24–26
Affiliation: HI-DJH
Regional office: Hannover
Extras: Table tennis, volleyball, basketball, badminton, parking, meals ($)

How to get there:
By bus: Contact hostel for transit details.
By car: Take Highway A7 to Fallingbostel exit.
By train: Take train to Fallingbostel. From Fallingbostel Station walk 1 mile to hostel. Or contact hostel for further transit details.

JUGENDHERBERGE FRIEDRICHRODA

(Friedrichroda Hostel)
Waldstrasse 25,
99894 Friedrichroda
Phone: 03623–304–410

Fax: 03623–305–003
E-mail: jugendherberge_friedrichroda @t-online.de
Rates: 21–26 DM per HI member (about $11–$13 US)
Beds: 125
Private/family rooms: No
Kitchen available: No
Season: Closed December 23–27
Affiliation: HI-DJH
Regional office: Thüringen
Extras: Grill, table tennis, volleyball, sled rentals, programs, breakfast, parking, meals ($)

How to get there:
By bus: Contact hostel for transit route.
By car: Take Highway B88 to Friedrichroda or Highway A4 to Waltershausen.
By train: Take train to Gotha. From Gotha Station change trains and continue to Friedrichroda and walk ¼ mile to hostel.

JUGENDHERBERGE FULDA

(Fulda Hostel)
Schirrmannstrasse 31,
36041 Fulda
Phone: 0661–73389

Fax: 0661–74811
E-mail: Fulda@djh-hessen.de
Rates: 23.50–28.50 DM per HI member (about $12–$14 US)
Beds: 122
Private/family rooms: Yes
Kitchen available: No
Season: Closed December 24–26
Affiliation: HI-DJH
Regional office: Hessen
Extras: Programs, parking, meals ($)

How to get there:
By bus/train: Take train to Fulda. From Fulda take #1 bus to Stadion stop. Or contact hostel for further transit details.
By car: Take Highway A7, exiting at signs for Fulda-Nord; follow signs in the direction of Stadtmitte (downtown), then follow signs to Deutsches Feuerwehrmuseum.

JUGENDHERBERGE GARDELEGEN

(Gardelegen Hostel)

Otto Reuter Haus Waldschnibbe,

39638 Gardelegen

Phone: 03907–712–629

Fax: 03907–712–629
Rates: 19–24 DM per HI member (about $10–$12 US)
Beds: 90
Private/family rooms: Yes
Kitchen available: No
Season: Closed December 24–26
Affiliation: HI-DJH
Extras: TV room, fireplace, disco, table tennis, volleyball, basketball, pool table, grill, parking, meals ($)

How to get there:
By bus: Contact hostel for transit route.
By car: Take Highway B71 to Highway B188 and continue to Gardelegen.
By train: Take train from Stendal or Gardelegen to Gardelegen, then walk 1½ miles in the direction of Letzlingen to Gardelegen.

JUGENDHERBERGE THÜLSFELDER TALSPERRE

(Garrel-Petersfeld Hostel)

Am Campingplatz 7,

49681 Garrel-Petersfeld

Phone: 04495–475

Fax: 04495–365
Rates: 26–31 DM per HI member (about $13–$16 US)
Beds: 174
Private/family rooms: No

Kitchen available: No
Season: Open year-round
Affiliation: HI-DJH
Regional office: Unterweser-Ems
Extras: Fireplace, basketball, beach nearby, programs, wheelchair, parking, meals ($)

How to get there:
By bus/train: Take train to Cloppenburg. From Cloppenburg Station take summer-only bus to hostel. Or contact hostel for transit details.
By car: Contact hostel for directions.

JUGENDHERBERGE GEYER

(Geyer Hostel)

Anton-Günther-Weg 3,

09468 Geyer

Phone: 037346–1364

Fax: 037346–1770
E-mail: servicecenter @djh-sachsen.de
Web site: www.djh-sachsen.de
Rates: 22–27 DM per HI member (about $11–$14 US)
Beds: 93
Private/family rooms: Yes
Kitchen available: No
Season: Open year-round
Affiliation: HI-DJH
Regional office: Sachsen
Extras: Sports programs, parking, meals ($)

How to get there:
By bus/train: Take train to Annaberg-Buchholz. From Annaberg-Buchholz Station take bus to Geyer bus station. Then walk ¾ mile to hostel. Or take bus from Chemnitz-Crottendorf station to Geyer Neumarkt stop

and walk to hostel.
By car: Contact hostel for directions.

JUGENDHERBERGE GIESSEN

(Giessen Hostel)
Richard-Schirrmann-Weg 53,
35398 Giessen
Phone: 0641–65879;
Buchung: 06441–71068

Fax: 0641–960–5502
E-mail: Giessen@djh-hessen.de
Rates: 22–27 DM per HI member
  (about $11–$14 US)
Beds: 75
Private/family rooms: Yes
Kitchen available: No
Season: Closed December 24–26
Affiliation: HI-DJH
Regional office: Hessen
Extras: Sports programs, parking,
  meals ($)

How to get there:
By bus/train: Take train to
  Giessen. From Giessen Station
  take #7 bus to Untere
  Hardthöhe stop, then walk 300
  yards to hostel.
By car: Take exit for Heuchelheim
  (Giessener Ring), following signs
  to Ev. Krankenhaus and then to
  Jugendherberge-Schild (hostel).

JUGENDHERBERGE GOMMERN

(Gommern Hostel)
Manheimerstrasse 12,
39245 Gommern
Phone: 039200–40080

Fax: 039200–40082
Rates: 24–29 DM per HI member
  (about $12–$15 US)
Beds: 100
Private/family rooms: No
Kitchen available: No
Season: Closed December 24–26
Affiliation: HI-DJH
Regional office: Hannover
Extras: Table tennis, volleyball,
  basketball, bike repair shop,
  parking, meals ($), laundry

How to get there:
By bus/train: From Magdeburg or
  Dessau take train to Gormern.
  Then take bus and walk ½ mile
  to hostel. Contact hostel for further transit details.
By car: Take Highway B184 and
  then Highway B246 to Gommern.

JUGENDHERBERGE GORENZEN

(Gorenzen Hostel)
Hagen 2–4,
06343 Gorenzen
Phone: 034782–20384
or 034782–21356

Fax: 034782–21357
Rates: 21–26 DM per HI member
  (about $11–$13 US)
Beds: 125
Private/family rooms: Yes
Kitchen available: No
Season: Closed December 24–26
Affiliation: HI-DJH
Regional office: Sachsen-Anhalt
Extras: Table tennis, grill, meals
  ($), parking, wheelchair access

How to get there:
By bus: Contact hostel for transit
  details.

By car: Contact hostel for directions.

By train: Take train to Hettstedt. Then contact hostel for further transit details.

JUGENDHERBERGE GOSLAR

(Goslar Hostel)

Rammelsberger Strasse 25, 38644 Goslar

Phone: 05321–22240

Fax: 05321–41376
Rates: 22–27 DM per HI member (about $11–$14 US)
Beds: 168
Private/family rooms: Yes
Kitchen available: No
Season: Closed December 24–26
Affiliation: HI-DJH
Regional office: Hannover
Extras: Table tennis, volleyball, grill, skiing nearby, meals ($), parking, wheelchair access

How to get there:
By bus/train: Take train to Goslar, then walk 1 mile to hostel. Or take C bus to Theresienhof stop.
By car: Contact hostel for directions.

JUGENDHERBERGE HAHNENKLEE

(Goslar-Hahnenklee Hostel)

Hahnenkleer Strasse 11, 38644 Goslar

Phone: 05325–2256

Fax: 05325–3524
Rates: 22–27 DM per HI member (about $11–$14 US)
Beds: 122

Private/family rooms: No
Kitchen available: No
Season: Closed December 24–26
Affiliation: HI-DJH
Regional office: Hannover
Extras: Programs, grill, skiing nearby, sports programs, parking, meals ($)

How to get there:
By bus/train: Take train to Goslar. From Goslar Station take bus to Bockswiese stop.
By car: Contact hostel for directions.

JUGENDHERBERGE GOTHA

(Gotha Hostel)

Mozartstrasse 1, 99852 Gotha

Phone: 03621–854–008

Fax: 03621–854–008
Rates: 21–26 DM per HI member (about $11–$13 US)
Beds: 150
Private/family rooms: Yes
Kitchen available: No
Season: Closed December 23–27
Affiliation: HI-DJH
Regional office: Thüringen
Extras: Table tennis, grill, musical instrument rentals, parking, meals ($)

How to get there:
By bus/train: Take train to Gotha. From Gotha Station walk 300 yards to hostel, or take S-Bahn line S1, S2, or S4 to hostel.
By car: Take Highway A4 to Gotha.

JUGENDHERBERGE GÖTTINGEN

(Göttingen Hostel)

Habichtsweg 2,

37075 Göttingen

Phone: 0551–57622

Fax: 0551–43887
Rates: 27–32 DM per HI member
(about $14–$16 US)
Beds: 161
Private/family rooms: Yes
Kitchen available: No
Season: Closed December 24–26
Affiliation: HI-DJH
Regional office: Hannover
Extras: Disco, table tennis, billiards, volleyball, basketball, grill, cafeteria ($), wheelchair access, parking

How to get there:
By bus/train: Take train to Göttingen. From Göttingen Station take #8 bus to Kornmarkt stop. Contact hostel for further transit details.
By car: Contact hostel for directions.

JUGENDHERBERGE "OLGA BENARIO"

(Gräfenroda Hostel)

Waldstrasse 134,

99330 Gräfenroda

Phone: 036205–76290

Fax: 036205–76421
Rates: 18–23 DM per HI member
(about $9.00–$12.00 US)
Beds: 60
Private/family rooms: Yes
Kitchen available: No
Season: Closed December 23–26

Affiliation: HI-DJH
Regional office: Thüringen
Extras: Grill, table tennis, meals
($), parking

How to get there:
By bus/train: Take train to Arnstadt. From Arnstadt Station take #352 bus to Gräfenroda (Dörrberg). Contact hostel for further transit details.
By car: Take Highway A4 to Erfurter Kreuz, continuing on Highway A71 in the direction of Arnstadt to exit for Arnstadt. Continue along Highway B88 to Gräfenroda.

NATURFREUNDEHAUS GRAFHORN

(Grafhorn Hostel)

Grafenhornerstrasse 30,

31275 Grafhorn-Lehrte

Phone: 05175–2790

Fax: 05175–93151
E-mail: h.ahlves@t-online.de
Rates: 25 DM per HI member
(about $13 US)
Beds: 28
Private/family rooms: No
Kitchen available: No
Season: Closed December 24–26
Affiliation: HI-DJH
Regional office: Hannover
Extras: Meals ($)

How to get there:
By bus: Contact hostel for transit details.
By car: Take Highway A2 to Lehrte-Ost exit, then continue to Immensen.
By train: Take train to Immensen/Arpke Station. Contact hostel for further transit details.

JUGENDHERBERGE GREIZ "JURI GAGARIN"

(Greiz Hostel)

Amselstieg 12,

07973 Greiz

Phone: 03661–2176

Fax: 03661–687–808
Rates: 21–26 DM per HI member (about $11–$13 US)
Beds: 92
Private/family rooms: Yes
Kitchen available: No
Season: Closed December 23–27
Affiliation: HI-DJH
Regional office: Thüringen
Extras: Grill, table tennis, disco, parking, laundry, bar/cafeteria, meals ($)

How to get there:
By bus: Contact hostel for transit details.
By car: Take Highway B92 to Greiz. Park at hostel.
By train: Take train to Greiz. From Greiz Station walk 1 mile to hostel.

JUGENDHERBERGE HALDENSLEBEN

(Haldensleben Hostel)

Bornsche Strasse 94,

39340 Haldensleben

Phone: 03904–40386

Fax: 03904–40386
Rates: 19–24 DM per HI member (about $10–$12 US)
Beds: 40
Private/family rooms: Yes
Kitchen available: Yes
Season: Closed December 24–January 1

Affiliation: HI-DJH
Regional office: Sachsen-Anhalt
Extras: Table tennis, volleyball, bike rentals, disco, tepees in summer, meals ($), laundry, parking

How to get there:
By bus: Contact hostel for transit details.
By car: Take Highway B71 to B245.
By train: Take S-Bahn train from Magdeburg to Haldensleben. Or contact hostel for transit details.

JUGENDHERBERGE HALLE

(Halle Hostel)

August-Bebel-Strasse 48a,

06108 Halle/Saale

Phone: 0345–202–4716

Fax: 0345–202–5172
Rates: 24–29 DM per HI member (about $12–$15 US)
Beds: 72
Private/family rooms: Yes
Kitchen available: No
Affiliation: HI-DJH
Regional office: Hannover
Season: Closed December 24–26
Extras: Laundry, parking, meals ($)

How to get there
By bus: Contact hostel for transit route.
By car: Take Highway A9 to A14, then to Highways B6 and B71.
By train: Contact hostel for transit route.

JUGENDHERBERGE HAMELN

(Hameln Hostel)

Jugendherberge Halle
Halle Hostel • Halle

(photo courtesy of Deutsches Jugendherbergswerk)

**Fischbecker Strasse 33,
31785 Hameln
Phone: 05151–3425**

Fax: 05151–42316
Rates: 22–27 DM per HI member
(about $11–$14 US)
Beds: 106
Private/family rooms: No
Kitchen available: No
Season: Closed December 24–26
Affiliation: HI-DJH
Regional office: Hannover
Extras: Table tennis, volleyball,
soccer field, pool table, basket-
ball, wheelchair access, parking,
meals ($)

How to get there:
By bus/train: Take train to
Hameln. From Hameln Station
take #2 bus to Wehler Weg
stop, then walk to hostel.
By car: Take Autobahn A2 to
Rehren, using Highway B83. Or
from Hannover take Highway

B217; or from Hildesheim take
Highway B1.

**JUGENDHERBERGE
HANKENSBÜTTEL**
(Hankensbüttel Hostel)
**Helmrichsweg 24,
29386 Hankensbüttel
Phone: 05832–2500**

Fax: 05832–6596
Rates: 22–27 DM per HI member
(about $11–$14 US)
Beds: 142
Private/family rooms: Yes
Kitchen available: No
Season: Closed December 24–26
Affiliation: HI-DJH
Regional office: Hannover
Extras: Table tennis, wheelchair
access, parking, meals ($)

How to get there:
By bus/train: Take train to

Wittingen. From Wittingen take bus to Hankensbüttel. Contact hostel for further transit details.

By car: From Celle take Highway B244, or from Braunschweig take Highway B4 to Wesendorf. Or from Lüneburg take Highway B4 to Sprakensehl.

JUGENDHERBERGE HANNOVER-MÜNDEN
(Hannover-Münden Hostel)
Prof.-Oelkers-Strasse 10,
34346 Hannover-Münden
Phone: 05541–8853

Fax: 05541–73439
Rates: 22–27 DM per HI member (about $11–$14 US)
Beds: 135
Private/family rooms: Yes
Kitchen available: No
Season: Contact hostel for current season
Affiliation: HI-DJH
Regional office: Hannover
Extras: Kids' play area, meals ($), parking

How to get there:
By bus/train: From Hannover-Münden Station take #135 bus to hostel. Or contact hostel for transit details.
By car: Take Highway A7 to Werratal or Lutterberg. Continue to Hannover-Münden and hostel via Highway B80, between Weser and Reinhardswald.

JUGENDHERBERGE HAREN
(Haren Hostel)

Nikolausweg 17,
49733 Haren (EMS)
Phone: 05932–2726

Rates: 21.50–26.50 DM per HI member (about $11–$13 US)
Beds: 85
Private/family rooms: Yes
Kitchen available: No
Season: Closed November 1– February 28
Affiliation: HI-DJH
Regional office: Unterweser-Ems
Extras: Grill, parking, meals ($), stove oven, bread-baking demonstrations

How to get there:
By bus/train: Take train to Haren (Ems) from Münster, Emden, or Norddeich. From Haren (Ems) Station walk 1½ miles to hostel, or take bus and walk ½ mile to hostel. Contact hostel for further transit details.
By car: Contact hostel for directions.

JUGENDHERBERGE "WASSERBURG"
(Heldrungen Hostel)
Schlossstrasse 13,
06577 Heldrungen
Phone: 034673–91224

Fax: 034673–98136
Rates: 19–24 DM per HI member (about $10–$12 US)
Beds: 52
Private/family rooms: Yes
Kitchen available: No
Season: Closed December 23–27
Affiliation: HI-DJH
Regional office: Thüringen
Extras: Paddleboats, grill, meals ($), parking

How to get there:

By bus/train: Take train to Heldrungen. From Heldrungen Station take #509, #510, or #520 bus to Jugendherberge (hostel) stop.

By car: Take Highway B86 to Heldrungen, between Sangerhausen and Erfurt.

JUGENDHERBERGE HILDESHEIM

(Hildesheim Hostel)

Schirrmannweg 4,

31139 Hildesheim

Phone: 05121–42717

Fax: 05121–47847
Rates: 24–29 DM per HI member (about $12–$15 US)
Beds: 104
Private/family rooms: Yes
Kitchen available: No
Season: Closed December 24–26
Affiliation: HI-DJH
Regional office: Hannover
Extras: Table tennis, playground, volleyball, piano, TV, VCR, parking, meals ($), wheelchair access

How to get there:

By bus/train: Take train to Hildesheim. From Hildesheim Station walk to hostel. Or take #1 bus to Schuhstrasse stop and change to #4 bus. Continue to Triftstrasse stop, then walk to hostel.

By car: Take Autobahn A7 to Hildesheim, then Highway B1 straight to Hildesheim. Or contact hostel for directions.

JUGENDHERBERGE GERSFELD

(Gersfeld Hostel)

Jahnstrasse 6,

36129 Gersfeld/Rhön

Phone: 06654–340

Fax: 06654–7788
E-mail: Gersfeld@djh-hessen.de
Rates: 22–27 DM per HI member (about $11–$14 US)
Beds: 107
Private/family rooms: Yes
Kitchen available: No
Season: Closed December 24–26
Affiliation: HI-DJH
Regional office: Hessen
Extras: Mountain bike tours, parking, meals ($)

How to get there:

By bus: Contact hostel for transit details.

By car: Take highway to Fulda Nord exit, or contact hostel for directions.

By train: Contact hostel for transit details.

JUGENDHERBERGE HORMERSDORF

(Geyer Hostel)

Am Greifenbachstauweiher,

09468 Geyer

Phone: 037346–1396

Fax: 037346–1645
E-mail: servicecenter @djh-sachsen.de
Web site: www.djh-sachsen.de
Rates: 25–30 DM per HI member (about $13–$15 US)
Beds: 205
Private/family rooms: Yes

Kitchen available: No
Season: Open year-round
Affiliation: HI-DJH
Regional office: Sachsen
Extras: Volleyball, pool table, grill, parking, meals ($)

How to get there:
By bus: Contact hostel for transit route.
By car: Take Highway A4 to Stollberg, continuing to Zwönitz-Geyer in the direction of Greifenbachstauweiher.
By train: Contact hostel for transit route.

JUGENDHERBERGE GRÄVENWIESBACH

(Grävenwiesbach Hostel)

Hasselborner Strasse 20,

61279 Grävenwiesbach

Phone: 06086–520

Fax: 06086–970–352
E-mail: Graevenwiesbach @djh-hessen.de
Rates: 23.50–28.50 DM per HI member (about $12–$14 US)
Beds: 150
Private/family rooms: Yes
Kitchen available: No
Season: Closed December 24–26
Affiliation: HI-DJH
Regional office: Hessen
Extras: Soccer fields, sports programs, grounds, garden, parking, meals ($)

How to get there:
By bus: Contact hostel for transit route.
By car: Take Highway A3 to exit for Limburg Nord (via Weilburg), or take Highway A5 to Butzbach (via Usingen) or Bad Homburger Kreuz (via Usingen).

By train: Take S-Bahn train from Frankfurt to Bad Homburg, then change to Taunus-Bahn and continue to Grävenwiesbach.

JUGENDHERBERGE SANDHATTEN

(Hatten Hostel)

Wöschenweg 28,

26209 Hatten

Phone: 04482–330

Fax: 04482–8498
Rates: 21.50–28.90 DM per HI member (about $11–$14 US)
Beds: 122
Private/family rooms: Yes
Kitchen available: No
Season: Open year-round
Affiliation: HI-DJH
Regional office: Unterweser-Ems
Extras: Basketball, volleyball, canoes, tepees, programs, parking, meals ($)

How to get there:
By bus: Contact hostel for transit details.
By car: From the direction of Bremen, take Highway A28 to Hude via Kirchhatten-Sandhatten. From the direction of Osnabrück, take Highway A29 to Oldenburg.
By train: Contact hostel for transit details.

JUGENDHERBERGE STARKENBURG

(Heppenheim Hostel)

64646 Heppenheim

Phone: 06252–77323

Fax: 06252–78185
E-mail: Starkenburg
@djh-hessen.de
Rates: 22–27 DM per HI member
(about $11–$14 US)
Beds: 121
Private/family rooms: Yes
Kitchen available: No
Season: Closed December 24–
January 1; also contact hostel
from December 15–March 1
Affiliation: HI-DJH
Regional office: Hessen
Extras: Grounds, table tennis,
parking, meals ($)

How to get there:
By bus: Contact hostel for transit
details.
By car: Take Highway A5 from
Frankfurt or Basel, exiting at
signs for Heppenheim or
Highway A67, exiting for
Lorsch.
By train: Take train from Frankfurt
or Mannheim to Starkenburg.
From Starkenburg walk 1½
miles to hostel.

JUGENDHERBERGE HILDERS

(Hilders Hostel)
36115 Hilders/Rhön

Phone: 06681–365

Fax: 06681–8429
E-mail: Hilders@djh-hessen.de
Rates: 22–27 DM per HI member
(about $11–$14 US)
Beds: 144
Private/family rooms: Yes
Kitchen available: No
Season: Closed December 24–26
Affiliation: HI-DJH
Regional office: Hessen

Extras: Skiing nearby, meals ($),
parking

How to get there:
By bus/train: Take train to Fulda.
Then take #5040 or #5033 bus
from Fulda to Hilders, then walk
1 mile from bus station to hostel.
By car: Take Autobahn A7 from
Schlitz/Hünfeld, exiting at signs
for Süden Fulda.

JUGENDHERBERGE HITZACKER

(Hitzacker Hostel)
Wolfsschlucht 2,

29456 Hitzacker

Phone: 05862–244

Fax: 05862–7767
Rates: 24–29 DM per HI member
(about $12–$15 US)
Beds: 165
Private/family rooms: Yes
Kitchen available: No
Season: Closed December 24–26
Affiliation: HI-DJH
Regional office: Hannover
Extras: Playground, basketball,
grill, meals ($), parking, wheel-
chair access, laundry

How to get there:
By bus: From Hitzacker walk 1
mile to hostel.
By car: Contact hostel for direc-
tions.
By train: Take train to Hitzacker.
From train station walk 2 miles
to hostel.

JUGENDHERBERGE BURG HOHNSTEIN

(Hohnstein Hostel)

Am Markt 1,

01848 Hohnstein

Phone: 035975–81202

Fax: 035975–81203
E-mail: servicecenter
  @djh-sachsen.de
Web site: www.djh-sachsen.de
Rates: 24–29 DM per HI member
  (about $12–$15 US)
Beds: 250
Private/family rooms: Yes
Kitchen available: No
Season: Open year-round
Affiliation: HI-DJH
Regional office: Sachsen
Extras: Meals ($), stage, grill, pro-
  grams

How to get there:

By bus/train: Take train to Pirna.
  From Pirna Station take bus to
  Hohnstein. Contact hostel for
  further transit details.
By car: Take Highway B172 from
  Dresden or Bad Schandau, then
  exit in the direction of Sebnitz
  to Hohnstein.

JUGENDHERBERGE HOLZMINDEN

(Holzminden Hostel)

Am Steinhof,

37603 Holzminden

Phone: 05531–4411

Fax: 05531–120–630
Rates: 22–27 DM per HI member
  (about $11–$14 US)
Beds: 123
Private/family rooms: Yes

Kitchen available: No
Season: Closed December 24–26
Affiliation: HI-DJH
Regional office: Hannover
Extras: Meeting room, disco, bike
  rentals, canoes, sports facilities,
  parking, meals ($)

How to get there:

By bus: Contact hostel for transit
  details.
By car: From Münden or
  Lutterberg drive via Göttingen,
  Northeim, Paderborn, Brakel, or
  Warburg. Or contact hostel for
  directions.
By train: Take train to
  Holzminden. From Holzminden
  Station walk ¾ mile to hostel.

JUGENDHERBERGE SILBERBORN

(Silberborn-Holzminden Hostel)

Schiesshäuser Strasse 4,

37603 Holzminden

Phone: 05536–568

Fax: 05536–1533
Rates: 22–27 DM per HI member
  (about $11–$14 US)
Beds: 161
Private/family rooms: Yes
Kitchen available: No
Season: Closed December 24–26
Affiliation: HI-DJH
Regional office: Hannover
Extras: Sauna, sports facilities,
  volleyball, basketball, table
  tennis, parking, meals ($)

How to get there:

By bus/train: Take train to
  Holzminden. From Holzminden
  Station take bus to Silberborn
  or Jugendherberge (hostel) stop.

By car: Contact hostel for directions.

JUGENDHERBERGE HUDE

(Hude Hostel)
Lintelner Strasse 3,

27799 Hude

Phone: 04408–414

Fax: 04408–970–322
E-mail: jh.hude.engstfeld
@t-online.de
Rates: 23.90–28.90 DM per HI
member (about $12–$14 US)
Beds: 90
Private/family rooms: No
Kitchen available: No
Season: Closed November 1–
February 28
Affiliation: HI-DJH
Regional office: Unterweser-Ems
Extras: Parking, meals ($)

How to get there:
By bus: Contact hostel for transit
details.
By car: Contact hostel for directions.
By train: From Oldenburg or
Bremen take train to Hude.
Then contact hostel for transit
details.

JUGENDHERBERGE ILMENAU

(Ilmenau Hostel)
Am Stollen 49,

98693 Ilmenau

Phone: 03677–884–681

Fax: 03677–884–682
E-mail: jh-ilmenau@t-online.de

Web site: home.t-online.de/home/
Jugendherberge-Ilmenau/index.htm
Rates: 25–30 DM per HI member
(about $13–$15 US)
Beds: 130
Private/family rooms: Yes
Kitchen available: No
Season: Closed December 23–28
Affiliation: HI-DJH
Regional office: Thüringen
Extras: Programs, table tennis,
parking, wheelchair access,
meals ($)

How to get there:
By bus: Contact hostel for transit
details.
By car: Take Highway A71 to
Ilmenau.
By train: Contact hostel for transit
details.

INTERNATIONALES JUGENDGÄSTEHAUS

(Jena Guest House Hostel)
Am Herrenberg 3,

07745 Jena

Phone: 03641–687–230

Fax: 03641–687–202
Rates: 26–31 DM per HI member
(about $13–$16 US)
Credit cards: Yes
Beds: 120
Private/family rooms: Yes
Kitchen available: No
Season: Closed December 19–
January 5
Affiliation: HI-DJH
Regional office: Thüringen
Extras: Table tennis, volleyball,
grill, VCR, TV, stereo, meals ($),
parking

How to get there:
By bus/train: Take train to

Jena-Saalebahnhof. From Jena-Saalebahnhof Station take #1 bus to Zentrum, then change to #10, #13, or #40 in the direction of Beutenbach/Ammerbach. Then walk ½ mile to hostel.

By car: Take Highway A4 to Jena-Göschwitz, then follow signs to Jena Zentrum and follow signs to Jugendgästehaus.

JUGENDHERBERGE JEVER

(Jever Hostel)

Mooshütter Weg 12,

26441 Jever

Phone: 04461–3590

Fax: 04461–3565
E-mail: jugendherberge-jever @t-online.de
Rates: 19.40–24.40 DM per HI member (about $10–$12 US)
Beds: 50
Private/family rooms: Yes
Kitchen available: No
Season: Closed November 1– March 31
Affiliation: HI-DJH
Regional office: Unterweser-Ems
Extras: Grill, playground, meals ($)

How to get there:

By bus: Contact hostel for transit details.
By car: Contact hostel for directions.
By train: Take train from Oldenburg to Wilhelmshaven, then change trains and continue to Sande in the direction of Wittmund to Jever. From Jever Station walk ¼ mile to hostel.

JUGENDHERBERGE JOHANNGEORGENSTADT

(Johanngeorgenstadt Hostel)

Hospitalstrasse 5,

08349 Johanngeorgenstadt

Phone: 03773–882–194

Fax: 03773–889–150
E-mail: servicecenter @djh-sachsen.de
Web site: www.djh-sachsen.de
Rates: 22–27 DM per HI member (about $11–$14 US)
Beds: 60
Private/family rooms: Yes
Kitchen available: No
Season: Contact hostel for current season
Affiliation: HI-DJH
Regional office: Sachsen
Extras: Sauna, sports facilities nearby, parking, laundry, meals ($)

How to get there:

By bus: Take bus from Aue to Johannesgeorgenstadt. Markt stop.
By car: Contact hostel for directions.
By train: Take train from Schwarzenberg to Johanngeorgenstadt.

JUGENDHERBERGE GRUMBACH

(Jöhstadt Hostel)

Jöhstädter Strasse 19,

09477 Jöhstadt

Phone: 037343–2288

Fax: 037343–88003
E-mail: servicecenter @djh-sachsen.de

Web site: www.djh-sachsen.de
Rates: 22–27 DM per HI member
(about $11–$14 US)
Beds: 62
Private/family rooms: Yes
Kitchen available: No
Season: Open year-round
Affiliation: HI-DJH
Regional office: Sachsen
Extras: Meeting room, volleyball,
ski rentals, music rooms

How to get there:
By bus/train: Take train to
Annaberg. From Annaberg take
bus to Grumbach or Jöhstadt.
By car: Take Highway B95 to
Morgensonne exit, then contin-
ue to Königswalde.

JUGENDHERBERGE JONSDORF "DREILÄNDERECK"
(Jonsdorf Hostel)
Hainstrasse 14,
02796 Jonsdorf
Phone: 035844–72130

Fax: 035844–72131
E-mail: servicecenter
@djh-sachsen.de
Web site: www.djh-sachsen.de
Rates: 22–27 DM per HI member
(about $11–$14 US)
Beds: 72
Private/family rooms: Yes
Kitchen available: Yes
Season: Open year-round
Affiliation: HI-DJH
Regional office: Sachsen
Extras: Sports facilities nearby,
parking, meals ($)

How to get there:
By bus/train: Take train to Zittau,
then change trains to local line
and continue to Jonsdorf (final

stop). From Jonsdorf Station
walk ¼ mile to hostel.
By car: Take Highway B96 and
Highway B178 to Zittau.

JUGENDHERBERGE JUIST
(Juist Hostel)
Loogster Pad 20,
26571 Juist
Phone: 04935–92910

Fax: 04935–8294
E-mail: DJugendherberge_Juist
@web.de
Rates: 37.70–47.20 DM per HI
member (about $19–$24 US)
Beds: 294
Private/family rooms: Yes
Kitchen available: No
Season: Closed November 1–
December 31
Affiliation: HI-DJH
Regional office: Unterweser-Ems
Extras: Beach nearby, programs,
meals ($)

How to get there:
By bus: Contact hostel for transit
details.
By car: Contact hostel for direc-
tions.
By train: Take train to Norddeich-
Mole. From Norddeich-Mole
Station take Fahre to Hafen
Juist.

JUGENDHERBERGE KASSEL
(Kassel Hostel)
Schenkendorfstrasse 18,
34119 Kassel
Phone: 0561–776–455
or 0561–776–933

Fax: 0561–776–832
E-mail: Kassel@djh-hessen.de
Rates: 24.50–32.50 DM per HI
member (about $12–$16 US)
Beds: 209
Private/family rooms: Yes
Kitchen available: Yes
Season: Closed December 24–26;
December 31–January 1
Affiliation: HI-DJH
Regional office: Hessen
Extras: Cafeteria ($), wheelchair
access

How to get there:
By bus: Contact hostel for further
transit details.
By car: Take Autobahn to Kassel-
Stadtmitte exit. Continue 2
miles to hostel.
By train: Take train to Kassel. Or
from Wilhelmshöhe take S-Bahn
line S4 or line S6 to
Annastrasse stop. Contact hostel
for further transit details.

JUGENDHERBERGE KATZHÜTTE
(Katzhütte Hostel)
Bahnhofstrasse 82,
98746 Katzhütte
Phone: 036781–37785

Fax: 036781–33806
Rates: 19–24 DM per HI member
(about $10–$12 US)
Beds: 70
Private/family rooms: No
Kitchen available: No
Season: Closed December 23–27
Affiliation: HI-DJH
Regional office: Thüringen
Extras: Programs, grill, table
tennis, meals ($)

How to get there:
By bus: Contact hostel for transit
route.
By car: Take Highway B281 to
Katzhütte.
By train: Take train to Katzhütte.
From Katzhütte Station walk
300 yards to hostel.

JUGENDHERBERGE KLINGENTHAL "ASCHBERG"
(Klingenthal Hostel)
Grenzweg 22,
08248 Klingenthal
Phone: 037467–22094

Fax: 037467–22099
E-mail: servicecenter
@djh-sachsen.de
Web site: www.djh-sachsen.de
Rates: 25–30 DM per HI member
(about $13–$15 US)
Beds: 122
Private/family rooms: Yes
Kitchen available: No
Season: Open year-round
Affiliation: HI-DJH
Regional office: Sachsen
Extras: Ski rentals, programs,
grill, parking, meals ($)

How to get there:
By bus: Take bus from Rodewisch
via Auerbach to Klingenthal. Or
contact hostel for transit details.
By car: Contact hostel for directions.
By train: Take train from Zwickau
to Klingenthal.

JUGENDHERBERGE KORBACH

(Korbach Hostel)

Enser Strasse 9,

34497 Korbach

Phone: 05631–8360

Fax: 05631–4835
E-mail: Korbach@djh-hessen.de
Rates: 23.50–31.50 DM per HI member (about $12–$16 US)
Beds: 98
Private/family rooms: Yes
Kitchen available: No
Season: Closed December 24–26
Affiliation: HI-DJH
Regional office: Hessen
Extras: Winter sports, meals ($), wheelchair access

How to get there:
By bus/train: Take train to Korbach. From Korbach Station walk ¾ mile to hostel, or take #1 bus to hostel.
By car: Take Highway A44 to Diemelstadt, then Highway B252 to Korbach.

JUGENDHERBERGE KRETZSCHAU

(Kretzschau Hostel)

Burgenlandkreis,

06712 Kretzschau

Phone: 03441–210–173
or 03441–212–678

Fax: 03441–210–174
Rates: 24–29 DM per HI member (about $12–$15 US)
Beds: 203
Private/family rooms: Yes
Kitchen available: No

Season: Closed December 24–26
Affiliation: HI-DJH
Regional office: Sachsen-Anhalt
Extras: Fitness center, pool table, grill, disco, water sports, laundry, parking, meals ($)

How to get there:
By bus/train: From Berlin or Magdeburg take train to Zeitz. Then take bus in the direction of Naumburg to Kretzschau stop and walk 1 mile to hostel.
By car: Take Autobahn A9 to Naumburg/Osterfeld exit, then Highway B180 in the direction of Zeitz and then toward Naumburg.

JUGENDHERBERGE GREETSIEL

(Krummhörn Hostel)

Kleinbahnstrasse 15,

26736 Krummhörn

Phone: 04926–550

Fax: 04926–1473
E-mail: u.magnitz@gmx.de
Web site: www.greetsiel.de
Rates: 21.20–26.20 DM per HI member (about $11–$13 US)
Beds: 88
Private/family rooms: No
Kitchen available: No
Season: Closed November 1–February 1
Affiliation: HI-DJH
Regional office: Unterweser-Ems
Extras: Bike rentals, playground, programs, parking, meals ($)

How to get there:
By bus/train: Take train Emden or Norden. From either train station take bus to Greetsiel and walk to hostel.

By car: Contact hostel for directions.

JUGENDHERBERGE LANGENWETZENDORF

(Langenwetzendorf Hostel)

Greizer Strasse (am Schwimmbad),

07957 Langenwetzendorf

Phone: 036625–20305

Rates: 18–23 DM per HI member (about $9.00–$12.00 US)
Beds: 72
Private/family rooms: No
Kitchen available: No
Season: Closed December 23–27
Affiliation: HI-DJH
Regional office: Thüringen
Extras: Sports facilities, table tennis, volleyball, grill, parking, meals ($)

How to get there:
By bus/train: Take train to Greiz. From Greiz Station take bus to Langenwetzendorf.
By car: Take Highway B92 to Kreuzung Dasslitz and then to Langenwetzendorf.

JUGENDHERBERGE LANGEOOG

(Langeoog Hostel)

Domäne Melkhörn,

26465 Langeoog

Phone: 04972–276

Fax: 04972–6694
Rates: 37.70–42.70 DM per HI member (about $19–$21 US)
Beds: 126
Private/family rooms: No

Kitchen available: No
Season: Closed October 1–April 1
Affiliation: HI-DJH
Regional office: Unterweser-Ems
Extras: Meals ($)

How to get there:
By bus: Contact hostel for transit details.
By car: Contact hostel for directions.
By train: Contact hostel for transit details.

JUGENDHERBERGE LAUBACH

(Laubach Hostel)

Felix-Klipstein-Weg 35,

35321 Laubach

Phone: 06405–1376

Fax: 06405–7046
E-mail: Laubach@djh-hessen.de
Rates: 22–27 DM per HI member (about $11–$14 US)
Beds: 122
Private/family rooms: No
Kitchen available: No
Season: Closed December 24–26
Affiliation: HI-DJH
Regional office: Hessen
Extras: Library, meals ($), parking

How to get there:
By bus: Contact hostel for transit details.
By car: Contact hostel for directions.
By train: Contact hostel for transit details.

NATURFREUNDEHAUS LAUENSTEIN

(Lauenstein Hostel)

Vogelsang 53,

31020 Lauenstein

Phone: 05153–6474

Fax: 05153–5029
Rates: Contact hostel for current rates
Beds: 73
Private/family rooms: Yes
Kitchen available: No
Season: Closed December 24–26
Affiliation: HI-DJH
Regional office: Hannover
Extras: Table tennis, basketball, volleyball, bocce, meals ($)

How to get there:
By bus/train: Take train from Voldagsen to Duingen or from Hameln to Hildesheim. Or contact hostel for further transit details.
By car: Contact hostel for directions.
By train: Take train to Voldagsen or Elze station. Contact hostel for further transit details.

JUGENDHERBERGE LAUTERBACH

(Lauterbach Hostel)

Fritz-Ebel-Allee 50,

36341 Lauterbach

Phone: 06641–2181

Fax: 06641–61200
E-mail: Lauterbach@djh-hessen.de
Rates: 22–27 DM per HI member (about $11–$14 US)
Beds: 172
Private/family rooms: Yes
Kitchen available: No
Season: Closed December 24–26
Affiliation: HI-DJH

Regional office: Hessen
Extras: Programs, grounds, meals ($), parking

How to get there:
By bus: Contact hostel for transit details.
By car: Contact hostel for directions.
By train: From Fulda or Giessen take train to Lauterbach. Contact hostel for further transit details.

JUGENDHERBERGE LEER

(Leer Hostel)

Süderkreuzstrasse 7,

26789 Leer

Phone: 0491–2126

Fax: 0491–61576
Rates: 21.50–26.50 DM per HI member (about $11–$13 US)
Beds: 94
Private/family rooms: No
Kitchen available: No
Season: Closed November 1–February 28
Affiliation: HI-DJH
Regional office: Unterweser-Ems
Extras: Table tennis, parking, meals ($)

How to get there:
By bus: Contact hostel for transit route.
By car: Take Highway A28 to Leer, then follow signs in the direction of the Altstadt.
By train: Take train to Leer. From Leer Station walk ¾ mile to the hostel.

JUGENDHERBERGE LICHTENSTEIN

(Lichtenstein Hostel)

An der Jugendherberge 3,

09350 Lichtenstein

Phone: 037204–2718

Fax: 037204–87387
E-mail: servicecenter
@djh-sachsen.de
Web site: www.djh-sachsen.de
Rates: 22–27 DM per HI member
(about $11–$14 US)
Beds: 80
Private/family rooms: Yes
Kitchen available: No
Season: Open year-round
Affiliation: HI-DJH
Regional office: Sachsen
Extras: Meeting room, disco, grill,
fields, parking, meals ($)

How to get there:
By bus/train: Take train to St.
Egidien, then take bus to
Lichtenstein. From Lichtenstein
Station walk 1 mile to hostel.
By car: Take Highway A4 from
Hohenstein to Ernstthal, then
continue 5 miles to
Lichtenstein. Or take Highway
A72 to Hartenstein and contin-
ue to Lichtenstein.

JUGENDHERBERGE LIMBURG

(Limburg Hostel)

Auf dem Guckucksberg,

65549 Limburg

Phone: 06431–41493

Fax: 06431–43873
E-mail: Limburg@djh-hessen.de

Rates: 23.50–28.50 DM per HI
member (about $12–$14 US)
Beds: 162
Private/family rooms: Yes
Kitchen available: No
Season: Closed December 24–26
Affiliation: HI-DJH
Regional office: Hessen
Extras: Hockey training, parking,
meals ($)

How to get there:
By bus/train: Take train to
Limburg from Koblenz, Giessen,
or Frankfurt. Contact hostel for
further transit details.
By car: Take Highway A3 from
Frankfurt or Köln, then follow
signs to Limburg-Süd.

JUGENDHERBERGE LINGEN

(Lingen Hostel)

Lengericher Strasse 62,

49811 Lingen

Phone: 0591–973–060

Fax: 0591–76954
E-mail: jhlingen@aol.com
Web site: www.lingen-ems.de/
verkehrsverein
Rates: 26.70–31.70 DM per HI
member (about $13–$16 US)
Beds: 152
Private/family rooms: Yes
Kitchen available: No
Season: Closed December 18–
January 5
Affiliation: HI-DJH
Regional office: Unterweser-Ems
Extras: Bike rentals, fitness room,
parking, meals ($), wheelchair
access, sauna, solarium, grill

How to get there:
By bus: Contact hostel for transit
details.

By car: Contact hostel for directions.

By train: Contact hostel for transit details.

JUGENDHERBERGE LINSENGERICHT

(Linsengericht Hostel)

OT Geislitz,

63589 Linsengericht

Phone: 06051–72029

Fax: 06051–75694
E-mail: Linsengericht@djh-hessen.de
Rates: 23.50–28.50 DM per HI member (about $12–$14 US)
Beds: 124
Private/family rooms: Yes
Kitchen available: No
Season: Closed December 24–26
Affiliation: HI-DJH
Regional office: Hessen
Extras: Grounds, parking, meals ($)

How to get there:
By bus: Take bus to Linsengericht. Contact hostel for further transit details.
By car: Take Highway A66 to Gelnhausen West, then continue to Linsengericht.
By train: Take train to Gelnhausen. Contact hostel for further transit details.

JUGENDHERBERGE LÜNEBURG

(Lüneburg Hostel)

Soltauer Strasse 133,

21335 Lüneburg

Phone: 04131–41864

Fax: 04131–45747
Rates: 22–27 DM per HI member (about $11–$14 US)
Beds: 105
Private/family rooms: No
Kitchen available: No
Season: Closed December 24–26
Affiliation: HI-DJH
Regional office: Hannover
Extras: Table tennis, foosball, pool table, volleyball, parking, meals ($)

How to get there:
By bus/train: Take train to Lüneburg. From Lüneburg Station walk 1½ miles to hostel down Berliner Strasse, or take #11 bus to Scharnhorststrasse/ Jugendherberge stop.
By car: From the south take Highway A7 to Soltau-Ost and continue to Lüneburg, or from the north take Highway A250 to exit for Stadtmitte/Lüneburg.

JUGENDGÄSTEHAUS MAGDEBURG

(Magdeburg Hostel)

Leiterstrasse 10,

39104 Magdeburg

Phone: 0391–532–1010

Fax: 0391–532–1020
E-mail: jugendherberge-magdeburg @gmx.de
Rates: 34–39 DM per HI member (about $17–$20 US)
Beds: 250
Private/family rooms: Yes
Kitchen available: No
Season: Closed December 24–26
Affiliation: HI-DJH
Regional office: Sachsen-Anhalt
Extras: Meeting room, TV room, cafe ($), kids' play room, VCR,

water sports, wheelchair access, meals ($)

How to get there:

By bus: Contact hostel for transit details.

By car: Take Highway A2 to exit for Magdeburg-Zentrum, then continue through Magdeburger Ring to Zentrum (center).

By train: Take train from Berlin, Frankfurt, Hannover, Cottbus, or Lübeck to Magdeburg and walk ¼ mile to hostel from Magdeburg Station.

JUGENDHERBERGE MARBURG

(Marburg Hostel)
Jahnstrasse 1,
35037 Marburg/Lahn
Phone: 06421–23461

Fax: 06421–12191
Rates: 27.50–32.50 DM per HI member (about $14–$16 US)
Beds: 164
Private/family rooms: Yes
Kitchen available: No
Season: Closed December 24–26
Affiliation: HI-DJH
Regional office: Hessen
Extras: Canoes, cafeteria ($), wheelchair access

How to get there:

By bus/train: Take train to Marburg. From Marburg Station take C bus to Softwarecenter stop, cross over Lahnbrücke bridge, and continue to hostel.

By car: Take Highway B3 to Marburg-Mitte exit, then follow signs to hostel.

JUGENDHERBERGE MARDORF

(Mardorf Hostel)
Umweltstudienplatz
Warteweg 2,
31535 Mardorf
Phone: 05036–457

Fax: 05036–1554
Rates: 24–29 DM per HI member (about $12–$15 US)
Beds: 164
Private/family rooms: Yes
Kitchen available: No
Season: Closed December 24–26
Affiliation: HI-DJH
Regional office: Hannover
Extras: Seminar room, disco, volleyball, table tennis, grill, meals ($), parking, wheelchair access

How to get there:

By bus/train: Take train to Neustadt. From Neustadt Station take bus to hostel. Contact hostel for further transit details.

By car: Take Highway A2 from Hannover to Herrenhausen or Highway A7 to Schwarmstedt; then continue on Highway B6 via Neustadt-Schneeren to Mardorf.

JUGENDHERBERGE MEISDORF

(Meisdorf Hostel)
Falkensteiner Weg 2b,
06463 Meisdorf
Phone: 034743–8257

Fax: 034753–92540
Rates: 21–26 DM per HI member (about $11–$13 US)

Beds: 108
Private/family rooms: Yes
Kitchen available: No
Season: Closed December 24–26
Affiliation: HI-DJH
Regional office: Sachsen-Anhalt
Extras: Table tennis, pool table, Basketball, volleyball, parking, meals ($), laundry

How to get there:
By bus/train: Take train to Aschersleben, then change trains and continue toward Gernode to Meisdorf Station. Or from Aschersleben take bus to Meisdorf. Contact hostel for further transit details.
By car: Take Highways B185, B6, and B242 to Meisdorf.

JUGENDHERBERGE "GRÖNENBURG" MELLE
(Melle Hostel)
Fr.-Ludwig-Jahn-Strasse 1, 49324 Melle
Phone: 05422–2434

Fax: 05422–3988
E-mail: djh-melle@t-online.de
Rates: 23.90–28.90 DM per HI member (about $12–$14 US)
Beds: 67
Private/family rooms: Yes
Kitchen available: No
Season: Open year-round
Affiliation: HI-DJH
Regional office: Unterweser-Ems
Extras: Sports facilities, fireplace, grill, meals ($), parking

How to get there:
By bus: Contact hostel for transit details.
By car: Contact hostel for directions.

By train: Contact hostel for transit details.

JUGENDHERBERGE MELSUNGEN
(Melsungen Hostel)
Lindenbergstrasse 23, 34212 Melsungen
Phone: 05661–2650

Fax: 05661–51928
E-mail: Melsungen@djh-hessen.de
Rates: 23.50–28.50 DM per HI member (about $12–$14 US)
Beds: 132
Private/family rooms: Yes
Kitchen available: No
Season: Closed December 24–26
Affiliation: HI-DJH
Regional office: Hessen
Extras: Library, sports facilities, meals ($), wheelchair access

How to get there:
By bus/train: Take bus to Melsungen. Contact hostel for further transit details.
By car: Take Highway A7 from Kassel, Fulda, or Frankfurt, exiting at signs for Melsungen.

JUGENDHERBERGE FALKENHAIN
(Mittweida Hostel)
An der Talsperre Kriebstein, 09648 Mittweida
Phone: 03727–2952

Fax: 03727–600–050
E-mail: servicecenter@djh-sachsen.de
Web site: www.djh-sachsen.de

MÜHLHAUSEN

Rates: 22–27 DM per HI member
(about $11–$14 US)
Beds: 220
Private/family rooms: Yes
Kitchen available: Yes
Season: Closed October 1–April 30
Affiliation: HI-DJH
Regional office: Sachsen
Extras: Volleyball, playground,
grill, parking, laundry, meals ($)

How to get there:
By bus/train: Hostel is 5 miles
from Mittweida Station; contact
hostel for further transit details.
By car: From Leipzig take
Highway A14, exiting at signs
for Döbeln Nord or Chemnitz-
Ost. Or from Dresden take
Highway A4. Contact hostel for
further details.

JUGENDHERBERGE MÜDEN

(Müden Hostel)
Wiesenweg 32,
29328 Müden/Oertze
Phone: 05053–225

Fax: 05053–1021
Rates: 24–29 DM per HI member
(about $12–$15 US)
Beds: 156
Private/family rooms: Yes
Kitchen available: No
Season: Closed December 24–26
Affiliation: HI-DJH
Regional office: Hannover
Extras: Conference room,
grounds, sports fields, meals
($), laundry, parking, wheelchair
access

How to get there:
By bus/train: Take train to Celle.
From Celle Station take bus to

Müden/Oertze. From Müden/
Oertze Station contact hostel for
further transit details.
By car: Take Highway A7, exiting
at signs for Soltau-Ost, and then
continue along Highway B71 via
Munster. From Dreilingen make a
right onto Alpen-Ostsee Strasse.

JUGENDHERBERGE MÜHLHAUSEN

(Mühlhausen Hostel)
Auf dem Tonberg 1,
99974 Mühlhausen
Phone: 03601–813–318

Fax: 03601–813–320
Rates: 21–26 DM per HI member
(about $11–$13 US)
Beds: 78
Private/family rooms: Yes
Kitchen available: No
Season: Closed December 22–27
Affiliation: HI-DJH
Regional office: Thüringen
Extras: Sports facilities, meals
($), parking, wheelchair access

How to get there:
By bus: Take train to
Mühlhausen. From Mühlhausen
Station take #5 or #6 bus to
Blobach stop and walk ⅓ mile
to hostel.
By car: Take Highway A4 to
Gotha, continuing along
Highway B247 to Mühlhausen
or Highway B249 to Eschwege-
Mühlhausen.

JUGENDHERBERGE/ JUGENDGÄSTEHAUS NAUMBURG

(Naumburg Guest House & Hostel)

Am Tennisplatz 9,

06618 Naumburg

Phone: 03445–703–422

Fax: 03445–703–422
Rates: 24–34 DM per HI member (about $12–$17 US)
Beds: 204
Private/family rooms: Yes
Kitchen available: No
Season: Closed December 24–26
Affiliation: HI-DJH
Regional office: Thüringen
Extras: Table tennis, tennis, volleyball, basketball, grill, parking, meals ($)

How to get there:
By bus: Contact hostel for transit details.
By car: Take Highway A9 and then Highway A4 to Naumburg.
By train: Take train to Naumburg. From Naumburg Station walk 2½ miles to hostel, or contact hostel for further transit details.

JUGENDHERBERGE NEBRA

(Nebra Hostel)
Altenburgstrasse 29,

06642 Nebra

Phone: 034461–25456

Fax: 034461–25456
Rates: 24–29 DM per HI member (about $12.00–$14.50 US)
Beds: 140
Private/family rooms: Yes

Kitchen available: No
Season: Closed December 24–26
Affiliation: HI-DJH
Regional office: Thüringen
Extras: Parking, laundry, meals ($)

How to get there:
By bus: Contact hostel for transit details.
By car: Take Highway B250 to Nebra.
By train: Take train to Nebra. From Nebra Station walk ¾ mile to hostel. Or contact hostel for further transit details.

JUGENDHERBERGE "AM RENNWEG"

(Neuhaus Hostel)
Apelsbergstrasse 54,

98724 Neuhaus am Rennweg

Phone: 03679–722–862

Fax: 03679–700–384
Rates: 19–24 DM per HI member (about $10–$12 US)
Beds: 80
Private/family rooms: Yes
Kitchen available: No
Season: Closed December 21–28
Affiliation: HI-DJH
Regional office: Thüringen
Extras: Grill, ski lessons nearby, parking, meals ($)

How to get there:
By bus/train: Take train to Saalfeld. From Saalfeld or Ernstthal Station take bus to Neuhaus. Contact for further transit details.
By car: Take Highway B241 to Neuhaus.

JUGENDHERBERGE NEUKIRCH "VALTENBERGHAUS"

(Neukirch Hostel)

Karl-Berger-Strasse 16,

01904 Neukirch

Phone: 035951–31484

Fax: 035951–37108
E-mail: servicecenter
  @djh-sachsen.de
Web site: www.djh-sachsen.de
Rates: Contact hostel for current
  rates
Beds: 112
Private/family rooms: No
Kitchen available: No
Season: Open year-round
Affiliation: HI-DJH
Regional office: Sachsen
Extras: Sports fields, basketball,
  volleyball, grill, meals ($)

How to get there:
By bus: Contact hostel for transit
  details.
By car: Take Highway A4 or
  Highway B98 to
  Neukirch/Lausitz.
By train: Contact hostel for transit
  details.

NATURFREUNDEHAUS NIENBURG

(Nienburg Hostel)

Luise-Wyneken-Strasse 4,

31582 Nienburg/Weser

Phone: 05021–2812

Fax: 05021–2812
Rates: 23–34 DM per HI member
  (about $12–$17 US)
Beds: 41
Private/family rooms: Yes

Kitchen available: No
Season: Closed January 1–31
Affiliation: HI-DJH
Regional office: Hannover
Extras: Piano, table tennis, play-
  ground, meals ($)

How to get there:
By bus/train: Take train to
  Nienburg/Weser. From Nienburg/
  Weser Station walk to hostel or
  take bus to Stadion stop.
By car: Contact hostel for direc-
  tions.

JUGENDHERBERGE NORDDEICH

(Norden Hostel)

Strandstrasse 1,

26506 Norden-Norddeich

Phone: 04931–8064

Fax: 04931–81828
Rates: 21.50–26.50 DM per HI
  member (about $11–$13 US)
Beds: 96
Private/family rooms: No
Kitchen available: No
Season: Open year-round
Affiliation: HI-DJH
Regional office: Unterweser-Ems
Extras: Grill, table tennis, park-
  ing, meals ($)

How to get there:
By bus: Contact hostel for transit
  details.
By car: Contact hostel for direc-
  tions.
By train: Take train to Norddeich-
  Mole Station then contact hos-
  tel for further transit details.

JUGENDHERBERGE NORDENHAM

(Nordenham Hostel)

Strandallee 12,

26954 Nordenham

Phone: 04731–88262

Fax: 04731–88034
E-mail: djhnham@aol.com
Rates: 23.90–28.90 DM per HI
member (about $12–$14 US)
Beds: 158
Private/family rooms: Yes
Kitchen available: No
Season: Closed December 20–
January 1
Affiliation: HI-DJH
Regional office: Unterweser-Ems
Extras: Volleyball, basketball,
table tennis, cafeteria ($),
wheelchair access, parking
How to get there:
By bus/train: Take train to
Nordenham. From Nordenham
Station contact hostel for transit
route.
By car: Contact hostel for direc-
tions.

JUGENDHERBERGE NORDERNEY "DÜNENSENDER"

(Norderney Dünensender
Hostel)

Am Dünensender 3,

26548 Norderney

Phone: 04932–2574

Fax: 04932–83266
Rates: 37.90–42.90 DM per HI
member (about $19–$21 US)
Beds: 142
Private/family rooms: No

Kitchen available: No
Season: Closed November 1–
February 28
Affiliation: HI-DJH
Regional office: Unterweser-Ems
Extras: Beach nearby, meals ($)
How to get there:
By bus: Contact hostel for transit
details.
By car: Contact hostel for transit
route.
By train: Take train to Norddeich-
Mole Station, then take ferry to
Hafen Norderney.

JUGENDHERBERGE NORDERNEY "SÜDSTRASSE"

(Norderney Südstrasse
Hostel)

Südstrasse 1,

26535 Norderney

Phone: 04932–2451

Fax: 04932–83600
Rates: 37.70–42.70 DM per HI
member (about $19–$21 US)
Beds: 121
Private/family rooms: Yes
Kitchen available: No
Season: Closed November 1–
February 1
Affiliation: HI-DJH
Regional office: Nordmark
Extras: Beach nearby, meals ($)
How to get there:
By bus: Contact hostel for transit
details.
By car: Contact hostel for direc-
tions.
By train: Take train to Norddeich-
Mole Station, then take ferry to
Hafen Norderney and walk ¾
mile to hostel.

JUGENDGÄSTE- UND BILDUNGSHAUS "ROTHLEIMMÜHLE"

(Nordhausen Hostel)

Parkallee 2,

99734 Nordhausen

Phone: 03631–902–391

Fax: 03631–902–393
E-mail: rothleimmuehle@t-online.de
Rates: 25–30 DM per HI member (about $13–$15 US)
Beds: 90
Private/family rooms: Yes
Kitchen available: No
Season: Closed December 20–January 10
Affiliation: HI-DJH
Regional office: Thüringen
Extras: Meeting room, TV room, table tennis, playground, grill, volleyball, meals ($), parking

How to get there:

By bus/train: Take train to Nordhausen. From Nordhausen Station take #6 bus to Altentor stop.
By car: Take Highway B4 to Nordhausen.

JUGENDHERBERGE NORTHEIM

(Northeim Hostel)

Brauereistrasse 1,

37154 Northeim

Phone: 05551–8672

Fax: 05551–911–108
Rates: 21.50–26.50 DM per HI member (about $11–$13 US)
Beds: 103
Private/family rooms: Yes
Kitchen available: No
Season: Closed December 15–January 31
Affiliation: HI-DJH
Regional office: Hannover
Extras: Parking, meals ($)

How to get there:

By bus: Contact hostel for transit details.
By car: Take Highway A7 to Northeim-Nord, following signs to Osterode.
By train: Take train to Northeim. From Northeim Station contact hostel for transit details.

JUGENDHERBERGE OBERBERNHARDS

(Oberbernhards Hostel)

Hauptstrasse 5,

36115 Hilders-Oberbernhards

Phone: 06657–240

Fax: 06657–8896
E-mail: Oberbernhards @djh-hessen.de
Rates: 23.50–28.50 DM per HI member (about $12–$14 US)
Beds: 257
Private/family rooms: Yes
Kitchen available: No
Season: Closed December 24–26
Affiliation: HI-DJH
Regional office: Hessen
Extras: Grounds, parking, meals ($)

How to get there:

By bus: Take #5033 bus from Fulda to Dörmbach (Oberbernhards) stop.
By car: Exit at signs for Fulda-Nord or Fulda-Süd and then travel toward Hilders through Petersberg, Dipperz, and Kleinsassen.

By train: Contact hostel for transit route.

JUGENDHERBERGE OBERODERWITZ
(Oberoderwitz Hostel)
Zur Lindenallee 5,
02791 Oberoderwitz
Phone: 035842–26544

Fax: 035842–27726
E-mail: servicecenter @djh-sachsen.de
Web site: www.djh-sachsen.de
Rates: 22–30 DM per HI member (about $11–$15 US)
Beds: 138
Private/family rooms: Yes
Kitchen available: No
Season: Open year-round
Affiliation: HI-DJH
Regional office: Sachsen
Extras: Meeting room, parking, meals ($)

How to get there:
By bus: Contact hostel for transit details.
By car: Take Highway B96 to Oberoderwitz and follow signs to hostel.
By train: Take train to Oberoderwitz from Dresden, Zittau, or Berlin. Then contact hostel for further transit details.

JUGENDHERBERGE OBERREIFENBERG
(Oberreifenberg Hostel)
Limesstrasse 14,
61389 Schmitten-Oberreifenberg
Phone: 06082–2440

Fax: 06082–3305
E-mail: Oberreifenberg @djh-hessen.de
Rates: 23.50–28.50 DM per HI member (about $12–$14 US)
Beds: 226
Private/family rooms: Yes
Kitchen available: Yes
Season: Closed December 24–26
Affiliation: HI-DJH
Regional office: Hessen
Extras: Fireplace, table tennis, game room, parking, meals ($)

How to get there:
By bus/train: Take train to Königstein. From Königstein Station take bus to Obereifenberg-Siedlung, then walk ½ mile to hostel.
By car: Contact hostel for directions.

JUGENDHERBERGE TALTITZ "TALSPERRE PIRK"
(Öelsnitz Hostel)
Dobenecker Weg 27,
08606 Öelsnitz
Phone: 037421–23019

Fax: 037421–20202
E-mail: servicecenter @djh-sachsen.de
Web site: www.djh-sachsen.de
Rates: 22–27 DM per HI member (about $11–$14 US)
Beds: 82
Private/family rooms: Yes
Kitchen available: No
Season: Open year-round
Affiliation: HI-DJH
Regional office: Sachsen
Extras: Water sports, fields, volleyball, grill, sports programs, meeting rooms, parking

How to get there:
By bus/train: Take train from Chemnitz via Plauen to Öelsnitz/West, then take bus to Taltitz Siedlung.
By car: Take Highway A72 to Chemnitz-Hof and continue to Öelsnitz.

JUGENDHERBERGE OLDENBURG

(Oldenburg Hostel)

Alexanderstrasse 65,

26121 Oldenburg

Phone: 0441–87135

Fax: 0441–885–2493
Rates: 23.90–28.90 DM per HI member (about $12–$14 US)
Beds: 104
Private/family rooms: Yes
Kitchen available: No
Season: Open year-round
Affiliation: HI-DJH
Regional office: Nordmark
Extras: Programs, grill, parking, meals ($)

How to get there:
By bus/train: Take train to Oldenburg. From Oldenburg Station take #302 or #303 bus toward Flughafen to Von-Fink-Strasse stop.
By car: Take Highway A28 to Oldenburg-Bürgerfelde, then follow signs in direction of Stadtzentrum (downtown). Hostel is ½ mile northwest of city center.

JUGENDHERBERGE OLDENBURG/HOLSTEIN

(Oldenburg/Holstein Hostel)

Göhlerstrasse 58a,

23758 Oldenburg/Holstein

Phone: 04361–7670

Fax: 04361–60731
Rates: 22–27 DM per HI member (about $11–$14 US)
Beds: 84
Private/family rooms: Yes
Kitchen available: No
Season: Closed December 23–January 5
Affiliation: HI-DJH
Regional office: Nordmark
Extras: Playground, grill, table tennis, volleyball, meals ($), parking, laundry

How to get there:
By bus: Contact hostel for transit details.
By car: Take Highway A1 to Oldenburg-Süd, then exit in direction of Göhl. Or contact hostel for directions.
By train: Contact hostel for transit details.

JUGENDGÄSTEHAUS OSNABRÜCK

(Osnabrück Guest House Hostel)

Iburger Strasse 183a,

49082 Osnabrück

Phone: 0541–54284

Fax: 0541–54294
Rates: 24.70–29.70 DM per HI member (about $12–$15 US)
Beds: 145
Private/family rooms: Yes
Kitchen available: No
Season: Open year-round
Affiliation: HI-DJH
Regional office: Unterweser-Ems

Extras: Programs, grill, game room, parking, wheelchair access, meals ($)

How to get there:

By bus/train: Take train to Osnabrück. From Osnabrück Station take #62, #463, #464, or #465 bus to Kinderhospital stop and walk 150 yards to hostel.

By car: Contact hostel for directions.

JUGENDHERBERGE OSSA

(Ossa Hostel)

Dorfstrasse 69,

04643 Ossa

Phone: 034346–60587

Fax: 034346–60587
E-mail: servicecenter @djh-sachsen.de
Web site: www.djh-sachsen.de
Rates: 22–27 DM per HI member (about $11–$14 US)
Beds: 52
Private/family rooms: Yes
Kitchen available: No
Season: Open year-round
Affiliation: HI-DJH
Regional office: Sachsen
Extras: Table tennis, volleyball, grill, meals ($), parking

How to get there:

By bus/train: From Leipzig or Chemnitz take train to Geithain, then change to bus (weekdays only) or walk 3 miles to Ossa. Contact hostel for further transit details.

By car: Take Highway B95 to Frohburg, then continue in direction of Ossa. Or take Highway B175 from Chemnitz, exiting at signs for Greithain-Ossa.

JUGENDHERBERGE PANSCHWITZ-KUCKAU

(Panschwitz Hostel)

Cisinskistrasse 1,

01920 Panschwitz-Kuckau

Phone: 035796–96963

Fax: 035796–96964
E-mail: servicecenter @djh-sachsen.de
Web site: www.djh-sachsen.de
Rates: 22–27 DM per HI member (about $11–$14 US)
Beds: 60
Private/family rooms: Yes
Kitchen available: No
Affiliation: HI-DJH
Regional office: Sachsen
Extras: Sports facilities, laundry, parking, meals ($)

How to get there:

By bus: Contact hostel for transit details.

By car: Contact hostel for directions.

By train: Contact hostel for transit details.

JUGENDHERBERGE PAPENBURG

(Papenburg Hostel)

Kirchstrasse 38–40,

26871 Papenburg

Phone: 04961–2793

Fax: 04961–916-554
Rates: 21.50–26.50 DM per HI member (about $11–$13 US)

Beds: 75
Private/family rooms: Yes
Kitchen available: No
Season: Closed November 1–
February 28
Affiliation: HI-DJH
Regional office: Unterweser-Ems
Extras: Programs, sports facilities,
parking, meals ($)

How to get there:
By bus: Contact hostel for transit
details.
By car: Contact hostel for directions.
By train: Take train to Papenburg.
From Papenburg Station walk ¾
mile to hostel.

JUGENDHERBERGE GRETHEN

(Parthenstein Hostel)
Herbergsweg 5,
04668 Parthenstein
Phone: 03437–763–449

Fax: 03437–763–449
E-mail: servicecenter
@djh-sachsen.de
Web site: www.djh-sachsen.de
Rates: Contact hostel for current
rates
Beds: 107
Private/family rooms: Yes
Kitchen available: No
Season: Open year-round
Affiliation: HI-DJH
Regional office: Sachsen
Extras: Meeting room, fitness
room, volleyball, grill, bike
rentals, meals ($), parking,
wheelchair access

How to get there:
By bus: From Leipzig or Grimma
take bus to Grethen, then walk
1 mile to hostel.

By car: Contact hostel for directions.
By train: From Leipzig or
Grossbothen take train to
Grosssteinberg, then walk 1½
miles to hostel.

JUGENDHERBERGE PIRNA-COPITZ "TOR ZUR SÄCHSISCHEN SCHWEIZ"

(Pirna-Copitz Hostel)
Birkwitzer Strasse 51,
01796 Pirna-Copitz
Phone: 03501–445–601

Fax: 03501–445–602
E-mail: servicecenter
@djh-sachsen.de
Web site: www.djh-sachsen.de
Rates: 25–30 DM per HI member
(about $13–$15 US)
Beds: 166
Private/family rooms: Yes
Kitchen available: No
Season: Open year-round
Affiliation: HI-DJH
Regional office: Sachsen
Extras: Children's room, television
room, videos, sports facilities
nearby, programs, parking,
meals ($)

How to get there:
By bus: Contact hostel for transit
details.
By car: Take Highway B172 from
Dresden to Pirna.
By train: Take train to Pirna. From
Pirna Station walk 1 mile to
hostel, across Elbbrücke bridge.

JUGENDHERBERGE PLAUEN

(Plauen Hostel)
Reusaer Waldhaus 1,
08529 Plauen
Phone: 03741–472–811

Fax: 03741–472–812
E-mail: servicecenter @djh-sachsen.de
Web site: www.djh-sachsen
Rates: 22–27 DM per HI member (about $11–$14 US)
Beds: 74
Private/family rooms: Yes
Kitchen available: No
Season: Open year-round
Affiliation: HI-DJH
Regional office: Sachsen
Extras: Programs, pool table, meals ($)

How to get there:
By bus/train: Take train to Plauen–Oberer. From train station take #4 bus to Schloss Reusa stop and walk ⅔ mile to hostel.
By car: Take Highway A72, exiting at signs for Plauen-Ost.

JUGENDHERBERGE "AM HAUSTEICH"

(Plothen Hostel)
07907 Plothen
Phone: 036648–22329

Fax: 036648–26013
Rates: 25–30 DM per HI member (about $13–$15 US)
Beds: 193
Private/family rooms: Yes
Kitchen available: No
Season: Closed December 23–27

Affiliation: HI-DJH
Regional office: Thüringen
Extras: Grill, programs, meals ($), parking

How to get there:
By bus: Contact hostel for transit details.
By car: Take Highway A9 to Dittersdorf, following signs toward Schleiz another 2½ miles to hostel.
By train: Contact hostel for transit details.

JUGENDHERBERGE QUEDLINBURG

(Quedlinburg Hostel)
Neuendorf 28,
06484 Quedlinburg
Phone: 03947–2881–0

Fax: 03947–91653
Rates: 24–29 DM per HI member (about $12–$15 US)
Beds: 54
Private/family rooms: Yes
Kitchen available: No
Season: Closed December 24–26
Affiliation: HI-DJH
Regional office: Sachsen
Extras: Meeting rooms, cafeteria ($), table tennis, parking

How to get there:
By bus: Contact hostel for transit details.
By car: Take Highway B6 or Highway B79 to Quedlinburg.
By train: Contact hostel for transit details.

JUGENDHERBERGE RADIS

(Radis Hostel)

ЗЗЗ ЗЗЗ

ЗЗЗ

Bahnofstrasse 18,
06773 Radis
Phone: 034953–39288

Fax: 034953–21429
Rates: 21–26 DM per HI member (about $11–$13 US)
Beds: 125
Private/family rooms: Yes
Kitchen available: No
Affiliation: HI-DJH
Regional office: Sachsen
Season: Closed December 24–26
Extras: TV room, disco, table tennis, bike rentals, meals ($), parking, laundry

How to get there:
By bus: Contact hostel for transit details.
By car: Take Highway B100 or Highway A9, exiting at signs for Dessau. Continue to Radis.
By train: From Leipzig or Berlin take train to Halle, then contact hostel for further transit details.

JUGENDHERBERGE WÜSTEWOHLDE
(Wüstewohlde-Ringstedt Hostel)
Wüstewohlde Nr. 20,
27624 Ringstedt
Phone: 04708–234

Fax: 04708–234
Rates: 21.10–26.10 DM per HI member (about $11–$13 US)
Beds: 72
Private/family rooms: Yes
Kitchen available: No
Season: Contact hostel for current season
Affiliation: HI-DJH

Regional office: None; owned by city of Bremerhaven
Extras: Playground, table tennis, grill

How to get there:
By bus: Contact hostel for transit route.
By car: From Bremen take Highway A27 to Debstedt; continue in direction of Bad Bederkesa through Hainmühlen to Wüstewohlde.
By train: Contact hostel for transit route.

JUGENDHERBERGE RINTELN
(Rinteln Hostel)
Am Bären 1,
31737 Rinteln
Phone: 05751–2405

Fax: 05751–44630
Rates: 22–27 DM per HI member (about $11–$14 US)
Beds: 96
Private/family rooms: Yes
Kitchen available: No
Season: Contact hostel for current season
Affiliation: HI-DJH
Regional office: Hannover
Extras: Program, table tennis, volleyball, basketball, meals ($), parking, wheelchair access

How to get there:
By bus: Contact hostel for transit details.
By car: Contact hostel for directions.
By train: Take train to Rinteln and contact hostel for transit details.

JUGENDHERBERGE RITTERSGRÜN

(Rittersgrün Hostel)

**Zur Jugendherberge 2,
08355 Rittersgrün**

Phone: 037757–7260

E-mail: servicecenter @djh-sachsen.de
Web site: www.djh-sachsen.de
Rates: 22–27 DM per HI member (about $11–$14 US)
Beds: 52
Private/family rooms: No
Kitchen available: No
Season: Contact hostel for current season
Affiliation: HI-DJH
Regional office: Sachsen
Extras: Parking, laundry, meals ($)

How to get there:
By bus: Take bus from Schwarzenberg to Rittersgrün, getting off at Arnoldshammer stop and walking to hostel.
By car: Contact hostel for directions.
By train: Take train to Antonsthal. From Antonsthal Station walk 2 miles to hostel in Rittersgrün.

JUGENDHERBERGE ROCHLITZ "SCHWEIZERHAUS"

(Rochlitz Hostel)

**Zassnitzer Strasse 1,
09306 Rochlitz**

Phone: 03737–42131

Fax: 03737–149–053
E-mail: servicecenter @djh-sachsen.de
Web site: www.djh-sachsen.de
Rates: 19–24 DM per HI member (about $10–$12 US)
Beds: 49
Private/family rooms: Yes
Kitchen available: No
Season: Open year-round
Affiliation: HI-DJH
Regional office: Sachsen
Extras: Volleyball, grill, parking, meals ($), laundry

How to get there:
By bus: Contact hostel for transit details.
By car: Take Highway A4 from Eisenach or Dresden to Glauchau, then continue on Highway B175 to Rochlitz.
By train: Take train from Leipzig or Chemnitz to Rochlitz, then contact hostel for further transit details.

NATURFREUNDEHAUS SCHNEEGRUND ROHDEN

(Rohden Hostel)

31840 Rohden/Hessen

Oldendorf

Phone: 05152–2607

Rates: Contact hostel for current rates
Beds: 42
Private/family rooms: No
Kitchen available: No
Season: Closed December 24–26
Affiliation: HI-DJH
Regional office: Hannover
Extras: Meals ($)

How to get there:
By bus/train: Take train to Hessen Oldendorf. From Hessen Oldendorf Station take bus to Rohdental.

By car: Contact hostel for directions.

JUGENDHERBERGE ROTENBURG AN DER FULDA

(Rotenburg an der Fulda Hostel)

Obertor 17,

36199 Rotenburg an der Fulda

Phone: 06623–2792

Fax: 06623–43177
E-mail: Rotenburg@djh-hessen.de
Rates: 22–27 DM per HI member (about $11–$14 US)
Beds: 125
Private/family rooms: Yes
Kitchen available: No
Season: Closed December 24–26
Affiliation: HI-DJH
Regional office: Hessen
Extras: Sports programs, meals ($)

How to get there:
By bus: Contact hostel for transit route.
By car: Take Autobahn Highway 7, exiting at signs for Bad Hersfeld or Melsungen; continue via B27 and B83.
By train: Take train to Rotenburg, then walk ¾ mile to hostel.

JUGENDHERBERGE ROTENBURG (Wümme)

(Rotenburg/Wümme Hostel)

Verdener Strasse 104,

27356 Rotenburg (Wümme)

Phone: 04261–83041

Fax: 04261–84233
E-mail: jh-rotenburg @djh-unterweser-ems.de
Rates: 26–31 DM per HI member (about $13–$16 US)
Beds: 224
Private/family rooms: Yes
Kitchen available: No
Season: Open year-round
Affiliation: HI-DJH
Regional office: Unterweser-Ems
Extras: Volleyball, sports programs, sports facilities, disco, meeting room, parking, laundry, meals ($)

How to get there:
By bus/train: Take train to Rotenburg (Wümme). From Rotenburg (Wümme) Station take #3 bus to Berufsschule stop, then walk 1½ miles to hostel.
By car: Take Highway A1 or Highway A27.

NATURFREUNDEHAUS ST. ANDREASBERG

(St. Andreasberg Hostel)

Am Gesehr 37,

37444 St. Andreasberg

Phone: 05582–269

Fax: 05582–517
Rates: Contact hostel for current rates
Beds: 53
Private/family rooms: Yes
Kitchen available: No
Season: Closed December 22–25
Affiliation: HI-DJH
Regional office: Hannover
Extras: Meals ($)

How to get there:
By bus/train: Take train to Goslar.

From Goslar Station take bus to Jordanshöhe stop and walk to hostel.
By car: Contact hostel for directions.

JUGENDHERBERGE SCHELLERHAU "ROTWASSERHÜTTE"

(Schellerhau Hostel)
Hauptstrasse 115,
01776 Schellerhau
Phone: 035052–64227

Fax: 035052–64227
E-mail: servicecenter @djh-sachsen.de
Web site: www.djh-sachsen.de
Rates: 22–27 DM per HI member (about $11–$14 US)
Beds: 46
Private/family rooms: Yes
Kitchen available: No
Season: Open year-round
Affiliation: HI-DJH
Regional office: Sachsen
Extras: Grill, parking, meals ($)

How to get there:
By bus: From Dresden take bus to Neu-Schellerhau.
By car: From Dresden exit for Kipsdorf (Highway E55), then exit at signs for Schellerhau.
By train: Take train to Dresden. From Dresden take bus to Neu-Schellerhau.

JUGENDGÄSTEHAUS SCHIERKE

(Schierke Guest House Hostel)
Brockenstrasse 48,
38879 Schierke

Phone: 039455–51066

Fax: 039455–51067
Rates: 28–33 DM per HI member (about $14–$17 US)
Beds: 272
Private/family rooms: Yes
Kitchen available: No
Season: Closed December 24–26
Affiliation: HI-DJH
Regional office: Sachsen
Extras: TV room, sports facilities, meals ($), laundry, wheelchair access, parking

How to get there:
By bus: Contact hostel for transit details.
By car: Take Highway B27 through Elend and Wernigerode to Schierke.
By train: From Berlin or Magdeburg take train to Wernigerode and then contact hostel for further transit details.

JUGENDHERBERGE MYLAU "WALDERHOLUNG"

(Schneidenbach Hostel)
08468 Schneidenbach
Phone: 03765–34584
or 03765–34875

Fax: 03765–64455
E-mail: servicecenter @djh-sachsen.de
Web site: www.djh-sachsen.de
Rates: 22–27 DM per HI member (about $11–$14 US)
Beds: 44
Private/family rooms: No
Kitchen available: No
Season: Open year-round
Affiliation: HI-DJH
Regional office: Sachsen
Extras: Meals ($)

How to get there:
By bus/train: Take train to Reichenbach/Vogtland. From Reichenbach/ Vogtland Station take T-74 or T-85 bus to Forsthaus Mylau stop.

By car: Take Highway A72, exiting at signs for Reichenbach and Schneidenbach.

JUGENDHERBERGE SCHÖNBRUNN/ EBERSDORF
(Schönbrunn/Ebersdorf Hostel)

Nr. 102 (Bellevue)

07368 Schönbrunn/Ebersdorf

Phone: 0172–368–2193

or 036651–87064

Fax: 036651–55413
Rates: 18–23 DM per HI member (about $9.00–$12.00 US)
Beds: 72
Private/family rooms: No
Kitchen available: No
Season: Closed December 23–27
Affiliation: HI-DJH
Regional office: Thüringen
Extras: Cafe ($), volleyball, table tennis, parking

How to get there:
By bus: Contact hostel for transit details.

By car: Take Highway A9 to Schleiz or Lobenstein and continue to Schönbrunn.

By train: Take train to Lobenstein or Unterlemnitz, then contact hostel for further transit details.

JUGENDHERBERGE SCHÖNECK
(Schöneck Hostel)

Am Stadtpark 52,

08261 Schöneck

Phone: 037464–8106

Fax: 037464–8107
E-mail: servicecenter @djh-sachsen.de
Web site: www.djh-sachsen.de
Rates: 25–30 DM per HI member (about $13–$15 US)
Beds: 63
Private/family rooms: Yes
Kitchen available: No
Affiliation: HI-DJH
Regional office: Sachsen
Extras: Tennis, volleyball, meals ($), parking, laundry

How to get there:
By bus: Contact hostel for transit details.

By car: Take Highway A72 from Plauen/Ost through Bergen to Schöneck or from Plauen/Süd through Oelsnitz/West to Schöneck.

By train: Take train from Zwickau, Falkenhain, Plauen, or Adorf to Schöneck.

JUGENDHERBERGE SCHÖNINGEN AM ELM
(Schöningen Hostel)

Richard-Schirrmann-Strasse 6a,

38364 Schöningen

Phone: 05352–3898

Fax: 05352–3752
Rates: 22–27 DM per HI member (about $11–$14 US)
Beds: 92
Private/family rooms: Yes
Kitchen available: No
Season: Closed December 24–26
Affiliation: HI-DJH
Regional office: Hannover

Extras: Meeting rooms, meals ($), parking

How to get there:

By bus: Take train to Schöningen. From Schöningen Station contact hostel for further transit details.

By car: Take Highway A2 to Helmstedt or Highway B82 from Braunschweig or Goslar.

By train: Take train to Schöningen. From Schöningen Station walk 2 miles to hostel or contact hostel for further transit details.

JUGENDHERBERGE HOHERODSKOPF

(Schotten-Hoherodskopf Hostel)

63679 Schotten

Phone: 06044–2760

Fax: 06044–784
E-mail: Hoherodskopf @djh-hessen.de
Rates: 22–27 DM per HI member (about $11–$14 US)
Beds: 125
Private/family rooms: Yes
Kitchen available: No
Season: Closed December 24–26
Affiliation: HI-DJH
Regional office: Hessen
Extras: Basketball, skiing nearby, parking

How to get there:

By bus/train: Take train to Nidda, then take bus to Breungeshain.

By car: Contact hostel for directions.

JUGENDHERBERGE "HANS BREUER"

(Schwarzburg Hostel)

Am Buschbach 2,

07427 Schwarzburg

Phone: 036730–22223

or 036730–22674

Fax: 036730–33555
E-mail: jugendherberge_schwarzburg @t-online.de
Rates: 19–24 DM per HI member (about $10–$12 US)
Beds: 163
Private/family rooms: Yes
Kitchen available: No
Season: Closed December 23–27
Affiliation: HI-DJH
Regional office: Thüringen
Extras: Volleyball, grill, parking, meals ($)

How to get there:

By bus: Contact hostel for transit details.

By car: Take Highway B88 to Bad Blankenburg, continuing to Schwarzburg.

By train: Take train to Schwarzburg. From Schwarzburg Station walk 1 mile to hostel.

JUGENDHERBERGE NEUDORF

(Sehmatal Hostel)

Vierenstrasse 26,

09465 Sehmatal

Phone: 037342–8282

Fax: 037342–8220
E-mail: servicecenter@djh-sachsen.de
Web site: www.djh-sachsen.de

Rates: 25–30 DM per HI member (about $13–$15 US)
Beds: 128
Private/family rooms: Yes
Kitchen available: No
Season: Contact hostel for current season
Affiliation: HI-DJH
Regional office: Sachsen
Extras: Disco

How to get there:
By bus: Take bus from Chemnitz or Annaberg to Neudorf, getting off at Vierenstrasse stop and walking to hostel.
By car: Take Highway B95 to Hammer-Unterwiesenthal and then Neudorf or Highway B101 to Scheibenberg, continuing through Crottendorf to Neudorf.
By train: Take train from Chemnitz, Flöha, or Annaberg to Neudorf. From train station walk ¼ mile along Vierenstrasse to hostel.

JUGENDHERBERGE SOSA "ROTE GRUBE"
(Sosa "Rote Grube" Hostel)
Rote Grube 1,
08326 Sosa
Phone: 03773–58019

Fax: 03773–882–540
E-mail: servicecenter @djh-sachsen.de
Web site: www.djh-sachsen.de
Rates: Contact hostel for current rates
Beds: 60
Private/family rooms: Yes
Kitchen available: No
Season: Open year-round
Affiliation: HI-DJH

Regional office: Sachsen
Extras: Volleyball, grill, parking, meals ($)

How to get there:
By bus: Take bus from Aue to Sosa.
By car: Contact hostel for directions.
By train: Take train from Aue to Blauenthal, then take bus to Sosa. Or contact hostel for transit details.

JUGENDHERBERGE SOSA "SKIHÜTTE"
(Sosa "Skihütte" Hostel)
Am Fröhlichwald 9,
08326 Sosa
Phone: 037752–8268

Fax: 037752–8268
E-mail: servicecenter@djh-sachsen.de
Web site: www.djh-sachsen.de
Rates: 22–27 DM per HI member (about $11–$14 US)
Beds: 28
Private/family rooms: Yes
Kitchen available: No
Season: Open year-round
Affiliation: HI-DJH
Regional office: Sachsen
Extras: Soccer, tennis, sports programs, parking, meals ($)

How to get there:
By bus: Take bus from Aue to Sosa.
By car: Contact hostel for directions.
By train: Take train from Aue ro Blauenthal, then take bus to Sosa.

JUGENDHERBERGE SPIEKEROOG

(Spiekeroog Hostel)

Bid` Utkiek,

26474 Spiekeroog

Phone: 04976–329

Rates: 37.70–42.70 DM per HI member (about $19–$21 US)
Beds: 47
Private/family rooms: Yes
Kitchen available: No
Season: Closed November 1– March 14
Affiliation: HI-DJH
Regional office: Unterweser-Ems

How to get there:
By bus/train: Take train to Esens. From Esens Station take bus or taxi to Neuharltingersie– Tideabhängige and take ferry to Spiekeroog. Contact hostel for further transit details.
By car: Contact hostel for directions.

JUGENDHERBERGE SPRINGE

(Springe Hostel)

In der Worth 25,

31832 Springe

Phone: 05041–1455

Fax: 05041–2963
Rates: 22–27 DM per HI member (about $11–$14 US)
Beds: 92
Private/family rooms: No
Kitchen available: No
Season: Closed December 24–26
Affiliation: HI-DJH
Regional office: Sachsen
Extras: Volleyball, table tennis, parking, meals ($)

How to get there:
By bus/train: Take train to Springe. From Springe Station walk 1 mile to hostel or take #504 bus to Auf dem Burghof stop and walk to hostel.
By car: Take Highway A2 from north or west, exiting at signs for Hann-Buchholz. From the west exit at signs for Lauenau.

JUGENDHERBERGE STREHLA

(Strehla Hostel)

Torgauer Strasse 33,

01616 Strehla

Phone: 035264–92030

Fax: 035264–92031
E-mail: servicecenter @djh-sachsen.de
Web site: www.djh-sachsen.de
Rates: 22–27 DM per HI member (about $11–$14 US)
Beds: 72
Private/family rooms: Yes
Kitchen available: No
Season: Open year-round
Affiliation: HI-DJH
Regional office: Sachsen
Extras: Volleyball, grill, meals ($), parking

How to get there:
By bus/train: Take train to Riesa. From Risa Station take bus to Strehla.
By car: Contact hostel for directions.

OSKAR-HEIDRICH-JUGENDHERBERGE

(Syke Hostel)

**Nordwohlder Strasse 59,
28857 Syke**

Phone: 04242–50314

Fax: 04242–66346
Rates: 23.90–28.90 DM per HI
member (about $12–$14 US)
Beds: 128
Private/family rooms: Yes
Kitchen available: No
Season: Open year-round
Affiliation: HI-DJH
Regional office: Unterweser-Ems
Extras: Fireplace, meeting room,
wheelchair access, parking,
meals ($)

How to get there:
By bus/train: Take train to Syke.
From Syke Station walk 1½ miles
to hostel or take bus. Contact
hostel further transit details.
By car: Contact hostel for directions.

JUGENDHERBERGE FRÖBERSGRÜN/ UMWELTSTUDIENPLATZ

(Syrau Hostel)
**Ortsstrasse 17,
08548 Syrau / OT Fröbersgrün**

**Phone: 037431–3256
or 3833**

Fax: 037431–88963
E-mail: servicecenter
@djh-sachsen.de
Web site: www.djh-sachsen.de
Rates: 22–27 DM per HI member
(about $11–$14 US)
Beds: 98
Private/family rooms: Yes
Kitchen available: No
Season: Closed November 1–
January 31

Affiliation: HI-DJH
Regional office: Sachsen
Extras: Meeting room, sports
programs, parking, laundry,
meals ($)

How to get there:
By bus: From Plauen take bus to
Jugendherberge in Fröbersgrün.
By car: Contact hostel for direc-
tions.
By train: Take train to Syrau.
Contact hostel for further transit
details.

JUGENDHERBERGE TAMBACH-DIETHARZ

(Tambach-Dietharz Hostel)
**Oberhoferstrasse 3,
99897 Tambach-Dietharz**

Phone: 036252–36149

Fax: 036252–36564
Rates: 25–30 DM per HI member
(about $13–$15 US)
Beds: 120
Private/family rooms: Yes
Kitchen available: No
Season: Closed December 20–27
Affiliation: HI-DJH
Regional office: Thüringen
Extras: Grill, table tennis,
programs, meals ($), parking,
bar/cafeteria, wheelchair access

How to get there:
By bus/train: Take train to
Georgenthal. From Georgenthal
Station take bus to Tambach-
Dietharz. Contact hostel for fur-
ther transit details.
By car: Take Highway B88 or
Highway B247 to Tambach-
Dietharz.

JUGENDHERBERGE THALE

(Thale Hostel)

Waldkater–Bodetal,

06502 Thale

Phone: 03947–2881

Fax: 03947–91653
E-mail: djh-thale@t-online.de
Rates: 24–29 DM per HI member (about $12–$15 US)
Beds: 204
Private/family rooms: Yes
Kitchen available: No
Season: Closed December 24–26
Affiliation: HI-DJH
Regional office: Hannover
Extras: Cafeteria ($), table tennis, disco, grill, musical instruments, parking, laundry

How to get there:
By bus: Contact hostel for transit route.
By car: Take Highway B6 to Thale.
By train: Contact hostel for transit route.

JUGENDHERBERGE THARANDT

(Tharandt Hostel)

Pienner Strasse 55,

01737 Tharandt

Phone: 035203–37272

Fax: 035203–37738
E-mail: servicecenter @djh-sachsen.de
Web site: www.djh-sachsen.de
Rates: 22–27 DM per HI member (about $11–$14 US)
Beds: 69
Private/family rooms: Yes
Kitchen available: No

Affiliation: HI-DJH
Regional office: Sachsen
Extras: Basketball, sports programs, grounds, parking, laundry, meals ($)

How to get there:
By bus: Contact hostel for transit details.
By car: Exit at signs for Wilsdruff. In Tharandt follow signs in the direction of Dippoldiswalde.
By train: Take train from Dresden or Chemnitz to Tharandt Edle Krone Station, then walk ¾ mile to hostel.

JUGENDHERBERGE UELSEN/GRAFSCHAFT BENTHEIM

(Uelsen Hostel)

Linnenbachweg 12,

49843 Uelsen

Phone: 05942–718

Fax: 05942–20960
Rates: 21.50–26.50 DM per HI member (about $11–$13 US)
Beds: 104
Private/family rooms: No
Kitchen available: No
Season: Closed November 1– February 1
Affiliation: HI-DJH
Regional office: None; locally owned
Extras: Grill, meals ($)

How to get there:
By bus: Contact hostel for transit route.
By car: Contact hostel for directions.
By train: Contact hostel for transit route.

JUGENDHERBERGE UELZEN

(Uelzen Hostel)

Fischerhof 1,

29525 Uelzen

Phone: 0581–5312

Fax: 0581–14210
Rates: 22–27 DM per HI member (about $11–$14 US)
Beds: 166
Private/family rooms: Yes
Kitchen available: No
Season: Closed December 24–26
Affiliation: HI-DJH
Regional office: Hannover
Extras: Bach volleyball, sports programs, pool table, grill, parking, laundry, meals ($)

How to get there:
By bus/train: Take train to Uelzen. From Uelzen Station take #1, #3, #4, #5, or #6 bus to Veersser Strasse stop, then change to #8 bus and continue to Fischerhof stop.
By car: Contact hostel for directions.

JUGENDHERBERGE VERDEN

(Verden Hostel)

Saumurplatz 1,

27283 Verden

Phone: 04231–61163

Fax: 04231–68121
E-mail: jh-verden @djh-unterweser-ems.de
Rates: 24.30–29.30 DM per HI member (about $12–$15 US)
Beds: 124
Private/family rooms: Yes
Kitchen available: No
Season: Open year-round
Affiliation: HI-DJH
Regional office: Unterweser-Ems
Extras: Sports facilities, sports programs, meals ($), parking, wheelchair access

How to get there:
By bus/train: Take train to Verden. From Verden Station take #714 bus to Haltest and Carl-Hesse-Strasse.
By car: Contact hostel for directions.

JUGENDHERBERGE "HOHE FAHRT AM EDERSEE"

(Vöhl/Assen Hostel)

34516 Vöhl/Assen

Phone: 05635–251

Fax: 05635–8142
E-mail: HoheFahrt@djh-hessen.de
Rates: 23.50–31.50 DM per HI member (about $12–$16 US)
Beds: 230
Private/family rooms: Yes
Kitchen available: No
Season: Closed December 24–26
Affiliation: HI-DJH
Regional office: Hessen
Extras: Disco, grill, sports programs, volleyball

How to get there:
By bus/train: Take train to Frankenberg, Korbach, or Bad Wildungen, then take bus or taxi to Vöhl/Asel. Contact hostel for further transit details.
By car: From the south travel via Frankenberg to Vöhl/Asel; from the north or the west travel via Korbach; from the east travel via Bad Wildungen.

JUGENDHERBERGE BURG HESSENSTEIN

(Vöhl/Ederbringhausen Hostel)

34516 Vöhl/Ederbringhausen

Phone: 06455–300

Fax: 06455–8771
E-mail: BurgHessenstein @djh-hessen.de
Rates: 22–27 DM per HI member (about $11–$14 US)
Beds: 126
Private/family rooms: Yes
Kitchen available: No
Season: Closed December 24–26
Affiliation: HI-DJH
Regional office: Hessen
Extras: Grill, parking, meals ($)

How to get there:
By bus: Contact hostel for transit details.
By car: From the north or the west, exit at signs for Diemelstadt/Arolsen. From the south exit at signs for Giessen/Marburg. From the north and east exit at signs for Bad Wildungen/Frankenberg.
By train: Contact hostel for transit details.

JUGENDHERBERGE MOSENBERG

(Wabern Hostel)

Umweltstudienplatz

Mosenberg,

34590 Wabern

Phone: 05681–2691

Fax: 05681–60208
E-mail: Mosenberg @djh-hessen.de
Rates: 23.50–28.50 DM per HI member (about $12–$14 US)
Beds: 130
Private/family rooms: Yes
Kitchen available: No
Season: Closed December 24–26
Affiliation: HI-DJH
Regional office: Hessen
Extras: Beach volleyball, parking, meals ($)

How to get there:
By bus/train: Take train to Wabern. From Wabern Station take bus to Homberg–Berge stop and walk ¾ mile to hostel.
By car: From the north exit at signs for Fritzlar, then take Highway B253 to Wabern–Falkenberg. From the south travel to Homberg, then follow signs to Wabern.

JUGENDHERBERGE WALDECK

(Waldeck Hostel)

Klippenberg 3,

34513 Waldeck

Phone: 05623–5313

Fax: 05623–6254
E-mail: Waldeck@djh-hessen.de
Rates: 23.50–31.50 DM per HI member (about $12–$16 US)
Beds: 161
Private/family rooms: Yes
Kitchen available: No
Season: Closed December 24–26
Affiliation: HI-DJH
Regional office: Hessen
Extras: Sports facilities, disco, parking, meals ($)

How to get there:
By bus/train: Take train to Bad Wildungen. From Bad

Wildungen Station take #503 bus toward Korbach to Waldeck-Mitte stop and walk to hostel.

By car: From the south travel through Marburg using highways B3 and B252 to Frankenberg/Korbach. From the west take Highway A44 to Diemelstadt, then Highway B252 through Bad Arolsen and Edertalsperre and Highway B485 to Waldeck. From the north or west take Highway A7 to Kassel, then Highway A49 to Fritzklar/Edersee.

JUGENDHERBERGE WALDHEIM

(Waldheim Hostel)

Breitenbergstrasse 21,

04736 Waldheim

Phone: 034327–92116

Fax: 034327–92116
E-mail: servicecenter @djh-sachsen.de
Web site: www.djh-sachsen.de
Rates: Contact hostel for current rates
Beds: 39
Private/family rooms: Yes
Kitchen available: No
Season: Open year-round
Affiliation: HI-DJH
Regional office: Sachsen
Extras: Meals ($)

How to get there:
By bus/train: From Chemnitz or Rochlitz/Döbeln take train to Waldheim; then from Waldheim take bus to Waldheim-Markt stop and walk to hostel.
By car: Contact hostel for directions.

JUGENDHERBERGE SCHILLIGHÖRN

(Wangerland Hostel)

Inselstrasse 6,

26434 Wangerland

Phone: 04426–371 or

04426–991–103

Fax: 04426–506
Rates: 23.30–28.30 DM per HI member (about $12–$14 US)
Beds: 132
Private/family rooms: No
Kitchen available: No
Season: Closed February 1–28
Affiliation: HI-DJH
Regional office: Unterweser-Ems
Extras: Laundry, playground, grill, table tennis, parking, meals ($)

How to get there:
By bus: Contact hostel for transit route.
By car: Contact hostel for directions.
By train: Take train to Wilhelmshaven. From Wilhelmshaven Station take "Jade-Sprinter" to Schillig Ortskern stop.

JUGENDHERBERGE WANGEROOGE

(Wangerooge Hostel)

Westturm,

26486 Wangerooge

Phone: 04469–439

Fax: 04469–8578
Rates: 37.70–42.70 DM per HI member (about $19–$21 US)
Beds: 136
Private/family rooms: No
Kitchen available: No

Season: Closed October 1–April 1
Affiliation: HI-DJH
Regional office: Unterweser-Ems
Extras: Table tennis, grill, meals ($)

How to get there:

By bus/train: Take train from Bremen or Oldenburg to Sande, then from either train station take bus to Harle. From Harle take ferry to Wangerooge.
By car/ferry: Contact hostel for directions.

JUGENDHERBERGE WARMBAD

(Warmbad-Gehringswalde Hostel)

Ortsteil Warmbad,

09429 Gehringswalde

(Warmbad)

Phone: 037369–9437

Fax: 037369–5665
E-mail: servicecenter @djh-sachsen.de
Web site: www.djh-sachsen.de
Rates: 25–30 DM per HI member (about $13–$15 US)
Beds: 62
Private/family rooms: Yes
Kitchen available: Yes
Season: Closed December 24–26
Affiliation: HI-DJH
Regional office: Sachsen

How to get there:

By bus: Take T218 bus to Gehringswalde, then walk to hostel. Contact hostel for further transit details.
By car: From Annaberg or Dresden take Highway #400 to Warmbad, exiting at signs for Gehringswalde. Or contact hostel for directions.
By train: Take train from Chemnitz or Bärenstein to Warmbad. Contact hostel for further transit details.

JUGENDHERBERGE WEILBURG

(Weilburg Hostel)

Am Steinbühl,

35781 Weilburg-Odersbach

Phone: 06471–7116

Fax: 06471–1542
E-mail: Weilburg@djh-hessen.de
Rates: 23.50–28.50 DM per HI member (about $12–$14 US)
Beds: 135
Private/family rooms: Yes
Kitchen available: No
Season: Closed December 24–26
Affiliation: HI-DJH
Regional office: Hessen
Extras: Parking, meals ($)

How to get there:

By bus: Contact hostel for transit details.
By car: Take Highway B49, exiting at signs for Weilburg.
By train: Take train to Weilburg. From Weilburg Station walk 2 miles to hostel.

JUGENDHERBERGE WERNIGERODE

(Wernigerode Hostel)

Am Eichberg 5,

38855 Wernigerode

Phone: 03943–606–176

Fax: 03943–606–177

Rates: 28–33 DM per HI member (about $14–$17 US)
Beds: 200
Private/family rooms: Yes
Kitchen available: No
Season: Open year-round
Affiliation: HI-DJH
Regional office: Sachsen-Anhalt
Extras: Cafeteria ($), parking, wheelchair access

How to get there:

By bus: Contact hostel for transit details.
By car: From Magdeburg take Highway B81, continuing to Highway B6 to Wernigerode or from Goslar take Highway B6 to Wernigerode.
By train: Contact hostel for transit details.

JUGENDHERBERGE WESTERSTEDE

(Westerstede Hostel)
Jahnallee 2,
26655 Westerstede
Phone: 04488–84690

Fax: 04488–78317
E-mail: hoessen-sportzentrum@t-online.de
Rates: 26–31 DM per HI member (about $13–$16 US)
Beds: 68
Private/family rooms: Yes
Kitchen available: No
Season: Closed December 20–January 2
Affiliation: HI-DJH
Regional office: None; locally owned
Extras: Grill, parking, wheelchair access, meals ($)

How to get there:

By bus/train Take train to Ocholt. From Ocholt Station contact hostel for transit details.
By car: Take Highway A28 to Westerstede.

JUGENDHERBERGE WETZLAR

(Wetzlar Hostel)
Richard-Schirrmann-Strasse 3,
35578 Wetzlar
Phone: 06441–71068

Fax: 06441–75826
E-mail: Wetzlar@djh-hessen.de
Rates: 24.50–32.50 DM per HI member (about $12–$16 US)
Beds: 190
Private/family rooms: Yes
Kitchen available: No
Season: Closed December 24–26
Affiliation: HI-DJH
Regional office: Hessen
Extras: Cafeteria ($), volleyball, soccer, wheelchair

How to get there:

By bus/train: Take train to Wetzlar. From Wetzlar Station take #12 bus to Sturzkopf.
By car: Take Autobahn Route 45 to Wetzlarer Kreuz, following signs to Stadtmitte; or take Highway B277 from Butzbach to Hallenbad, then follow signs to hostel.

JUGENDHERBERGE WIESBADEN

(Wiesbaden Hostel)
Blücherstrasse 66,
65195 Wiesbaden
Phone: 0611–449–081

or 0611–48657

Fax: 0611–441–119
E-mail: Wiesbaden@djh-hessen.de
Rates: 24–29 DM per HI member
(about $12–$15 US)
Beds: 161
Private/family rooms: Yes
Kitchen available: No
Season: Closed December 24–
January 1
Affiliation: HI-DJH
Regional office: Hessen
Extras: Tennis, fields, parking,
meals ($)

How to get there:
By bus: Contact hostel for transit
details.
By car: From the south take
Highway A9 to Nürnberg, then
Highway A3 to Wiesbadener Kreuz
and Highway A66 to Wiesbaden.
From the north take Highway B27
to Hannover, Highway A7 to
Giessen, Highway A5 to Frankfurt,
and Highway A66 to Wiesbaden.
By train: Contact hostel for transit
details.

JUGENDHERBERGE WILHELMSHAVEN

(Wilhelmshaven Hostel)

Freiligrathstrasse 131,

26386 Wilhelmshaven

Phone: 04421–60048

Fax: 04421–64716
Rates: 23.90–28.90 DM per HI
member (about $12–$14 US)
Beds: 126
Private/family rooms: No
Kitchen available: No
Season: Closed November 1–
March 3
Affiliation: HI-DJH

Regional office: Unterweser-Ems
Extras: Programs, volleyball, bike
rentals, parking, meals ($)

How to get there:
By bus: Contact hostel for transit
route.
By car: Contact hostel for directions.
By train: Contact hostel for transit
route.

JUGENDHERBERGE WILLINGEN

(Willingen Hostel)

Am Lukasheim 9–12,

34508 Willingen

Phone: 05632–6347

Fax: 05632–4343
E-mail: Willingen@djh-hessen.de
Rates: 23.50–28.50 DM per HI
member (about $11.75–$14.25
US)
Beds: 124
Private/family rooms: Yes
Kitchen available: No
Season: Closed December 24–26
Affiliation: HI-DJH
Regional office: Hessen
Extras: Tennis, mountain bikes,
parking, meals ($)

How to get there:
By bus/train: From Willingen
Station take bus to Schwalefeld.
By car: Take Highway 480 to
Dortmund or Highway B251 to
Kassel, then Highway B252 to
Marburg and B251 to Korbach.

JUGENDHERBERGE WINDISCHLEUBA
(Windischleuba Hostel)
Pestalozziplatz 1,
04603 Windischleuba
Phone: 03447–834–471

Fax: 03477–832–702
E-mail: jugendherberge-windischleu-ba
@t-online.de
Rates: 21–26 DM per HI member (about $11–$13 US)
Beds: 145
Private/family rooms: Yes
Kitchen available: No
Season: Closed December 23–27
Affiliation: HI-DJH
Regional office: Sachsen
Extras: Sports facilities, table tennis, pool table, meals ($), wheelchair access, laundry

How to get there:
By bus/train: Take train to Altenburg. From Altenburg Station take bus toward Geithain to Windischleuba.
By car: Take Highway A4 to Ronneburg, then continue on Highway B7 to Windischleuba.

JUGENDHERBERGE WITTENBERG SCHLOSS
(Wittenberg Hostel)
06886 Lutherstadt
(Wittenberg)
Phone: 03491–403–255

Fax: 03491–403–255
Rates: 21–26 DM per HI member (about $11–$13 US)
Beds: 104

Private/family rooms: No
Kitchen available: No
Season: Closed December 22–27
Affiliation: HI-DJH
Regional office: Unterweser-Ems
Extras: Piano, pool table, parking, laundry, meals ($)

How to get there:
By bus: Contact hostel for transit route.
By car: Take Highway A9 to B2, then B100 and finally B187.
By train: From Berlin, Leipzig, or Halle take train to Elbtor Station, then walk ½ mile to hostel.

JUGENDHERBERGE CAROLINENSIEL
(Wittmund Hostel)
Herbergsmense 13,
26409 Wittmund
Phone: 04464–252

Fax: 04464–655
Rates: 21.50–26.50 DM per HI member (about $11–$13 US)
Beds: 123
Private/family rooms: No
Kitchen available: No
Season: Closed December 1–January 31
Affiliation: HI-DJH
Regional office: Unterweser-Ems
Extras: Playground, programs, grill, parking, meals ($)

How to get there:
By bus/train: Take train to Jever. From Jever Station take bus to Carolinensiel.
By car: Contact hostel for directions.

JUGENDHERBERGE WOLFSBURG

(Wolfsburg Hostel)

Lessingstrasse 60,

38440 Wolfsburg

Phone: 05361–13337

Fax: 05361–16630
Rates: 24–29 DM per HI member
(about $12–$15 US)
Beds: 68
Private/family rooms: No
Kitchen available: No
Season: Closed December 24–26
Affiliation: HI-DJH
Regional office: Unterweser-Ems
Extras: Pool table, foosball, vol-
leyball, grill, meals ($), parking,
wheelchair access

How to get there:
By bus/train: From station walk ¾
mile to hostel, or take #3 bus
and walk to hostel.
By car: Contact hostel for directions.

JUGENDHERBERGE WORPSWEDE

(Worpswede Hostel)

Hammeweg 2,

27726 Worpswede

Phone: 04792–1360

Fax: 04792–4381
E-mail: jh-worpswede
@djh-unterweser-ems.de
Rates: 23.90–28.90 DM per HI
member (about $12–$14 US)
Beds: 164
Private/family rooms: Yes
Kitchen available: No
Season: Open year-round
Affiliation: HI-DJH
Regional office: Unterweser-Ems
Extras: Meals ($), parking, wheel-
chair access

How to get there:
By bus/train: Take train to
Bremen. From Bremen take
#670 bus to Worpswede.
By car: From Hamburg take A1
exiting at signs for Stucken-
borstel and continuing to
Worpswede. From Hannover or
Osnabrück take Highway A27,
exiting at signs for Horn and
continuing through Lehe and
Lilienthal to Worpswede.

JUGENDHERBERGE RUTTELERFELD

(Zetel Hostel)

Zollweg 27,

26340 Zetel-Neuenburg

Phone: 04452–416

Fax: 04452–8230
Rates: 21.50–26.50 DM per HI
member (about $11–$13 US)
Beds: 111
Private/family rooms: Yes
Kitchen available: No
Season: Open year-round
Affiliation: HI-DJH
Regional office: Unterweser-Ems
Extras: Grounds, meals ($),
parking

How to get there:
By bus/train: Take train to Varel.
From Varel Station take bus to
Neuenburg; then take taxi or
walk 2 miles to hostel.
By car: Contact hostel for direc-
tions.

JUGENDHERBERGE ZEVEN-BADEMÜHLEN
(Zeven-Bademühlen Hostel)
Nr. 1,
27404 Zeven-Bademühlen
Phone: 04281–2550

Fax: 04281–80293
Rates: 23.90–28.90 DM per HI member (about $12–$14 US)
Beds: 130
Private/family rooms: Yes
Kitchen available: No
Season: Open year-round
Affiliation: HI-DJH
Regional office: Unterweser-Ems
Extras: Grill, programs, basketball, volleyball, parking, wheelchair access, meals ($)
How to get there:
By bus/train: From Bremen Station take #630 bus to Zeven.
By car: Take A1 Bremen-Hamburg to Bockel-Zeven.

JUGENDHERBERGE ZWINGENBERG
(Zwingenberg Hostel)

Die Lange Schneise 11,
64673 Zwingenberg
Phone: 06251–75938

Fax: 06251–788–113
E-mail: Zwingenberg @djh-hessen.de
Rates: 22–27 DM per HI member (about $11–$14 US)
Beds: 125
Private/family rooms: No
Kitchen available: No
Season: Closed December 24–26
Affiliation: HI-DJH
Regional office: Hessen
Extras: Meals ($)
How to get there:
By bus: Contact hostel for transit details.
By car: Take Highway A5 from Frankfurt, Darmstadt, or Heidelberg, then continue to Zwingenberg.
By train: From Zwingenberg Station walk ½ mile to hostel, or take bus to Mitte Station and walk to hostel. Or contact hostel for transit details.

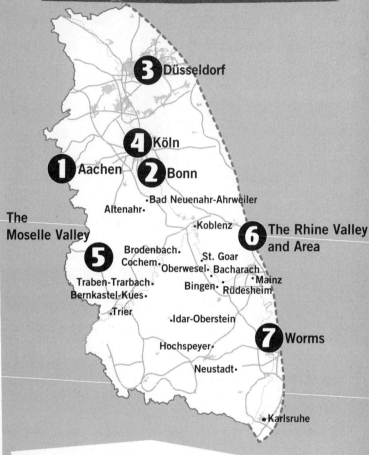

RHINELAND/WEST

3 Düsseldorf

4 Köln

1 Aachen

2 Bonn

·Bad Neuenahr-Ahrweiler

Altenahr·

The
Moselle Valley

·Koblenz

6 The Rhine Valley
and Area

Brodenbach·

Cochem·

·St. Goar

5

Oberwesel· Bacharach·

Traben-Trarbach·

Bingen·

·Mainz

Bernkastel-Kues·

·Rüdesheim

·Trier

·Idar-Oberstein

Hochspeyer·

7 Worms

Neustadt·

·Karlsruhe

Page numbers follow town names

RHINELAND/WEST

Rhineland and the west of Germany (also known as West-phalia) is one of the places you immediately think of when you think of Germany: big rivers with slow-moving barges; cliffs and wine-covered hills; rocky castles at every turn. It's a tremendously touristed region—the Germans themselves can't seem to get enough of it, never mind the rest of us—so hostel beds are gonna be tight in summer. Fall is a very pleasant time to come, due to the all the grape harvesting and its associated merriment, but remember that German kids are back in school, and that means one thing: field trips, and lots of 'em.

In addition to the main cities of western Germany—places brimming in history like Aachen and Mainz—we have focused on two river valleys in this guidebook: the Rhine and the Moselle, two rivers joined at the hip but quite different in character. The hostels along both valleys are rich in character (a couple are even inside castles!) and among the best in the country. There's no age limitation, and you'll find people pretty friendly. So what are you waiting for?

AACHEN

Aachen (known as Aix-la-Chapelle in French) is a lively university city *and* spa town snuggled up to the borders of both Belgium and France. As a result locals speak German, French, and Dutch interchangeably—English, too. Drawing admirers as far back as the Romans and King Charlemagne (they liked to soak in the local mineral waters), it's now a vibrant and diverse place, much less German than most others in the country. While you're here, dive into the multinational vibe—and bite into the local gingerbready cookies.

EUREGIONALES JUGENDGÄSTEHAUS AACHEN (AACHEN GUEST HOUSE HOSTEL)

Maria-Theresia-Allee 260,

52074 Aachen

Phone: 0241–711–010

Fax: 0241–711–0120
Rates: 38.50–63.50 DM per Hostelling International member (about $19–$32 US)
Credit cards: No
Beds: 180
Private/family rooms: Yes

Kitchen available: No
Season: Closed December 24–26
Office hours: Open twenty-four hours
Curfew: 1:00 A.M.
Affiliation: Hostelling International-DJH
Regional office: Rheinland-Palatinate
Extras: Table tennis, volleyball, foosball table, bistro ($), bar, TV, breakfast, lockers, parking

Situated on a cute hilltop north of the city center, this place is nowhere near historic and interesting downtown Aachen, but at least it's a nice place. Very nice, actually; you might think you've stumbled upon a hotel instead of a hostel.

They've really pulled out all the stops. Beds come in rooms containing from two to six bunks apiece (the eight-bedded rooms tend to be reserved for school groups). There's a kitchen, dining room, several lounges, a game room—yeah, a foosball table and table tennis setup in there—plus grounds outside. Families will love the fact that many of the rooms are quads or doubles.

The cool bar area has a great television set and they serve restaurant meals here, too. Breakfast is free in the morning. Only drawback? A 1:00 A.M. curfew, but with a location this distant you're likely not gonna be staying out late anyway.

Once Charlemagne's great and strategic capital, Aachen is quieter today but still retains a thousand-year-old church and other mementos of his reign as emperor. There's also more nightlife than you can shake a stick at, thanks to legions of students here; dive in, but remember that curfew and the long bus trip back out to the hostel when you do.

Best bet for a bite:
Café Chico Mendes

Insiders' tip:
News museum

What hostellers say:
"Great!"

Gestalt:
On the border

Safety:

Hospitality:

Cleanliness:

Party index:

KEY TO ICONS

 Attractive natural setting

 Ecologically aware hostel

Superior kitchen facilities or cafe

Offbeat or eccentric place

Superior bathroom facilities

Romantic private rooms

Comfortable beds

Editors' choice: among our very favorite hostels

A particularly good value

Wheelchair accessible

Good for business travelers

 Especially well suited for families

 Good for active travelers

 Visual arts at hostel or nearby

 Music at hostel or nearby

Great hostel for skiers

 Bar or pub at hostel or nearby

How to get there:

By bus/train: Take train to Aachen, then take bus to Finanzamt stop and change to #2 bus toward Preusswald to Ronheide stop or #12 bus toward Diepenbenden to Colynshof stop. Or walk 1½ miles from train station to hostel.

By car: Take Highway A4 to Aachener Kreuz, then take Highway A44 in the direction of Lüttich.

BONN

Frankly speaking, Bonn is not all that interesting a place—although, as the once-but-now-former capital of a great nation, it does have many more than its share of museums. The Landesmuseum, for instance, is Germany's national museum and the exhibits are heavy on German natural history (of which there's a lot to tell). And the nightlife, a relic from the time when diplomats, lobbyists, and other loaded types danced and drank the night away, is actually still quite good—more like that of a much bigger city.

JUGENDGÄSTEHAUS BONN VENUSBERG/KULTURSTUDIENPLATZ (BONN GUEST HOUSE HOSTEL)

Haager Weg 42,
53127 Bonn
Phone: 0228–289–970

Fax: 0228–289–9714
E-mail: jgh-Bonn@t-online.de
Rates: 39–65 DM per Hostelling International member (about $20–$33 US)
Beds: 249
Private/family rooms: Yes
Kitchen available: Yes
Season: Closed December 24–26
Office hours: 7:30 A.M.–midnight
Curfew: 1:00 A.M.
Affiliation: Hostelling International-DJH
Regional office: Rheinland
Extras: Programs, bar, meals ($), laundry

This hostel's in a lovely green part of town south of the Bonn train station, far from the madding crowds and close to the intriguing Godesburg castle. It's a clean, leafy location at the edge of the woods that you'll love—unless you're a night owl wanting to bar-hop all night. Otherwise, check it out.

Inside a complex of brick buildings, they've installed lots of room here: nine lounges, five dining rooms, and about sixty bunkrooms. We're talking forty-eight quads (good for families or friends traveling together), then twenty-four double rooms perfect for couples, and even nine single rooms for misanthropes or bus drivers. The kitchen serves filling, good meals; there's a bar on-premises too—even a laundry if you need one.

As we've mentioned, Bonn has lots more culture and nightlife than you'd expect of a sleepy ex-capital. And, didja know it? Ludwig van Beethoven was born right here (not at the hostel, but in town). His home is a little-known museum.

Ladies and gentlemen, we have another winner.

Best bet for a bite:
In-house restaurant

Insiders' tip:
Brauhaus Bònnsch (bar)

What hostellers say:
"Greater!"

Gestalt:
Bonn voyage

Safety: 👍

Hospitality: 👍

Cleanliness: 👍

Party index:

How to get there:

By bus/train: Take train to Bonn. From Bonn Station take #621 bus in the direction of Ippendorf-Altenheim to Jugendgästehaus (hostel) stop.

By car: Take Highway A565 from Bonn or Poppelsdorf, exiting at signs in the direction of Uniklinik/ Jugendherberge. Continue to hostel.

DÜSSELDORF

At first glance—a 700-foot TV tower and some sky-scrapers in the heart of the industrial north—Düsseldorf doesn't seem like a must-visit. It's more a business town than anything else.

But the smell of money here has brought other stuff, too, and the history plus nightlife might make for a good night's visit if you want a taste of urban Germany. After all, it was good enough for Napoleon; the little guy considered relocating his operations here from France at one point. And the hostel here's excellent.

The Alstadt (Old Town) area is where to find food and drink: There are hundreds of bars and restaurants packed in this compact section; this being Germany, be sure to try the local beer. Inside the Basilican Church of St. Lambertus, you can find items related to Düsseldorf's patron saint (Apollinaris) plus tombs. Got cash? Yeah, right. Well, even if you don't, stroll down the Königsalle and pretend you do—this is one of Europe's tonier addresses. Need to move around? This city has Germany's best subway (U-Bahn) system, efficient and entertaining.

The surrounding countryside is lovely, as well, if you can get out there.

Jugendgästehaus Düsseldorf
Düsseldorf Guest House Hostel • Düsseldorf

(photo courtesy of Deutsches Jugendherbergswerk)

JUGENDGÄSTEHAUS DÜSSELDORF
(DÜSSELDORF GUEST HOUSE HOSTEL)

Düsseldorfer Strasse 1,

40545 Düsseldorf

Phone: 0211–557–310

Fax: 0211–572–513

E-mail: jgh-duesseldorf@t-online.de

Rates: 38–47 DM per Hostelling International member (about $19–$24 US)

Credit cards: No

Beds: 272

Private/family rooms: Yes

Kitchen available: No

Season: Closed December 22–January 2

Office hours: 6:00–1:00 A.M.

Curfew: 1:00 A.M.

Affiliation: Hostelling International-DJH

Regional office: Rheinland

Extras: Programs, table tennis, meeting room, laundry, luggage storage, breakfast, TV room, meals ($)

Wow, the good hostels just keep on coming along the Rhine.

This hostel, parked (heh, heh) in the middle of a high-priced Oberkassel neighborhood that's full of car executives, really stands out—and it's so central, without being noisy.

The handsome white building, tucked behind trees and a driveway, is packed with dorms containing one to six beds each, many of them well suited to be family rooms. We're talking nine single rooms, twenty-seven (wow!) doubles, ten triples, thirty-seven quads, and eight more rooms with five, six, or more beds in 'em. They've got a common room here with (of course) a television, as well as a dining room, a game room, a laundry room, and river views, too. Breakfast is included with your bed. Finally, the place is wheelchair accessible. What the heck else do you want? Sure, there's a curfew at 1:00 A.M., but otherwise we can't find anything to complain about here.

Although Düsseldorf flexes its moneyed muscles downtown—the city's rich love to strut their designer cars and clothes—you can take refuge from all the conspicuous consumption in museums, beer halls, and a surprising concentration of Japanese restaurants and teahouses. Do take note that restaurant prices in this town are higher than they should be because of all the hoity-toity trade shows and the suits attending them.

Best bet for a bite:
Im Alten Bierhaus

Insiders' tip:
Lotsa fashion shows
in this city

What hostellers say:
"Baby, you can drive
my car!"

Gestalt:
Ober and above

Safety:

Hospitality:

Cleanliness:

Party index:

How to get there:

By bus/train: Take train to Düsseldorf. From Düsseldorf Station take U-Bahn line U70, U74, U75, U76, or U77 to Luegplatz stop, then walk south along Kaiser-Wilhelm-Ring to bridge and hostel. Or take U-Bahn to Belsenplatz and change to #835 or #836 bus; continue to Jugendherberge stop.

By car: Take Autobahn to Düsseldorf, then follow signs in the direction of Oberkassel to hostel.

KEY TO ICONS

 Attractive natural setting

 Ecologically aware hostel

 Superior kitchen facilities or cafe

 Offbeat or eccentric place

Superior bathroom facilities

Romantic private rooms

 Comfortable beds

 Editors' choice: among our very favorite hostels

 A particularly good value

 Wheelchair accessible

Good for business travelers

 Especially well suited for families

 Good for active travelers

 Visual arts at hostel or nearby

 Music at hostel or nearby

Great hostel for skiers

 Bar or pub at hostel or nearby

KÖLN

Köln is more of a way station than anything else: If you're taking a train from Brussels to Copenhagen, or Amsterdam to points south, you're probably going to pass through Köln at some point and at least change trains in the station.

There's only one other immediately obvious reason to leave the station and see the town—the enormous gray Dom (that's cathedral to you and me), which stands head and shoulders above its own little plaza right across from the station.

But also take note of a few other things. First, there's the hopping (literally) local beer scene: There are an amazing two dozen breweries here, and though the local style of brew is kinda wimpy, it is refreshing on a hot day. Second, there are three (count 'em) hostels, all not too far from the main station, so breaking up a long journey here is easy.

Finally, add this to your travel calendars: Each spring, just before Lent, a huge parade takes over these dour streets and transforms the city into a huge international party. If you're gonna be in northern Germany anytime around now, come for this—needless to say, though, the hostels get pretty busy that week.

KÖLN HOSTELS at a glance

	RATING	COST	IN A WORD	PAGE
Köln-Riehl	👍👍	39–65 DM	quiet	213
Station Backpackers	👍	27–50 DM	hoppin'	215
Köln-Deutz	👍	33–38 DM	decent	211

JUGENDHERBERGE KÖLN–DEUTZ (KÖLN–DEUTZ HOSTEL)

Siegestrasse 5 a,
50679 Köln

Phone: 0221–814–711
Fax: 0221–884–425
E-mail: jh-deutz@t-online.de
Rates: 33–38 DM per Hostelling International member (about $17–$19 US)
Credit cards: No

Jugendherberge Köln-Deutz
Köln-Deutz Hostel • Köln-Deutz

(photo courtesy of Deutsches Jugendherbergswerk)

Beds: 374
Private/family rooms: Yes
Kitchen available: No
Season: Closed December 24–26
Office hours: Open twenty-four hours
Curfew: 1:00 A.M.
Affiliation: Hostelling International-DJH
Regional office: Rheinland
Extras: Programs, table tennis, game room, pinball, laundry, meals
($), breakfast, patio, parking, TV room, meeting rooms, lockers,
Internet access

This low-slung, two-story hostel looks, at first glance, more like a
Motel 6 just off the interstate than a place of happiness and social
mixing. (Feels like it at times, too, but at least there are plenty of
nice big trees around.)

Yet the boring stone building turns out to be extremely well
stocked inside and not too far removed from the city's action, either.
Want amenities like those you know and love at home? Try a kitchen,
a laundry (which is sometimes free!), meal service, and free breakfast, for starters.

Rooms break out this way: We counted four singles, four doubles,
twenty triple rooms, and three quads. The remaining forty or so
rooms contain six or more beds, so there is some possibility you'll
get sequestered in a huge room with lots of other bodies. Each
comes with its own set of wooden furniture and in-room lockers.

Bathrooms are in the hallway, and—pretty inconveniently—the showers are all down in the basement. (Only the singles and doubles, which are normally reserved for bus drivers and group leaders—but ask if one's available—contain their own bathrooms and showers.)

To get away from the crowds, there are five separate lounging-around areas here. The most popular one, at the moment, is the one with the Internet-access terminal. The gaming area is stocked with table tennis paddles and even a pinball machine. Or, if that's still too much exercise for ya, the television room requires no effort whatsoever: Throw your stuff in the handy laundry and check out what's on the tube (though you may need a German phrasebook to understand it).

Best bet for a bite:
HL (grocery store)

Insider's tip:
Cathedral opens at 6:00
A.M. daily

What hostellers say:
"Nice and close."

Gestalt:
Pinball Wizard

Safety:

Hospitality:

Cleanliness:

Party index:

Lunch and dinner are served daily for 7.00 DM (about $3.50 US); it's a self-serve buffet, with both meat-based and vegetarian options. Still hungry? It's only a hundred yards to the nearest supermarkets.

You're within easy walking distance of the Dom and other great sights, too; only the curfew might be a slight annoyance. In case you haven't overdosed on sight-seeing already, head into town and check out the Roman-German museum, which sports some great old jewelry (if you're into that sort of thing).

As a final note, we have learned that the hostel association wants to begin constructing a brand-new building on this same location. Call ahead to make sure the place isn't closed for renovations.

How to get there:

By bus: Easier by train.

By car: From Düsseldorf, Dortmund, or Oberhausen, take Highway A3 to Autobahnkreuz Köln-Ost, then take Stadtautobahn toward Köln-Centrum to Köln-Deutz exit, following signs for Köln Messe and Deutz-Mülheimer Strasse. Past Eisenbahnbrücke, make a right onto Kasemattenstrasse, then continue to Siegestrasse.

By train: Take train to Köln. From Köln Station take S-Bahn line S6, S11, or S12 to Köln-Deutz Station. Walk along Neuhöffer-strasse to first right and turn; continue to hostel.

JUGENDGÄSTEHAUS KÖLN-RIEHL (KÖLN-RIEHL GUEST HOUSE HOSTEL)

An der Schanz 14,
50735 Köln
Phone: 0221–767–081

Fax: 0221–761–555
E-mail: jgh-koeln-riehl@t-online.de
Rates: 39–65 DM per Hostelling International member (about $20–$33 US)
Beds: 366
Private/family rooms: Yes
Kitchen available: No
Season: Closed December 24–26
Office hours: Open twenty-four hours
Affiliation: Hostelling International-DJH
Regional office: Rheinland
Extras: Foosball table, grill, disco, table tennis, TV, VCR, piano, meeting room, programs, bistro ($), lockers, breakfast, laundry

There are three great hostels in Köln, but if you're wanting a little peace and quiet—or if you're traveling by car or with kids—this huge one's probably your best pick. It's also, not coincidentally, the most distant from the center of town, though it's not too far.

It's right by the Rhine River, where the landscaping and trees in front only partly conceal a functional, modern building. Dorms come in rooms with two to six beds apiece, so families are well taken care of here; single rooms provide an option for lone travelers who don't mind paying more (but much less than at a hotel). Every room has its own shower, sink, and bathroom—a welcome switch from the usual situation. They've also got some huge lounges, a music room with piano, a TV room with movies to play on a VCR, lockers for your stuff, a little restaurant, and a game room stocked with goodies. Don't forget the free breakfast or the small "disco" area. Pretty good.

Best bet for a bite:
Früh am Dom
(beer hall)

Insiders' tip:
Gaffelhaus brewery

What hostellers say:
"Very family-friendly."

Gestalt:
Dom Perignon

Safety: 👍

Hospitality: 👍

Cleanliness: 👍

Party index: 🎉🎉🎉

What to do now? Why, you've gotta see that cathedral, of course! How big is this place (the cathedral, not the hostel)? Try this statistic, for starters: It took more than *600 years* to build the thing. Yeah, that's right. Six. Hundred. Years. Remember that it closes each day around 12:30 in the afternoon and doesn't open again until the next morning.

Not into that huge hulking church? Never fear—you've got another choice close by, the city zoo.

How to get there:

By bus: Take #16 or #18 streetcar to hostel.

By car: From Zoobrücke follow signs to Zoo/Flora and take next left to Colonia Hochhaus. Or contact hostel for directions.

By train: From Köln Station take U-Bahn line U16 toward Ebertplatz to Boltensternstrasse Station, then walk ¼ mile to hostel.

STATION BACKPACKERS HOSTEL

Marzellenstrasse 44-48,

50668 Köln

Phone: 0221–912–5301 or 0221–230–247 (annex)

Fax: 0221–912–5303

E-mail: station@t-online.de

Rates: 27–50 DM per person (about $14–$25 US); doubles 70–80 DM (about $35–$40 US)

Credit cards: No

Beds: Number varies

Private/family rooms: Yes

Kitchen available: Yes

Season: Open year-round

Office hours: Open twenty-four hours

Affiliation: None

Extras: Internet access, laundry, tours, travel information desk, breakfast ($), storage room, bar, bike rentals

There's no question that this is the most central of Köln's three hostels—it's practically on top of the train station and you'll hear the comings and goings of cross-European trains and be within spitting distance of downtown Köln's considerable supply of churches. The no-rules vibe and absolutely partyin' bar just might draw you in.

Enter at the funky pink reception desk, where you start to get a sense that this isn't the usual overserious hostel. Past the cramped but happy and happenin' lounge, descend into the innards of the place: You'll find your room's brightly painted, and it contains actual single beds spread around the rooms, *not* bunks for once. Beds come in a variety of configurations—everything from singles to doubles, triples, quads, and more; the most beds in one dorm are six.

There are actually two buildings that make up the place. At the main hostel compound, right at the big train station, beds in a dorm cost from 27 DM to 32 DM (about $14 to $16 US), depending on how many beds are in them, and doubles cost just 70 DM (about $35 US) for two—an outstanding deal, as are the singles at 40 DM (about $20 US) a pop. The hotel-style annex, just ⅓ mile from the station (that's about

Best bet for a bite:
Magnus

Insiders' tip:
Päffgen brewery

What hostellers say:
"He's Dom. I'm Dommer."

Gestalt:
Cheap Cologne

Safety:

Hospitality:

Cleanliness:

Party index:

a five to ten minutes' walk) is much in the same style. Beds here cost 33 DM (about $17 US) in a quad, 36 DM (about $18 US) in a triple, or 80 DM (about $40 US) for two in a double. Singles run you 50 DM (about $25), again a pretty good deal for the privacy.

It's a very laid-back sort of place, so if you're a Mr. Dude or Ms. Dudette type of hosteller—let's call you a Type D personality, OK?—then this is gonna be your kinda place. It's not out-of-control wild, though, with people throwing up and passing out from too much drink, thank goodness. Things really have been put together for the hosteller's comfort and ease, though. There's Internet access, a really affordable laundry, a little tour desk with maps and travel material, bikes for rent, and a kitchen. Reception's always open, you can always get food any time of day or night, and—check this out (literally)—you don't have to check out until noon. You have the option of paying for breakfast (you've also gotta pay for sheets unless you've brought some). They've got free lockers in a storage room, too.

The bar is here very hip, with a wide range of drinks and cocktails—anything from a relative sedate Whiskey Sour to a Screaming Orgasm. On Tuesday they're currently showing English movies on a big screen; on Wednesday it's techno and house music night; Friday brings a retro '70s thing (think *Shaft*) with hip-hop, too; Saturday is ska/punk night; and Sunday features dub music.

As we've noted previously, there are a ton of cathedrals around town, including Gross St. Martin (built around 1150, they tell us), St. Andreas, and the interesting St. Georg. The Köln city hall's 200-foot tower is worth a look, too, as are the city walls and gates—some ruined, some still quite intact. First and foremost among them is the brick Romerturm, a Roman fortification that dates from around the time of the death of Jesus, if you can believe that.

How to get there:

By bus: Contact hostel for transit details.

By car: Contact hostel for directions.

By train: Take train to Köln. From Köln Station walk west down Trankgasse or Dompropst-Ketzer-Strasse 1 block to Marzellenstrasse; turn right and continue to hostel on right.

MOSELLE VALLEY

Think of the Moselle as a poorer, lesser-known, but actually more attractive cousin—a wallflower, if you will. But make the time to get here, connecting from the Rhine Valley, because these tiny wine towns are as equally authentic as anything the Rhine can throw out there. Hostels here on this stretch of river tend to be simpler, but that might be part of the fun.

Note that although Koblenz is technically at the junction of the Rhine and the Moselle, we're sticking it here because it's the logical (and, in fact, only) entry point to the Moselle. (Also, this is *our* book.)

JUGENDHERBERGE BERNKASTEL-KUES (BERNKASTEL-KUES HOSTEL)

Jugendherbergsstrasse 1,

54470 Bernkastel-Kues

Phone: 06531–2395

Fax: 06531–1529

E-mail: jh-bernkastel-kues@djh-info.de

Web site: www.djh-info.de

Rates: 22.80 DM per Hostelling International member (about $11 US); doubles 64 DM (about $32 US)

Credit cards: No

Beds: 96

Private/family rooms: Yes

Kitchen available: No

Season: Closed December 24–26

Affiliation: Hostelling International-DJH

Regional office: Rheinland

Extras: Table tennis, soccer, basketball, volleyball, grill, meals ($)

There's a good supply of double, quad, and six-bedded rooms in this unassuming but surprisingly large hostel high above the Moselle. It's hard to imagine a better position; you're wayyyy up top, looking down even on the castle.

Some dorms here are bigger, with eight beds, but it's all run well enough by the management. And every single room has its own bathroom, a surprisingly modern attitude—yet the place is inexpensive, as hostels go. Bathrooms are on the hallway, and they've got a game room stocked with table tennis tables, plus a grilling area and outdoor sports area. Don't forget to check out the kitchen and lounge.

The linked town of Bernkastel-Kues is a bit overrun with wine-sucking tourists in summer and fall, but it still makes a good trip. As a bonus, there's a boat dock right in town—you don't even need to take the train. Or you might check out the ruins of Burg Landshut down in the valley.

Good town, and a good-choice hostel, too.

Best bet for a bite:
Eulenspiegel

Insiders' tip:
Wine museum with wine-tasting cellar next door

What hostellers say:
"Pass the glass."

Gestalt:
Vino vedi vici

Hospitality:

Cleanliness:

Party index:

How to get there:

By bus:/train From Koblenz or Trier take train to Wittlich, then transfer to bus to Bernkastel-Kues. Contact hostel for further transit details.

By car: Take Highway B50 and Hunsrück-Höhenstrasse to Bernkastel-Kues. From Trier take Autobahn A48 to Wittlich or Highway B53.

JUGENDHERBERGE BRODENBACH (BRODENBACH HOSTEL)

Im Moorkamp 7,

56332 Brodenbach

Phone: 02605–3389

Fax: 02605–4244
E-mail: Jugendherberge-Brodenbach@djh-info.de
Web site: www.djh-info.de
Rates: 21.30 DM per Hostelling International member (about $11 US)
Credit cards: No
Beds: 106
Private/family rooms: Yes
Kitchen available: No
Season: Closed December 24–26
Affiliation: Hostelling International-DJH
Regional office: Rheinland
Extras: Table tennis, grill, meals ($)

Located about 12 miles southwest of Koblenz is the quiet little hamlet of Brodenbach. There's no compelling reason to come here, but the hostel is certainly welcoming with its rustic half-timber construction, spacious rooms, and friendly young staff. It's pretty cheap, too.

The hostel, like most others in Germany, is immaculately clean. If you're lucky you'll have a room on the east side, where you'll wake to a tugboat horn and a majestic sunrise over the placid Moselle River—a lovely view worthy of the finest of hotels. If unlucky you'll be stuck looking at an overgrown hillside. Either way, though, the room will very likely contain either four or six beds—the standard sizes here.

Within walking distance, you'll find few affordable restaurants, so although the food here isn't spectacular, it *is* cheap and filling. Dig in. And before you leave, plan out your next day's journey using the huge map on the wall in one of the lounges. You'll discover some interesting local roads and trails that aren't on even the best German road maps.

Best bet for a bite:
Right here

Insiders' tip:
Take a hike

What hostellers say:
"Another sandwich, please."

Gestalt:
Clean and serene

Hospitality:

Cleanliness:

Party index:

How to get there:

By bus/train: From Koblenz or Trier Station take bus to Brodenbach, or walk 2½ miles to hostel.

By car: Take Highway A61 or Highway B49.

JUGENDHERBERGE COCHEM (COCHEM HOSTEL)

Klottener Strasse 9,

56812 Cochem

Phone: 02671–8633

Fax: 02671–8568

E-mail: jh-cochem@djh-info.de

Web site: www.djh-info.de

Rates: 22.80 DM per Hostelling International member (about $11 US per person)

Credit cards: No

Beds: 146

Private/family rooms: No

Kitchen available: No

Season: Closed December 24–26

Affiliation: Hostelling International-DJH

Regional office: Rheinland

Extras: Table tennis, sports field, basketball, grill, breakfast, meals ($)

S 🚲

Yet another supertouristed Moselle Valley town, Cochem attracts plenty of Germans in summer and fall; you won't be alone in these streets. It's still nice enough to merit some snapshots, though.

The hostel isn't bad, either. Beds here come mostly in quad or six-bedded rooms, though there are a few singles and doubles as well. There are five lounge areas in all, they serve a free breakfast with your bed price, and the basketball hoop and grill offer opportunities for social mixing. There's a game room, as well.

Best bet for a bite:
Kochlöffel

Insiders' tip:
Moselbad water park

What hostellers say:
"Staff was alright."

Gestalt:
Cochem and a smile

Hospitality:

Cleanliness:

Party index:

How to get there:

By bus: Contact hostel for transit details.

By car: Take Highway A48 to Kaisersesch or Ulmen or Highway B49 from the direction of Koblenz or Trier.

By train: From Koblenz or Trier take the train to Cochem and walk ½ mile across bridge to hostel.

JUGENDHERBERGE KOBLENZ
(KOBLENZ HOSTEL)

Festung Ehrenbreitstein,

56077 Koblenz

Phone: 0261–972–870

Fax: 0261–972–8730
E-mail: jh-koblenz@djh-info.de
Web site: www.djh-info.de
Rates: 25.20–31.20 DM per Hostelling International member (about $13–$16 US)
Credit cards: Yes
Beds: 166
Private/family rooms: Yes
Kitchen available: No
Season: Closed December 24–26
Office hours: 7:00 A.M.–11:30 P.M.
Affiliation: Hostelling International-DJH
Regional office: Rheinland
Extras: Table tennis, grill, cafeteria ($), luggage storage, information desk, TV room, garden, playground, meeting rooms

You can see this low-slung, practically windlowless hostel from just about anywhere in Koblenz. Then, again, it's pretty hard to miss: It's located inside the famed Ehrenbreitstein Fortress high on a bluff overlooking the city and the river. It's got to be one of the most dramatic settings for a hostel anywhere in the country, and it's part of one of the biggest fortresses in all of Europe.

That's right, it's located in the fort—yet another of Germany's tippy-top-of-the-rock hostels—though you've gotta watch the clock with this one. That's because the cross-Rhine ferry service and the gondola up the cliff both stop running early in the evening. At that point you'll have to resign yourself to taking a city bus and then slogging up-up-uphill to get back to bed. At least you'll be tired when you get there. (If you're driving, just look for the FESTUNG (fortress) signs and park outside the walls. Signage is terrible here, so just walk inside—and walk and walk—until you can see the city, then turn left.)

Best bet for a bite:
Winningen Weinstuben

Insiders' tip:
River fireworks in early August

What hostellers say:
"Darned schoolkids . . ."

Gestalt:
River rugrats

Hospitality:

Cleanliness:

Party index:

The original foundations for the hostel—oops, we mean the fort—were laid in the 1100s. Later, during the relatively recent 1500s, most of it was added on; this remains one of the biggest forts in the whole damn world! (Cool.) Once used as a barracks by Prussian, French, and German troops, the location now hosts armies of German

Jugendherberge Koblenz
Koblenz Hostel • Koblenz

(photo courtesy of Deutsches Jugendherbergswerk)

school groups and Boy Scouts as well as a motley assortment of travelers like you. It's a busy, frantic place, and all in all it's not really surprising that it has an institutional feel with very little personality. But it is a warm, cheap bed nonetheless. There are lots of doubles, quad rooms, and six- and eight-bedded dorms; each has wood furniture, but only the family rooms have en suite bathrooms.

The in-house cafeteria serves rib-sticking, unremarkable meals. Yeah, that's right, big surprise: The food is bland and expensive, though the outdoor tables overlooking the city at the confluence of the Rhine and Moselle Rivers make for a spectacular dining view at least. Within a few minutes' drive there are a few pizza shops, pubs, and nondescript cafes if you want to try to find something better.

Koblenz's strong point is its old town, snuggled up against the river but insulated from it by a belt of greenery that makes for fine walking. Check out the Liebfrauenkirche's stained-glass work or the Florianskirche for starters.

Note that if you're going to be cruising up and down the Rhine (that's what we'd do from here), the boat docks are just across the river from the hostel. But the train station, where you'll likely arrive, is a good mile and a half inland (i.e., west) of the river, so allow extra time and energy to get to the ferry or hostel.

How to get there:

By bus/train: Take train to Koblenz. From Koblenz Station take #7, #8, or #9 bus to Ehrenbreitstein stop and walk uphill ½ mile to hostel.

By car: Take Highway A3 or A 61 to Highway A48, following signs in the direction of Koblenz-Ehrenbreitstein fortress (Festung).

JUGENDHERBERGE TRABEN-TRARBACH (TRABEN-TRARBACH HOSTEL)

Hirtenpfad 6,

56841 Traben-Trarbach

Phone: 06541–9278

Fax: 06541–3759
E-mail: jh-traben-trarbach@djh-info.de
Web site: www.djh-info.de
Rates: 26.90–32.90 DM per Hostelling International member (about $13–$16 US); doubles 64 DM (about $32 US)
Credit cards: Yes
Beds: 176
Private/family rooms: Yes
Kitchen available: Yes
Season: Closed December 24–26
Office hours: 8:00–9:00 A.M.; 6:30–7:00 P.M.
Curfew: Midnight
Affiliation: Hostelling International-DJH
Regional office: Rheinland
Extras: Piano, table tennis, basketball, kids' playroom, cafeteria ($), grill, breakfast

This is a small town—a pair of linked towns, actually—which you'll probably only find if you're hot on the trail of obscure German wines. The rooms at the hostel here are mostly quads and six-bedded rooms—all with bathrooms—and they've got plenty of stretching-out lounge space, plus two dining rooms and a playroom for kiddies. The game room has table tennis, the music room has a piano, the patio has a grill, and the cafeteria serves food.

Any questions? It's all kinda institutional, sure, but we heard no complaints. Breakfast is included for free, by the way, and meals can be purchased for about an extra $5.00 US (one per day) or $8.00 US (for lunch *and* dinner). Make sure you check in during the short office hours, though.

This double-team of towns offers a little something different from your average set of wine villages, with some interesting architectural details on the buildings (even some Art Deco–type touches) in addition to the usual wine cellars, tastings, and rustic eateries.

How to get there:

By bus/train: From Koblenz or Trier take train to Bullay Station and change to bus for

Best bet for a bite:
In-house grub

Insiders' tip:
Museum on Casinostrasse

What hostellers say:
"Plain and simple."

Gestalt:
Dynamic duo

Hospitality:

Cleanliness:

Party index:

Traben-Trarbach. Take #6206 bus to Schulzentrum stop and walk uphill less than 1 mile to hostel.

By car: Take Highway A48, exiting at signs for Wittlich, and continue to Traben-Trarbach. Or take Highway B53 from Trier, exiting in the direction of Zell. Take Highway A61, exiting at signs for Rheinböllen, then continue on Highway B50 to Traben-Trarbach.

JUGENDGÄSTEHAUS TRIER (TRIER GUEST HOUSE HOSTEL)

An der Jugendherberge 4,
54292 Trier/Mosel
Phone: 0651–146–620

Fax: 0651–146–6230
E-mail: jh-trier@djh-info.de
Web site: www.djh-info.de
Rates: 29.10–38.60 DM per Hostelling International member (about $15–$19 US); doubles 73 DM (about $37 US)
Credit cards: Yes
Beds: 248
Private/family rooms: Yes
Kitchen available: No
Season: Closed December 24–26
Office hours: 7:00 A.M.–midnight
Curfew: Midnight
Affiliation: Hostelling International-DJH
Regional office: Rheinland
Extras: Breakfast, piano, table tennis, volleyball, basketball, playground, grill, cafeteria ($), laundry

No, it's not central (hey, what did you expect?), but it's pretty nice as hostels go, despite the size. Yeah, this place is absolutely huge. There are sixty-plus rooms here, all containing from one to six beds; the hostel has doubles up the wazoo, plus singles, triples, quad rooms, and six-bedded dormitories, too. Every single honkin' one of 'em has its own private bathroom, private shower, and wooden furniture. There's no kitchen to cook in, but you've got the option of taking the free breakfast, paying a little more for another meal each day, or paying more still and getting all three meals served to you in the hostel cafeteria's two dining rooms.

Best bet for a bite:
Havanna

Insiders' tip:
Great Roman ruins

What hostellers say:
"Good value, but only so-so."

Gestalt:
Trier house

Hospitality:

Either inside or out, you've got sports opportunities in the form of volleyball nets, basketball hoops, and a playground. There's also a nice meadow and a soccer field.

The main sight here in Trier—the oldest city in Germany, you know—is the Porta Nigra, a Roman gate of not-quite-black stone. If you're a budding Communist, be sure to check out the Karl Marx Museum, located in the house where the soon-to-be-reviled thinker grew up. (It should be free for the masses, but it's not.) Afterward, grab food on the fast-food strip or hit the Edekka market for snacks.

Cleanliness:

Party index:

How to get there:

By bus/train: From Köln or Koblenz take train to Trier. From Trier Station walk 1 mile to hostel via Theodor-Haus-Allee, Nordallee, and then Lindenstrasse. Or take #3 bus to Zur Laubener Ufer stop and walk ½ mile along river to hostel.

By car: Take Highway A48 from Koblenzor or Highway A1 from Saarbrücken. Exit onto Highway A602 and continue to Trier.

JUGENDGÄSTEHAUS KOLPINGNHAUS (TRIER KOLPINGNHAUS GUEST HOUSE HOSTEL)

Dietrichstrasse 42,
54292 Trier/Mosel
Phone: 0651–975–250
Fax: 0651–975–2540
Rates: 27–39 DM per Hostelling International member (about $14–$20 US); doubles 78 DM (about $39 US)
Credit cards: No
Beds: 120
Private/family rooms: Yes
Kitchen available: No
Season: Open year-round
Office hours: 8:00 A.M.–11:00 P.M.
Affiliation: None
Extras: Breakfast, restaurant ($), pool table, table tennis

This hostel goes toe-to-toe with the "official" joint in Trier—and holds its own. It's run by the same folks as the attached hotel, so you do get some hotel-style services (like breakfast) but hostel-style beds.

There are two kinds of rooms in this renovated old building "hotel" style doubles, more expensive and private, and then the dorms of course. Bathroom facilities are great, and the restaurant on the premises stays open quite late if you've got the munchies.

This is not a fancy place at all, but it is about the same price as the other hostel—and *much* more centrally located (it's practically in the dead-center of town)—so you should give it a look, particularly if you want to sample bars, clubs, or other stuff you can only do if you're staying right in the thick of the action. Bear in mind that word is getting out about this place, so it can be quite busy.

Fur fun, as we've previously said, hit one of the numerous bars or pubs in the area. There's an Irish one on Jakobstrasse, for example, and many other styles nearby as well.

Best bet for a bite:
Astarix

Insiders' tip:
Zur Glocke for beer

What hostellers say:
"Not bad."

Gestalt:
Centrally parked

Hospitality:

Cleanliness:

Party index:

How to get there:

By bus: Contact hostel for transit route.
By car: Contact hostel for directions.
By train: From Trier Station walk ½ mile directly into center of town. Then continue west on Dietrichstrasse, toward the Moselle River; hostel is on right.

RHINE VALLEY

Most hostellers associate the Rhine River with big wine, or the Lorelei Rocks that nineteenth-century sailors couldn't resist. This long river has actually long been one of Europe's most important transportation corridors, however, with a lot of industrial traffic—and now, tourist traffic, too—as it rolls from the mountains of French Switzerland north to the North Sea. The tourists come for the kitschy towns, and the wine keeps them in good spirits (sorry); but you'll probably still find the area worth a stop anyway.

NATURSCHUTZ-JUGENDHERBERGE (ALTENAHR HOSTEL)

Langfigtal 8,
53505 Altenahr
Phone: 02643–1880

Fax: 02643–8136
E-mail: jh-altenahr@djh-info.de
Web site: www.djh-info.de
Rates: 21.30 DM per Hostelling International member (about $11 US)
Credit cards: No
Beds: 98
Private/family rooms: No
Kitchen available: No
Season: Closed December 24–26
Affiliation: Hostelling International-DJH
Regional office: Rheinland
Extras: Table tennis, basketball, game room, grill, meals ($)

$

Not quite in the Rhine Valley, but over in the adjacent and lesser-touristed Ahr Valley, this hostel's in one cute town. Walking trails, vineyards, old ruins . . . you've got it all in one compact package here.

Best bet for a bite:
Eat here now

Insiders' tip:
Cafe Lang dance club

What hostellers say:
"Pretty town."

Gestalt:
Say Ahr

Hospitality:

Cleanliness:

Party index:

The hostel rooms are kept to a maximum of eight beds and a minimum of two beds, which is excellent for families and couples. Two of these dorms have their own bathrooms, plus their own keys to ensure protection of valuables and all rooms have a closet. The remaining hostellers have to shower on the first floor.

Other neat stuff here includes a grill, a game room with table tennis, and a basketball hoop. Meals are served and available to all guests, not just those in groups. Speaking of groups, they are present mostly during the week—so weekends are relatively calm (hint, hint). As for meals, the hostel serves them in different stages for all hostellers: You can purchase just break-

KEY TO ICONS

Attractive natural setting

Ecologically aware hostel

Superior kitchen facilities or cafe

Offbeat or eccentric place

Superior bathroom facilities

Romantic private rooms

Comfortable beds

Editors' choice: among our very favorite hostels

A particularly good value

Wheelchair accessible

Good for business travelers

Especially well suited for families

Good for active travelers

Visual arts at hostel or nearby

Music at hostel or nearby

Great hostel for skiers

Bar or pub at hostel or nearby

fast; a half board, which includes dinner; and a full board, which includes three squares.

The town itself has a surprising amount of nightlife for a little riverside village, so hit the wine bars and pubs and try to remember to get up in the morning.

How to get there:

By bus/train: Take train to Altenahr. From Altenahr Station contact hostel for transit route.

By car: Take Highway A61 to Autobahn Meckenheim, continuing in the direction of Altenahr. Exit over the narrow bridge to hostel.

JUGENDBURG STAHLECK (BACHARACH HOSTEL)

55422 Bacharach

Phone: 06743–1266

Fax: 06743–2684
E-mail: jh-bacharach@djh-info.de
Web site: www.djh-info.de
Rates: 25.20–31.20 DM per Hostelling International member (about $13–$16 US); doubles 73 DM (about $37 US)
Credit cards: No
Beds: 166
Private/family rooms: Yes
Kitchen available: No
Season: Closed December 24–26
Affiliation: Hostelling International-DJH
Regional office: Rheinland-Pfalz/Saarland
Extras: Table tennis, piano, cafeteria ($), patio,

Located inside a romantic castle high above the romantic Rhine River and staffed by terrific management, this one gets our vote as one of the Top Two hostels in Germany. (You'll have to read through the rest of this book to find the other one. Sorry.)

Beds come in everything from doubles to quads, six-bedded rooms, or eight-bedded dormitories. Every single room has a shower and bathroom. There's a kitchen, dining room, cafeteria, music room with concert piano, terrace with views . . . get the idea? This place is special. And the owners couldn't be friendlier if they tried (and they *do* try.) Even if the hostel is full, the owner will try to make space for you and all your crazy buddies.

What to see? The famous Lorelei rocks are very nearby, reachable by boat, bike, or foot. Or take in the half-timbered

Best bet for a bite:
Hotel Kranenturm

Insiders' tip:
Fritz's wine bar
(Weingut)

What hostellers say:
"The best I've ever seen!"

Gestalt:
Bacharach on track

structures along the medieval main street. There are a number of churches, like the ruins of the Wernerkapelle, worth seeing, too. Not of a religious bent? No problem. You'll be in good company at popular wine/beer gardens like Fritz Bastian's on Oberstrasse.

Hospitality:

Cleanliness:

Party index:

How to get there:

By bus: Contact hostel for transit details.

By car: Take Autobahn A61 or Highway B9 to the Rhine. Bacharach is halfway between Koblenz and Mainz.

By train: From Koblenz or Mainz take train to Bacharach. Walk ¾ mile uphill to hostel.

JUGENDGÄSTEHAUS BAD NEUENAHR-AHRWEILER (BAD NEUENAHR-AHRWEILER GUEST HOUSE HOSTEL)

St. Piusstrasse 7,

53474 Bad Neuenahr-Ahrweiler

Phone: 02641–34924

Fax: 02641–31574

E-mail: Jugendherberge-Bad-Neuenahr-Ahrweiler@djh-info.de

Web site: www.djh-info.de

Rates: 29.10–38.60 DM per Hostelling International member (about $15–$19 US); doubles 73 DM (about $37 US)

Credit cards: Yes

Beds: 140

Private/family rooms: Yes

Kitchen available: No

Season: Closed December 24–26

Affiliation: Hostelling International-DJH

Regional office: Rheinland-Pfalz/Saarland

Extras: Piano, bike rentals, table tennis, basketball, cafeteria ($), breakfast

This is a really nice, modern hostel in yet another quaint Ahr Valley town. The rooms come in singles, doubles, or quads—everything with private bath and shower. There are eight separate lounging areas, including a game room, cafeteria, music room, and more. They've got table tennis, a piano, a basketball hoop; they serve free breakfast and rent you bikes to explore the gorgeous green countryside.

Best bet for a bite: Both's

Insiders' tip: Soak in spa for a splurge

What hostellers say: "Excellent and modern."

Also be sure to check out the Roman ruins nearby, which are open to the public daily except Monday from April to October.

How to get there:

By bus: Contact hostel for transit details.

By car: Take Highway A61 to Bad Neuenahr-Ahrweiler.

By train: Take train from Remangen or Kreuzberg to Ahrweiler. From Ahrweiler Station walk ½ mile east to hostel.

Gestalt:
Ahr kind of place

Hospitality:

Cleanliness:

Party index:

JUGENDHERBERGE
BINGEN-BINGERBRÜCK (BINGEN HOSTEL)

Herterstrasse 51,

55411 Bingen-Bingerbrück

Phone: 06721–32163

Fax: 06721–34012
E-mail: djh-bingen-bingerbrueck@jh-info.de
Rates: 21.30 DM (about $11 US) per Hostelling International member
Credit cards: No
Beds: 176
Private/family rooms: Yes
Kitchen available: No
Season: Closed December 24–26
Office hours: 8:00–10:00 P.M.; 5:00–10:00 P.M.
Curfew: 10:00 P.M.
Affiliation: Hostelling International-DJH
Regional office: Rheinland
Extras: Table tennis, grill, meals ($), breakfast

This hilltop hostel isn't in the most obvious location—it's in an adjacent burb uphill from the city of Bingen—but it's actually closer than you'd think to the train station, from where you can get into the city pretty easily.

The rooms are generally six- or eight-bedded ones. There's a grill, a small game room, free breakfast, and the option of a full meal plan. Staff is cool, though they do have to administrate stupid rules like the absurdly early 10:00 P.M. curfew (which is even stupider once you've been clued in to the huge, fun disco down by the river).

Best bet for a bite:
Prina's

Insiders' tip:
Enormous disco at river

What hostellers say:
"#%@& curfew!!!"

Gestalt:
Early to bed

Bingen's not much to see, mainly a hub to get to the rest of the river valley. Use the ferry to hit adjacent towns like St. Goar and

Hospitality:

Cleanliness:

Party index:

Bacharach, each with its own hostels, yes, but those might be full. Or, if you're stuck in town, check out the Mouse Tower. Yes, that's what it's called. Anyone can point you. (Hint: *Maus* is "mouse" in German.)

How to get there:

By bus: Contact hostel for transit details.

By car: Take Highway A61 from the north, exiting at Waldalgesheim, or take Highway A60 via Highway B9 from the direction of St. Goar.

By train: Take train from Koblenz or Mainz to Bingen. From the Bingen Station walk ⅓ mile to hostel.

JUGENDHERBERGE HOCHSPEYER— NATURPARK/WALDJUGENDHERBERGE (HOCHSPEYER PARK HOSTEL)

Trippstadter Strasse 150,

67691 Hochspeyer

Phone: 06305–336–0

Fax: 06305–5152

E-mail: jh-hochspeyer@djh-info.de

Web site: www.djh-info.de

Rates: 22.80–32.90 DM (about $11–$16 US) per Hostelling International member

Credit cards: No

Beds: 149

Private/family rooms: Yes

Kitchen available: No

Season: Closed December 24–26

Affiliation: Hostelling International-DJH

Regional office: Rheinland

Extras: Programs, cafeteria ($), grill, table tennis

Set in a wooded park in the tiny little town of Hochspeyer, this is a good hostel for getting away from it all.

Best bet for a bite:
Hostel cafeteria

Insiders' tip:
Next town over has more nightlife

What hostellers say:
"Quiet town."

Gestalt:
Woody

Beds are arranged in a series of four- and six-bedded rooms mostly, though they also have some single and double rooms, too. Every room in the joint comes with its own private bathroom, a nice touch. There are three lounges, a small game area, a grill, and a cafeteria serving meals. Occasional programs at the hostel explain the ecology of the surrounding woods, though they're almost exclusively in German, of course.

Hochspeyer isn't too well known by the tourists, and it sits right on the so-called "German Wine Road," a neat winding track that isn't actually on the Rhine but a little west of it. The nearby town of Kaiserlautern has more to do (there's a huge U.S. military base there), but either way you're smack dab in the Palatinate Forest—Germany's biggest. Check it out.

Hospitality:

Cleanliness:

Party index:

How to get there:

By bus: Contact hostel for transit details.

By car: Take Highway A6 from Mannheim, Saarbrücken, Enkenbach, or Alsenborn in the direction of Hochspeyer.

By train: Take train to Hochspeyer from Mannheim, Saarbrücken, or Bingen. From Hochspeyer Station walk 1 mile to hostel, or contact hostel for further transit details.

JUGENDHERBERGE IDAR-OBERSTEIN (IDAR-OBERSTEIN HOSTEL)

Alte Treibe 23,

55743 Idar-Oberstein

Phone: 06781–24366

Fax: 06781–26712

E-mail: jh-idar-oberstein@djh-info.de

Web site: www.djh-info.de

Rates: 26.90–32.90 DM (about $13–$16 US) per Hostelling International member

Credit cards: No

Beds: 128

Private/family rooms: Yes

Kitchen available: No

Season: Closed December 24–26

Affiliation: Hostelling International-DJH

Regional office: Rheinland

Extras: Piano, table tennis, playground, basketball, volleyball, grill, cafeteria ($), breakfast

Located in a pretty little side valley west of the Rhine, Idar-Oberstein wouldn't be your first stop on a German vacation—unless you'd been there, and then it might. The town boasts some amazing local rocks (geology students take note), plus a famous baby was born here. We'll get to that in a minute.

The hostel's nothing special, but it's perfectly acceptable. Architecturally, take note of the stone floor as you enter. Inside, rooms contain the usual mixture of singles, doubles, quad rooms, and six-bedded dormitories—but most of them are four-bedded—which is a good range of choice for families, lone travelers, or couples. All have the much-coveted private bathroom and shower facilities and wooden furniture, too, and there's plenty of common space.

Best bet for a bite:
Along Haupstrasse

Insiders' tip:
Armageddon

What hostellers say:
"Look who's talking, too."

Gestalt:
Moonlighting

Hospitality:

Cleanliness:

Party index:

Breakfast comes free, too. (As in many other German hostels, you can choose to pay about $5.00 US more here for lunch or dinner each day or $8.00 US more to get served both meals in the in-house cafeteria. Eat in one of five dining rooms.) Other pluses here include a game room with table tennis, some outdoor space to shoot hoops and so forth, and a piano for tinkling at (not *on*).

The highlight of your visit will probably be the local rocks and gems. Hit one of several museums to see them under special lights that play up their sparkly qualities; watch the cutting of the precious stones; and view a monster gem from Brazil. (Why are monster gemstones always from Brazil, anyway? Just wondering.) When you get tired of the museums, walk up to the chapel in the cliff—anyone can direct you—or keep strolling through woods to the two old castles way up top looking down on the valley.

Oh, and the famous guy who was said to have been born here? Here's a hint: He starred in the two of the highest-grossing Hollywood films of 1999 and 2000. As for how and why he was born in this little place, well, sorry; you're gonna have to take it from there.

How to get there:

By bus: Take #6440 bus from Trier to Idar-Oberstein. From Idar-Oberstein Station take #5 bus to Weber stop, walk to hostel.

By car: Take Highway B41 from Bingen in the direction of Neunkirchen toward Finsterheck/Hohl to Idar-Oberstein.

By train: Take train to Idar-Oberstein from Mainz or Saarbrücken. From Idar-Oberstein Station take #5 bus to Weber stop or walk ¾ mile to hostel.

JUGENDHERBERGE KARLSRUHE (KARLSRUHE HOSTEL)

Moltkestrasse 24,
76133 Karlsruhe
Phone: 0721–28248
Fax: 0721–27647

Rates: 24–29 DM (about $12–$15 US) per Hostelling International member
Beds: 164
Private/family rooms: Yes
Kitchen available: No
Season: Closed December 24–26
Curfew: 11:30 P.M.
Lockout: 9:00 A.M.–5:00 P.M.
Affiliation: DJH-Hostelling International
Regional office: Baden-Württemberg
Extras: Breakfast ($), meals ($), parking

Quite close to the city of Karlsruhe's castle, this place is well kept and acceptable if you really need to stay the night in town. But it's a bit of a ride from the center of town, dorms are rather standard, and they charge you for the breakfast. There's also a brutal all-day lockout to contend with.

The city itself is no big deal, either. It only dates from the eighteenth century, so that yellow castle is cool but not terribly old. At least there's an attached museum and some expansive grounds to relax in. Of more interest, perhaps, the city university is pretty close—affording you the opportunity for plenty of cheap food and entertainment and maybe, just maybe, friendship with a local young 'un.

Best bet for a bite:
Mensa

Insiders' tip:
Great art museum

What hostellers say:
"Like the hostel, hate the lockout."

Gestalt:
Neat 'n' tidy

Hospitality:

Cleanliness:

Party index:

How to get there:

By bus/train: Take train to Karlsruhe from Frankfurt, Basel, München, or Strasbourg. From Karlsruhe Station take S-Bahn line S1 or S11 to Europaplatz stop, then walk up Karlstrasse to Stevenienstrasse and turn left; make a right on Seminarstrasse, then go left on Moltkestrasse.

By car: Take Autobahn Highway A5 to Karlsruhe.

KEY TO ICONS

 Attractive natural setting

 Ecologically aware hostel

 Superior kitchen facilities or cafe

Offbeat or eccentric place

 Superior bathroom facilities

 Romantic private rooms

 Comfortable beds

 Editors' choice: among our very favorite hostels

 A particularly good value

 Wheelchair accessible

 Good for business travelers

 Especially well suited for families

 Good for active travelers

 Visual arts at hostel or nearby

 Music at hostel or nearby

Great hostel for skiers

 Bar or pub at hostel or nearby

RHEIN–MAIN–JUGENDHERBERGE UND JUGENDGÄSTEHAUS MAINZ (MAINZ GUEST HOUSE AND HOSTEL)

Otto-Brunfels-Schneise 4,
55130 Mainz
Phone: 06131–85332
Fax: 06131–82422
E-mail: jh-mainz@djh-info.de
Web site: www.djh-info.de
Rates: 29.10–38.60 DM (about $15–$19 US) per Hostelling International member
Credit cards: Yes
Beds: 166
Private/family rooms: Yes
Kitchen available: Yes
Season: Closed December 24–26
Office hours: 6:30 A.M.–midnight
Curfew: Midnight
Affiliation: Hostelling International-DJH
Regional office: Rheinland
Extras: Table tennis, playground, grill, piano, breakfast, TV room, playground, meals ($), meeting rooms, garden

First things first, bub: It's pronounced "Mines," not "Maine's." There. We feel better. The hostel here—a white, prisonlike complex forming an "L" with a slightly scraggly lawn—is located in a city park, not exactly central but nice and quiet at least. Rooms are all doubles (twenty-two of them) or quads (twenty-seven), and all have private bathrooms and showers. Breakfast is included, and there's a whole host of services here, such as a game room, playroom for kids, playground area, grill, and piano. The field across the way is perfect for booting a soccer ball around. Don't know how? Ask anyone in these parts. They probably can teach you.

Best bet for a bite:
Central Cafe

Insiders' tip:
Beers at Eisgrub

What hostellers say:
"Peaceful setting."

Gestalt:
Land Mainz

Hospitality:

Cleanliness:

Party index:

Not everyone reports being crazy about it, but if you're staying in Mainz you're probably gonna hit the Gutenberg Museum, which purports to lay out the history of printing with a copy of Gutenberg's original press and a *very* old Bible. That's right, the book you're holding in your hands might not have been possible without the invention of Mainz's most famous native; Gutenberg developed the idea of movable pieces of type sometime around 1450 and printed the first "mass-produced" Bibles with his simple press.

Other cool stuff in Mainz includes a museum showcasing some Roman ships that were dug up here in the early '80s. Or you could head for the city docks and catch a boat or hydrofoil up the Rhine to more interesting places. The so-called K-D ferries are, as we've mentioned before, free for Eurailpass holders; so go nuts. Literally.

How to get there:

By bus/train: From Mainz Station take #1 or #22 bus to Weisenau stop and walk ¼ mile to hostel.

By car: Take Autobahnring A60 to Mainz from Darmstadt, then follow signs through Weisenau/Grossberg in the direction of the Volkspark.

PFALZ-JUGENDHERBERGE/ JUGENDGÄSTEHAUS NEUSTADT (NEUSTADT GUEST HOUSE AND HOSTEL)

Hans-Geiger-Strasse 27,

67434 Neustadt

Phone: 06321–2289

Fax: 06321–82947
E-mail: jh-neustadt@djh-info.de
Web site: www.djh-info.de
Rates: 29.10–38.60 DM (about $15–$19 US) per Hostelling International member
Credit cards: No
Beds: 122
Private/family rooms: Yes
Kitchen available: No
Season: Closed December 24–26
Affiliation: Hostelling International-DJH
Regional office: Rheinland
Extras: Piano, cafeteria ($), basketball, volleyball, table tennis, grill, breakfast

This nicely done hostel is located in a fairly touristed region, but if you can get past all the visitors, you'll like the place well enough.

It's the usual collection of singles, doubles, and quad rooms here, all with private bathrooms. Among the common areas are a dining room, a game room, and a cafeteria; there's also a piano for the musically inclined and some

Best bet for a bite:
Wespennest

Insiders' tip:
Wine taverns abound

What hostellers say:
"Grab my corkscrew."

Gestalt:
Winer

Hospitality: 👍

Cleanliness: 👍

Party index:

🎉 🎉

sports facilities for the athletically inclined. Breakfast is free with your bed.

Neustadt is supposedly the country's biggest wine-producing town, and so it's therefore a little bigger than other wine towns in the area. That means less charm, yes, but also a few more services and options at night.

How to get there:

By bus: Contact hostel for transit details.

By car: Take Highway A65 to Neustadt-Süd exit and continue to hostel.

By train: Take train to Neustadt from Mannheim or Saarbrücken. From Neustadt Station walk ¾ mile to hostel.

JUGENDGÄSTEHAUS OBERWESEL 👍
(OBERWESEL GUEST HOUSE HOSTEL)

Auf dem Schönberg,

55430 Oberwesel

Phone: 06744–93330

Fax: 06744–7446

E-mail: jh-oberwesel@djh-info.de

Web site: www.djh-info.de

Rates: 29.10–38.60 DM (about $15–$19 US) per Hostelling International member

Credit cards: Yes

Beds: 179

Private/family rooms: Yes

Kitchen available: No

Season: Closed December 24–26

Office hours: 8:00 A.M.–8:00 P.M.

Curfew: Midnight

Affiliation: Hostelling International-DJH

Regional office: Rheinland

Extras: Table tennis, cafeteria ($), photo darkroom, volleyball, basketball, grill, music practice room, swimming pool access

Best bet for a bite:
Eat here

Insiders' tip:
Bring the earplugs

What hostellers say:
"Ah, the pitter-patter of little feet . . ."

There's not much to say about this hostel, which lays out a lot of bunks in small rooms of one, two, or four beds—all with private bathroom facilities—and tops off the mix with a game room, cafeteria, sports area, music room, and a grill. It's another of those German places designed for school groups, so expect lots of kiddies romping around. If you hit it on a lucky day, though, and it's empty you can use the services yourself. Don't forget a dip in the pool, to which you have access as a hostel guest.

Don't expect luxury here, but *do* expect great stuff to do in the area. You're on a stretch of the Rhine just five minutes by train or boat from St. Goar, and not much farther to other towns of similar ilk. You could hike or laze around all day here soaking up the wine, castles, river views, and local characters—and feel like never leaving Germany.

Gestalt: Romper room

Hospitality:

Cleanliness:

Party index:

How to get there:

By bus: Contact hostel for transit details.

By car: Take Highway A61 from Köln to Ludwigshafen or Highway B9 from Mainz or Koblenz.

By train: Take train to Oberwesel from Mainz or Koblenz. Contact hostel for further transit details.

JUGENDHERBERGE RÜDESHEIM (RÜDESHEIM HOSTEL)

Am Kreuzberg,

65385 Rüdesheim

Phone: 06722–2711

Fax: 06722–48284

E-mail: Ruedesheim@djh-hessen.de

Rates: 22–27 DM (about $11–$14 US) per Hostelling International member

Credit cards: No

Beds: 176

Private/family rooms: Yes

Kitchen available: No

Season: Closed December 24–26

Curfew: 11:30 P.M.

Affiliation: Hostelling International-DJH

Regional office: Rheinland

Extras: Breakfast, meals ($), parking

It's actually fun to get to this hostel, if a bit exerting: You hike uphill (always, always, hostels are *up*hill) from the train station through vineyards to the place. And that tells you all you need to know about the town—They Grow Grapes.

Once here, you'll find that the bunks are arranged in a variety of doubles, quads, and six- and eight-bedded dormitories. There are several dining rooms and breakfast is included with your bed, but there are few other concessions to modern life. Think simplicity and good views.

The white wine from this town is widely renowned, and so your primary activity here is probably going to be somehow related to it. Check out the local Wine Museum—located right inside the town's thirteenth-century castle and open from March until around late November—then head for a winery or eat and drink in town. You'll likely end up on hypertouristed Drosselgasse, a street we'd normally avoid like the plague, but in a town this small, eating choices are limited.

If you're a teetotaler, or you already ate something on the train, you could instead take the local cable car to the top of a small rise and get a better view on things. Another small museum in town showcases windup musical instruments if you're into that sort of thing.

Best bet for a bite:
Beats us

Insiders' tip:
Breuer winery offers
tastings

What hostellers say:
"Not bad."

Gestalt:
Wine and dine

Hospitality:

Cleanliness:

Party index:

How to get there:

By bus: Contact hostel for transit details.
By car: Contact hostel for directions.
By train: Contact hostel for transit details.

JUGENDHERBERGE ST. GOAR (ST. GOAR HOSTEL)

Bismarckweg 17,
65385 St. Goar
Phone: 06741–388

Fax: 06741–2869
Rates: 22–27 DM (about $11–$14 US) per Hostelling International member
Credit cards: No
Beds: 130
Private/family rooms: Yes
Kitchen available: No
Season: Closed December 24–26
Curfew: 10:00 P.M.
Affiliation: Hostelling International-DJH
Regional office: Rheinland
Extras: breakfast, meals ($)

This redding, unremarkable building is another of those German hostels that's marvelously located but quite simple in its layout. Free breakfast is really the only major bonus, and the dorms and private rooms are as normal as you'll find anywhere else.

Ah, but the setting! You couldn't be any closer to the Rheinfels Castle—it's right over your head—so pay a few bucks for a ticket, buy a candle, and walk through the spooky-yet-dripping-with-medieval-atmo place. The other obvious thing to do here is grab a ferry and shuttle across the river to the famous Lorelei rocks.

How to get there:

By bus: Contact hostel for transit details.

By car: Contact hostel for directions.

By train: From Mainz take local train to St. Goar. From St. Goar Station walk down Oberstrasse to Schlossberg; continue to Bismarckweg on right.

Best bet for a bite:
Vielharmonie (in castle)

Insiders' tip:
Keutmann

What hostellers say:
"What a town!"

Gestalt:
Go-Goar

Hospitality:

Cleanliness:

Party index:

WORMS

Worms is world famous for Martin Luther's tacking of certain antichurch edicts up on a certain local church door—the act that touched off the Reformation—yet there's no Martin Luther museum, and you have to do some poking around to find out more about him, which struck us as a bit odd. But, hey—there's a tremendous wine party each late August, which is loads of fun if you can find a bunk here, and a summertime jazz fest, too.

JUGENDGÄSTEHAUS WORMS (WORMS GUEST HOUSE HOSTEL)

Dechaneigasse 1,

67547 Worms

Phone: 06241–25780

Fax: 06241–27394

E-mail: jh-worms@djh-info.de

Web site: www.djh-info.de

Rates: 28.20–37.70 DM (about $14–$19 US) per Hostelling International member

Credit cards: Yes

Beds: 114

Private/family rooms: Yes

Kitchen available: No

Season: Closed December 24–26
Office hours: 7:00 A.M.–11:30 P.M.
Curfew: 11:30 P.M.
Affiliation: Hostelling International-DJH
Regional office: Rheinland
Extras: Table tennis, piano, cafeteria ($)

This hostel's smack dab in the center of Worms (that's Voorms, not "worms," but you knew that, right?)—centrally located right near the city's best church, and mighty well equipped too.

Best bet for a bite:
Weinkeller

Insiders' tip:
Hagenbräu for beer

What hostellers say:
"Hotel rooms at hostel prices."

Gestalt:
Tough love

Hospitality:

Cleanliness:

Party index:

Rooms come in singles, doubles, quads, and six-bedded rooms. This is a great stop for any family, single traveler, couple, or businessperson, as all rooms come with their own private bathrooms and showers. There are five lounging areas, a cafeteria serving decent food, a game room, a piano for noodling on, and so forth. The tight-butt staff, though, sometimes interferes with the fun by clamping down on rules, such as the early door-closing at night.

How to get there:

By bus: Contact hostel for transit details.
By car: Take Highway A61 to Worms.
By train: Take train to Worms from Mainz or Ludwigshafen. From Worms Station walk 1 mile to hostel.

BURG-JUGENDHERBERGE JUGENDGÄSTEHAUS ALTLEININGEN

(Altleiningen Guest House Hostel)

Burgberg,

67317 Altleiningen

Phone: 06356–1580

Fax: 06356–6364
E-mail: jh-altleiningen @djh-info.de
Web site: www.djh-info.de
Rates: 24.50–29.50 DM per HI member (about $12–$15 US)
Beds: 160
Private/family rooms: Yes
Kitchen available: No
Season: Closed March 1; December 24–26
Affiliation: HI-DJH
Regional office: Rheinland
Extras: Cafeteria ($), table tennis, playground, wheelchair access

How to get there:

By bus/train: Take train to Grünstadt. From Grünstadt Station take bus to Altleiningen. Contact hostel for further transit details.
By car: Take Autobahn A6 to Wattenheim, following signs to hostel.

JUGENDHERBERGE BURG ALTENA

(Altena Hostel)

Fritz-Thomee-Strasse 80,

58762 Altena

Phone: 02352–23522

Fax: 02352–26330
E-mail: jh-burg.altena@djh-wl.de
Rates: 24.50–29.50 DM per HI member (about $12–$15 US)
Beds: 59
Private/family rooms: No
Kitchen available: No
Season: Closed December 20– January 3
Affiliation: HI-DJH
Regional office: Rheinland
Extras: Table tennis, parking, meals ($)

How to get there:

By bus: Contact hostel for transit details.
By car: Take Highway A45 to Lüdenscheid-Nord or Highway A46 to Iserlohn-Oestrich.
By train: From Altena Station walk ¾ mile to hostel.

JUGENDHERBERGE ARNSBERG

(Arnsberg Hostel)

Rumbecker Höhe 1,

59821 Arnsberg

Phone: 02931–10627

Fax: 02931–13589
E-mail: jh-arnsberg@djh-wl.de
Rates: 22–27 DM per HI member (about $11–$14 US)
Beds: 132
Private/family rooms: No

Kitchen available: No
Season: Closed December 18–
January 13
Affiliation: HI-DJH
Regional office: Rheinland
Extras: Grill, table tennis, park-
ing, meals ($)

How to get there:

By bus: Contact hostel for transit
details.
By car: Take Highway A44 from
Ruhrgebiet to Kassel, then continue from Werl to Arnsberg and
take Highway B7, exiting in the
direction of Meschede and
Warstein. Pass through
Oeventrop, turn left and go over
bridge.
By train: Contact hostel for transit
details.

JUGENDHERBERGE
BAD BERGZABERN

(Bad Bergzabern Hostel)
Altenbergweg,
76887 Bad Bergzabern
Phone: 06343–8383

Fax: 06343–5184
E-mail: jh-bad-bergzabern
@djh-info.de
Web site: www.djh-info.de
Rates: 22.80 DM per HI member
(about $11 US)
Beds: 140
Private/family rooms: Yes
Kitchen available: No
Season: Closed December 24–26
Affiliation: HI-DJH
Regional office: Rheinland
Extras: Table tennis, meals ($)

How to get there:

By bus: Contact hostel for transit
details.
By car: From north take Highway

A65, going from Landau-Süd to
Bad Bergzabern. From south
take Highway A65, going from
Kandel-Nord to Bad Bergzabern.
By train: Contact hostel for transit
details.

JUGENDHERBERGE
BAD BERLEBURG

(Bad Berleburg Hostel)
Goetheplatz 1,
57319 Bad Berleburg
Phone: 02751–7340

Fax: 02751–2076
E-mail: jh-bad.berleburg
@djh-wl.de
Rates: 24.50–29.50 DM per HI
member (about $12–$15 US)
Beds: 61
Private/family rooms: Yes
Kitchen available: No
Season: Closed December 1–
January 1
Affiliation: HI-DJH
Regional office: Rheinland
Extras: Table tennis, grill, meals
($), parking

How to get there:

By bus: Contact hostel for transit
details.
By car: From Köln take Highway
A4/A45 to Wenden, exiting in
the direction of Kreuztal, then
continue to Bad Berleburg. Or
from Frankfurt take Highway
B253 to Bad Berleburg.
By train: Contact hostel for transit
details.

KULTURSTUDIENPLATZ
JUGENDHERBERGE
BAD DRIBURG

(Bad Driburg Hostel)

Schirrmannweg 1,
33014 Bad Driburg
Phone: 05253–2570

Fax: 05253–3882
E-mail: jh-bad.driburg@djh-wl.de
Rates: 24.50–29.50 DM per HI member (about $12–$15 US)
Beds: 124
Private/family rooms: Yes
Kitchen available: No
Season: Closed December 15–January 15
Affiliation: HI-DJH
Regional office: Rheinland
Extras: Theater workshops, rink nearby, musical instruments, sports facilities, parking, meals ($)

How to get there:
By bus: Contact hostel for transit details.
By car: Take Highway A44/A33, exiting at signs for Büren. Or from Paderborn take Highway B64 to Bad Driburg. Or take Highway A44, exiting at signs for Diemelstadt/Bad Driburg.
By train: Take train to Bad Driburg. From Bad Driburg Station walk 1 mile to hostel.

JUGENDHERBERGE BAD EMS
(Bad Ems Hostel)
Alte Kemmenauer Strasse 41,
56130 Bad Ems
Phone: 02603–2680

Fax: 02603–50384
E-mail: jh-bad-ems@djh-info.de
Web site: www.djh-info.de
Rates: 26.90–32.90 DM per HI member (about $13–$16 US)
Beds: 120
Private/family rooms: Yes
Kitchen available: No
Season: Closed December 24–26
Affiliation: HI-DJH
Regional office: Rheinland
Extras: Cafeteria ($), kids' playroom, table tennis, soccer, volleyball, basketball, grill

How to get there:
By bus: Contact hostel for transit details.
By car: Take Highway A3 to Montabaur, then continue in the direction of Bad Ems. Or take Highway B260 to Bad Ems, between Limburg and Lahnstein.
By train: From Koblenz or Limburg, take train to Bad Ems and walk to hostel.

JUGENDHERBERGE BAD HONNEF
(Bad Honnef Hostel)
Selhofer Strasse 106,
53604 Bad Honnef
Phone: 02224–71300

Fax: 02224–79226
E-mail: Jugendherberge-Bad-Honnef @t-online.de
Rates: 22.50–30 DM per HI member (about $11–$15 US)
Beds: 210
Private/family rooms: Yes
Kitchen available: Yes
Season: Closed December 4–January 2
Affiliation: HI-DJH
Regional office: Rheinland
Extras: Programs, table tennis, meals ($), parking

How to get there:
By bus: Contact hostel for transit details.
By car: Take Autobahn from Köln or Frankfurt, exiting at signs for Bad Honnef-Linz.

By train: Take train to Bad
Honnef. From Bad Honnef
Station walk 1 mile to hostel.

JUGENDHERBERGE BAD KREUZNACH
(Bad Kreuznach Hostel)
Rheingrafenstrasse 53,

55543 Bad Kreuznach

Phone: 0671–62855

Fax: 0671–75351
E-mail: Jugendherberge-
Bad-Kreuznach@djh-info.de
Web site: www.djh-info.de
Rates: 28.20–37.70 DM per HI
member (about $14–$19 US)
Credit cards: Yes
Beds: 136
Private/family rooms: Yes
Kitchen available: No
Season: Closed December 24–26
Affiliation: HI-DJH
Regional office: Rheinland
Extras: Piano, cafeteria ($), fire-
place, table tennis, volleyball,
tennis, basketball, playground,
grill, wheelchair access
How to get there:
By bus: Contact hostel for transit
details.
By car: Take Highway A61 from
Koblenz or Ludwigshafen to Bad
Kreuznach. Follow signs to hos-
tel.
By train: Contact hostel for transit
details.

JUGENDHERBERGE BAD MARIENBERG
(Bad Marienberg Hostel)

Erlenweg 4,

56470 Bad Marienberg

Phone: 02661–5008

Fax: 02661–61898
E-mail: jh-bad-marienberg
@djh-info.de
Web site: www.djh-info.de
Rates: 20 DM per HI member
(about $10 US)
Beds: 122
Private/family rooms: Yes
Kitchen available: No
Season: Contact hostel for current
season
Affiliation: HI-DJH
Regional office: Rheinland
Extras: Meals ($)
How to get there:
By bus/train: Take train to
Erbach. From Erbach Station
take bus to Marienberg and
walk ½ mile to hostel.
By car: Take Highway A3 from
Dierdorf to Highway B414, con-
tinuing in in the direction of
Hachenburg. Or take A3 from
Montabaur, continuing along
Highway B255 in the direction
of Rennerod. Or take Highway
A45 from Haiger or Burbach.

JUGENDHERBERGE BAD MÜNSTEREIFEL
(Bad Münstereifel-Rodert Hostel)
Herbergsweg 1–5,

**53902 Bad Münstereifel-
Rodert**

Phone: 02253–7438

Fax: 02253–7483
Rates: 23.00–31.50 DM per HI
member (about $12–$16 US)

Beds: 164
Private/family rooms: Yes
Kitchen available: Yes
Season: Closed December 24–26
Affiliation: HI-DJH
Regional office: Rheinland
Extras: Programs, disco, mountain bike rentals, sports facilities nearby, meals ($), parking

How to get there:

By bus: Contact hostel for transit details.
By car: Take Highway A1 to Bad Münstereifel/Mechernich.
By train: Take train to Bad Münstereifel. From Bad Münstereifel Station walk 1 mile to hostel.

JUGENDHERBERGE BIELEFELD

(Bielefeld Hostel)
Oetzer Weg 25,
33605 Bielefeld
Phone: 0521–22227

Fax: 0521–25196
E-mail: jh-bielefeld@djh-wl.de
Rates: 23.40–28.40 DM per HI member (about $12–$14 US)
Beds: 164
Private/family rooms: Yes
Kitchen available: No
Season: Closed December 18–January 4
Affiliation: HI-DJH
Regional office: Rheinland
Extras: Table tennis, piano, grill, sports facilities, parking, meals ($)

How to get there:

By bus/train: Take S-Bahn line S2 to Sieker Station, final stop. From Sieker Station take #118

bus to Waldkrug, then walk down Osningstrasse and Oetzer Weg to hostel.
By car: Take Highway A2 through Sennestadt, then Highway B68 in the direction of Bielefeld-Ost. Or take Highway A2 to Bielefeld, then Highway B66 in the direction of the Innenstadt to Sieker, then follow signs Osningstrasse and Tiroler Weg.

JUGENDHERBERGE BURG BLANKENHEIM

(Blankenheim Hostel)
Burg 1,
53945 Blankenheim
Phone: 02449–95090

Fax: 02449–950–910
E-mail: Jugendherberge-BurgBlankenheim@t-online.de
Rates: 23.50– 31.00 DM per HI member (about $12–$16 US)
Beds: 158
Private/family rooms: Yes
Kitchen available: No
Season: Closed December 23–26
Affiliation: HI-DJH
Regional office: Rheinland
Extras: Programs, sports facilities, volleyball, table tennis, bike rentals, fireplace, bistro ($), parking

How to get there:

By bus/train: Take train to Blankenheim-Wald Station, then take bus to hostel. Contact hostel for further transit details.
By car: Take Autobahn A1 from Köln or Trier, exiting at signs for Blankenheim.

SPORT-JUGENDHERBERGE BLOMBERG

(Blomberg Hostel)

Ulmenallee 15,

32825 Blomberg

Phone: 05235–7255

Fax: 05235–2130

E-mail: jh-blomberg@djh-wl.de

Rates: 24.50–29.50 DM per HI member (about $12–$15 US)

Beds: 163

Private/family rooms: No

Kitchen available: No

Affiliation: HI-DJH

Regional office: Rheinland

Extras: Programs, sports facilities, parking, meals ($)

How to get there:

By bus/train: Take train to Schieder or Detmold, then take bus to Blomberg. Contact hostel for further transit details.

By car: From northeast take Highway B1 to exit for Rinteln, then continue through Bielefeld, Sennestadt, and Paderborn.

JUGENDHERBERGE BOLLENDORF

(Bollendorf Hostel)

Auf der Ritschlay 1,

54669 Bollendorf

Phone: 06526–200

Fax: 06526–1204

E-mail: jh-bollendorf@djh-info.de

Web site: www.djh-info.de

Rates: 26.90–32.90 DM per HI member (about $14–$16 US)

Beds: 156

Private/family rooms: Yes

Kitchen available: No

Season: Closed December 24–26

Affiliation: HI-DJH

Regional office: Rheinland

Extras: Table tennis, pool table, basketball, grill, soccer, cafeteria ($)

How to get there:

By bus:/train Take train to Trier. From Trier Station take bus to Bollendorf.

By car: Take Highway B257 from Bitburg or Highway B51 from Trier to Bollendorf.

JUGENDHERBERGE GLÖRSEE

(Breckerfeld Hostel)

58339 Breckerfeld

Phone: 02338–434

Fax: 02338–3674

E-mail: jh-gloersee@djh-wl.de

Rates: 23.40–28.40 DM per HI member (about $12–$14 US)

Beds: 124

Private/family rooms: No

Kitchen available: No

Season: Closed December 18–26

Affiliation: HI-DJH

Regional office: Rheinland

Extras: Table tennis, sports facilities, parking, meals ($)

How to get there:

By bus/train: Take train to Hagen. From Hagen Station take #84 bus to Breckerfeld Branten stop. Or from Dahlerbrück Station walk 2 ½ miles to hostel. Contact hostel for further transit details.

By car: Take Autobahn in the direction of Beckerfeld, then go in the direction of Halver to Branten; follow signs to hostel.

EURO-UMWELTSTUDIENPLATZ BRILON

(Brilon Hostel)

Hölsterloh 3,

59929 Brilon

Phone: 02961–2281

Fax: 02961–51731
E-mail: jh-brilon@djh-wl.de
Rates: 24.50–29.50 DM per HI member (about $12–$15 US)
Beds: 165
Private/family rooms: No
Kitchen available: No
Season: Closed December 15– January 15
Affiliation: HI-DJH
Regional office: Rheinland
Extras: Volleyball, table tennis, meals ($), parking

How to get there:

By bus/train: Take train to Brilon-Wald. From Brilon-Wald Station take #482 bus to hostel.
By car: Take Highway A44 to Kreuz Erwitte-Anröchte exit, or exit at Kreuz Wünnenberg-Haaren, then head in the direction of Brilon.

JUGENDHERBERGE BRÜGGEN

(Brüggen Hostel)

Auf dem Eggenberg 1,

41379 Brüggen

Phone: 02163–5161

Fax: 02163–59967
Rates: 21.60–30.00 DM per HI member (about $11–$15 US)
Beds: 134
Private/family rooms: Yes
Kitchen available: Yes
Season: Closed February 1–28; December 23–26
Affiliation: HI-DJH
Regional office: Rheinland
Extras: Programs, table tennis, TV, VCR, grill, piano, bike rentals, sports facilities, disco, parking, meals ($)

How to get there:

By bus/train: Take train to Mönchengladbach. From Mönchengladbach Station take #83-012 bus to hostel. Or take train to Dülken, then take #074 bus to hostel. Or take train to Kaldenkirchen, then take #074 bus to hostel.
By car: Take Highway A6, exiting at signs for Kaldenkirchen-Süd, then continue to Brüggen.

JUGENDHERBERGE DAHN

(Dahn Hostel)

Am Wachtfelsen 1,

66994 Dahn

Phone: 06391–1769

Fax: 06391–5122
E-mail: Jugendherberge-Dahn @djh-info.de
Web site: www.djh-info.de
Rates: 23.80 DM per HI member (about $12 US)
Beds: 108
Private/family rooms: Yes
Kitchen available: No
Season: Closed December 24–26
Affiliation: HI-DJH
Regional office: Rheinland
Extras: Table tennis, basketball, playground, grill, cafeteria ($)
Must be under age twenty-seven to stay

How to get there:

By bus/train: Take train from Bingen or Kaiserslautern to Pirmasens, or from Mannheim or Saarbrücken to Hinterweidenthal. From Pirmasens or Hinterweidenthal take bus to Dahn and walk to hostel.

By car: Take Highway B10 to Kandel, then take Highway B427 to Dahn.

JUGENDHERBERGE DETMOLD

(Detmold Hostel)

Schirrmannstrasse 49,

32756 Detmold

Phone: 05231–24739

Fax: 05231–28927
E-mail: jh-detmold@djh-wl.de
Rates: 24.50–29.50 DM per HI member (about $12–$15 US)
Beds: 126
Private/family rooms: Yes
Kitchen available: No
Season: Closed December 14– January 15
Affiliation: HI-DJH
Regional office: Rheinland
Extras: Volleyball, table tennis, TV, VCR, grill, meals ($), parking

How to get there:

By bus: Contact hostel for transit route.

By car: Take Highway A2 to Autobahn at Bielefeld, then continue to Highway A33 in the direction of Paderborn. Or contact hostel for directions.

By train: Take train to Detmold Station, then walk 1½ miles to hostel.

JUGENDHERBERGE SCHLOSS DIEZ

(Diez Hostel)

Schlossberg,

65582 Diez

Phone: 06432–2481

Fax: 06432–4504
E-mail: jh-diez@djh-info.de
Web site: www.djh-info.de
Rates: 22.80 DM per HI member (about $11 US)
Beds: 91
Private/family rooms: Yes
Kitchen available: No
Season: Closed December 24–26
Affiliation: HI-DJH
Regional office: Rheinland
Extras: Table tennis, grill, sports facilities, playground, meals ($)
Must be under age twenty-seven to stay

How to get there:

By bus: Contact hostel for transit details.

By car: Take Highway A3 from Köln or Frankfurt to Diez. Or take Highway B54 from Montabaur or Siegen.

By train: Direct trains from Koblenz or Limburg to Diez. Contact hostel for further transit details.

JUGENDHERBERGE ZUR SAARSCHLEIFE/ JUGENDGÄSTEHAUS DREISBACH

(Dreisbach Guest House Hostel)

Herbergstrasse 1,

66693 Mettlach-Dreisbach

Phone: 06868–270

Fax: 06868–556

E-mail: jh-dreisbach@djh-info.de
Web site: www.djh-info.de
Rates: 28.20–37.70 DM per HI
member (about $14–$19 US)
Beds: 136
Private/family rooms: No
Kitchen available: No
Season: Contact hostel for current
season
Affiliation: HI-DJH
Regional office: Rheinland-
Pfalz–Saarland
Extras: Playground, grill, meeting
rooms, cafeteria ($)

How to get there:

By bus:/train Take train to Mettlach
or Merzig, then walk to bus stop
and take bus to hostel. Contact
hostel for further details.
By car: Take Highway B51 to
Besseringen and Schwemlingen-
Dreisbach or Highway B406/E42
to Schwemlingen and Dreisbach.

JUGENDHERBERGE DORSTEN-WULFEN

(Dorsten Hostel)
Im Schöning 83,
46286 Dorsten
Phone: 02369–8722

Fax: 02369–23867
E-mail: jh-dorsten@djh-wl.de
Rates: 23.40–28.40 DM per HI
member (about $12–$14 US)
Beds: 104
Private/family rooms: Yes
Kitchen available: No
Season: Closed December 21–
January 7
Affiliation: HI-DJH
Regional office: Rheinland
Extras: Piano, table tennis, grill,
volleyball, parking, meals ($)

How to get there:

By bus: Contact hostel for transit
details.
By car: Take Highway A43 or
Highway A31 to Highway B58.
By train: Take train to Deuten or
Wulfen Stations, then walk 2
mile to hostel. Or contact hostel
for further transit details.

JUGENDHERBERGE DUISBURG

(Duisburg Hostel)
Kalkweg 148 E,
47279 Duisburg
Phone: 0203–724–164

Fax: 0203–720–834
E-mail: jh.duisburg@usa.net
Rates: 24.50–32 DM per HI
member (about $12–$16 US)
Beds: 134
Private/family rooms: Yes
Kitchen available: No
Season: Closed December 23–
January 1
Affiliation: HI-DJH
Regional office: Rheinland
Extras: Programs, table tennis,
disco, parking, laundry, meals
($)

How to get there:

By bus/train: Take train to
Duisburg. From Duisburg
Station take #934 or #944 bus
or S-Bahn to Schlenk stop. Or
take #943 bus or S-Bahn to
Buchholz stop.
By car: Take Highway A3, exiting
at signs for Duisburg-Wedau, or
A59, exiting at signs for Wan-
heimerort. Follow signs to Städt-
Klinik.

JUGENDHERBERGE ESSEN-WERDEN

(Essen Hostel)

Pastoratsberg 2,

45239 Essen

Phone: 0201–491–163

Fax: 0201–492–505
Rates: 24–32 DM per HI member (about $12–$16 US)
Beds: 130
Private/family rooms: Yes
Kitchen available: No
Season: Closed December 23–January 6
Affiliation: HI-DJH
Regional office: Rheinland
Extras: Programs, table tennis, sports facilities, TV, VCR, grill, piano, meeting room, parking, meals ($)

How to get there:

By bus/train: From Essen or Köln Station, take S-Bahn line S6 to Essen-Werden Station, then take #190 bus in the direction of Ruhrlandklinik to hostel.
By car: Take Highway A52, exiting at signs for Essen-Rüttenscheid or Highway A40 to exit at Essen-Stadtmitte. Continue in the direction of Wuppertal-Solingen on Highway B224.

JUGENDHERBERGE FINNENTROP-BAMENOHL

(Finnentrop-Bamenohl Hostel)

Herbergsweg 1,

57413 Finnentrop-Bamenohl

Phone: 02721–7293

Fax: 02721–5486
Rates: 24.50–29.50 DM per HI member (about $12–$15 US)
Beds: 30
Private/family rooms: No
Kitchen available: No
Season: Closed December 24–26
Affiliation: HI-DJH
Regional office: Rheinland
Extras: Piano, guitar, playground, table tennis, parking, meals ($)

How to get there:

By bus: Contact hostel for transit details.
By car: Take Highway A45 to Olpe or Meinerzhagen, then head through Attendorn in the direction of Finnentrop-Bamenohl. Use Highway B236 and Killeschlader Weg in the direction of Rathaus to Herbergsweg.
By train: Take train to Finnentrop Station. Contact hostel for further transit details.

JUGENDHERBERGE FINNENTROP-HEGGEN

(Finnentrop-Heggen Hostel)

Ahauser Strasse 22–24,

57405 Finnentrop

Phone: 02721–50345

Fax: 02721–79460
E-mail: jh-finnentrop.heggen @djh-wl.de
Rates: 24.50–29.50 DM per HI member (about $12–$15 US)
Beds: 223
Private/family rooms: Yes
Kitchen available: No
Affiliation: HI-DJH
Regional office: Rheinland
Extras: Piano, table tennis, volleyball, disco, meals ($), parking, wheelchair access

How to get there:

By bus: Contact hostel for transit details.

By car: Take Highway A45, exiting for Olpe or Meinerzhagen. Go down Landstrasse through Attendorn.

By train: Take train to Finnentrop-Heggen; contact hostel for further transit details.

JUGENDHERBERGE GEROLSTEIN

(Gerolstein Hostel)

Zur Büschkapelle 1,

54568 Gerolstein

Phone: 06591–4745

Fax: 06591–7243
Rates: 22.80 DM per HI member (about $11 US)
Beds: 180
Private/family rooms: Yes
Kitchen available: No
Season: Closed December 24–26
Affiliation: HI-DJH
Regional office: Rheinland
Extras: Sports facilities nearby, meals ($), wheelchair access
Must be under age twenty-seven to stay

How to get there:

By bus/train: Direct trains run from Köln, Trier, and Saarbrücken to Gerolstein. From Gerolstein Station walk ¾ mile to hostel. Or take bus or taxi.

By car: Take highway A 48, exiting at signs for Ulmen. Or from the direction of Köln, take A1 to Bliesheimer Kreuz and continue to Euskirchen and Gerolstein.

JUGENDGÄSTEHAUS GÜTERSLOH

(Gütersloh Hostel)

Wiesenstrasse 40,

33330 Gütersloh

Phone: 05241–822–181

Fax: 05241–822–184
E-mail: 05241532704-1 @t-online.de
Web site: members.aol.com/jghgt/welcome.html
Rates: 23.00–35.50 DM per HI member (about $12–$18 US)
Beds: 67
Private/family rooms: Yes
Kitchen available: No
Season: Closed December 11– January 7
Affiliation: HI-DJH
Regional office: Rheinland
Extras: Tennis, table tennis, squash, fitness programs, sports facilities, parking, wheelchair access, meals ($)

How to get there:

By bus/train: Take train to Gütersloh. From Gütersloh Station take #41 bus to Hallenbad stop and walk to hostel.

By car: Take Highway A2 from Rheda or Wiedenbrück to Gütersloh-Süd, then continue in the direction of Bielefeld.

JUGENDHERBERGE HAGEN

(Hagen Hostel)

Eppenhauser Strasse 65 a,

58093 Hagen

Phone: 02331–50254

Fax: 02331–588–576
E-mail: jh-hagen@djh-wl.de
Rates: 23.40–28.40 DM per HI
member (about $12–$14 US)
Beds: 131
Private/family rooms: Yes
Kitchen available: No
Affiliation: HI-DJH
Regional office: Rheinland
Extras: Table tennis, basketball,
volleyball, soccer, foosball, grill,
parking, meals ($)

How to get there:

By bus/train: Take train to Hagen.
From Hagen Station take #522 or
#523 bus to Emster Strasse stop
and walk to hostel.
By car: Take Highway A45 to
Hagener Kreuz, then take
Highway A46 to Hagen
Emst/Feithstrasse Or contact hostel for directions.

JUGENDHERBERGE HALTERN

(Haltern/Stausee Hostel)
Stockwieser Damm 255,
45721 Haltern/Stausee
Phone: 02364–2258

Fax: 02364–169–604
E-mail: jh-haltern@djh-wl.de
Rates: 23.40–28.40 DM per HI
member (about $12–$14 US)
Beds: 138
Private/family rooms: Yes
Kitchen available: No
Season: Closed December 24–26
Affiliation: HI-DJH
Regional office: Rheinland
Extras: Table tennis, volleyball,
parking, meals ($)

How to get there:

By bus/train: Take train to
Haltern. From Haltern Station
take #272 bus toward Hullern
to Haus Niemen stop.
By car: From the south take
Highway A43 to exit for Marl-
Nord; continue to Haltern-
Flaesheim and head in the
direction of Sythen. From the
north take Highway A43 and
exit for Haltern-Lavesum.

JUGENDHERBERGE HELLENTHAL

(Hellenthal Hostel)
Studienplatz für
Erlebnispädagogik
Platiss 3,
53940 Hellenthal
Phone: 02482–2238 or
02482–911–582

Fax: 02482–2557
E-mail: Jugendherberge-
Hellenthal @t-online.de
Rates: 22.50–30.00 DM per HI
member (about $11–$15 US)
Beds: 161
Private/family rooms: Yes
Kitchen available: Yes
Season: Closed December 27–
January 1
Affiliation: HI-DJH
Regional office: Rheinland
Extras: Programs, sports camps,
sports facilities, family apart-
ment, laundry, wheelchair
access, parking, meals ($)

How to get there:

By bus/train: Take train to Kall.
From Kall Station take bus to
Hellenthal and walk 1½ miles to
hostel.
By car: Take Autobahn A1 to exit
for Euskirchen-Wisskirchen, then

take Highway B266 to Gemünd
and B265 to Hellenthal.

JUGENDHERBERGE HERMESKEIL
(Hermeskeil Hostel)
**Adolf-Kolping-Strasse 4,
54411 Hermeskeil
Phone: 06503–3097**

Fax: 06503–6146
E-mail: jh-hermeskeil@djh-info.de
Web site: www.djh-info.de
Rates: 26.90–32.90 DM per HI member (about $13–$16 US)
Beds: 111
Private/family rooms: Yes
Kitchen available: No
Season: Closed December 24–26
Affiliation: HI-DJH
Regional office: Rheinland
Extras: Grounds, volleyball, table tennis, chess set
How to get there:
By bus/train: Take train to Trier or Türkismühle (weekdays only). From Trier or Türkismühle Station take bus to Hermeskeil and walk to hostel. Contact hostel for further transit details.
By car: Take Highway A1 from Trier or Saarbrücken to Hermeskeil, at junction of B327 and B52.

JUGENDHERBERGE HILCHENBACH
(Hilchenbach Hostel)
**Wilhelm-Münker-Strasse 9,
57271 Hilchenbach
Phone: 02733–4396**

Fax: 02733–8085
E-mail: jh-hilchenbach@djh-wl.de
Rates: 23.40–28.40 DM per HI member (about $12–$14 US)
Beds: 86
Private/family rooms: Yes
Kitchen available: No
Season: Closed January 1–31
Affiliation: HI-DJH
Regional office: Rheinland
Extras: Table tennis, sports facilities, parking, meals ($)
How to get there:
By bus: Contact hostel for transit details.
By car: Take Highway A45 to exit for Wenden-Kreuztal, or take Highway A4 to exit for Wenden. Continue in the direction of Kreuztal Hilchenbach, or use Highway B508.
By train: Direct trains run from Köln, Siegen, and Kreuztal to Hilchenbach. Contact hostel for further transit details.

JUGENDHERBERGE HOMBURG
(Homburg Hostel)
**Sickinger Strasse 12,
66424 Homburg
Phone: 06841–3679**

Fax: 06841–120–220
E-mail: jh-homburg@djh-info.de
Web site: www.djh-info.de
Rates: 21.30 DM per HI member (about $11 US)
Beds: 76
Private/family rooms: Yes
Kitchen available: No
Season: Closed December 24–26
Affiliation: HI-DJH
Regional office: Rheinland

Jugendherberg Homburg
Homburg Hostel • Homburg

(photo courtesy of Deutsches Jugendherbergswerk)

Extras: Table tennis, grill, sports fields, meals ($)

Must by under age twenty-seven to stay

How to get there:

By bus/train: Direct trains run from Mannheim and Saarbrücken. From Homburg Station take bus to hostel. Contact hostel for further details.

By car: Take Highway A6 from Bexbach to Homburg to or Bruchdorf to Homburg.

JUGENDHERBERGE HORN-BAD MEINBERG
(Horn-Bad Meinberg Hostel)

Jahnstrasse 36,

32805 Horn-Bad Meinberg

Phone: 05234–2534

Fax: 05234–69199

E-mail: jh-horn.bad.meinberg @djh-wl.de

Rates: 23.40– 28.40 DM per HI member (about $12–$14 US)

Beds: 122

Private/family rooms: No

Kitchen available: No

Season: Closed December 27– January 19

Affiliation: HI-DJH

Regional office: Rheinland

Extras: Programs, e-mail, table tennis, foosball, playground, grill, parking, meals ($)

How to get there:

By bus: Contact hostel for transit details.

By car: Take Highway A33, exiting at signs for Paderborn-Elsen, then take Highway B1 to Horn.

By train: Take train to Horn. From Horn Station walk 2 miles to hostel.

EURO-UMWELTSTUDIENPLATZ HÖXTER
(Höxter Hostel)

An der Wilhelmshöhe 59,

37671 Höxter

Phone: 05271–2233

Fax: 05271–1237
E-mail: jh-hoexter@djh-wl.de
Rates: 24.50–29.50 DM per HI
   member (about $12–$15 US)
Beds: 130
Private/family rooms: No
Kitchen available: No
Season: Closed December 23–
   January 5
Affiliation: HI-DJH
Regional office: Rheinland
Extras: Water sports nearby, park-
   ing, meals ($)

How to get there:
By bus: Contact hostel for transit
   details.
By car: Take Highway B64, B83,
   or B239 to Höxter.
By train: Take train to Höxter
   Rathaus Station; contact hostel
   for further transit details.

JUGENDHERBERGE KEVELAER
(Kevelaer Hostel)

Am Michelsweg 11,

47626 Kevelaer

Phone: 02832–8267

Fax: 02832–899–432
Rates: 22–29 DM per HI member
   (about $11–$15 US)
Beds: 130
Private/family rooms: Yes
Kitchen available: Yes
Season: Closed December 24–26

Affiliation: HI-DJH
Regional office: Rheinland
Extras: Programs, table tennis,
   sports facilities, basketball, volleyball, TV, VCR, parking, meals
   ($)

How to get there:
By bus: Contact hostel for transit
   details.
By car: Take Highway A57 from
   Kölnor Nijmwegen, exiting for
   Sonsbeck-Winnekendonk.
By train: Take train to Kevelaer,
   then walk 1 mile to hostel.

JUGENDHERBERGE FREUSBURG
(Kirchen-Freusburg Hostel)

Burgstrasse 46,

57548 Kirchen-Freusburg

Phone: 02741–61094

Fax: 02741–63135
E-mail: jh-freusburg@djh-wl.de
Rates: 24.50–29.50 DM per HI
   member (about $12–$15 US)
Beds: 219
Private/family rooms: Yes
Kitchen available: No
Affiliation: HI-DJH
Regional office: Rheinland
Extras: Programs, piano, volley-
   ball, basketball, table tennis,
   parking, meals ($)

How to get there:
By bus: Contact hostel for further
   transit details.
By car: Take Highway A45, exiting
   at signs for Freudenberg and
   going in the direction of Betzdorf
   or exiting for Siegen and taking
   Highway B62.
By train: Take train to Freusberg-
   Siedlung or Kirchen. Contact hostel for further transit details.

JUGENDHERBERGE OBERHUNDEM

(Kirchhundem Hostel)

Wilhelm-Münker-Weg 1,

57399 Kirchhundem

Phone: 02723–72640

Fax: 02723–73597
E-mail: jh-oberhundem@djh-wl.de
Rates: 23.40–28.40 DM per HI
member (about $12–$14 US)
Beds: 106
Private/family rooms: No
Kitchen available: No
Season: Closed December 15–
January 15
Affiliation: HI-DJH
Regional office: Rheinland
Extras: Parks nearby, parking,
meals ($)

How to get there:

By bus/train: Take train to
Lennestadt-Althundem. From
Lennestadt-Althundem Station
take bus to Oberhundem.
By car: Take Highway A45 from
Olpe or Lennestadt to B55 to
Lennestadt, heading in the
direction of Kirchhundem-
Oberhundem.

JUGENDHERBERGE KLEVE-MATERBORN

(Kleve Hostel)

St. Annaberg 2,

47533 Kleve

Phone: 02821–23671

Fax: 02821–24778
Rates: 22–29 DM per HI member
(about $11–$15 US)
Beds: 106
Private/family rooms: Yes

Kitchen available: No
Season: Closed December 24–26
Affiliation: HI-DJH
Regional office: Rheinland
Extras: Programs, table tennis,
piano, volleyball, basketball, TV,
VCR, parking, meals ($)

How to get there:

By bus/train: Take train to Kleve.
From Kleve Station take #57
bus to hostel.
By car: Take Highway A3, exiting
at signs for Emmerich-Kleve or
Highway A57, exiting at signs
for Kleve.

JUGENDHERBERGE BURG BILSTEIN

(Lennestadt Hostel)

Von-Gevore-Weg 10,

57368 Lennestadt

Phone: 02721–81217

Fax: 02721–83016
E-mail: jh-burg,bilstein@djh-wl.de
Rates: 24.50–29.50 DM per HI
member (about $12–$15 US)
Beds: 227
Private/family rooms: Yes
Kitchen available: No
Season: Closed December 2–
January 2
Affiliation: HI-DJH
Regional office: Rheinland
Extras: Fireplace, music room,
instruments, piano, basketball,
skiing nearby, sports facilities,
parking, meals ($)

How to get there:

By bus: Contact hostel for transit
details.
By car: Take Highway A45 from
Olpe to Lennestadt, or take
Highway B55 in the direction of
Lennestadt.

By train: Take train to Lennestadt-Altenhundem Station, or contact hostel for further transit details.

JUGENDHERBERGE LINDLAR – UMWELTSTUDIENPLATZ (Lindlar Hostel)

Jugendherberge 30,

51789 Lindlar

Phone: 02266–5264

Fax: 02266–45517
E-mail: jugendherberge@lindlar.de
Web site: www.jugendherberge-lindlar.de
Rates: 23.50–31 DM per HI member (about $12–$16 US)
Beds: 170
Private/family rooms: Yes
Kitchen available: No
Season: Closed December 24–26
Affiliation: HI-DJH
Regional office: Rheinland
Extras: Programs, table tennis, TV, grill, movies, parking, meals ($)

How to get there:

By bus/train: Take train to Engelskirchen. From Engelskirchen Station take #332 bus or another bus from Wipperfürth, Gummersbach, or Köln. Contact hostel for further transit details.
By car: Take Highway A4 from Köln or Olpe, exiting for Lindlar or Engelskirchen.

NATURFREUNDEHAUS "CARL SCHRECK" LÖHNE-GOHFELD (Löhne Hostel)

In den Tannen 63,

32584 Löhne

Phone: 05731–81012

Fax: 05731–81031
Rates: 18.50– 27.00 DM per HI member (about $9.00–$14.00 US)
Beds: 84
Private/family rooms: Yes
Kitchen available: No
Season: Closed December 24–26
Affiliation: HI-DJH
Regional office: Rheinland
Extras: Sauna, piano, music room, parking, wheelchair access, meals ($)

How to get there:

By bus/train: Take train to Bad Oeynhausen. From Bad Oeynhausen Station take #406 or #429 bus to Hartsiekerweg stop and walk to hostel.
By car: Take Highway A2, exiting at signs for Löhne, then continuing in the direction of Gohfeld. Or take Highway A30, exiting at signs for Gohfeld.

JUGENDHERBERGE CAPPENBERGER SEE (Lünen Hostel)

Richard-Schirrmann-Weg 7,

44534 Lünen

Phone: 02306–53546

Fax: 02306–73000
E-mail: jh-cappenberger.see @djh-wl.de
Rates: 22–27 DM per HI member (about $11–$14 US)
Beds: 122
Private/family rooms: Yes
Kitchen available: No

Season: Closed December 23–
January 14
Affiliation: HI-DJH
Regional office: Rheinland
Extras: Volleyball, basketball,
table tennis, grill, parking,
meals ($)

How to get there:

By bus/train: Take train to Lünen.
From Lünen Station take R11
bus to Cappenberger See.
By car: Take Highway A2 from
Dortmund northeast to Lünen-
Cappenberg, or take Highway
A1 from Werne, Bockum, and
Hövel to Lünen.

VULKANEIFEL-JUGENDHERBERGE / JUGENDGÄSTEHAUS MANDERSCHEID

(Manderscheid Guest House
Hostel)

**Mosenbergstrasse 17,
54531 Manderscheid**

Phone: 06572–557

Fax: 06572–4759
E-mail: jh-manderscheid@djh-
info.de
Web site: www.djh-info.de
Rates: 28.20–37.70 DM per HI
member (about $14–$19 US)
Beds: 105
Private/family rooms: Yes
Kitchen available: No
Season: Closed December 24–26
Affiliation: HI-DJH
Regional office: Rheinland
Extras: Grounds, table tennis,
grill, cafeteria ($)

How to get there:

By bus/train: Take train to Wittlich,
then take bus to Manderscheid.

Or contact hostel for transit
details.
By car: Take Highway A48 Koblenz
or Trier to Manderscheid; drive
through town and go in the direction of Grosslittgen.

JUGENDHERBERGE MAYEN

(Mayen Hostel)

**Am Knüppchen 5,
56727 Mayen**

Phone: 02651–2355

Fax: 02651–78378
E-mail: jh-mayen@djh-info.de
Web site: www.jugendherberge-
mayen.de
Rates: 22.80 DM per HI member
(about $11 US)
Beds: 130
Private/family rooms: Yes
Kitchen available: No
Season: Closed December 24–26
Affiliation: HI-DJH
Regional office: Rheinland
Extras: Piano, table tennis, bolz-
platz (sports field), grill, cafete-
ria ($)
**Must be under age twenty-seven
to stay**

How to get there:

By bus/train: Take train to
Andernach or Koblenz. Then take
bus to Mayen and walk ½ mile to
hostel.
By car: Take Highway A48 from
Koblenz or Trier or Highway A61
to Highway B258 to Mayen.

JUGENDHERBERGE MEINERZHAGEN

(Meinerzhagen Hostel)

Bergstrasse 1,
58540 Meinerzhagen
Phone: 02354–2280

Fax: 02354–14341
E-mail: jh-meinerzhagen @djh-wl.de
Rates: 24.50–29.50 DM per HI member (about $12–$15 US)
Beds: 150
Private/family rooms: No
Kitchen available: No
Season: Closed November 1–30
Affiliation: HI-DJH
Regional office: Rheinland
Extras: Programs, grounds, table tennis, basketball, volleyball, parking, meals ($), wheelchair access

How to get there:
By bus/train: Take train to Brügge. From Brügge Station take #58 bus to Meinerzhagen; get off at Stadion stop and walk to hostel.
By car: Take Highway A45 to Meinerzhagen, following signs in the direction of Stadtmitte-Gerichtstrasse-Bergstrasse.

JUGENDHERBERGE MERZALBEN
(Merzalben Hostel)
Tannenstrasse 20,
66978 Merzalben
Phone: 06395–6271

Fax: 06395–7089
E-mail: jh-merzalben@djh-info.de
Web site: www.djh-info.de
Rates: 21.30 DM per HI member (about $11 US)
Beds: 103
Private/family rooms: No
Kitchen available: No
Season: Closed December 24–26
Affiliation: HI-DJH

Regional office: Rheinland
Extras: Table tennis, volleyball, basketball, grill, meals ($)
Must be under age twenty-seven to stay

How to get there:
By bus/train: Take train to München-weiler, Pirmasens, or Rodalben, then take bus to Merzalben. Contact hostel for further details.
By car: Take Highway B10 from Karlsruhe or Saarbrücken or Highway B270 from Kaierslautern or Hochspeyer. Or take Highway A62 via Thaleischweiler.

JUGENDHERBERGE "HAUS DORTMUND"
(Meschede Hostel)
Warsteiner Strasse,
59872 Meschede
Phone: 0291–6666

Fax: 0291–1589
Rates: 23.40–28.40 DM per HI member (about $12–$14 US)
Beds: 100
Private/family rooms: Yes
Kitchen available: No
Season: Closed December 24–26
Affiliation: HI-DJH
Regional office: Rheinland
Extras: Foosball, table tennis, volleyball, basketball, meals ($), parking

How to get there:
By bus: Contact hostel for transit details.
By car: Take Autobahn from Dortmund or Kassel to Arnsberg, continuing in the direction of Meschede to Meschede; then take Highway B55 in the direction of

Wartstein. Or take Highway A44
to Erwitte/Anröchte, then Highway
B55 through Belecke and
Warstein to Meschede.

By train: Contact hostel for transit
details.

JUGENDHERBERGE MÖHNESEE
(Möhnesee Hostel)

Südufer 20,

59519 Möhnesee-Körbecke

Phone: 02924–305

Fax: 02924–2788
E-mail: jh-moehnesee@djh-wl.de
Rates: 23.40–28.40 DM per HI
member (about $12–$14 US)
Beds: 203
Private/family rooms: Yes
Kitchen available: No
Season: Closed December 24–26
Affiliation: HI-DJH
Regional office: Rheinland
Extras: Sports facilities, parking,
meals ($)

How to get there:

By bus/train: Take train to Soest.
From Soest Station take bus to
Körbecke and get off at
Jugendherberge (hostel) stop.
Note: Bus runs weekdays only.
By car: Take Highway A44 to Soest
or Soest-Ost, following signs in
the direction of Möhnesee.

UMWELTSTUDIENPLATZ MÖNCHENGLADBACH
(Mönchengladbach Hostel)

Brahmsstrasse 156,

41169 Mönchengladbach

Phone: 02161–560–900

Fax: 02161–556–464
Rates: 26–31 DM per HI member
(about $13–$16 US)
Beds: 131
Private/family rooms: No
Kitchen available: No
Season: Closed December 24–26
Affiliation: HI-DJH
Regional office: Rheinland
Extras: Table tennis, TV, VCR,
grill, sports facilities, meals ($)

How to get there:

By bus/train: Take train to
Mönchengladbach. From
Mönchengladbach Station take
#13 or #23 bus to Hardter
Markt and walk ¾ mile to hostel.
By car: Take Autobahn to
Mönchengladbach-Roermond,
exiting at signs for Hardt, then
take Highway B230 to Hardt.

JUGENDHERBERGE MONSCHAU-HARGARD
(Monschau Hargard Hostel)

Hargardsgasse 5,

52156 Monschau

Phone: 02472–2180

Fax: 02472–4527
E-mail: jh-monschau-hargard
@t-online.de
Rates: 24–31 DM per HI member
(about $12–$16 US)
Beds: 148
Private/family rooms: No
Kitchen available: No
Season: Closed December
4–January 1
Affiliation: HI-DJH
Regional office: Rheinland
Extras: Programs, grounds, grill,
sports facilities, parking, meals
($)

How to get there:

By bus/train: Take train to
Aachen. From Aachen take
Aachen-Monschau bus to
Hargard stop and walk to hostel.

By car: Take Highway A44 to
Aachen-Lichtenbusch, then take
Highway B258 in the direction
of Monschau.

JUGENDHERBERGE BURG MONSCHAU
(Burg Monschau Hostel)
Auf dem Schloss 4,
52156 Monschau
Phone: 02472–2314

Fax: 02472–4391
Rates: 21.60–27.80 DM per HI
member (about $11–$14 US)
Beds: 96
Private/family rooms: No
Kitchen available: No
Season: Closed December 24–26
Affiliation: HI-DJH
Regional office: Rheinland
Extras: Table tennis, TV, VCR,
grill, grounds, meals ($)

How to get there:

By bus/train: Take train to
Aachen. From Aachen Station
take bus to Monschau and walk
¼ mile to hostel.

By car: Take Highway A44, exit-
ing at signs for Aachen-
Lichtenbusch, then take
Highway B258 toward
Monschau.

JUGENDHERBERGE MONTABAUR
(Montabaur Hostel)

Richard-Schirrmann-Strasse,
56410 Montabaur
Phone: 02602–5121

Fax: 02602–180–176
E-mail: jh-montabaur@djh-info.de
Web site: www.djh-info.de
Rates: 23.80 DM per HI member
(about $12 US)
Beds: 136
Private/family rooms: Yes
Kitchen available: No
Season: Closed December 24–26
Affiliation: HI-DJH
Regional office: Rheinland
Extras: Piano, table tennis,
volleyball, playground, grill,
cafeteria ($)
**Must be under age twenty-seven
to stay**

How to get there:

By bus: Contact hostel for transit
details.

By car: Take Highway A3 to
Montabaur, then Highway B49
to Limburg/Gelbachtal.

By train: Take train from Limburg
or Siersheim to Montabaur.
From Montabaur Station walk
1½ miles to hostel.

JUGENDHERBERGE MORSBACH
(Morsbach Hostel)
Obere Kirchstrasse 21,
51597 Morsbach
Phone: 02294–8662

Fax: 02294–7807
Rates: 22.50–30.50 DM per HI
member (about $11–$15 US)
Beds: 166
Private/family rooms: Yes
Kitchen available: No
Season: Closed December 24–26

Jugendgästehaus Aasee Münster
Münster Hostel • Münster
(photo courtesy of Deutsches Jugendherbergswerk)

Affiliation: HI-DJH
Regional office: Rheinland
Extras: Programs, TV, VCR, table tennis, grounds, grill, volleyball, basketball, meals ($), parking

How to get there:

By bus:/train Take train to Wissen/Sieg, then take bus to Morsbach. Or take bus from Siegen, Gummersbach, or Waldbröl.

By car: Take Highway A4 from Köln or Olpe, exiting at signs for Reichshof/Morsbach or Reichshof/Eckenhagen

JUGENDGÄSTEHAUS AASEE MÜNSTER
(Münster Hostel)
Bismarckallee 31,
48151 Münster
Phone: 0251-532-470
or 0251-532-477

Fax: 0251-521-271
E-mail: jgh-muenster@djh-wl.de
Rates: 40.50– 50.50 DM per HI member (about $20–$25 US)
Beds: 208
Private/family rooms: Yes
Kitchen available: No
Season: Closed December 25–26
Affiliation: HI-DJH
Regional office: Rheinland
Extras: Table tennis, pool table, bike rentals, disco, piano, bar/cafeteria, wheelchair access, parking, laundry

How to get there:

By bus/train: Take train to Münster. From Münster Station take #10 or #34 bus to Hoppendamm and walk to hostel.

By car: Take Highways A1 and A43 to Autobahn Münster-Süd, or exit for Münster-Nord and go straight along Weseler Strasse to Handwerkskammer; then go in the direction of Aasee.

JUGENDHERBERGE HINSBECK

(Nettetal Hostel)

Heide 1,

41334 Nettetal

Phone: 02153–6492

Fax: 02153–89598
Rates: 22.75–32.00 DM per HI
member (about $11–$16 US)
Beds: 161
Private/family rooms: Yes
Kitchen available: No
Season: Closed December 23–26
Affiliation: HI-DJH
Regional office: Rheinland
Extras: Volleyball, circus tent,
parking, meals ($)

How to get there:

By bus/train: Take train to
Kempen or Kaldenkirchen; from
train station take #093 bus to
Hinsbeck and walk to hostel.
By car: Take Highway A40 in the
direction of Venlo-Duisburg, exiting at signs for Wankum-
Wachtendonk, then continue
toward Viersen and go another 1
mile toward Hinsbeck to
Ortsschild. Or take Highway A61
from Koblenz or Venlo, exiting at
signs for Nettetal.

JUGENDHERBERGE NEUSS-UEDESHEIM

(Neuss Hostel)

Macherscheider Strasse 113,

41468 Neuss

Phone: 0211–577–0349

Fax: 0211–577–0350
E-mail: service-center@djh-
rheinland.de

Rates: 24.50–32.00 DM per HI
member (about $12–$16 US)
Beds: 131
Private/family rooms: No
Kitchen available: Yes
Season: Contact hostel for current
season
Affiliation: HI-DJH
Regional office: Rheinland
Extras: Grill, bistro ($), parking

How to get there:

By bus/train: Take local train or S-
Bahn train to Neuss
Hauptbahnhof (train station),
then change to #851 bus to
Uedesheim and walk to hostel.
By car: Take Autobahn from Köln
or Krefeld, exiting in the direction of Wuppertal, then exit
again for Neuss-Uedesheim.

JUGENDHERBERGE NIDEGGEN

(Nideggen Hostel)

Rather Strasse 27,

52385 Nideggen

Phone: 02427–1226

Fax: 02427–8453
Rates: 22–29 DM per HI member
(about $11–$15 US)
Beds: 126
Private/family rooms: No
Kitchen available: No
Season: Closed December 24–26
Affiliation: HI-DJH
Regional office: Rheinland
Extras: Basketball, grill, table
tennis, bike storage room, disco,
parking, meals ($)

How to get there:

By bus/train: Take train to Düren.
From Düren Station take local
train to Nideggen-Brück, and take

bus to Nideggen or walk 1½ miles to hostel. Or, also from Düren Station, take #21 bus to Jugendherberge (hostel) stop.

By car: Take Highway A1/A61 to Erftstadt, then head in the direction of Zülpich (via the B265), past Erp in the direction of Froisheim/ Nideggen (the L33).

JUGENDHERBERGE NOTTULN

(Nottuln Hostel)

St. Amand-Montrond-Strasse 6,

48301 Nottuln

Phone: 02502–7878

Fax: 02502–9619
E-mail: jh-nottuln@djh-wl.de
Rates: 23.40– 28.40 DM per HI member (about $12–$14 US)
Beds: 132
Private/family rooms: Yes
Kitchen available: No
Season: Closed December 22– January 8
Affiliation: HI-DJH
Regional office: Rheinland
Extras: Table tennis, grill, playground, parking, meals ($)

How to get there:

By bus: Take #560 or #561 bus from Münster or Coesfeld to Rhodeplatz stop, then walk ½ mile to hostel.

By car: Take Highway A43 to Nottuln.

By train: Contact hostel for transit details.

JUGENDHERBERGE OERLINGHAUSEN

(Oerlinghausen Hostel)

Auf dem Berge 11,

33813 Oerlinghausen

Phone: 05202–2053

Fax: 05202–15456
E-mail: jh-oerlinghausen @djh-wl.de
Rates: 23.40–28.40 DM per HI member (about $12–$14 US)
Beds: 127
Private/family rooms: Yes
Kitchen available: No
Season: Closed December 21– January 3
Affiliation: HI-DJH
Regional office: Rheinland
Extras: Table tennis, parking, meals ($)

How to get there:

By bus/train: Take train to Oerlinghausen, then bus to Marktplatz stop and walk to hostel. Or contact hostel for transit details.

By car: Take Highway A2 to Oerlinghausen or Highway A33.

JUGENDHERBERGE BIGGESEE

(Olpe Hostel)

Auf dem Mühlenberg,

57462 Olpe

Phone: 02761–6775

Fax: 02761–64714
E-mail: jh-biggesee@djh-wl.de
Rates: 24.50– 29.50 DM per HI member (about $12–$15 US)
Beds: 240
Private/family rooms: Yes
Kitchen available: No
Affiliation: HI-DJH
Regional office: Rheinland
Extras: Programs, volleyball, disco, piano, parking, meals ($)

How to get there:

By bus: Take train to Olpe. From Olpe Station walk to hostel, or take bus from Eichhagen Station.

By car: Take Highway A45 in the direction of Attendorn. Or contact hostel for directions.

By train: Take train to Olpe. From Olpe Station walk to hostel, or take bus from Eichhagen Station.

JUGENDHERBERGE PADERBORN

(Paderborn Hostel)

Meinwerkstrasse 16,

33098 Paderborn

Phone: 05251–22055

Fax: 05251–280–017
E-mail: jh-paderborn@djh-wl.de
Rates: 23.40– 28.40 DM per HI member (about $12–$14 US)
Beds: 108
Private/family rooms: Yes
Kitchen available: No
Season: Closed December 4– January 1
Affiliation: HI-DJH
Regional office: Rheinland
Extras: Piano, guitar, table tennis, grill, meals ($), parking

How to get there:

By bus/train: Take train to Paderborn. From Paderborn Station walk 1 mile to hostel. Or take #2 bus to Detmolder Tor stop or #5 bus to Maspernplatz stop, then walk to hostel.

By car: Take Highway A33 in the direction of Innenstadt, then from Inneren Ring take Harthumarstrasse to Maspernplatz.

JUGENDHERBERGE PORTA WESTFALICA

(Porta Westfalica Hostel)

Kirchsiek 30,

32457 Porta Westfalica

Phone: 0571–70250

Fax: 0571–710–0047
E-mail: jh-porta.westfalica @djh-wl.de
Rates: 22–27 DM per HI member (about $11–$14 US)
Beds: 95
Private/family rooms: No
Kitchen available: No
Season: Open year-round
Affiliation: HI-DJH
Regional office: Rheinland
Extras: Table tennis, parking, meals ($)

How to get there:

By bus/train: From Porta-Westfalica or Minden Station, take bus to Hausberge and walk ¾ mile to hostel.

By car: Take Highway A2 from Porta-Westfalica, then Highway B482 to Hausberge.

JUGENDHERBERGE PRÜM

(Prüm Hostel)

Pferdemarkt,

54595 Prüm

Phone: 06551–2500

Fax: 06551–70030
E-mail: jh-prüm@djh-info.de
Web site: www.djh-info.de
Rates: 22.80 DM per HI member (about $11 US)
Beds: 74
Private/family rooms: Yes

Kitchen available: No
Season: Closed December 24–26
Affiliation: HI-DJH
Regional office: Rheinland
Extras: Table tennis, grounds, basketball, grill, meals ($)
Must be under age twenty-seven to stay

How to get there:

By bus/train: From Gerolstein or Trier Station walk to bus stop and take bus to Prüm.
By car: Take Highway A48 from Daun to Mehren, going via Gerolstein, to Prüm.

JUGENDHERBERGE RADEVORMWALD

(Radevormwald Hostel)

Telegrafenstrasse 50,

42477 Radevormwald

Phone: 02195–1063

Fax: 02195–6323
Rates: 21–29 DM per HI member (about $11–$15 US)
Beds: 97
Private/family rooms: Yes
Kitchen available: No
Season: Closed December 24–26
Affiliation: HI-DJH
Regional office: Rheinland
Extras: Programs, playground, table tennis, grill, piano, parking, meals ($)

How to get there:

By bus/train: Take train to Wuppertal. From Wuppertal Station take bus to Radevormwald and walk ½ mile to hostel.
By car: Take Highway A1 from Köln or Wuppertal, exiting at signs for Remscheid/Radevormwald, going

in the direction of Radevormwald-Zentrum.

JUGENDHERBERGE RATINGEN

(Ratingen Hostel)

Götschenbeck 8,

40882 Ratingen

Phone: 02102–20400

Fax: 02102–204–010
Rates: 23.50–31.00 DM per HI member (about $12–$16 US)
Beds: 167
Private/family rooms: Yes
Kitchen available: No
Season: December 24–26
Affiliation: HI-DJH
Regional office: Rheinland
Extras: Programs, table tennis, foosball, pinball, garden, grill, disco, meals ($), parking, wheelchair access

How to get there:

By bus/train: From Düsseldorf or Essen take S-Bahn line S6 to Ratingen Ost Station, or take #750 bus to Götschenbeck.
By car: Take Highway A3/A52 from Tiefenbroich in the direction of Ratingen.

JUGENDHERBERGE BLOCKHAUS

(Reichshof-Eckenhagen Hostel)

51580 Reichshof-Eckenhagen

Phone: 02265–8628

Fax: 02265–9042
E-mail: mrschneider@t-online.de
Rates: 22–27 DM per HI member (about $11–$14 US)
Beds: 58

Private/family rooms: No
Kitchen available: No
Season: Closed December 1–27
Affiliation: HI-DJH
Regional office: Rheinland
Extras: Table tennis, skiing near-
by, parking, meals ($)

How to get there:

By bus/train: From
Gummersbacht or
Dieringhausen Station take bus
via Derschlag to Eckenhagen.
Contact hostel for further transit
details.
By car: Take Highway A4 from
Köln to Olpe, Reichshof-
Eckenhagen.

JUGENDHERBERGE GROSS REKEN

(Reken Hostel)
Coesfelder Strasse 18,
48734 Reken
Phone: 02864–1023

Fax: 02864–2044
E-mail: jh-gross.reken@djh-wl.de
Rates: 23.40–28.40 DM per HI
member (about $12–$14 US)
Beds: 126
Private/family rooms: Yes
Kitchen available: No
Affiliation: HI-DJH
Regional office: Rheinland
Extras: Table tennis, skateboard-
ing, parking, meals ($)

How to get there:

By bus: Contact hostel for transit
details.
By car: Take Highway A43 from
Dülmen or Coesfeld via Merfeld,
then take A31 to Reken via
B67 N to Gross Reken. Or contact hostel for directions.

By train: Take train to Maria Veen.
From Maria Veen Station walk 2
miles to hostel.

JUGENDHERBERGE RHEINE

(Rheine Hostel)
Mühlenstrasse 75,
48431 Rheine
Phone: 05971–2407

Fax: 05971–13526
E-mail: jh-rheine@djh-wl.de
Rates: 23.40–28.40 DM per HI
member (about $12–$14 US)
Beds: 53
Private/family rooms: No
Kitchen available: No
Affiliation: HI-DJH
Regional office: Rheinland
Extras: Meals ($), parking,
wheelchair access

How to get there:

By bus: Contact hostel for transit
details.
By car: Take Highway A1 to exit
for Greven and then continue
along B481 or via Kreuz Lotte
and Osnabrück on the A30,
exiting at signs for the Rheine.
By train: Take train to Rheine
Station. Contact hostel for further transit details.

JUGENDHERBERGE RÖDINGHAUSEN

(Rödinghausen Hostel)
Zum Nonnenstein 21,
32289 Rödinghausen
Phone: 05746–8173

Fax: 05746–920–425
Rates: Contact hostel for current
rates

Beds: 80
Private/family rooms: Yes
Kitchen available: No
Season: Closed December 21–26
Affiliation: HI-DJH
Regional office: Rheinland
Extras: Meals ($), parking
How to get there:
By bus: From Bünde Station take bus to Rödinghausen, then walk ½ mile to hostel.
By car: Take Highway A30 to Rödinghausen, then continue north 4 miles to the hostel.
By train: Contact hostel for transit details.

JUGENDHERBERGE RÜTHEN
(Rüthen Hostel)
Am Rabenknapp 4,
59602 Rüthen
Phone: 02952–483

Fax: 02952–2717
E-mail: jh-ruethen@djh-wl.de
Rates: 23.40–28.40 DM per HI member (about $12–$14 US)
Beds: 121
Private/family rooms: No
Kitchen available: No
Season: Closed December 15– January 14
Affiliation: HI-DJH
Regional office: Rheinland
Extras: Programs, parking, meals ($)
How to get there:
By bus/train: From Lippstadt Station take #562 bus to Rüthen. Or take S-Bahn line S60 to Belecke and then regional train R71 to Rüthen. Or take train to Paderborn Station,

then Schnellbus (express bus) #400 to Rüthen.
By car: Take Highway A44 to Anröchte, then Highway B55 in the direction of Meschede, exiting at signs for Belecke; continue on B516 to Rüthen or on B64 in the direction of Rüthen (exiting at Möhnebrücke).

EUROPA-JUGENDHERBERGE / JUGENDGÄSTEHAUS SAARBRÜCKEN
(Saarbrücken Guest House and Hostel)
Meerwiesertalweg 31,
66123 Saarbrücken
Phone: 0681–33040

Fax: 0681–374–911
E-mail: jh-saarbrücken @djh-info.de
Web site: www.djh-info.de
Rates: 29.10–38.60 DM per HI member (about $15–$19 US)
Beds: 192
Private/family rooms: Yes
Kitchen available: No
Season: Closed December 24–26
Affiliation: HI-DJH
Regional office: Rheinland-Pfalz/Saarland
Extras: Piano, cafeteria ($), table tennis, playground, grill, wheelchair access
How to get there:
By bus/train: From Saarbrücken Station take #49 or #69 bus in the direction of Uni to Prinzenweiher stop and walk to hostel.
By car: Take Highway A1 in the direction of Köln/Trier or Highway A8 and then A623 in the direction of Saarbrücken to

Europa-Jugendherberge/Jugendgästehaus Saarbrücken
Saarbrücken Guest House and Hostel • Saarbrücken

(photo courtesy of Deutsches Jugendherbergswerk)

Highway B4. Continue to hostel. Or contact hostel for directions.

WALDJUGENDHERBERGE SARGENROTH

(Sargenroth Hostel)

Kirchweg 1,

55471 Sargenroth

Phone: 06761–2500

Fax: 06761–6378
E-mail: jh-sargenroth@djh-info.de
Web site: www.djh-info.de
Rates: 23.80 DM per HI member (about $12 US)
Beds: 134
Private/family rooms: Yes
Kitchen available: No
Season: Closed December 24–26
Affiliation: HI-DJH
Regional office: Rheinland
Extras: Grill, table tennis, volleyball, basketball, playground, meals ($), wheelchair access

Must be under age twenty-seven to stay

How to get there:

By bus/train: Take train to Koblenz or Bingen. From train station walk to bus stop and take regional bus to Simmern and get off at hostel.

By car: Take Highway A61 to Rheinböllen via Argenthal, then continue through Riesweiler to Sargenroth.

JUGENDHERBERGE GEMÜND

(Schleiden-Gemünd Hostel)

Im Wingertchen 9,

53937 Schleiden-Gemünd

Phone: 02444–2241

Fax: 02444–3386
E-mail: Jugendherberge.Gemuend @t-online.de
Rates: 22–30 DM per HI member (about $11–$15 US)

Beds: 163
Private/family rooms: Yes
Kitchen available: Yes
Season: Contact hostel for current season
Affiliation: HI-DJH
Regional office: Rheinland
Extras: Programs, grill, table tennis, volleyball, piano, parking, meals ($)

How to get there:

By bus/train: Take train to Kall. From Kall Station walk to bus stop and take bus to Gemünd, then walk 1 mile to hostel.

By car: Take Highway A1 from Köln or Trier, exiting at signs for Wisskirchen, then continue to Schleiden/Gemünd using Highway B266 from Kommern to Gemünd.

JUGENDHERBERGE SCHMALLENBERG

(Schmallenberg Hostel)
Im Lenningshof 20,
57392 Schmallenberg
Phone: 02972–6098

Fax: 02972–4918
E-mail: jh-schmallenberg @djh-wl.de
Rates: 24.50–29.50 DM per HI member (about $12–$15 US)
Beds: 134
Private/family rooms: Yes
Kitchen available: No
Season: Closed December 1– January 1
Affiliation: HI-DJH
Regional office: Rheinland
Extras: Table tennis, basketball, volleyball, playground, grill, parking, meals ($)

How to get there:

By bus/train: From Altenhundem Station take bus to Schmallenberg and walk to hostel. Or contact hostel for further transit details.

By car: Take Highway A45 exiting for Olpe, then Highways B55 and B236 to Schmallenberg. Or take Highway A445 to Arnsberg, then B7 to Meschede, B55 to Bremke, and Highways B511 and B236 to Schmallenberg.

JUGENDHERBERGE SOEST

(Soest Hostel)
Kaiser-Friedrich-Platz 2,
59494 Soest
Phone: 02921–16283

Fax: 02921–14623
E-mail: jh-soest@djh-wl.de
Rates: 22–27 DM per HI member (about $11–$14 US)
Beds: 70
Private/family rooms: Yes
Kitchen available: No
Season: Closed December 24–26
Affiliation: HI-DJH
Regional office: Rheinland
Extras: Table tennis, volleyball, sports facilities, parking, meals ($)

How to get there:

By bus/train: Take train to Soest. From Soest Station take #549/550 bus in the direction of Stadthalle to hostel. Contact hostel for further transit details.

By car: Take Highway A44 from Soest or Möhnesee.

JUGENDHERBERGE RURBERG FÜR NATUR-UND ABENTEUERSPORT

(Simmerath-Rurberg Hostel)

52152 Simmerath-Rurberg

Phone: 02473-2200

Fax: 02473-4911
Rates: 22.50-30.00 DM per HI member (about $11-$15 US)
Beds: 161
Private/family rooms: Yes
Kitchen available: Yes
Season: Closed December 24-26
Affiliation: HI-DJH
Regional office: Rheinland
Extras: Programs, climbing wall, canoe rentals, volleyball, basketball, bistro ($), children's theater, parking

How to get there:

By bus/train: Take train to Aachen, then take bus to Rurberg and walk to hostel. Contact hostel for further transit details.
By car: Take Highway A44 from Aachen or Lichtenbusch to Highway B258, going in the direction of Monschau, then take road in the direction of Simmerath/Rurberg. Or take Highway A1 from Köln, Euskirchen, or WissKirchen to Highway B266, going in the direction of Gemünd and Rurberg.

JUGENDHERBERGE BURG AN DER WUPPER

(Burg an der Wupper Solingen Hostel)

An der Jugendherberge 11, 42659 Solingen

Phone: 0212-41025

Fax: 0212-49449
E-mail: Jugendherberge-Burg-an-der-Wupper@t-online.de
Rates: 22.60-30.00 DM per HI member (about $11-$15 US)
Beds: 118
Private/family rooms: Yes
Kitchen available: No
Season: Closed December 24-26
Affiliation: HI-DJH
Regional office: Rheinland
Extras: Programs, table tennis, playground, disco, TV, VCR, piano, campground, parking, meals ($)

How to get there:

By bus/train: Take train to Köln. From Köln Station take #260 bus to Wermelskirchen (Eich). Or take #681 or #682 bus from Solingen or Ohligs to Graf-Wilhelm-Platz stop or #683 bus to Burg Brücke stop.
By car: Take Highway A1 to Schloss Burg.

JUGENDHERBERGE SOLINGEN-GRÄFRATTH

(Solingen-Gräfratth Hostel)

Flockertsholzer Weg 10, 42653 Solingen

Phone: 0212-591-198

Fax: 0212-594-179
Rates: 22.60-30.00 DM per HI member (about $11-$15 US)
Beds: 120
Private/family rooms: No
Kitchen available: No
Season: Closed December 24-26
Affiliation: HI-DJH
Regional office: Rheinland
Extras: Programs, table tennis, volleyball, grill, parking, meals ($)

How to get there:

By bus/train: Take train to Wuppertal Vohwinkel, then take #683 bus to Gräfrath. Or take train to Solingen-Ohligs, then change to #695 bus to Eugen-Maurer-Heim.

By car: Take Highway A46, exiting at signs for Solingen and continuing through Haan/Ost.

KURPFALZ-JUGENDHERBERGE / JUGENDGÄSTEHAUS SPEYER

(Speyer Guest House and Hostel)

Geibstrasse 5,

67346 Speyer

Phone: 06232–61597

Fax: 06232–61596
E-mail: jh-speyer@djh-info.de
Web site: www.djh-info.de
Rates: 29.10–38.60 DM per HI member (about $15–$19 US)
Beds: 160
Private/family rooms: No
Kitchen available: No
Affiliation: HI-DJH
Regional office: Rheinland
Extras: Table tennis, playground, grill, cafeteria ($), wheelchair access

How to get there:

By bus/train: Take train from Ludwigshafen to Speyer. From Speyer Station walk to city-shuttle and take bus to hostel.

By car: Take Highway A61 to Speyer, exiting in the direction of Dom/Museum or Highways B9 and B39, exiting for Dom/Museum. Continue past the Technikmuseum and make a right toward Freibad. The entrance is off Geibstrasse.

JUGENDHERBERGE SORPESEE

(Sundern Hostel)

Am Sorpesee 7,

59846 Sundern

Phone: 02935–1776

Fax: 02935–7254
E-mail: jh-sorpesee@djh-wl.de
Rates: 24.50–29.50 DM per HI member (about $12–$15 US)
Beds: 166
Private/family rooms: Yes
Kitchen available: No
Season: Closed December 18–January 18
Affiliation: HI-DJH
Regional office: Rheinland
Extras: Sports facilities, parking, meals ($)

How to get there:

By bus: From Arnsberg Station take Balve-Arnsberg bus line to Sundern stop and walk to hostel.

By car: Take Highway A445 from Arnsberg or Hüsten, then Highway B229 in the direction of Sundern. Or take Highway A45 to Olpe, then Highway B236.

By train: Contact hostel for transit directions.

JUGENDHERBERGE STEINBACH

(Steinbach Hostel)

Südwestausgang,

67808 Steinbach

Phone: 06357–360

Fax: 06357–1583
E-mail: jh-steinbach@djh-info.de
Web site: www.djh-info.de
Rates: 23.80 DM per HI member (about $12 US)
Beds: 104
Private/family rooms: Yes
Kitchen available: No
Season: Closed December 24–26
Affiliation: HI-DJH
Regional office: Rheinland
Extras: Table tennis, basketball, volleyball, grill, cafeteria ($)
Must be under age twenty-seven to stay

How to get there:

By bus/train: Take train from Bad Kreuznach or Kaiserslautern to Winnweiler. From Winnweiler Station take bus to hostel. Contact hostel for further transit details.
By car: Take Highway A63 to Göllheim, continuing in the direction of Göllheim-Kaiserslautern; or take B40 through Dreisen to Steinbach.

JUGENDHERBERGE TECKLENBURG
(Tecklenburg Hostel)
Am Herrengarten 5,
49545 Tecklenburg
Phone: 05482–360

Fax: 05482–7937
E-mail: jh-tecklenburg@djh-wl.de
Rates: 24.50–29.50 DM per HI member (about $12–$15 US)
Beds: 128
Private/family rooms: Yes
Kitchen available: No
Season: Closed December 24–26
Affiliation: HI-DJH
Regional office: Rheinland

Extras: Disco, stage, basketball, table tennis, meeting room, meals ($), parking

How to get there:

By bus: From Ibbenbüren or Lengerich Station take #145 bus to Tecklenburg and walk to hostel.
By car: Take Highway A1 to Tecklenburg, exiting at signs for Stadtgebiet Schildern.
By train: Contact hostel for transit details.

SCHAUMBERG-JUGENDHERBERGE / JUGENDGÄSTEHAUS THOLEY
(Tholey Guest House and Hostel)
Am Schaumberg 9,
66636 Tholey
Phone: 06853–2271

Fax: 06853–5534
E-mail: jh-tholey@djh-info.de
Web site: www.djh-info.de
Rates: 22.80–32.90 DM per HI member (about $11–$16 US)
Beds: 141
Private/family rooms: Yes
Kitchen available: No
Season: Closed December 24–26
Affiliation: HI-DJH
Regional office: Rheinland
Extras: Table tennis, pool table, foosball, volleyball, basketball, cafeteria ($), wheelchair access

How to get there:

By bus: From train station in St. Wendel, walk to bus stop and take bus to Jugendgästehaus Tholey. Contact hostel for further transit details.
By car: Take Highway A1 to Tholey.

By train: Contact hostel for transit details.

JUGENDHERBERGE VLOTHO (Vlotho Hostel)

Oeynhauser Strasse 15,

32602 Vlotho

Phone: 05733–4063

Fax: 05733–18139
E-mail: jh-vlotho@djh-wl.de
Rates: 22–27 DM per HI member (about $11–$14 US)
Beds: 108
Private/family rooms: Yes
Kitchen available: No
Season: Closed December 24–26
Affiliation: HI-DJH
Regional office: Rheinland
Extras: Sports facilities, parking, meals ($)

How to get there:

By bus: Contact hostel for transit details.
By car: From north take Highway A2 to Vennebeck. From south take Highway A2 to Vlotho-Exter.
By train: Take train from Hameln or Bielefeld to Vlotho. Contact hostel for further transit details.

JUGENDHERBERGE WEISKIRCHEN

(Weiskirchen Hostel)
Jugendherbergsstrasse 12,

66709 Weiskirchen

Phone: 06876–231

Fax: 06876–1444
E-mail: jh-weiskirchen@djh-info.de
Web site: www.djh-info.de

Rates: 23.80 DM per HI member (about $12 US)
Beds: 126
Private/family rooms: Yes
Kitchen available: No
Season: Closed December 24–26
Affiliation: HI-DJH
Regional office: Rheinland
Extras: Table tennis, playground, grill, cafeteria ($), wheelchair access

How to get there:

By bus: From Saarbrücken or Trier Station take bus to Weiskirchen. Or contact hostel for transit details.
By car: Take Highway A1 from Primstal to Weiskirchen or through Hunsrückhöhenstrasse in the direction of Saarburg to Weiskirchen.
By train: Contact hostel for transit details.

JUGENDHERBERGE ESBORN

(Wetter Hostel)
Wacholderstrasse 11,

58300 Wetter

Phone: 02335–7718

Fax: 02335–73519
E-mail: jh-esborn@djh-wl.de
Rates: 22–27 DM per HI member (about $11–$14 US)
Beds: 60
Private/family rooms: No
Kitchen available: No
Season: Closed December 16–January 14
Affiliation: HI-DJH
Regional office: Rheinland
Extras: VCR, accordion, guitar, table tennis, volleyball, grill,

grounds, parking, meals ($)

How to get there:

By bus/train: Take train to Wetter. From Wetter Station take bus to Wetter-Hasslinghausen.

By car: Take Highway A43 to Sprockhövel, then Highway A1 to Gevelsberg.

JUGENDHERBERGE WEWELSBURG

(Wewelsburg Hostel)

Burgwall 17,

33142 Büren (Wewelsburg)

Phone: 02955–6155

Fax: 02955–6946

E-mail: jh-wewelsburg@djh-wl.de

Rates: 24.50–29.50 DM per HI member (about $12–$15 US)

Beds: 210

Private/family rooms: Yes

Kitchen available: No

Season: Closed January 10– February 10

Affiliation: HI-DJH

Regional office: Rheinland

Extras: Piano, TV, VCR, grill, sports field, table tennis, bike rentals, photo darkroom, parking, meals ($)

How to get there:

By bus: Contact hostel for transit details.

By car: Take Highway A44 from Büren to Salzkotten.

By train: Take train to Paderborn. From Paderborn Station contact hostel for transit details.

JUGENDHERBERGE WIEHL

(Wiehl Hostel)

An der Krähenhardt 6,

51674 Wiehl

Phone: 02262–93410

Fax: 02262–91598

Rates: 22.60–30.00 DM per HI member (about $11–$15 US)

Beds: 175

Private/family rooms: Yes

Kitchen available: No

Season: Closed January 2– February 5; December 24–26

Affiliation: HI-DJH

Regional office: Rheinland

Extras: Programs, meeting rooms, parking, meals ($)

How to get there:

By bus/train: Take train from Köln to Dieringshausen, then from Dieringshausen Station take #302 bus to Wiehl. Get off at Hotel Post or Zirrerstrasse stop and walk to hostel.

By car: Take Highway A4 from Köln to Olpe, exiting at signs for Wiehl/Gummersbach, then exit for Birkenstrasse.

JUGENDHERBERGE WINDECK-ROSBACH

(Windeck-Rosbach Hostel)

Herbergsstrasse 19,

51570 Windeck-Rosbach

Phone: 02292–5042

Fax: 02292–6569

E-mail: jh-windeck@t-online.de

Rates: 23.60–32.10 DM per HI member (about $12–$16 US)

Beds: 142

Private/family rooms: Yes

Kitchen available: Yes

Season: Closed December 22– January 7

Affiliation: HI-DJH
Regional office: Rheinland
Extras: Programs, table tennis, piano, grill, fireplace, meeting rooms, parking, wheelchair access, meals ($)

How to get there:

By bus: Contact hostel for transit details.
By car: Contact hostel for directions.
By train: From Köln Station or Köln-Deutz Station, take S-Bahn to Rosbach Station, then walk 2 miles to hostel or contact hostel for transit details.

JUGENDHERBERGE WINTERBERG

(Winterberg Hostel)

Astenberg 1,

59955 Winterberg

Phone: 02981–2289

Fax: 02981–569
E-mail: jh-winterberg@djh-wl-de
Rates: 24.50–29.50 DM per HI member (about $13–$15 US)
Beds: 170
Private/family rooms: No
Kitchen available: No
Season: Closed November 1–31
Affiliation: HI-DJH
Regional office: Rheinland
Extras: Piano, TV, VCR, table tennis, bike rentals, ski rentals, disco, parking, meals ($)

How to get there:

By bus/train: From Winterberg Station take bus in the direction of Bad Berleburg-Siegen to Jugendherberge-Winterberg stop.
By car: Take Highway A44 Autobahn from Hamm to Werl in the direction of Arnsberg through Velmede. Or take Highway A45, exiting at signs for Olpe and continue through Lennestadt and Schmallenberg.

JUGENDHERBERGE WIPPERFÜRTH

(Wipperfürth Hostel)

Ostlandstrasse 34,

51688 Wipperfürth

Phone: 02267–1228

Fax: 02267–80977
Rates: 23–30 DM per HI member (about $12–$15 US)
Beds: 144
Private/family rooms: No
Kitchen available: No
Season: Closed December 24–26
Affiliation: HI-DJH
Regional office: Rheinland
Extras: Programs, table tennis, wheelchair access, parking, meals ($)

How to get there:

By bus: Take hourly bus from Köln to Wipperfürth, or twice-hourly bus from Remscheid or Lennep to Wipperfürth.
By car: Take Highway A1 from Köln, Dortmund, or Bremen, exiting at signs for Burg/Wupper and continue to Wermeskirchen. Or exit at Remscheid, then continue through Hückeswagen to Wipperfürth.
By train: Take train to Bergisch or Gladbach, then bus to Wipperfürth.

JUGENDHERBERGE WOLFSTEIN

(Wolfstein Hostel)

Rötherweg 24,

67752 Wolfstein

Phone: 06304–1408

Fax: 06304–683
E-mail: jh-wolfstein@djh-info.de
Web site: www.djh-info.de
Rates: 22.80 DM per HI member
(about $12 US)
Beds: 160
Private/family rooms: Yes
Kitchen available: No
Season: Closed December 24–26
Affiliation: HI-DJH
Regional office: Rheinland
Extras: Cafeteria ($), table tennis,
basketball, volleyball, grill,
meals ($), laundry, wheelchair
access
**Must be under age twenty-seven
to stay**

How to get there:

By bus: Contact hostel for transit
route.
By car: Take Highway A6 to
Bingen, Highway B50 to Bad
Kreuznach, Highway B48 to
Alsenz, Highway B420 to
Lauterecken, and Highway
B270 to Wolfstein. Or take
Highway A6 to Kaiserslautern-
Ost, then Highway B270 in the
direction of Idar-Oberstein to
Wolfstein.
By train: Trains from
Kaiserslautern or Lauterecken.
From Wolfstein Station walk 1
mile to hostel.

JUGENDHERBERGE WUPPERTAL
(Wuppertal Hostel)
Obere Lichtenplatzer

Strasse 70,

42287 Wuppertal

Phone: 0202–552–372

Fax: 0202–557–354
Rates: 23–31 DM per HI member
(about $12–$16 US)
Beds: 140
Private/family rooms: No
Kitchen available: Yes
Season: Open year-round
Affiliation: HI-DJH
Regional office: Rheinland
Extras: Programs, soccer, basket-
ball, table tennis, meals ($)

How to get there:

By bus: From Wuppertal Barmen
Station take #640 bus in the
direction of Ronsdorf to
Jugendherberge (hostel) stop.
By car: Take Highway A46, exiting at signs for Wuppertal-
Barmen and continuing in the
direction of Zentrum (center of
town).
By train: Contact hostel for transit
details.

BADEN/ SOUTHWESTERN GERMANY

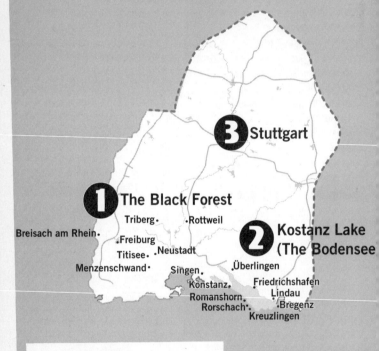

3 Stuttgart

1 The Black Forest

Triberg·   ·Rottweil

Breisach am Rhein·

·Freiburg

Titisee· ·Neustadt

Menzenschwand·   ·Singen

Überlingen

2 Kostanz Lake (The Bodensee

Konstanz·

Romanshorn·   Friedrichshafen

Rorschach·   Lindau

·Bregenz

Kreuzlingen

BADEN/SOUTHWESTERN GERMANY

The southwestern corner of Germany, also known generally as the Baden-Württemberg region, is basically famous for one area: the Black Forest, a still-wooded forest (one of the only big ones left in the country) where you'll stumble over cuckoo clocks every 10 feet, it seems, even though this clock wasn't actually invented in Germany at all. What you will also find, however, are pretty lakes, tiny towns, and a surprisingly "left" (as in way-left) culture of vegetarians, Birkenstocks, communes, and the like. Must be something in the water. Anyway, speaking of the water, the other claim to fame around here are the baths. Baden *means* "baths," for gosh sakes, and there are plenty of opportunities to just sit 'n' soak.

BLACK FOREST (SCHWARZVALD)

The Black Forest ("Schvortz-vold" in German) is one of Germany's most characteristic regions. Think cuckoo clocks and you're thinking about this area—actually pretty small, but close enough to bigger cities in France and Switzerland that you can get here in half a day. The hostels here are almost all pretty simple affairs, but as a bonus they're often placed close to attractive lakes with good swimming and hiking options. A small train line goes into the mountains and forest from Freiburg, which you can reach from Basel or many points in Germany.

JUGENDHERBERGE BREISACH (BREISACH HOSTEL)

Rheinuferstrasse 12,

79206 Breisach

Phone: 07667–7665

Fax: 07667–1847
Rates: 26–31 DM per Hostelling International member (about $13–$16 US)
Credit cards: No
Beds: 158
Private/family rooms: No
Kitchen available: No
Season: Closed December 23–27

Office hours: 8:00–10:00 A.M.; 5:00–10:00 P.M.
Curfew: 11:30 P.M.
Affiliation: Hostelling International-DJH
Regional office: Baden-Württemberg
Extras: Parking, meals ($)

Breisach, placed carefully between the bigger cities of Strasbourg and Basel, is almost forgotten today—and that means you might think about taking a gander. This hostel's great, if somewhat lacking in character, and makes a perfect budget bunk while resting between more famous places.

Best bet for a bite:
Meals at hostel

Insiders' tip:
Wine festival in August

What hostellers say:
"Well run."

Gestalt:
Münster mash

Hospitality:

Cleanliness:

Party index:

Set right beside the river that divides France from Germany, this was once a very contested land; you could ask locals about the many times this area has changed hands between France and Germany, though it's a bit of a sore subject for some—the huge local church was bombed.

Yeah, that's right, this town has a huge cathedral overlooking the town—ask anyone to point you toward the Münster, or just keep walking *up*—with views back down across the river to France and even, on exceptionally clear days, of the Vosges and Alps mountain ranges. A number of hiking trails range from town up into the weird surrounding hills, a freak of local geology; inquire at the tourist office about maps and conditions. Wine is also a big draw; those vineyards trailing down the hills have storefronts here. Really bored? Take a bus or bike across the (usually unguarded) border to beautiful Colmar, France, or take a ship from the town docks upriver to Strasbourg or downriver to Basel.

KEY TO ICONS

 Attractive natural setting

 Ecologically aware hostel

Superior kitchen facilities or cafe

Offbeat or eccentric place

Superior bathroom facilities

 Romantic private rooms

 Comfortable beds

 Editors' choice: among our very favorite hostels

 A particularly good value

Wheelchair accessible

Good for business travelers

 Especially well suited for families

Good for active travelers

 Visual arts at hostel or nearby

 Music at hostel or nearby

Great hostel for skiers

 Bar or pub at hostel or nearby

Jugendherberge Freiburg
Freiburg Hostel • Freiburg

(photo courtesy of Deutsches Jugendherbergswerk)

How to get there:

By bus: Take bus from Freiburg to Breisach. Or contact hostel for transit details.

By car: Take Highway A31 or Autobahn A5, exiting at signs for Bad Krozingen.

By train: Take train to Breisach from Freiburg (Monday–Saturday only). From Breisach Station walk ¾ mile along river to hostel.

JUGENDHERBERGE FREIBURG
(FREIBURG HOSTEL)

Karthäuserstrasse 151,

79104 Freiburg

Phone: 0761–67656

Fax: 0761–60367
Rates: 26–31 DM per Hostelling International member (about $13–$16 US)
Credit cards: no
Beds: 443
Private/family rooms: Yes
Kitchen available: No
Season: Closed December 24–26
Office hours: 7:00 A.M.–11:30 P.M.

Curfew: 1:00 A.M.
Affiliation: Hostelling International-DJH
Regional office: Baden-Württemberg
Extras: Meeting rooms, breakfast, disco, table tennis, laundry, parking, information desk, TV room, meals ($)

There are two parts to this huge and distant hostel, but either way it's not your greatest pick in the world. Unfortunately, as is often the case, it's the only hostel in town, so you may end up out here anyway.

Right out in the middle of a field beneath a small hill, the hostel is a three-story modern building with a yard and little pitched roof on top. The interior has about a dozen common spaces, most of them filled with obedient (or not-so-obedient) school kiddies. It's pretty boring throughout, despite the included breakfast. The price goes up—and the beds slightly improve—in the "Guest house" section of the place, but this is still a cattle-call situation at the very best. We'd ignore the in-house disco or television room and head for town. Speaking of town, you'll love the quiet location of this place if you like quiet—but if you want to experience downtown Freiburg's considerable charms, get a hotel instead.

Best bet for a bite:
Schlappen

Insiders' tip:
Local Kirsche-Torte (Black Cherry Chocolate Cake)

What hostellers say:
"C'mon, man, it's too far out."

Gestalt:
French Freiburg

Safety: 👎

Hospitality: 👍 👎

Cleanliness: 👍 👎

Party index:

That's because Freiburg's one cool city: lots of eateries, coffeehouses, bars, university types, and alternative lifestyles, and check out the interesting canals that water the sloping city streets. Those canals once put out fires, cooled locals, or were drunk from by cows, depending on whom you ask. One thing's for sure, though—they're deeper than they look, so step carefully. For eats there's a market square around the cathedral—tons of fruit, vegetables, crafts, honey, sausage stands, and that kind of stuff. And that cathedral makes a good visit, too: There are four pipe organs, some of which are occasionally played in concerts. There are interesting paintings on the pillars, too.

A place as great as Freiburg sure deserves a good hostel. This ain't it.

How to get there:

By bus/train: From train station, take S-Bahn line S1 toward Littenweiler to Römerhof stop, then walk to Fritz-Geiges-Strasse and turn right onto it. Cross bridge and make another right; continue to hostel.

By car: Take Highway A5, exiting for Freiburg-Mitte, then follow signs toward Titisee-Neustadt to Highway B31.

JUGENDHERBERGE MENZENSCHWAND (MENZENSCHWAND HOSTEL)

Vorderdorstrasse 10,

79837 Menzenschwand (St. Blasien)

Phone: 07675–326

Fax: 07675–1435
E-mail: Jugendherberge-menzenschwand@t-online.de
Rates: 24–29 DM per Hostelling International member (about $12–$15 US)
Credit cards: No
Beds: 102
Private/family rooms: Yes
Kitchen available: No
Season: Closed December 23–26
Affiliation: Hostelling International-DJH
Regional office: Baden-Württemberg
Extras: Breakfast, meals ($), parking

Why? That's the question we want an answer to. Why on Earth does tiny St. Blasien possess this honking-huge cathedral (the "Dom") that looks more like it belongs in Rome or Montreal or something? Our crack sleuths have been at it, and they say it has something to do with some religious items brought here by monks about, oh, a thousand years ago.

Set inside an absolutely beautiful wooden farmhouse that dates back to 1658, the hostel here is no slouch, either. It's set in pretty countryside, with access to cross-country skiing and hiking trails, and they serve breakfast for free each morning. There are the usual bunk beds and family rooms—two to eight beds per room, all bathrooms and showers located on the hallway—plus three lounges to get to know fellow Dom-gawkers. Both meat-based and vegetarian meals are served at dinner, and they'll honor special requests if they can.

Obviously you're gonna fork over a few bucks to check out that cathedral while you're here—catch the semiregular bus over to St. Blasien to do it. But also save the time for a hike into the hills, not to mention a look at the area waterfalls and maybe a taste of wine. We counted about a dozen pubs and restaurants in the town of Menzenschwand, giving you additional nighttime options.

Best bet for a bite:
Edeka (store)

Insiders' tip:
Free classical music concerts in summer

What hostellers say:
"Nice Dom!"

Gestalt:
Chrome Dom

Hospitality:

Cleanliness:

Party index:

How to get there:

By bus/train: From Seebrugg or Aha Station take #7613 bus to Menzenschwand.

By car: Take Highway B31 to Titisee-Neustadt, then the B500 to Aha and the Landstraseee (Route 168 A).

JUGENDHERBERGE SCHLUCHSEE IM WOLFSGRUND (SCHLUCHSEE HOSTEL)

Im Wolfgrund 28,
79859 Schluchsee
Phone: 07656–329

Fax: 07656–9237
Rates: 24–29 DM per Hostelling International member (about $12–$15 US)
Credit cards: No
Beds: 133
Private/family rooms: Yes
Kitchen available: No
Season: Closed December 23–26
Office hours: 7:00 A.M.–2:00 P.M.; 5:00–11:00 P.M.
Curfew: 11:00 P.M.
Affiliation: Hostelling International-DJH
Regional office: Baden-Württemberg
Extras: Beach access, water sports, breakfast, meals ($), laundry, parking

Best bet for a bite:
Schmidt's (store)

Insiders' tip:
SCUBA diving allowed in lake

What hostellers say:
"So peaceful."

Gestalt:
See side

Hospitality:

Cleanliness:

Party index:

Any hostel that comes complete with its own walkway to the beach automatically gets our *Hostels Germany* consideration; we sit up and take notice at this stuff. Of course the hostel still has to deliver on the basics—friendliness, safety, decent bunks—to get the coveted Thumb Up.

And this one does, certainly, yet another case where simplicity isn't a bad thing. The bunks are standard-issue, yeah, but four common areas help you get away from 'em. One caveat: The place is pretty popular with school outings. Come during the height of summer, though, and you won't have to worry about that.

The draw here, obviously, is the beach and the cool water of the lake. Back inside the hostel, they give you breakfast free and serve other meals for an extra charge; the laundry is a major bonus when you've been wearing that swimsuit just a little *too* long.

How to get there:

By bus: Easier by train.

By car: From Freiburg take Highway B31 to Titisee-Neustadt, then take B500 to the Schluchsee lake and follows signs to Wolfsgrund.

By train: From Freiburg, Titisee, or Seebrugg, take local train to Schluchsee Station. Walk around lake (counterclockwise) about ½ mile to parking lot; turn left onto trail and continue up to railroad crossing. Walk another 100 yards to hostel.

JUGENDHERBERGE SEEBRUGG (SEEBRUGG HOSTEL)

Haus Nr. 9,
79859 Schluchsee
Phone: 07656–494

Fax: 07656–1889
Rates: 24 –29 DM per Hostelling International member (about $12–$15 US)
Beds: 134
Private/family rooms: Yes
Kitchen available: No
Season: Closed December 23–26
Office hours: 7:00–9:00 A.M.; 5:00–10:00 P.M.
Curfew: 10:00 P.M.
Affiliation: Hostelling International-DJH
Regional office: Baden-Württemberg
Extras: Lake, water sports, breakfast, bike tours, parking, meals ($)

Hostel Number Two on the Schluchsee lake is every bit as good as the other one back up the line in Wolfsgrund. Rooms are eight bedded, and there are four common areas to spread out in. They serve breakfast here for free, and you get to use the lake, of course, for whatever you want. (Just don't pee in it, okay?)

Don't come expecting a crowd, though. The hostel is the town, basically, even if the beach gets surprisingly crowded during the daytime. The only thing to do is swim or, if you wanna get sweaty first, hike over the hill to the adjacent lake town. Nightlife is nonexistent, making the unfairly early 10:00 P.M. curfew basically irrelevant; you come for quiet and lake views, and that's it.

Best bet for a bite:
Dinner on-site

Insiders' tip:
Buy a hiking map at tourist office

What hostellers say:
"Another good one."

Gestalt:
Scluchy duck

Hospitality:

Cleanliness:

Party index:

How to get there:

By bus: Contact hostel for transit details.

By car: From Freiburg take Highway B31 to Titisee-Neustadt, then change to Highway B500 and continue to Seebrugg.

By train: Take train to Seebrugg from Freiburg, Titisee, or Schluchsee. From Seebrugg Station walk ¼ mile to hostel.

JUGENDHERBERGE VELTISHOF (TITISEE-NEUSTADT HOSTEL)

Bruderhalde 27,

79822 Titisee-Neustadt

Phone: 07652–238

Fax: 07652–756
E-mail: jh-veltishof@t-online.de
Rates: 24–29 DM per Hostelling International member (about $12–$15 US)
Credit cards: No
Beds: 128
Private/family rooms: Yes
Kitchen available: No
Season: Closed December 23–26
Office hours: Hours vary; contact hostel for current office hours
Curfew: 10:00 P.M.
Affiliation: Hostelling International-DJH
Regional office: Baden-Württemberg
Extras: Playground, disco, table tennis, bike storage, ski storage, breakfast, fields, lake, parking, meals ($)

This place, situated in a pretty area on lovely lake Titisee (no snickering!), is one of the Black Forest's nicer hostels.

Best bet for a bite:
Imbiss takeout

Insiders' tip:
Paddleboat rentals at lake

What hostellers say:
"Love the lake."

Gestalt:
Titiseeside

Dorms are mostly eight-bedded rooms. They've got three lounges here, too, not to mention a disco (try out your John Travolta impression on the ladies), a game room with table tennis, storage space for your bikes and skis, and fields outdoors where you can practice the perfect soccer kick or sling around a ball.

There's not much to do in the area except vegetate, hike around the lakeside trail, or swim right in the thing, but that's OK. The town beside the lake offers little of anything—souvenirs, fast-food, the usual.

How to get there:

By bus/train: Take local train from Freiburg to Titisee. From Titisee Station take #7300 bus (occasional) toward Toltnau to Feuerwehrheim/Jugendherberge stop and walk ¼ mile to hostel. Or walk 1½ miles from station to hostel, going along Strandbadstrasse to Burderhalde and continuing around lake.

By car: Take Highway B31 from Freiburg toward Donaueschingen to Titisee.

Hospitality:

Cleanliness:

Party index:

JUGENDHERBERGE TRIBERG (TRIBERG HOSTEL)

Rohrbacher Strasse 3,
78098 Triberg
Phone: 07722–4110

Fax: 07722–6662
Rates: 24–29 DM per Hostelling International member (about $12–$15 US)
Credit cards: No
Beds: 125
Private/family rooms: Yes
Kitchen available: No
Season: Closed December 23–26
Office hours: 7:00–9:00 A.M.; 5:00–7:00 P.M.
Affiliation: Hostelling International-DJH
Regional office: Baden-Württemberg
Extras: Hiking trails, breakfast, laundry, meals ($), parking

There are two things you'll quickly find out about Triberg, so we'll clue you in on both right here and now. One, it's the oldest city in Germany, a designation most obvious at the so-called Porta Negra—a series of stone gates that were put here by the Romans. Yeah, them. The other thing you won't be able to avoid is the local waterfall—sorry, Wassergall—known as the Gusacher; Germans come from miles around to see this thing, but if you've recently been to Switzerland's Alps you might wonder just what the heck all the fuss is about.

Anyhow, this is a good hostel with very nice facilities—the usual bunk beds, three lounges, a kitchen—and knockout views. They serve breakfast free, too, and can direct you to local hiking

Best bet for a bite:
Schwarzwaldstübel

Insiders' tip:
Some of the clocks weren't made here

What hostellers say:
"Pretty good."

Gestalt:
Nice Triberg

Safety:

trails. The only drawback is getting there, which *could* be fun—if you're not carrying anything. Get our drift? It's, like, straight up, so plan extra time and energy for the climb.

Hospitality:

Cleanliness:

Party index:

Yet another thing about Triberg is, well, tourists like it. A lot. They pour in to buy their little souvenir clocks and leave again by nightfall.

How to get there:

By bus: Easier by train.

By car: Take Highway B33 from Offenburg, Villinge, or Schwenningen to Triberg.

By train: From Triberg Station walk to tourist office, then from Friedrichstrasse continue 1 mile uphill to hostel.

KONSTANZ LAKE
(LAKE CONSTANCE; THE BODENSEE)

The Bodensee (which comes with two other names, as you can clearly see) is Europe's huge, central lake—so big it had to be split among three countries, but Germany got the best part.

If you've got lots of time, rent a bike and do the three-country lake circuit on the neat bike path. Be forewarned, it's gonna take a couple of days, although there are some very interesting vineyards, churches, sights, and even a hip town or two to stop at along the way.

The lake is also home to some of the best hostelling in Germany, with at least three fantastic places. Why not string 'em together in a round-the-lake itinerary?

JUGENDGÄSTEHAUS BREGENZ
(BREGENZ GUEST HOUSE HOSTEL)

Mehrerauerstrasse 3-5,

A-6900 Bregenz (Austria)

Phone: (43)5574–42867 from outside Austria

Fax: (43)5574–428674 from outside Austria

E-mail: jgh.bregenz@jgh.at

Rates: 230–330 AS (about $18–$25 US) per Hostelling International member; doubles 600 AS (about $46 US)

Credit cards: Yes

Beds: 142

Season: May 1–December 31
Office hours: 7:00 A.M.–midnight
Affiliation: Hostelling International-ÖJHV
Extras: Meals ($), breakfast, bar, snacks, Internet access, play area, volleyball, currency exchange, TV

This brand-new hostel, located in an Austrian town that tickles the lake borders of both Germany and Switzerland, is blessed with a good facility and one of the nicest staffs we've met in all of Europe. Unfortunately, it's also inundated with bunches of very young schoolkids from time to time, so you might not get to enjoy it at all if they're booked full (summer can be especially rough). Snag a bunk, though, and you're sure to have a good time hanging out around big Lake Konstanz/Constance/Bodensee/whatever-ya-wanna-call it.

The hostel occupies a former textile mill. It seems like just another drab brick schoolhouse-style hostel on the outside, but they've done a beautiful restoration job throughout—polishing up old wooden floors till they shine, putting in all-new windows and thick sound-muffling doors, and installing brand-new pine bunks. There's lots of comfort here, bathrooms in every single room, an ultramodern key system (you wave a key before a sensor and the lock magically opens), and—for some reason—bad pop music pumping through the hallway speakers.

We loved the supercomfortable dorms, all with not just their own bathrooms but also some with amazing touches like thick comforters, airy windows, lofts, and fancy new showers. There are four doubles, four quads, sixteen nice six-bedded dorms, and one great big one. Each floor has a nice TV room with a new set that gets about a jillion stations—in languages including, but not limited to, French Swiss, German Swiss, German, Italian, Austrian, Turkish, Hungarian (we think), and (yes!) the Cartoon Channel in plain English. Train buffs will love some of the back rooms, which have views of the tracks and various trains going off to Innsbruck, Vienna, etc., without tooting or otherwise disturbing your slumber.

Down by reception there's a great little bar that serves local beer on tap, ice cream sundaes, and snacks round the clock. You can cruise the Internet in the same area by popping schilling (yeah, you're in Austria, remember?) coins into one of the machines. And did we mention the neato laundry that both washes AND dries the clothes in the same machine? We'd never seen that before.

Finally, we'd be remiss if we didn't point out that this hostel is extremely close to Bregenz's well-connected rail station (four direct trains a day to Munich and Zurich, plus others to Innsbruck and Vienna). And we gotta give props to the really good dinners, which cost just 65 AS (about $5.00 US—a steal). Cooked by a professional chef who actually enjoys feeding the masses good stuff, they feature a vegetarian and meat entree each night, both usually Austrian specialties. Breakfast is included, too—bread and hot chocolate and muesli. You have to pay for drinks, but the vending machines stock great mineral water and sodas.

Though it doesn't look that way today, Bregenz has actually been settled for a very, very long time. Let's put it this way: When the Romans got here right around the time B.C. was becoming A.D., there had already been Celts here for centuries. Today this is a wealthy town, and most folks come here for the upscale beach, quaint and touristed streets, or other sights. Dadgum if there isn't a casino right across the street, too, though you probably won't be blowing your dough there. A better idea: Get a bike and haul it over to pretty Lindau, Germany, a few miles around the lake on an island. Bring that passport just in case, though the border guards rarely check or stamp.

Best bet for a bite:
Bella Napoli, downtown

Insiders' tip:
Underwear outlet store next door

What hostellers say:
"More of everything!"

Gestalt:
Bregenz Sie Deutsch?

Hospitality:

Cleanliness:

Party index:

Make a trek a few hundred yards over to Seebühne, a giant floating stage on the lake that was being used in 1999 for a giant skeleton turning the pages of a book—the backdrop for a year-long opera. That's typical of this area: Things peak each summer around August, when the month-long Bregenz Festival gets going.

The town's a bit uppity, we'll concede, but you'll find some nice shops—and friendly people—if you poke a little. Also poke into the pretty good museum of Vorarlberg history, where Celtic and Roman ruins are all carefully explained. They've got some work from local hero painter Angelika Kaufmann, too, who made a big splash in the man's world of eighteenth-century art.

How to get there:

By bus: Contact hostel for transit route.

KEY TO ICONS

Attractive natural setting

Ecologically aware hostel

Superior kitchen facilities or cafe

Offbeat or eccentric place

Superior bathroom facilities

Romantic private rooms

Comfortable beds

Editors' choice: among our very favorite hostels

A particularly good value

Wheelchair accessible

Good for business travelers

Especially well suited for families

Good for active travelers

Visual arts at hostel or nearby

Music at hostel or nearby

Great hostel for skiers

Bar or pub at hostel or nearby

By car: Contact hostel for directions.

By train: From Bregenz Station walk up to long corridor in station, crossing tracks. Follow signs toward "am See" (away from City); walk to end of corridor, down stairs, and turn left. Walk past casino and through casino parking lot to main road (Meeraurergasse); cross street. Hostel entrance is just across the road.

GRAF-ZEPPELIN-JUGENDHERBERGE (FRIEDRICHSHAFEN HOSTEL)

Lindauer Strasse 3,

88046 Friedrichshafen

Phone: 07541–72404

Fax: 07541–74986

Rates: 26–31 DM per Hostelling International member (about $13–$16 US)

Credit cards: No

Beds: 235

Private/family rooms: No

Kitchen available: No

Season: Closed December 16–31

Office hours: Contact hostel for current hours

Lockout: 9:00 A.M.–noon

Affiliation: Hostelling International-DJH

Regional office: Baden-Württemberg

Extras: Cafeteria ($), patio, campground, laundry, parking, laundry

This place is deservedly popular, and so you might want to make some advance reservations, especially in summertime. It's got everything—a lakeside position, seven common rooms, a cafeteria serving meals on a terrasse, and a ton of rooms with private bathrooms—that you could possibly want in a place.

Dorms are mostly four- or six-bedded, but more than twenty of them come with those private bathroom facilities; the rest have sinks. Did we mention the laundry? No? What about the free breakfast?

The town is the usual Bodensee thing, actually less interesting than many of the rest but for one salient fact: This is dirigible country. The inventor of the ill-fated airship was from around here, evidently, as the town's Zeppelinmuseum explains the entire history of dirigibles in careful detail.

Best bet for a bite:
Naturkost

Insiders' tip:
Kultur-Blätter lists
stuff to do

What hostellers say:
"Excellent!"

Gestalt:
Bed Zeppelin

Hospitality:

How to get there:

Cleanliness:

Party index:

By bus/train: From station walk 2 miles to hostel, or take #7587 bus toward Kressbronn to Jugendherberge (hostel) stop and walk 150 yards to hostel.

By car: From Meersburg or Lindau take Highway B31 to Friedrichshafen; or from Ulm take Highway B30 to Friedrichshafen.

JUGENDHERBERGE KONSTANZ (KONSTANZ HOSTEL)

Zur Allmannshöhe 18,
78464 Konstanz
Phone: 07531–32260
Fax: 07531–31163
Rates: 22 –27 DM per Hostelling International member (about $11–$14 US)
Credit cards: No
Beds: 96
Private/family rooms: Yes
Kitchen available: No
Season: Open year-round
Office hours: 7:00–9:30 A.M.; 5:00–10:00 P.M.
Curfew: 10:00 P.M.
Lockout: 9:30 A.M.–noon
Affiliation: Hostelling International-DJH
Regional office: Baden-Württemberg
Extras: Breakfast, meals ($), parking

Located not in hip, happenin', and attractive Konstanz—but rather in the blander suburb known as Allmansdorf—this place is a little strange. For starters, it's built from an old water tower, which right away might give you the creeps.

Best bet for a bite:
Seekuh

Insiders' tip:
Etch gravestones next door

What hostellers say:
"Great town, so-so hostel."

Gestalt:
Eat a Peach

Hospitality:

Cleanliness:

It's a rather simple place, too. However, you gotta like this—dinner is included! And so is breakfast! That kinda makes up for the otherwise unimpressive place, especially if you're on a tight budget.

Konstanz has several good points: an active student life during the school year, a nice beach during the summer, and boat docks from which several lines of ferries chug to and fro around the lake to various destinations in the three countries that share its boundaries.

How to get there:

By bus/train: From Konstanz Station walk 2½ miles to hostel. Or take #4 bus to Jugendherberge stop or #1 bus to Allmansdorf post office stop, then walk to hostel.

By car: Contact hostel for directions.

Party index:

JUGENDWOHNEIM DON BOSCO

Salesianerweg 5,
78464 Konstanz
Phone: 07531–62252

Fax: 07531–60688
Rates: 30 DM per person (about $15 US)
Beds: Number varies
Private/family rooms: No
Kitchen available: No
Season: Contact hostel for current season
Office hours: Contact hostel for current office hours
Affiliation: None
Extras: Television lounge

This place is bare bones but money-saving and is more central than the water-tower place elsewhere in town. They charge you for sheets, as though that were a privilege and not a right, which sticks in our craw a little bit. At least there's a lounge with a television, but it's little compensation.

Ah, forget it. We'd pick the Kreuzlingen hostel (it's just across the Swiss border, easy walking distance from downtown) over this—or the other Konstanz hostel—in a heartbeat.

Best bet for a bite: Tengelmann
What hostellers say: "Is that all there is?"
Gestalt: Konstanz hassle
Hospitality:
Cleanliness:
Party index:

How to get there:

By bus/train: From Konstanz Station take #1 bus to Salzberg stop and walk down Mainaustrasse to hostel. Or take #4 bus and walk down Mainaustrasse to hostel.

By car: Contact hostel for directions.

VILLA HORNLIGERG (KREUZLINGEN HOSTEL)

Promenadenstrasse 7,
CH-8280 Kreuzlingen (Switzerland)
Phone: 071–688–2663

Fax: 071–688–4761
E-mail: kreuzlingen@youthhostel.ch
Rates: 20.80–22.80 CHF per Hostelling International member (about $15–$16 US)
Credit cards: Yes
Beds: 97
Private/family rooms: No
Kitchen available: No
Season: March 1–November 30
Office hours: 8:00–9:00 A.M.; 5:00–9:00 P.M.
Affiliation: Hostelling International-SJ (Switzerland)
Extras: Breakfast, meals ($), bike rentals, kayak rentals

This hostel's in Switzerland, but oddly enough you are much more likely to use it if you are visiting Germany. See, the interesting German city of Konstanz (or Constance to language-challenged Anglos) is a heckuva interesting place, but its hostel is not too great. And if you're older than twenty-six, you can't stay there anyway. Bingo! Instant short walking trip across the border to the Swiss city of Kreuzlingen, where you'll have to show a passport to the unsmiling Swiss guards, but they probably won't give you a hard time.

Once there you'll find this to be a pretty good hostel: a homey old three-story building in quiet surroundings right on the lake. The dorms are a little too big for our taste, with many of them containing eight or more beds (and they get a lot of school groups here, to boot), but we liked the emphasis on fresh air here—staff will rent you a bicycle, a kayak, or both.

If you're not on a bike or on the lake, you'll probably be spending most of your free time over in Konstanz. It's a cool town, fueled by scores of university students—that means more and later-night bars, discos, and clubs than you'll often find in a small European city. Good beaches on the lake, too.

Konstanz is also the starting point for numerous excursions around the lake, which is served by a tremendous network of ferries, trains, and bus lines; get all the details at the hostel. We recommend a bus over to Mainau in Germany, with its terrific gardens, or a ferry ride over to the old and spooky medieval town of Meersburg.

Best bet for a bite:
Rheingasse, in Konstanz

Insiders' tip:
Gardens in Mainau, Germany

What hostellers say:
"Perfect base for seeing Germany."

Gestalt:
Konstanz comment

Hospitality:

Cleanliness:

Party index:

How to get there:

By bus: Call hostel for transit route.
By car: Call hostel for directions.
By ferry: Take ferry to the Kreuzlingen-Hafen ferry dock and walk ¼ mile to hostel.

By train: From Kreuzlingen-Hafen Station walk ¼ mile to hostel. Or from Konstanz walk 1 mile around lake path to park; turn right and walk away from water, turning again to hostel entrance.

JUGENDHERBERGE LINDAU (LINDAU HOSTEL)

Herbergsweg 11,
88131 Lindau
Phone: 08382–96710

Fax: 08382–967–150
E-mail: jhlindau@djh-bayern.de
Rates: 29 DM per Hostelling International member (about $15 US)
Credit cards: No
Beds: 240
Private/family rooms: Yes
Kitchen available: No
Season: Open year-round
Affiliation: Hostelling International-DJH
Regional office: Bavaria
Extras: Water sports, pool table, foosball table, restaurant ($), piano, basketball, table tennis, meeting rooms, laundry, parking

Lindau's one of our very favorite towns on the Bodensee, so it's only appropriate that this hostel should become one of our very favorites, too. It's just super in every regard—well equipped and fun, with good rooms and beds. (The doubles are basically hotel rooms at hostel prices.) And, for once, it's not located miles from nowhere.

Rooms come in a wide variety of configurations; there's everything from a single to a double to a quad to a six-bedded room, but nothing bigger than that. There are five meeting rooms, two dining rooms (dinner is served nightly around six o'clock), and a piano. The laundry is mighty handy, so are the sports grounds.

Lindau may not be excitement city, but it is a handy transportation link to Munich or Zurich—the big train linking both passes through about four or five times a day.

How to get there:

By bus/train: From Lindau Station take #1 or #2 bus to Anheggerstrasse stop, then walk to hostel or switch to #3 bus to get closer still; get off at the Jugendherberge (hostel) stop.

Best bet for a bite:
Alte Schule (for pizza)

Insiders' tip:
Baboo's has email access

What hostellers say:
"Can't believe how close to town it is!"

Gestalt:
Sport haus

Hospitality:

Cleanliness:

Party index:

By car: From Munich take Highway B12 or Autobahn to the Bodensee, then take B31.

JUGENDHERBERGE VEITSBURG (RAVENSBURG HOSTEL)

Veitsburgstrasse 1,
88212 Ravensburg
Phone: 0751–25363

Rates: 24–29 DM per Hostelling International member (about $12–$15 US)
Credit cards: No
Beds: 110
Private/family rooms: Yes
Kitchen available: No
Season: Closed December 18–31
Office hours: 7:00–9:00 A.M.; 5:00–10:00 P.M.
Curfew: 10:00 P.M.
Affiliation: Hostelling International-DJH
Regional office: Baden-Württemberg
Extras: Laundry, parking, meals ($)

Best bet for a bite:
Thai at Tom's

Insiders' tip:
Internet access nearby

What hostellers say:
"Too harsh."

Gestalt:
Full court press

Hospitality:

Cleanliness:

Party index:

This place is pretty simple and, quite frankly, run in an all-too-German manner; it feels more like punishment than fun, which is what we want our European vacations to be at least *once* in a while.

They've got four common rooms but offer little extra comfort—no free meals, few kind words; you get the picture. With all the other great places dotting the lake, this one's quite missable, we'd say.

How to get there:

By bus/train: From Ravensburg Station take bus or walk 2 miles to hostel.
By car: Take Highway B32 toward Wangen, then toward Veitsburg.

ROMANSHORN HOSTEL

Gottfried Keller-Strasse 6,
CH-8590 Romanshorn (Switzerland)
Phone: 071–463–1717

Fax: 071–461–1990
E-mail: romanshorn@youthhostel.ch
Rates: 11–20 CHF per Hostelling International member (about $8.00–$14.00 US)
Credit cards: No
Beds: 114
Private/family rooms: No
Kitchen available: No
Season: March 1–October 31
Office hours: 7:00–10:00 A.M.; 5:00–10:00 P.M.
Affiliation: Hostelling International-SJ (Switzerland)
Extras: Breakfast, meals ($), bike storage, bike rentals

We can't imagine getting excited about this centrally located place, which packs you in dorms that typically average fifteen beds per room. Obviously it's a tour-group leader's dream—but it might be your nightmare.

They do rent bikes and let you store 'em , and serve meals for a charge. The only reason you might come is that Romanshorn in on big Lake Konstanz, and you can take boats from this seaside town to others. We'd recommend staying in one of the others, if only because we don't like huge warehouse dorm rooms.

How to get there:

By bus: Call hostel for transit route.
By car: Call hostel for directions.
By ferry: Take ferry to Romanshorn; from dock walk ½ mile to hostel.
By train: From Romanshorn Station walk ¼ mile to hostel.

Best bet for a bite:
Breakfast and dinner here

Insiders' tip:
Use that eyeshade and earplugs

What hostellers say:
"Now I know what cattle feel like."

Gestalt:
Romanshorn 'o plenty

Hospitality:

Cleanliness:

Party index:

RORSCHACH–SEE HOSTEL

Churerstrasse 4,

CH-9400 Rorschach (Switzerland)

Phone: 071–844–9712

Fax: 071–844–9713
E-mail: rorschach.see@youthhostel.ch
Rates: 32.00 CHF per Hostelling International member (about $22 US)
Credit cards: No
Beds: 32
Private/family rooms: Yes
Kitchen available: No

Season: April 1–October 31
Office hours: 7:00–10:00 A.M.; 5:00–10:00 P.M.
Affiliation: Hostelling International-SJ (Switzerland)
Extras: Breakfast, meals ($), bike rentals

This is a rather bland building at first glance, but you've got to like a hostel that almost literally touches a lake.

Best bet for a bite:
Strap on the feed bag at hostel

What hostellers say:
"Nice grounds."

Insiders' tip:
Old Grange Museum

Gestalt:
Rorschach test

Hospitality:

Cleanliness:

Party index:

Basically a house in a green field, this new Swiss hostel augments the other one in town, which is open only to groups; we applaud the division of labor (and hostellers) here, having been awakened one too many times by the trampling feet of kiddies arriving back off their bus in the middle of the night. Anyhow, the place enjoys great position right next to the lake and a small beach, practically touching Lake Konstanz and the bike trail that encircles it. Yet you're in a green field at the edge of woods, too. Nice.

It's a rather small joint, though, just thirty-two beds doled out as seven quad rooms and two coveted doubles. None have private bathroom facilities, unfortunately. They serve meals and rent bikes—probably the best way to explore the lake at your leisure if you've got the time.

Rorschach as a town is no big deal at all, just a few churches and museums and the usual lake-resort resturants. We'd likely opt instead for a boat trip over to the gardens of Mainau, Germany, or maybe a night boat to another lake town nearby. Just make sure you know when the last boat to Rorschach runs.

How to get there:

By bus: From the port take postbus to Jugendherberge (hostel) stop and walk ¼ mile to hostel.
By car: Call hostel for directions.
By ferry: Take ferry to Rorschach; from dock walk ½ mile to hostel.
By train: From Rorschach Station walk ¼ mile to hostel.

JUGENDHERBERGE ROTTWEIL

Lorenzgasse 8,
78628 Rottweil
Phone: 0741–7664
Fax: 0741–7604

Rates: 22–27 DM per Hostelling International member (about $11–$14 US)
Credit cards: No
Beds: 62
Private/family rooms: No
Kitchen available: No
Season: Closed December 20–January 7
Office hours: 7:00–9:00 A.M.; 5:00–10:00 P.M.
Affiliation: Hostelling International-DJH
Regional office: Baden-Württemberg
Extras: Breakfast, meals ($)

Right by the river cliffs, this handsome old house-turned-hostel isn't great and it isn't bad, either; it's okay. Dorms are nothing special, containing six or eight beds in most cases and—actually—feel a bit cramped and musty. They serve breakfast in the dining room and have two lounges, but otherwise we find nothing remarkable about it one way or the other.

The city that gave us mean doggies (Rottweilers, ya know?) is actually a pretty interesting—and very ancient—place, though. Witness the persistence of several crazy festivals, such as Fasnet (a wild carnival in late February or March, roughly around the time of Mardi Gras).

Best bet for a bite:
Rotuvilla

Insiders' tip:
Free paper lists stuff to do

What hostellers say:
"Bark is more impressive than its bite."

Gestalt:
Dog daze

Safety: 👍

Hospitality: 👍

Cleanliness: 👍

Party index: 🎉🎉

How to get there:

By bus/train: From Rottweil Station walk 1 mile to hostel, or take bus to Obere Hauptstrasse stop and walk 200 yards to hostel.

By car: Take Highway A81 or Highways B14 and B27 to Rottweil.

JUGENDHERBERGE SINGEN (SINGEN HOSTEL)

Friedinger Strasse 28,
78224 Singen
Phone: 07731–42590

Fax: 07731–48842
Rates: 22–27 DM per Hostelling International member (about $11–$14 US)
Credit cards: No

Beds: 105
Private/family rooms: Yes
Kitchen available: No
Season: Open year-round
Affiliation: Hostelling International-DJH
Regional office: Baden-Württemberg
Extras: Sports facilities nearby, parking, meals ($)

Singen is notable only as a "train town"—that is, a place where major train lines come and go frequently—and thus a useful place to bunk down when you're heading elsewhere (say Munich) the next day.

However, this hostel—some distance northeast of the town center in the Waldrand suburb—doesn't take advantage of this fact. It is really useful only for its proximity to the local sports stadium—which is useful if you're, say, a German schoolkid training for a future Olympics but pretty useless for you, the hosteller.

They do maintain four lounges of various sorts, however, and can point you to various biking trails and water sports endeavors.

Best bet for a bite:
Hostel kitchen

Insiders' tip:
Singen's a bore

What hostellers say:
"What's the point?"

Gestalt:
Singen the blues

Hospitality:

Cleanliness:

Party index:

How to get there:

By bus/train: From Singen Station walk 1 mile to hostel, or take #7364 bus or #1 tram to Hallenbad-Waldeckstrasse stop.

By car: Take Highway A81, exiting at the Singen-Mühlhausen sign, then follow Highway B33 to Singen.

MARTIN-BUBER-JUGENDHERBERGE/ JUGENDHERBERGE-BEGEGNUNGSSTÄTTE (ÜBERLINGEN HOSTEL)

Alte Nussdorfer Strasse 26,

88662 Überlingen

Phone: 07551–4204

Fax: 07551–1277
Rates: 26–31 DM per Hostelling International member (about $13–$16 US)
Credit cards: No
Beds: 259
Private/family rooms: Yes
Kitchen available: No

> **Season:** Closed December 24–26
> **Affiliation:** Hostelling International-DJH
> **Regional office:** Baden-Württemberg
> **Extras:** Water sports, lake, disco, parking, laundry, meals ($)

Once again we have here the mysterious case of a hostel being located in a nothing town for no apparent reason. This time it's in Überlingen, a town near (but not on) Lake Konstanz and important only as a connection between other towns with train or bus stations.

The hostel is huge, so it must gets loads of schoolkids during the academic year. There are nine (count 'em) lounges, plus some sports facilities and (gasp) a disco, though you likely won't be shakin' it till the wee hours; this is a hostel disco, after all, not a real one.

Best bet for a bite:
Dine here

Insiders' tip:
Platform shoes went out in '70s

What hostellers say:
"Again, what's the point??"

Gestalt:
Disco duck

Party index:

How to get there:

By bus/train: From train station walk 2 miles to hostel, or take bus to Kramerwerke stop and walk ¼ mile to hostel.

By car: Take Highway A81 to A98 and then B31.

STUTTGART

If you were expecting just a skyscraper city full of buttoned-down car execs, Stuttgart might surprise you. Of course it *is* a skyscraper city full of buttoned-down car execs—but that's not all it is.

For one thing, it's as lush as a city could probably be in this part of the world. Lots of parks and surrounding hills and vineyards contribute to the feeling that you're not really in a crass capitalistic capital (if you know what we mean) where the main business is the manufacture of smoke-breathing boxes of metal too expensive for the mortal hosteller to even consider owning.

All right, we'll get off the soapbox. There are three hostels here—each different in character and very different in quality. Buyer beware, as usual: With increasing comfort and cleanliness, you'll pay more as you move up the hostelling food chain.

Jugendherberge Stuttgart
Stuttgart Hostel • Stuttgart

(photo courtesy of Deutsches Jugendherbergswerk)

JUGENDHERBERGE STUTTGART (STUTTGART HOSTEL)

Haussmannstrasse 27,

70188 Stuttgart

Phone: 0711–241–583

Fax: 0711–236–1041

Rates: 26–31 DM per Hostelling International member (about $13–$16 US)

Credit cards: No

Beds: 285

Private/family rooms: Yes

Kitchen available: No

Office hours: 7:00 A.M.–midnight

Lockout: 9:00 A.M.–noon

Curfew: 11:30 P.M.

Affiliation: Hostelling International-DJH

Regional office: Baden-Württemberg

Extras: Breakfast, meals ($), TV room, meeting rooms, table tennis

It's almost unheard of for a hostel to be placed in such a location as this—among the hoity-toity homes of auto executives—yet here

it is. Right across the river from central Stuttgart, this is the berries. But that fact makes the hostel deservedly popular, so get your dibs before arrival by making that all-important reservation phone call.

The hostel has nice gardens in front, behind which rises the tiny-windowed, blocklike hostel. Within, rooms are mostly four-bedded in style (there are forty-five of those), plus a total of fifteen six-bedded rooms, seven doubles, and one single room—not to mention four common rooms. Staff serves breakfast for free each morning but also enforces the sorts of rules that make your head ache—an 11:30 curfew, for example, which makes no sense at all since this is a *city*. Other pluses here include a game room and the obligatory television lounge.

Trying to find the danged place? Here's a tip: Ignore the street address listed above and head, instead, for the corner of Kernerstrasse and Werastrasse as described below.

How to get there:

By bus: From station walk ⅓ mile to hostel. Or take #15 tram or #42 bus toward Humaden to Eugenplatz stop; walk down Kernerstrasse and make a right on Werastrasse. Hostel is on right.

By car: Contact hostel for directions.

By train: From station walk ⅓ mile to hostel. Or take #15 tram or #42 bus toward Humaden to Eugenplatz stop; walk down Kernerstrasse and make a right on Werastrasse. Hostel is on right.

Best bet for a bite:
Bacchus

Insiders' tip:
Beer museum near
Vaihingen Station

What hostellers say:
"OK; could be better."

Gestalt:
Mercedes beds

Safety:

Hospitality:

Cleanliness:

Party index:

JUGENDGÄSTEHAUS STUTTGART

Richard-Wagner-Strasse 2,
Stuttgart
Phone: 0711–241–132

Fax: 0711–236–1110
Rates: 35–45 DM per person (about $18–$23 US); doubles 70–90 DM (about $35–$45 US)
Credit cards: No
Beds: 100
Private/family rooms: Yes
Kitchen available: No
Affiliation: None
Season: Closed December 24–26
Office hours: 9:00 A.M.–8:00 P.M.
Extras: Garden, laundry

This place sure ain't cheap, but it's pretty good. Located inside an old house close to downtown action yet still relatively quiet, it's also a *lot* friendlier than the other two hostels in town. Combined. Sometimes that's just why you wanna go for an independent hostel over an HI-affiliated place: the cooler groove.

Some of the rooms here come with their own private bathrooms—you gotta pay extra for that, but it's a big bonus—and even so, they're very nice singles and doubles. Consider the splurge. Cleanliness doesn't suffer at all.

We won't dwell too much on the city's sight-seeing here—a 650-foot TV tower is typical of the offerings, which aren't all that great—but one neat thing we did turn up was the Wilhelma botanical gardens and zoo. If you're into that sort of thing, this place is huge: more than 80 critters who walk, slither, gambol, swim, climb, or otherwise get around the expansive and attractive grounds.

Best bet for a bite:
Ketterer

Insiders' tip:
Lotsa wineries outside city

What hostellers say:
"Okay with me."

Gestalt:
Stutt-great

Hospitality:

Cleanliness:

Party index:

How to get there:

By bus/train: From Stuttgart Station take #15 tram toward Humaden to Bubenbad stop; hostel is at corner.

By car: Contact hostel for directions.

TRAMPER POINT HOSTEL

Wiener Strasse 317,
Stuttgart
Phone: 0711–817–7476

Fax: 0711–231–2810
Rates: 13 DM per person (about $7.00 US)
Beds: 30
Private/family rooms: No
Kitchen available: Yes
Season: June 1–September 5
Office hours: 8:00–9:00 A.M.; 5:00–11:00 P.M.
Affiliation: None
Extras: Breakfast

Note: **Must be ages sixteen to twenty-seven to stay**

This is probably Germany's cheapest hostel, but before you begin salivating and booking that direct flight to Stuttgart, consider this a moment: You often get what you pay for in life, and that's certainly true here. Also bear in mind that it's open only for about two months out of the year—and that you have to be between the ages of sixteen and twenty-seven even to snag a bunk.

Blankets cost extra, for gosh sakes, and the most luxurious bed here isn't anything better than the flimsy cot or fold-out couch you slept at in your brother's bachelor apartment. If they're full you'll have to sleep on the floor on an inflatable mattress. Hey, what did you expect for seven bucks? The only freebie here is the breakfast. It isn't terrible, not a dive, but the design of the place is, well, *strange*.

Best bet for a bite:
Markthalle for groceries

Insiders' tip:
Festival each August

What hostellers say:
"Nice 'n cheap."

Gestalt:
Point-less

Party index:

How to get there:

By bus: Easier by train.

By car: Contact hostel for directions.

By train: From Stuttgart Station take U-Bahn line U6 toward Gehrlingen to Sportpark Feuerbach stop; walk across tracks toward sports facility to hostel.

BADEN-SOUTHWEST
OTHER HOSTELS

SCHUBART-JUGENDHERBERGE
(Aalen Hostel)

Stadionweg 8,

73430 Aalen

Phone: 07361–49203

Fax: 07361–44682
Rates: 22–27 DM per HI member (about $11–$14 US)
Beds: 125
Private/family rooms: Yes
Kitchen available: No
Season: Closed November 20–December 26
Affiliation: HI-DJH
Regional office: Baden-Württemberg
Extras: Meals ($)

How to get there:

By bus/train: Take train to Aalen. From Aalen Station walk 2 miles to hostel. Or take bus to hostel stop (ask driver) and walk ⅓ mile to hostel.
By car: Take Highways A6, A7, or A8 to Aalen.

JUGENDHERBERGE ALPIRSBACH
(Alpirsbach Hostel)

Reinerzauer Steige 80,

72275 Alpirsbach

Phone: 07444–2477

Fax: 07444–1304
Rates: 24–29 DM per HI member (about $12–$15 US)
Beds: 125
Private/family rooms: No
Kitchen available: No
Season: Closed December 23–31
Affiliation: HI-DJH
Regional office: Baden-Württemberg
Extras: Disco, playground, meals ($)

How to get there:

By bus/train: Take train to Alpirsbach. From Alpirsbach Station take bus to hostel. Contact hostel for further transit details.
By car: Contact hotel for directions.

EVANG. FERIENHEIM ASCHENHÜTTE
(Bad Herrenalb Hostel)

Aschenhüttenweg 44,

76332 Bad Herrenalb

Phone: 07083–2430

Fax: 07083–51031
Rates: 26–31 DM per HI member (about $13–$16 US)
Beds: 87
Private/family rooms: Yes
Kitchen available: No
Season: Contact hostel for current season
Affiliation: HI-DJH
Regional office: Baden-Württemberg
Extras: Meals ($), parking, wheelchair accessibility

How to get there:

By bus/train: Take train to Karlsruhe. From Karlsruhe Station take S-Bahn line S1 to

Bahnhofsvorplatz stop and walk 3 miles to hostel or take summer-only bus to Gasthaus Linde stop.

By car: Take Highway A5 from Karlsruhe to Rüppurr and Ettlingen, going through Alb Valley 12 miles. Or take Highway A8, exiting at signs for Pforzheim-West and continuing through Enztal and over Dobel 20 miles to Bad Herrenalb.

JUGENDHERBERGE BAD URACH
(Bad Urach Hostel)
Burgstrasse 45,
72574 Bad Urach
Phone: 07125–8025

Fax: 07125–40358
Rates: 22–26 DM per HI member (about $11–$13 US)
Beds: 123
Private/family rooms: Yes
Kitchen available: No
Season: Closed December 18–31
Affiliation: HI-DJH
Regional office: Baden-Württemberg
Extras: Volleyball, meals ($), parking, laundry
How to get there:
By bus/train: Take train to Bad Urach. From Bad Urach Station take bus to Krankenhaus stop and walk 300 yards to hostel.
By car: Take Highway B28 from Reutlingen or Ulm to Bad Urach.

JUGENDHERBERGE BADEN-BADEN
(Baden-Baden Hostel)
Hardbergstrasse 34,
76532 Baden-Baden
Phone: 07221–52223

Fax: 07221–60012
Rates: 24–29 DM per HI member (about $12–$15 US)
Beds: 151
Private/family rooms: Yes
Kitchen available: No
Season: Contact hostel for current season
Affiliation: HI-DJH
Regional office: Baden-Württemberg
Extras: Meals ($), parking
How to get there:
By bus/train: Take train to Baden-Baden from Frankfurt or Basel. From Baden-Baden Station take #1 bus to Grosse Dollenstrasse stop and walk ⅓ mile to hostel.
By car: Take Highway A5, exiting at signs for Baden-Baden.

JUGENDHERBERGE BALINGEN
(Balingen Hostel)
Schlossstrasse 5,
72336 Balingen
Phone: 07433–20805

Fax: 07433–5911
Web site: www.balingen.de/juhe/juhebl.htm
Rates: 24–29 DM per HI member (about $12–$15 US)
Beds: 46
Private/family rooms: Yes
Kitchen available: No
Season: Closed January 1–3; December 1–31
Affiliation: HI-DJH
Regional office: Baden-

Württemberg

Extras: Meals ($), parking

How to get there:

By bus/train: Take train to
Balingen. From train station walk
½ mile to hostel. Or take bus to
Volksbank/ Zollernschloss stop
and walk 50 yards to hostel.

By car: Contact hostel for directions.

JUGENDHERBERGE BIBERACH

(Biberach Hostel)

Heusteige 40,

88400 Biberach

Phone: 07351–21885

Fax: 07351–21315
E-mail: juhe.biberach.a.r@gmx.de
Rates: 24–29 DM per HI member
  (about $12–$15 US)
Beds: 139
Private/family rooms: Yes
Kitchen available: No
Season: Closed January 10–
  February 6
Affiliation: HI-DJH
Regional office: Baden-
  Württemberg
Extras: Meals ($), parking

How to get there:

By bus: Contact hostel for transit
route.

By car: Take Highway A7 to
Highway B30 and then Highway
312 or 465. Or contact hostel for
directions.

By train: Take train from Ulm or
Friedrichshafen to Biberach.
From Biberach Station walk 1
mile to hostel.

JUGENDHERBERGE BONNDORF

(Bonndorf Hostel)

Waldallee 27,

79848 Bonndorf

Phone: 07703–359

Fax: 07703–1686
Rates: 22–27 DM per HI member
  (about $11–$14 US)
Beds: 214
Private/family rooms: Yes
Kitchen available: No
Season: Contact hostel for current
  season
Affiliation: HI-DJH
Regional office: Baden-
  Württemberg
Extras: Gym, pool, sports pro-
  grams, meals ($), laundry

How to get there:

By bus/train: Take train to
Neustadt. From Neustadt Station
take bus to Bonndorf stop and
walk ½ mile to hostel.

By car: Take Highway A5, exiting at
signs for Freiburg-Mitte, then fol-
low Highway B31 (Höllental) to
Highway B315, then to Highway
A81. Or take Highway A864 to
Bad Dürrheim, then Highway
B27 to Hüfingen and Highway
B31 to Löffingen and Bonndorf.

JUGENDHERBERGE CREGLINGEN

(Creglingen Hostel)

Erdbacher Strasse 30,

97993 Creglingen

Phone: 07933–336

Fax: 07933–1326
Rates: 24–29 DM per HI member
  (about $12–$15 US)

Beds: 153
Private/family rooms: Yes
Kitchen available: No
Season: Closed December 4–26
Affiliation: HI-DJH
Regional office: Baden-Württemberg
Extras: Gym, volleyball, sports programs, wheelchair accessibility, meals ($)

How to get there:

By bus/train: Take train to Weikersheim or Rothenburg. Then take bus to Schulzentrum stop and walk ½ mile to hostel.
By car: Take Highways A6, A13, A81, or A7 or Romantische Strasse to Creglingen.

JUGENDHERBERGE DILSBERG

(Dilsberg Hostel)

Untere Strasse 1,

69151 Neckargemünd (Dilsberg)

Phone: 06223–2133

Fax: 06223–74871
Rates: 27 DM per HI member (about $14 US)
Beds: 77
Private/family rooms: No
Kitchen available: No
Season: Contact hostel for current season
Affiliation: HI-DJH
Regional office: Baden-Württemberg
Extras: Meals ($)

How to get there:

By bus: Contact hostel for transit details.
By car: Take Highway B37 to Autobahn A5, then Highway A656 or B45 to Autobahn A6.

By train: Take train from Heidelberg or Würzburg to Neckargemünd, or from Heidelberg or Heilbronn to Neckargemünd. Then walk ¾ mile to hostel.

JUGENDHERBERGE "PFAHLBERG"

(Dornstetten Hostel)

Auf dem Pfahlberg 39,

72280 Hallwangen-Dornstetten

Phone: 07443–6469

Fax: 07443–20212
Rates: 24–29 DM per HI member (about $12–$15 US)
Beds: 125
Private/family rooms: Yes
Kitchen available: No
Season: Closed December 11–26
Affiliation: HI-DJH
Regional office: Baden-Württemberg
Extras: Music room, meals ($), parking, wheelchair access

How to get there:

By bus/train: Take train from Stuttgart, Freudenstadt, or Karlsruhe to Dornstetten. From Dornstetten Station walk 2 miles to hostel or take bus to Grüner Baum stop and walk ⅓ mile to hostel.
By car: Take Highway B28 from Freudenstadt or Stuttgart or Highway B294 from Pforzheim or Schramberg.

JUGENDHERBERGE EBERBACH

(Eberbach Hostel)

Richard-Schirrmann-Strasse 6, 69412 Eberbach

Phone: 06271–2593

Fax: 06271–71393
Rates: 22–27 DM per HI member (about $11–$14 US)
Beds: 127
Private/family rooms: Yes
Kitchen available: No
Season: Contact hostel for current season
Affiliation: HI-DJH
Regional office: Baden-Württemberg
Extras: Parking, meals ($)

How to get there:

By bus: Contact hostel for transit details.

By car: Take Highway B37 from Autobahn A5, exiting at signs for Heidelberg; continue to Eberbach.

By train: Take train to Eberbach from Heidelberg, Würzburg, or Heilbronn. From Eberbach Station walk 1 mile to hostel, or contact hostel for transit details.

JUGENDHERBERGE ERPFINGEN

(Erpfingen Hostel)

Auf der Reute,

72820 Erpfingen-Sonnenbühl

Phone: 07128–1652

Fax: 07128–3370
Rates: 24–29 DM per HI member (about $12–$15 US)
Beds: 149
Private/family rooms: Yes
Kitchen available: No
Season: Closed December 4–31
Affiliation: HI-DJH

Regional office: Baden-Württemberg
Extras: Tennis, ski rentals, mountain bike rentals, sports facilities, laundry, meals ($), parking

How to get there:

By bus/train: Take train to Reutlingen. From Reutlingen Station take bus to Erpfingen, getting off at Marktplatz stop and walking 1 mile to hostel.

By car: Take Highway B27 from Stuttgart to Reutlingen, then take Highway B312 to Pfullingen, following signs to Sonnenbühl. Or, from the direction of München, take Highway A8 to Merklingen exit, continuing from Münsingen through Bärenhöhle to Erpfingen.

JUGENDHERBERGE ESSLINGEN

(Esslingen Hostel)

Neuffenstrasse 65,

73734 Esslingen

Phone: 0711–381–848

Fax: 0711–388–886
Rates: 22–27 DM per HI member (about $11–$14 US)
Beds: 104
Private/family rooms: Yes
Kitchen available: No
Season: Closed November 25–December 31
Affiliation: HI-DJH
Regional office: Baden-Württemberg
Extras: Meals ($), parking

How to get there:

By bus/train: Take train to Esslingen. From Esslingen Station take #119 or #120 bus

to Zollberg stop. Or
(Monday–Friday only) take #118
bus to Zollernplatz and walk ⅓
mile to hostel.
By car: Take Highway B10 from
Stuttgart or München or Highway
A8 from Karlsruhe.

JUGENDHERBERGE HEBELHOF

(Feldberg Hostel)
Passhöhe 14,
79868 Feldberg
Phone: 07676–221

Fax: 07676–1232
Rates: 23–28 DM per HI member
(about $12–$14 US)
Beds: 270
Private/family rooms: Yes
Kitchen available: No
Season: Contact hostel for current
season
Affiliation: HI-DJH
Regional office: Baden-
Württemberg
Extras: Disco, swimming, parking,
meals ($)

How to get there:

By bus/train: Take train to
Feldberg-Bärental from Freiburg.
From Bärental Station take bus to
Hebelhof stop and walk ½ mile to
hostel.
By car: Take Highway A5, exiting at
signs for Freiburg-Mitte, then
continue along Highway B31 to
Titisee and Highway B317, exit-
ing at signs for Donaueschingen.
Continue to Feldberg.

TURNERHEIM ALTGLASHÜTTEN

Am Sommerberg 26,
79868 Feldberg
Phone: 07655–90010

Fax: 07655–900–199
Rates: 26–31 DM per HI member
(about $13–$16 US)
Beds: 91
Private/family rooms: Yes
Kitchen available: No
Season: Contact hostel for current
season
Affiliation: HI-DJH
Regional office: Baden-
Württemberg
Extras: Meals ($), parking

How to get there:

By bus: Contact hostel for transit
details.
By car: Take Highway B31 to
Titisee-Neustadt, then Highway
B317 to Bärental, continuing via
Highway B500 to Feldberg.
By train: Take train from Freiburg
via Bärental, Schluchsee, and
Seebrugg. From train station
walk ¾ mile to hostel. Or contact
hostel for further transit details.

FRANZ-KÖBELE-JUGENDHERBERGE HERRENWIES

(Forbach Hostel)
Environment Study Center
Haus Nr. 33,
76596 Forbach
Phone: 07226–257

Fax: 07226–1318
Rates: 24–29 DM per HI member
(about $12–$15 US)

Beds: 143
Private/family rooms: Yes
Kitchen available: No
Season: Contact hostel for current season
Affiliation: HI-DJH
Regional office: Baden-Württemberg
Extras: TV room, meals ($), environmental programs, parking

How to get there:

By bus/train: Take train to Bühl/Baden from Karlsruhe or Freibur. From Bühl Station take bus to Herrenwies Jugendherberge stop.

By car: Take Highway A5, exiting at signs for Bühl, then continuing in direction of Bühlertal-Schwarzwaldhochstrasse to Sand. Or from Rastatt/Freudenstadt take Highway B462.

JUGENDHERBERGE FREUDENSTADT

(Freudenstadt Hostel)
Eugen-Nägele-Strasse 69,
72250 Freudenstadt
Phone: 07441–7720

Fax: 07441–85788
Rates: 24–29 DM per HI member (about $12–$15 US)
Beds: 130
Private/family rooms: Yes
Kitchen available: No
Season: Closed November 11–December 26
Affiliation: HI-DJH
Regional office: Baden-Württemberg
Extras: Table tennis, laundry, meals ($)

How to get there:

By bus: Take train to Freudenstadt. From Stadtbahnhof Station walk ⅓ mile to hostel. From Hauptbahnhof Station take bus to Berufsschule stop and walk 200 yards to hostel.

By car: Contact hostel for directions.

By train: Take train to Freudenstadt. From Stadtbahnhof Station walk ⅓ mile to hostel. From Hauptbahnhof Station take bus to Berufsschule stop and walk 200 yards to hostel.

JUGENDHERBERGE HEIDELBERG

(Heidelberg Hostel)
Tiergartenstrasse 5,
69120 Heidelberg
Phone: 06221–412–066

Fax: 06221–402–559
Rates: 24–29 DM per HI member (about $12–$15 US)
Beds: 441
Private/family rooms: Yes
Kitchen available: No
Season: Closed December 24–26
Affiliation: HI-DJH
Regional office: Baden-Württemberg
Extras: Cafeteria ($), disco, TV room, laundry, parking

How to get there:

By bus/train: Take train from Frankfurt, Karlsruhe, Mannheim, or Stuttgart to Heidelberg. From Heidelberg Station take #33 bus to Jugendherberge (hostel) stop.

By car: Take Autobahn A5 and Highway A656 to Heidelberg.

JUGENDHERBERGE HEIDENHEIM

(Heidenheim Hostel)

Liststrasse 15,

89518 Heidenheim

Phone: 07321–42045

Fax: 07321–949–045
Rates: 24–29 DM per HI member
(about $12–$15 US)
Beds: 128
Private/family rooms: Yes
Kitchen available: No
Season: Closed November 11–
December 26
Affiliation: HI-DJH
Regional office: Baden-
Württemberg
Extras: Meals ($), wheelchair
access

How to get there:

By bus/train: Take train to
Heidenheim. From Heidenheim
Station take bus to Liststrasse
stop or bus toward Göppingen to
Ratskeller stop.
By car: Take Highway A7 from
Fernziel or Highway B466 from
Göppingen.

REINHARDT-JUGENDHERBERGE

(Heilbronn Hostel)

Schirrmannstrasse 9,

74074 Heilbronn

Phone: 07131–172–961

Fax: 07131–164–345
Rates: 24–29 DM per HI member
(about $12–$15 US)
Beds: 126
Private/family rooms: No
Kitchen available: No

Season: Contact hostel for current
season
Affiliation: HI-DJH
Regional office: Baden-
Württemberg
Extras: Table tennis tables, meals
($), parking, laundry

How to get there:

By bus/train: Take train to
Heilbronn. From Heilbronn
Station walk 3 miles to hostel, or
take #1 bus to last station
(Trappensee) and walk 200 yards
to hostel.
By car: Take Highway A6, exiting at
signs for Heilbronn/Neckarsulm,
or take Highway A81, exiting at
signs for Heilbronn/ Unter-
gruppenbach.

JUGENDHERBERGE HOHENSTAUFEN

(Hohenstaufen Hostel)

Schottengasse 45,

73037 Hohenstaufen-

Göppingen

Phone: 07165–438

Fax: 07165–1418
Rates: 24–29 DM per HI member
(about $12–$15 US)
Beds: 128
Private/family rooms: No
Kitchen available: Yes
Season: Closed November 27–
December 31
Affiliation: HI-DJH
Regional office: Baden-
Württemberg
Extras: Parking, meals ($)

How to get there:

By bus/train: Take train to
Göppingen. From Göppingen
Station take bus to

Jugendherberge (hostel) stop, and walk 50 yards to hostel.

By car: Contact hotel for directions.

JUGENDHERBERGE IGERSHEIM

(Igersheim Hostel)

Erlenbachtalstrasse 44,

97999 Igersheim

Phone: 07931–6373

Fax: 07931–52795

Rates: 24–29 DM per HI member (about $12–$15 US)

Beds: 162

Private/family rooms: Yes

Kitchen available: No

Season: Closed November 11–December 31

Affiliation: HI-DJH

Regional office: Baden-Württemberg

Extras: Parking, meals ($)

How to get there:

By bus/train: Take train to Igersheim. From Igersheim Station walk 1 mile to hostel. Or, from Bad Mergentheim, walk 1 mile to hostel or take bus to Solymar stop and walk ⅓ mile to hostel.

By car: Take Highway A81 to Tauberbischofsheim or Boxberg.

GEORG-SULZBERGER-JUGENDHERBERGE

(Isny Hostel)

Dekan-Marquardt-Strasse 18,

88316 Isny/Allgäu

Phone: 07562–2550

Fax: 07562–55547

Rates: 24–29 DM per HI member (about $12–$15 US)

Beds: 131

Private/family rooms: No

Kitchen available: No

Season: Closed November 27–December 31

Affiliation: HI-DJH

Regional office: Baden-Württemberg

Extras: Meals ($), parking

How to get there:

By bus/train: Take train to Leutkirch or Kempten. From either train station take bus to Isny. From Marktplatz walk 1 mile to hostel.

By car: Take Highway A7 to Memmingen, then Highway A96 to Lindau, exiting at signs for Leutkirch-Süd Isny.

JUGENDHERBERGE PLATZHOF

(Kandern Hostel)

Auf der Scheideck,

79400 Kandern

Phone: 07626–484

Fax: 07626–6809

Rates: 22–29 DM per HI member (about $11–$15 US)

Beds: 69

Private/family rooms: Yes

Kitchen available: No

Season: Closed December 24–26

Affiliation: HI-DJH

Regional office: Baden-Württemberg

Extras: Meals ($), parking

How to get there:

By bus/train: Take train to Kandern from Basel, Lörrach, or Steinen. From Steinen Station take bus to Jugendherberge (hostel).

By car: Take Highway A5, exiting at signs for Neuenburg-Mühlheim, then take Highway B3 to Schliengen, through Liel and Riedlingen to Kandern. Or take Highway B317 via Schlächtenhaus.

JUGENDHERBERGE KEHL

(Hostel Kehl)

Altrheinweg 11,

77694 Kehl

Phone: 07851–2330

Fax: 07851–76608
Rates: 24–29 DM per HI member (about $12–$15 US)
Beds: 122
Private/family rooms: Yes
Kitchen available: No
Season: Contact hostel for current season
Affiliation: HI-DJH
Regional office: Baden-Württemberg
Extras: Parking, meals ($)

How to get there:

By bus: Contact hostel for transit details.
By car: Take Autobahn A5, exiting at signs for Appenweier (using Highway B28) or Offenburg.
By train: Take train from Offenburg or Strasburg to Kehl. From Kehl Station walk 1 mile to hostel.

JUGENDHERBERGE KIRCHBERG/JAGST

(Hostel Kirchberg)

Gaggstatter Strasse 35,

74592 Kirchberg/Jagst

Phone: 07954–230

Fax: 07954–1319
Rates: 22–27 DM per HI member (about $11–$14 US)
Beds: 90
Private/family rooms: No
Kitchen available: No
Season: Closed December 23–31
Affiliation: HI-DJH
Regional office: Baden-Württemberg
Extras: Disco, meals ($), parking

How to get there:

By bus/train: Take train to Crailsheim or Schwäbisch Hall. From either train station take bus to Kirchberg/Jagst and get off at Frankenplatz stop, then walk ⅓ mile to hostel. From Kirchberg/Jagst center walk ¾ mile over Jagstbrücke bridge to hostel.
By car: Take Highway A6, exiting at signs for Kirchberg.

JUGENDHERBERGE KÖNIGSBRONN

(Königsbronn Hostel)

Weilerweg 12,

89551 Königsbronn-Ochsenberg

Phone: 07328–6600

Fax: 07328–7451
Rates: 24–29 DM per HI member (about $12–$15 US)
Beds: 116
Private/family rooms: Yes
Kitchen available: No
Season: Closed December 11–26
Affiliation: HI-DJH
Regional office: Baden-Württemberg
Extras: Meals ($), parking, wheelchair access

How to get there:

By bus: Contact hostel for transit details.

By car: Take Autobahn A7 to Ulm-West, continuing in the direction of Heidenheim or Highway A7 from Würzburg to Ulm, exiting at signs for Heidenheim-Königsbronn.

By train: Take train to Königsbronn. From Königsbronn Station walk 2 miles to hostel or take bus to Ochsenberg, getting off at Im Weiler stop and walking 300 yards to hostel.

JUGENDHERBERGE BURG WILDENSTEIN

(Leibertingen Hostel)

88637 Leibertingen

Phone: 07466–411

Fax: 07466–417
Rates: 24–29 DM per HI member (about $12–$15 US)
Beds: 163
Private/family rooms: Yes
Kitchen available: No
Season: Closed November 11– December 26
Affiliation: HI-DJH
Regional office: Baden-Württemberg
Extras: Laundry, parking, meals ($)

How to get there:

By bus/train: Take train to Beuron, then walk 3 miles to hostel or take bus. Contact hostel for further transit details.

By car: Contact hostel for directions.

JUGENDHERBERGE LOCHEN

(Lochen Hostel)

Auf der Lochen 1,

72336 Lochen

Phone: 07433–37383

Fax: 07433–382–296
Web site: www.balingen.de/ juhe/juheloch.htm
Rates: 24–29 DM per HI member (about $12–$15 US)
Beds: 102
Private/family rooms: Yes
Kitchen available: No
Season: Closed December 11–26
Affiliation: HI-DJH
Regional office: Baden-Württemberg
Extras: Fireplace, wood-fired oven, disco, sports programs, bike rentals, parking, meals ($)

How to get there:

By bus/train: Take train to Balingen. From Balingen Station take bus to Lochen stop.

By car: Take Highway A81 to Lochen.

JUGENDHERBERGE LÖRRACH

(Lörrach Hostel)

Steinenweg 40,

79540 Lörrach

Phone: 07621–47040

Fax: 07621–18156
Rates: 24–29 DM per HI member (about $12–$15 US)
Beds: 168
Private/family rooms: Yes
Kitchen available: No
Season: Contact hostel for current season
Affiliation: HI-DJH
Regional office: Baden-Württemberg

Extras: Meals ($), parking, wheel-
chair access

How to get there:

By bus:/train Take train to
Lörrach. From Lörrach Station
take #7 bus to Jugendherberge
(hostel) stop or walk 1 mile to
hostel.

By car: Take Autobahn A5, or
from east take Highway B34,
exiting at signs for Rheinfelden
and continuing along Highway
B316. Or travel through
Wiesental via Highway B317.

JUGENDHERBERGE UND JUGENDGÄSTEHAUS LUDWIGSBURG

(Ludwigsburg Hostel/Guest
House)

Gemsenbergstrasse 21,

71640 Ludwigsburg

Phone: 07141–51564

Fax: 07141–59440
Rates: 24–33 DM per HI member
(about $12–$17 US)
Beds: 121
Private/family rooms: Yes
Kitchen available: No
Season: Closed December 23–31
Affiliation: HI-DJH
Regional office: Baden-
Württemberg
Extras: Meals ($), parking

How to get there:

By bus/train: Take train to
Ludwigsburg. From Ludwigsburg
Station take #422 bus to
Schlösslesfeld stop (last stop),
then walk 300 yards to hostel.

By car: Take Highway A8, exiting
at signs for: Ludwigsburg-Nord

and following signs in
the direction of Stadtmitte,
Backnang, Neckarbrücke,
and finally Krankenhaus.

JUGENDHERBERGE MANNHEIM

(Mannheim Hostel)

Rheinpromenade 21,

68163 Mannheim

Phone: 0621–822–718

Fax: 0621–824–073
Rates: 22–27 DM per HI member
(about $11–$14 US)
Beds: 112
Private/family rooms: Yes
Kitchen available: No
Season: Closed December 24–26
Affiliation: HI-DJH
Regional office: Baden-
Württemberg
Extras: Parking, meals ($)

How to get there:

By bus/train: Take train to
Mannheim. From Mannheim
Station take #71 or #75 bus in
the direction of Lindenhof to
Gontardplatzstop and walk ¼
mile to hostel. Or from Neckar-
West take #7 line and get off at
Lindenhofplatz, then walk ¼
mile to hostel.

By car: Take Highways A5, A6,
and B36 to Highways B38 and
B44. Continue to Mannheim.

JUGENDHERBERGE MUTSCHLER'S MÜHLE

(Mosbach Hostel)

Beim Elzstadion,

74821 Mosbach

Phone: 06261–7191

Fax: 06261–61812
Rates: 26–31 DM per HI member
(about $13–$16 US)
Beds: 147
Private/family rooms: Yes
Kitchen available: No
Season: Contact hostel for current
season
Affiliation: HI-DJH
Regional office: Baden-
Württemberg
Extras: Disco, bicycle repair shop,
parking, laundry, meals ($)

How to get there:

By bus: Contact hostel for transit
details.
By car: Take Highway A6, exiting
at signs for Neckarsulm, or take
Highway A81, exiting at signs
for Osterburken. Continue along
Highway B27 or Highway B292
to Neckarelz-Mitte. Follow signs
to Elzstadion/Jugendherberge.
By train: Take train to Neckarelz
from Heidelberg or Würzburg.
From Neckarelz Station walk ½
mile to hostel.

SCHLOSS ORTENBERG HOSTEL

(Ortenberg Hostel)
Burgweg 21,
77799 Ortenberg
Phone: 0781–31749

Fax: 0781–948–1031
E-mail: schloss-ortenberg
@t-online.de
Rates: 24–29 DM per HI member
(about $12–$15 US)
Beds: 146
Private/family rooms: Yes
Kitchen available: No
Season: Contact hostel for current
season
Affiliation: HI-DJH

Regional office: Baden-
Württemberg
Extras: Meals ($), parking

How to get there:

By bus/train: Take train to
Offenburg or Gengenbach. From
either station take bus to
Ortenberg and walk ½ mile to
castle. Hostel is inside.
By car: Take Highway A5, exiting at
signs for Offenburg, then continue
along Highway B33 in the direction of Donaueschingen, exiting at
signs for Ortenberg-Elgersweiler.

JUGENDHERBERGE SOHLBERG

(Ottenhöfen Hostel)
Sohlberg 5,
77883 Ottenhöfen
Phone: 07842–2629

Fax: 07842–30008
Rates: 22–27 DM per HI member
(about $11–$14 US)
Beds: 73
Private/family rooms: Yes
Kitchen available: No
Season: Contact hostel for current
season
Affiliation: HI-DJH
Regional office: Baden-
Württemberg
Extras: Walking trails, ski trails
nearby, parking, meals ($)

How to get there:

By bus: Contact hostel for transit
details
By car: Take Highway A5, exiting at
signs for Achern, then continuing
in direction of Schwarzwaldhochstrasse to Ottenhöfen.
By train: Take train to Ottenhöfen
from Nebenbahn or Achern. From
Ottenhöfen Station take bus in

the direction of Allerheiligen to
St. Ursula and walk to hostel.

JUGENDHERBERGE BURG RABENECK

(Pforzheim Hostel)

Kräheneckstrasse 4,

75180 Pforzheim

Phone: 07231–972–660

Fax: 07231–972–661
Rates: 26–31 DM per HI member
(about $13–$16 US)
Beds: 96
Private/family rooms: Yes
Kitchen available: No
Season: Closed December 24–26
Affiliation: HI-DJH
Regional office: Baden-
Württemberg
Extras: Programs, meals ($), parking

How to get there:

By bus/train: Take train to
Pforzheim. From Pforzheim
Station take #3 bus to
Burggartenstrasse stop and walk
short distance to hostel.

By car: Take Highway A8, exiting
at signs for Pforzheim-West,
then continue along Highway
B10 to Pforzheim, joining up
with Highway B463. Continue
in the direction of Calaw to
Weissensteiner Nagoldbrücke.

JUGENDHERBERGE SCHLOSS RECHENBERG

(Stimpfach Hostel)

Zum Schloss 7,

74597 Stimpfach

Phone: 07967–372

Fax: 07967–8985
Rates: 22–27 DM per HI member
(about $12–$15 US)
Beds: 100
Private/family rooms: No
Kitchen available: No
Season: Closed December 11–31
Affiliation: HI-DJH
Regional office: Baden-Württemberg
Extras: Disco

How to get there:

By bus/train: Take train to
Crailsheim. From Crailsheim
Station take bus to Jugendherberge (hostel) stop and walk
300 yards to hostel. Or take
train to Jagstzell and walk 2½
miles to hostel.

By car: Take Highway A6 to
Crailsheim or Highway A7 to
Ellwangen, then take Highway
B290 to Stimpfach.

JUGENDHERBERGE SCHWÄBISCH HALL

(Schwäbisch Hall Hostel)

Langenfelderweg 5,

74523 Schwäbisch Hall

Phone: 0791–41050

Fax: 0791–47998
Rates: 24–29 DM per HI member
(about $11–$15 US)
Beds: 143
Private/family rooms: Yes
Kitchen available: No
Season: Closed December 11–31
Affiliation: HI-DJH
Regional office: Baden-Württemberg
Extras: Laundry, meals ($), parking, laundry

How to get there:

By bus/train: Take train to
Schwäbisch Hall. From
Schwäbisch Hall Station walk 1

mile to hostel. Or take #1 bus to Bausparkasse stop and walk 1 mile to hostel.

By car: Take Highway B14 from Stuttgart or Nürnberg; or take Highway A8 from Nürnberg to Heilbronn, then continue to Schwäbisch Hall and follow signs in the direction of Bausparkasse.

JUGENDHERBERGE TAUBERBISCHOFSHEI M (Tauberbischofsheim Hostel)

Schirrmannweg 2,

97941 Tauberbischofsheim

Phone: 09341–3152

Fax: 09341–95052
Rates: 22–27 DM per HI member (about $11–$14 US)
Beds: 106
Private/family rooms: Yes
Kitchen available: No
Season: Contact hostel for current season
Affiliation: HI-DJH
Regional office: Baden-Württemberg
Extras: Game room, table tennis, disco, parking, meals ($)

How to get there:

By bus: Contact hostel for transit details.
By car: Take Highway A81, exiting at signs for Tauber-bischofsheim.
By train: Take train to Tauber-bischofsheim from Aschaffen-burg, Lauda, or Würzburg. From Tauberbischofsheim Station walk ¾ mile to hostel.

JUGENDHERBERGE TÜBINGEN

(Tübingen Hostel)

Gartenstrasse 22/2,

72074 Tübingen

Phone: 07071–23002

Fax: 07071–25061
Rates: 26–31 DM per HI member (about $13–$16 US)
Beds: 163
Private/family rooms: Yes
Kitchen available: No
Season: Closed December 24–27
Affiliation: HI-DJH
Regional office: Baden-Württemberg
Extras: Meals ($), parking

How to get there:

By bus/train: Take train to Tübingen. From Tübingen Station walk ½ mile to Europaplatz and take #11 bus to Jugendherberge (hostel) stop.
By car: Take Highway B27 or Highway A81.

GESCHWISTER-SCHOLL-JUGENDHERBERGE

(Ulm Hostel)

Grimmelfinger Weg 45,

89077 Ulm/Donau

Phone: 0731–384–455

Fax: 0731–384–511
Rates: 24–29 DM per HI member (about $12–$15 US)
Beds: 147
Private/family rooms: No
Kitchen available: No
Season: Closed December 11–31
Affiliation: HI-DJH
Regional office: Baden-Württemberg

Extras: Laundry, meals ($), parking
How to get there:
By bus/train: Take train to Ulm.
From Ulm Station take S-Bahn
line S1 in the direction of
Söfingen to Ehinger Tor stop,
then change to #4 bus in the
direction of Kuhberg to
Schulzentrum stop or #8 bus in
the direction of Wiblingen.
By car: Take Highway A8 from
Stuttgart or München, exiting at
signs for Ulm-West.

JUGENDHERBERGE VILLINGEN
(Hostel Villingen)
St. Georgener Strasse 36,
78048 Villingen-Schwenningen
Phone: 07721–54149

Fax: 07721–52616
Rates: 22–27 DM per HI member
(about $11–$14 US)
Beds: 134
Private/family rooms: Yes
Kitchen available: No
Season: Contact hostel for current
season
Affiliation: HI-DJH
Regional office: Baden-
Württemberg
Extras: Playground, meals ($),
parking, laundry
How to get there:
By bus/train: Take train from
Offenburg or Konstanz to
Villingen. From Villingen Station
take #3 or #4 bus to Triberger
Strasse stop and walk short dis-
tance to hostel. Or walk 1½ miles
from train station to hostel.
By car: Take Autobahn A5, exiting
at signs for Offenburg and taking
Highway B33 or Highway A81,

exiting at signs for Villingen-
Schwenningen.

JUGENDHERBERGE WALLDÜRN
(Walldürn Hostel)
Auf der Heide 37,
74731 Walldürn
Phone: 06282–283

Fax: 06282–40194
Rates: 24–29 DM per HI member
(about $12–$15 US)
Beds: 102
Private/family rooms: Yes
Kitchen available: No
Season: Contact hostel for current
season
Affiliation: HI-DJH
Regional office: Baden-
Württemberg
Extras: Bike rentals, TV, VCR,
meals ($), parking
How to get there:
By bus: Contact hostel for transit
details.
By car: Take Highway B47 and
then Highway B27 to Walldürn.
By train: From Miltenberg or
Seckach, take train to Walldürn.
From Walldürn Station walk 1½
miles to hostel or contact hostel
for further transit details.

JUGENDGÄSTEHAUS "HAUS DER MUSIK"
(Weikersheim Guest House Hostel)
Im Heiligen Wöhr 1,
97990 Weikersheim
Phone: 07934–7025

Fax: 07934–7709
Rates: 24–29 DM per HI member
(about $12–$15 US)
Beds: 143
Private/family rooms: Yes
Kitchen available: No
Season: Closed November 11–
December 26
Affiliation: HI-DJH
Regional office: Baden-
Württemberg
Extras: Beach volleyball, laundry,
parking, meals ($), wheelchair
access

How to get there:

By bus/train: Take train to
Weikersheim. From Weikersheim
Station take bus to Marktplatz
and walk 200 yards to hostel.
By car: Take Highway A81 from
Heilbronn or Würzburg, continu-
ing through Boxberg and Bad
Mergentheim to Weikersheim.

JUGENDHERBERGE WEINHEIM

(Weinheim Hostel)

Breslauer Strasse 46,

69469 Weinheim

Phone: 06201–68484

Fax: 06201–182–730
Rates: 26–31 DM per HI member
(about $13–$16 US)
Beds: 129
Private/family rooms: Yes
Kitchen available: No
Season: Contact hostel for current
season
Affiliation: HI-DJH
Regional office: Baden-
Württemberg
Extras: Game room, disco, laundry,
meals ($), parking

How to get there:

By bus/train: Take train to
Weinheim from Heidelberg or
Frankfurt. From Weinheim
Station take bus in the direction
of Mannheim to Stahlbad stop,
then walk to hostel.
By car: Take Highway A5.

JUGENDHERBERGE FRANKENLAND

(Wertheim Hostel)

Alte Steige 16,

97877 Wertheim

Phone: 09342–6451

Fax: 09342–7354
Rates: 22–27 DM per HI member
(about $11–$14 US)
Beds: 99
Private/family rooms: Yes
Kitchen available: No
Season: Contact hostel for current
season
Affiliation: HI-DJH
Regional office: Baden-
Württemberg
Extras: Parking, meals ($)

How to get there:

By bus: Contact hostel for transit
route.
By car: Take Highway A3 or Highway A81, exiting at signs for
Tauberbischofsheim.
By train: Take train to Wertheim
from Aschaffenburg, Lauda or
Würzburg. From Wertheim Station
walk ¾ mile to hostel.

JUGENDHERBERGE BELCHEN

(Wieden Hostel)

Oberwieden 16,

79695 Wieden

Phone: 07673–538

Fax: 07673–504
Rates: 22–27 DM per HI member
(about $11–$14 US)
Beds: 167
Private/family rooms: Yes
Kitchen available: No
Affiliation: HI-DJH
Regional office: Baden-Württemberg
Extras: Disco, sports programs, parking, meals ($)

How to get there:

By bus: From Waldmünster, take bus to Wiedener Eck stop and walk to hostel.

By car: Take Highway A5, exiting at signs for Bad Krozingen and continuing through Münstertal to Wieden.

By train: Take train to Münstertal from Bad Krozingen or Untermünstertal. From Münstertal Station contact hostel for transit route.

JUGENDHERBERGE ZUFLUCHT

(Zuflucht Hostel)

Schwarzwaldhochstrasse,

72250 Zuflucht

Phone: 07804–611

Fax: 07804–1323
Rates: 24–29 DM per HI member
(about $12–$15 US)
Beds: 218
Private/family rooms: No
Kitchen available: No
Season: Closed November 11–December 26
Affiliation: HI-DJH
Regional office: Baden-Württemberg
Extras: Laundry, playroom, ski trips

How to get there:

By bus/train: Take train to Freudenstadt. From Freudenstadt Station take bus (daily; runs May to September only) to hostel.

By car: Contact hostel for directions.

MÜNCHEN (MUNICH)

Page numbers follow hostel names

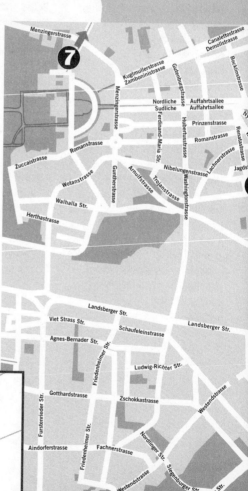

MÜNCHEN (MUNICH)

Ah, Munich, city of monks. That's what the name means. Honest. Of course you'd never know it—it's the least German of German cities. In other words, it's easygoing, fun-loving and (relatively) sunny compared to the rest of 'em—this ain't fast-paced Berlin, it's the kind of place where people sit around for three hours in the midday sun drinking beer. And those are people with jobs.

Still, it's a little hard at times to reconcile all this merrymaking with a recent past as the nerve center of Nazi activity during the dark years of World War II.

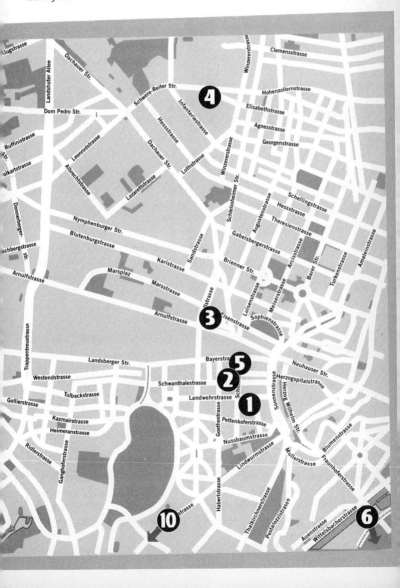

ORIENTATION AND GETTING AROUND

You'll most likely start your visit at the big and confusing Munich **Hauptbahnhof,** one of the busiest train stations in Europe. Getting off the train, you're confronted with a jumble of tracks, each bunch earmarked for a specific type of travel: slow local trains, slick inter-city trains, speedy international trains, and ultramodern overnight trains all have their own areas.

Before you even leave, make your first stop the **EurAide** office, on the quiet side of the station beside track #11. The staff at this American-run office (funded by the Germans) speaks perfect English and helps you find your way through train schedules, make train reservations for a small charge (it's worth it, trust us), or book a tour. The station itself contains any services you need under one roof—a travel agency, twenty-four-hour lockers and luggage storage, restaurants, a currency exchange, a cool Internet cafe (upstairs near the exit), a newsstand, a tourist office, and bike rentals. There are public phones everywhere that accept German phone cards (buy 'em at the post office or newsstand).

Surprisingly, the immediate area surrounding the train station is not as shabby as it could be. But there's not much to see here if your hostel is elsewhere; you'll probably be making a beeline for the U-Bahn or S-Bahn station to check into your hostel. Wanna get an immediate taste of the city? Head straight out of the station and follow the crowds to Marienplatz through a no-car walking zone. This is where most of the tourist action can be found (see What to See, below).

Of the in-town neighborhoods, **Schwabing** is by far the coolest. It's the heart and soul of Munich, located between the enormous and lively English Garden and even bigger Olympic Park. The "Jugendstil" of art was born here, and many beautiful buildings survived World War II bombings. Though Schwabing has gotten a little too hip for its own good—there are suits and cell phones all over the place now—the area still has Munich's best cafes, pubs, good-value restaurants, and cinemas. Bottom line? This is as laid-back as Germany ever gets. Come here.

GETTING AROUND

Getting around should be no trouble, as the city maintains a topflight transit network of buses, commuter trains **(S-Bahn)** and subway cars **(U-Bahn)**. The system is efficient, fairly clean, and always busy. Look for an "S" on a green circle for commuter rail stations and a "U" on a blue square for subway stations. **Bus stops** are marked by street signs with an "H" on them.

You can purchase **single tickets** for this system for 3.50 DM (about $1.75 US) or—to save time and money while hopping around—a transit pass such as the following:

- The one-day pass **(Single-Tageskarte)** costs 9.00 DM (about $4.50 US) or 12.50 DM for two adults (a **Partner-Tageskarte,** about $6.00 US).
- The three-day pass **(3-Day Pass)** goes for 21 DM (about $10.50 US).

- The three-day **Welcome Card** costs 29 DM (about $14.50 US) and gets you half-price museum entry and bike rentals.

It's probably better to buy one of these passes rather than going for the complicated **Streifenkarte** ("strip ticket") book of ten tickets, which can work out cheaper but is also a pain to use if you're not a local.

Remember to "validate" (punch) your ticket at the blue box as soon as you board your streetcar, bus, or subway car. Don't forget to do this. Secret transit police may be riding alongside you, dressed like normal Munichers, and they'll fine you big if you "forgot" to stamp your ticket.

There are two things to keep in mind when using the subways and commuter trains:

Number one. This is one of those rare cities where the S-Bahn's aboveground trains are actually handier for getting to most of the sights and hostels than the subway, so when in doubt go for the S-Bahn signs instead of the U-Bahn signs.

Number two. If you've got a Eurail pass, you can use the S-Bahns for free—yes, free!—as long as you have penciled in the current date in the box. This is *not* a good idea normally because it wastes a day. However, if you have already used the pass to get into town, pencil in that date.

Feeling flush? In a hurry? Taxis troll for passengers at the exit near track #11. They are beige, clean, and fairly inexpensive.

WHAT TO SEE, DRINK, and EAT

The main tourism information office is located just outside the train station (follow the signs). It's open Monday to Saturday, 8:00 A.M. to 8:00 P.M., and 9:00 A.M. to 6:00 P.M. Sunday. They are among the friendliest and most helpful tourist officers we've ever met.

After picking up maps and getting their advice, begin in the **Altstadt** ("old town"), where the Marienplatz plaza is the focal point for the worthwhile sights and beer. Even without much time, you can taste the mood of the city within a few minutes in this sunshine-filled pedestrian zone containing the majestically twin-towered Frauenkirche, St. Michael's Kirche, the Rathaus and the royal Residenz.

A little southeast and you'll be walking through the Isartor—a gate built in the early fourteenth century, the last remaining piece of the ring that formerly closed Munich—towards the **Viktualienmarkt**. You've gotta see this place: an open market teeming with foodies in search of plump olives, freshly squeezed carrot juice, shaded beer gardens, and tons of small restaurants. Eat here now!

Culture vultures might head in the other direction, to art museums such as the Alte and Neue Pinakotheks and the modern Haus der Kunst. You'd also do well to entertain yourself at the huge and fun Deutsches Museum (on the other side of the Isar River) or the informative BMW and Siemens museums.

If the weather's good, skip the museums and head instead for the **Englischer Garten** (English Garden), Europe's oldest public park,

MUNICH HOSTELS at a glance

	RATING	COST	IN A WORD	PAGE
Hotel Helvetia Hostel	👍👍	25–65 DM	nice	335
Pullach Burg Schwaneck Hostel	👍👍	23 DM	regal	341
Euro Youth Hotel	👍	25–36 DM	beery	331
Kapuziner (The Tent) Hostel	👍	14–18 DM	groovy	337
CVJM Jugendgästehaus Hostel	👍	42–61 DM	Catholic	329
Neuhausen Hostel	👍	30–48 DM	institutional	338
Haus International Hostel	👍👎	42–85 DM	big	333
4 You München	👍👎	26–79 DM	green	332
Thalkirchen Hostel	👍👎	32.50–37.50	strict	342
Jump In Hostel	NR	29–39 DM	friendly	336

with several great beer gardens, fields, and sunbathers—basically one of the best places to discover Munich in a nutshell.

Note that almost all the Munich museums and sights are closed on Monday, so do something else.

The beer, of course, flows in a never-ending river through this town. This is arguably the best beer in the world—if you like dark beers, it *is* the best in the world—so suck it up and suck some down. You can get a draft or bottle or keg of the stuff anytime anywhere, but it's especially obvious during beery festivals in March (March Beer Festival), May (Maibock), and September (Oktoberfest). Beer garden listings are included in some of the hostel writeups below.

Finally, know that Munich's restaurants are pricey—even more so in crowded areas such as around the station, as there are loads of tourists to rip off there. A better choice might be the many pizza and falafel take-out joints, the Wienerwald fast-food chain, or the McJunk outlets in the station, if you can stand them.

THE HOSTELS

Munich's hostels are, for the most part, clean and safe. Some even manage to be fun and interesting. Despite the huge annual beer fest, they don't have the same fluctuations in standards that similar party-oriented cities like Amsterdam do.

There's a big difference between DJH hostels and the rest here. Travelers older than twenty-six will be turned away at the "official" DJH-affiliated hostels but not at most of the more laid-back independent ones. The DJH joints here also tend to have inconvenient locations, harsher rules, and loads of noisy (sometimes bratty) schoolchildren. On the other hand, the independent places tend to slide a bit in terms of quietness and cleanliness. You make the choice.

Be aware, too, that during Oktoberfest—which actually takes place the last two weeks of *September,* strangely enough—all hostel prices listed here probably jump at least 10 percent and as much as 50 percent, depending on the greed of the hostel managers. (We're kidding. In reality the jump will probably be something like 15 percent. The point is, they could charge the moon and you'd still *pay* it, wouldn't you?)

Note that a number of these hostels are located very close to the main train station. There's lots of red-light business to be found here, as well as the usual suspects hanging out in the station, so one should be a bit more cautious at night—though Munich is, generally speaking, a very safe place.

CVJM JUGENDGÄSTEHAUS HOSTEL (YMCA GUEST HOUSE HOSTEL)

Landwehrstrasse 13,

80336 Munich

Phone: 089–552–1410

Fax: 089–550–4282
E-mail: muenchen@cvjm.org or hotel@cvjm-muenchen.org
Rates: 42–61 DM per person (about $21–$31 US); doubles 90–104 DM (about $45–$52 US)
Credit cards: Yes
Beds: 85
Private/family rooms: Yes
Kitchen available: No
Season: Closed December 25–January 6
Office hours: 7:00 A.M.–midnight
Curfew: 12:30 A.M.
Affiliation: None
Extras: Restaurant ($), breakfast

$

Bring those rosary beads if you wanna stay at this hostel, 'cause it's run by the local Catholics.

After a complete renovation last year, the place looks more like a posh bank than a hostel. Staff is surprisingly friendly and keeps everything looking as though no hosteller had ever used it before. There are only single rooms, doubles, and triples available; none of them are very large, but all sport new furniture. They actually resemble nice hotel rooms, not barnyard floors (which a couple other places in town resemble); try to ask for an off-the-street room, some of which face a courtyard and are pleasantly quieter.

Best bet for a bite:
La Vecchia Masseria for pizza

Insiders' tip:
Head for the Augustinerkeller beer garden

What hostellers say:
"Jeez—I mean, gosh—too many rules."

Gestalt:
Church chat

Safety:

Hospitality:

Cleanliness:

Party index:

However, note that there are only two showers on each floor (there are sinks in the room). The hostel also has its own restaurant, bar, and common room. The reception area and restaurant had just been renovated when we stopped by.

But while even some HI-affiliated hostels have recently trashed their ridiculously outdated rules, these folks are Catholic enough to hold the line. You'll have to deal with rules, rules, rules—among them: strict curfews, no unmarried couples sharing a room, no smoking, single male travelers are discouraged, no booze, and you have to be in by 12:30 at night. There are also no scandalous, licentious extras like Internet access or a laundry. That's just the beginning. The whole attitude here really is almost like being back in Catholic school (for those who remember such a thing); you half expect nuns to bring out the rulers and begin whacking your knuckles.

But, OK, the staff is friendly. Sheets and breakfast are included for free. And everything's kept spic-and-span, just as you'd expect. As usual, there's an extra charge here if you're over twenty-six years old.

At least it's mighty central, just steps from that huge train station where you're undoubtedly going to be arriving.

KEY TO ICONS

 Attractive natural setting

 Ecologically aware hostel

Superior kitchen facilities or cafe

Offbeat or eccentric place

Superior bathroom facilities

Romantic private rooms

 Comfortable beds

Editors' choice: among our very favorite hostels

 A particularly good value

Wheelchair accessible

 Good for business travelers

 Especially well suited for families

Good for active travelers

Visual arts at hostel or nearby

 Music at hostel or nearby

 Great hostel for skiers

 Bar or pub at hostel or nearby

Party? You'll have to pray for one.

How to get there:

By bus: Contact hostel for transit details.

By car: Contact hostel for directions.

By train: From the main train station turn right and walk down Schillerstrasse; take the second street on the left.

EURO YOUTH HOTEL

Senefelderstrasse 5,

80336 Munich

Phone: 089–599–0880

Fax: 089–5990–8877

E-mail: info@euro-youth-hotel.de

Rates: 25–36 DM per person (about $13–$18 US); doubles 84 DM (about $42 US)

Credit cards: No

Beds: Number varies

Private/family rooms: Yes

Kitchen available: No

Season: Open year-round

Office hours: Open twenty-four hours

Affiliation: None

Extras: Bar, breakfast ($), laundry, information

We heard very good reports of this place, but when we finally got there we were greeted by an extremely rude receptionist who refused to give us any info at all (too busy playing video games). That's unfortunate, because it's said to be one of the best choices in town—if you don't mind a little noise and beer.

Housed inside a once-posh hotel just next to Munich's train station, the place opened in 1999. Already they've got everything from a cheap, monsterlike thirty-bed dormitory to more expensive quad and double room digs (with shared bathrooms, of course; this ain't the Ritz). The best thing of all here, though, isn't the bed or the company—it's the beer. It is owned lock, stock, and barrel by one of Munich's (and Germany's) finest breweries, Augustiner. Needless to say, there's a constant flow of the suds, and the price isn't

Best bet for a bite:
Mövenpick at Karlsplatz

Insiders' tip:
Beer gardens in
Viktualienmarkt

What hostellers say:
"Pour me another!"

Gestalt:
Beer guardian

Safety:

Hospitality:

Cleanliness:

Party index:

bad: Less than 4.00 DM for a half-liter draft is less than you'll pay just about anywhere else in town.

Friendly? Central? Absolutely yes on both counts. The laundry is a huge bonus after traveling on the train, and you can pay extra for breakfast. It's a little expensive by Munich standards, however, so bring a few extra bucks and you'll be all right.

How to get there:

By bus: Contact hostel for transit details.

By car: Contact hostel for directions.

By train: From main train station exit right-hand side and turn down Bayerstrasse; continue to Senefelderstrasse.

4 YOU MÜNCHEN HOSTEL

Hirtenstrasse 18,

80335 Munich

Phone: 089–552–1660

Fax: 089–552–16666
E-mail: info@the4you.de
Rates: 26–79 DM per person (about $13–$40 US); doubles 80–129 DM (about $40–$65 US)
Credit cards: Yes
Beds: 212
Private/family rooms: Yes
Kitchen available: No
Season: Open year-round
Office hours: Open twenty-four hours
Affiliation: None
Extras: Cafeteria ($), bar, breakfast ($), tours, luggage storage, kindergarten, lockers

A few years ago a group of enthusiasts took over a run-down 1950s-era hotel with a mission: Start up Munich's first independent hostel. But they focused so much on ecology, on making it a "green hostel"—they even added wooden light switches—that they forgot to use a little business sense. And "green" didn't always equal "clean."

The project flopped economically. The place changed hands, passing to newer, more savvy (if less idealistic) management. Bottom line? Things look to be straightening out and services should be improving here soon.

The place *needs* improvement: Right now, it's only so-so. The building, located on a quiet little street just inches from the train station's craziness, has seen better days, and the somewhat beat-up dorm rooms (which have large lockers, by the way) are just too used-looking. The bunk beds are decent but not superior. At least everything is kept clean, a very recent improvement after the cleanliness and upkeep standards had really begun to slide. Check out the walls, floors, beds, and everything else while you're here; it's probably been recycled, depesticided, and left unpainted. You get the drift.

Prices are cheaper for younger folks; more expensive as you age or your room improves. Breakfast and meals—you have to pay for both—are organic and healthful, possibly as an antidote to all the beer and city fumes you'll be swilling the rest of the time. A huge bar in the basement is now waiting for live music and partying crowds, and a few basic extras like Internet access and a laundry are also planned; by press time they might have been added.

The place is still very politically and ecologically correct, too: Smoking is allowed only in a "smoker room," and the hostel kindergarten takes care of kiddies during the daytime. Nevertheless, we've gotta admit one thing: This is already one of Munich's best hostels in which to meet fellow travelers.

Note that the hostel also includes a pricier "hotel" section upstairs, part of the same complex but with better-equipped single and double rooms (they're more expensive, of course); these rooms all come with private bathrooms, and breakfast is included.

All things considered, this is one to consider, especially since it's very close to the city's central train station.

Best bet for a bite:
Buxs (near Viktualienmarkt) for veggie

Insiders' tip:
Sussman's has newspapers in English

What hostellers say:
"Duuuuude."

Gestalt:
2 cool 2 be 4gotten

Safety:

Hospitality:

Cleanliness:

Party index:

How to get there:

By bus: Contact hostel for transit route.
By car: Contact hostel for directions.
By train: From main train station exit left-hand side to Arnulfstrasse; take an immediate right onto Pfeffenstrasse, then another quick right onto Hirtenstrasse.

HAUS INTERNATIONAL HOSTEL

Elisabethstrasse 87,

80797 Munich

Phone: 089–120–060

Fax: 089–1200–6251
E-mail: info@haus-international.de
Rates: 42–85 DM per person (about $21–$43 US); doubles 98–138 DM (about $49–$69 US)
Credit cards: Yes
Beds: 545

Private/family rooms: Yes
Kitchen available: No
Season: Open year-round
Office hours: Open twenty-four hours
Affiliation: None
Extras: Restaurant ($), swimming pool, TV room, disco, bar, garden, patio, breakfast

In one word, this hostel is huge and ugly—and inconveniently located, too. Wait, that's more than one word.

You can't believe how huge this '70s-style building is—it's one of two hostels in town with 500-odd beds—yet, remarkably, it's often quite full due to the unending parade of school kiddies who provide the hostel with its bread-and-butter.

Best bet for a bite:
Pizzeria da Tanino

Insiders' tip:
BMW museum near Olympic park

What hostellers say:
"Big but bland."

Gestalt:
Haus of horrors

Safety:

Hospitality:

Cleanliness:

Party index:

The place was designed for school groups and congresses, and it shows. The common area on the ground floor looks practically Soviet, and the rooms and floors have taken lots of abuse. Double rooms here are in an acceptable condition, though the bigger ones are overpriced for what you get: cigarette burns through the carpets, loose closet doors, and graffiti. For "fun" there's a large, mostly empty disco in the basement, where you can also improve your skills in '80s video games (think Pac-Man, Ms. Pac-Man, Frogger, Super Mario). Teenyboppers congregate there, so *you* head downtown instead.

Despite the incredibly bland and beat-up fixtures and rooms, though, it's surprisingly expensive—twenty bucks a night?!—and the U-Bahn doesn't come anywhere near here, so you've gotta hoof it quite a ways or take a bus (#33 bus from Rotkreuzplatz) that doesn't run at night. You might have to split a taxi, kiddies, so factor that into your budget.

The only good things are the swimming pool, beer garden area, meals in a cafeteria, and a television lounge. Not good enough. Perhaps most important, though, the hostel's in approximately—and we stress approximately, not exactly—the same part of town as the Schwabing neighborhood, which some have compared with Greenwich Village, it's so cool (though it's a *lot* cleaner and safer). Okay, Schwabing actually stretches from the city center to Munich's northern border, and the Haus International is even quite a bit north of this hoppin' district, but you could conceivably see Schwabing on the same journey you're making out to the hostel.

The hostel *is* exceptionally close to the city's Olympic Stadium, however, with its awe-inspiring tinted-glass suspended roof. You can take a dip in the swimming pool, too, which is open to the public;

in winter rent skates and take to the ice. Other highlights of the park include tours of the grounds and a speedy lift to the top of the Olympic Tower.

How to get there:

By bus/train: Take U-Bahn line U2 toward Feldmoching to Hohenzollernplatz stop, then walk to hostel or change to #12 tram or #33 bus and continue to Barbara Strasse stop. Hostel is next to gas station.

By car: From any highway into the city, take Mittlerer Ring to Schwabing exit and continue to hostel.

HOTEL HELVETIA HOSTEL

Schillerstrasse 6,

80336 Munich

Phone: 089–590–6850

Fax: 089–5906–8570
E-mail: Hotel-Helvetia@t-online.de
Rates: 25–65 DM per person (about $13–$33 US); doubles 100 DM (about $50 US)
Credit cards: Yes
Beds: 100
Private/family rooms: Yes
Kitchen available: No
Season: Open year-round
Office hours: Open twenty-four hours
Affiliation: None
Extras: Breakfast ($), TV room, free Internet access, luggage storage

If you're sick of noisy youth hostels, this low-end but friendly hotel might be your Munich alternative. Its doubles aren't luxurious, but they're clean and well maintained and among the cheapest you can get in the city.

For the budget traveler who doesn't want a double room, there's only one dorm room. It contains ten beds—*real* beds, not bunk beds—but unfortunately the shower is on the other end of the floor, and it only dispenses water until 10:00 at night! Yikes! The reception staff is very helpful and friendly, though, and Net-addicts can take full advantage of *free* (yes, you read right) Internet access.

The whole operation is miles better than you'd expect any hostel to be, in fact. (The fact that it's part of a hotel doesn't even explain that fact, since many hotels tack on a few

Best bet for a bite:
Diät Reformhaus (veggie)

Insiders' tip:
Be safe in this neighborhood

What hostellers say:
"Didn't we meet in Berlin?"

Gestalt:
Swiss bliss

Safety:

Hospitality:

Cleanliness:

Party index:

cheapo rooms to make a buck and then leave the hostellers in freezing, drafty, damp digs.) Breakfast is included with your bed, and the bedding is good quality for a change. It's all very close to the train station, too.

The only problem is, well, absolutely everybody knows about it. That means everyone—including a Europe-wide bus circuit that stops here. So it's often too full to take you in high season. The lesson? Book ahead, of course! Also note that safety is a bit of a concern here—there are no lockers at all in which to store your stuff, and this a red-light neighborhood besides.

How to get there:

By bus: Contact hostel for transit route.

By car: Contact hostel for directions.

By train: From main train station exit main exit to Bahnofsplatz and look for the Vereinsbank; hostel is next door, on Schillerstrasse.

JUMP IN HOSTEL

Hochstrasse 51,

81541 Munich

Phone: 089–489–53437

Rates: 29–39 DM per person (about $15–$20 US); doubles 78 DM (about $39 US)

Credit cards: No

Beds: 30

Private/family rooms: Yes

Kitchen available: Yes

Season: Closed November 1–March 1

Office hours: 10:00 A.M.–1:00 P.M., 5:00–10:00 P.M.

Affiliation: None

Extras: Laundry, coffee

The newest entry in Munich's hostelling lottery, we hear that this one is supremely fun but not the plushest. Translation? You come here for the company, not great bunks.

Best bet for a bite:
Englischer Garten
beer garden

Insiders' tip:
Check out Deutsches
Museum

What hostellers say:
"Good place."

They've done themselves right by outfitting a laundry and kitchen, which—as we all know—are the number one and number two concerns of the wayward hosteller. It almost makes up for dorm rooms and beds that could best be described as, well, so-so. Also know that there are few rules here, no breakfast, and they charge extra for sheets.

The location is prime, though, on the southern edge of the city center within easy reach of public transport and spitting distance of the Deutsches Museum, the Gasteig (lots of concerts and exhibitions), and the Müllersches Volksbad—a beautiful hundred-year-old public swimming bath with everything from Turkish steam bath to massage. The Isar River, with parks on both sides, is just 2 blocks away.

Gestalt: Jump street

Hospitality:

Party index:

How to get there:

By bus: Contact hostel for transit details.

By car: Contact hostel for directions.

By train: Take S-Bahn to Karlsplatz Station, then change to the #27 tram and continue to the Ostfriedhof stop. Walk downhill to Hochstrasse, turn and right, and walk to hostel. Or take any S-Bahn from Hauptbahnhof to Rosenheimer Platz; exit back of station to Rosenheimer Strasse, and take first left onto Hochstrasse.

KAPUZINER (THE TENT)

In den Kirschen 30,

Munich

Phone: 089–141–4300

Fax: 089–175–090

Rates: 14–18 DM per person (about $7.00–$9.00 US)

Credit cards: No

Beds: Nobody's sure how many

Private/family rooms: No

Kitchen available: Yes

Season: Open June 15–August 31

Office hours: Open twenty-four hours

Affiliation: None

Extras: Bike rentals, lockers, breakfast, meals ($), campfires, movies, campground, transit pass discounts, Internet access, city tours

Must be under age twenty-seven to stay

Note: This hostel is sponsored by the city of Munich and kept on a tight budgetary leash, so its future is not secure. It could be gone by the time you crack this book, or it could be around forever.

Spartans have found a new joint in town to celebrate: "The Tent." This place, quite simply put, is a regular three-ring circus (minus the animals)—very appropriate, given that it is located beneath, yes, a giant tent.

That's right: A bed here isn't really a bed; what it is is a mattress on the floor of the tent—talk about urban camping—with a skimpy blanket. On warm nights you might not mind, though you're obviously sacrificing tons of privacy and amenities and security. Oh, they've got some plain bunk beds, too, marginally more like home but not much. Still, it's all in good fun and the skank-factor isn't too too high. Plumbing facilities consist of camp-style showers and toilets.

They show movies, sell cheap city transit passes (that city ownership really comes in handy), offer free breakfast, rent bikes, have an Internet terminal, and maintain lockers for your stuff. The real draw, though, is the ambience, which is as groovy as they come. They light bonfires at night, grill stuff, bring out the guitars and the red wine . . . what a great feeling developing under the stars.

It's in a bit of an inconvenient location, but there's always space, and the enthusiastic staff is great. They are soooo laidback here, it's scary. Age limit? Chances are 50-50 that these folks won't even care. There's a three-night maximum stay rule, too, but we imagine that's flexible, depending on the mood of the receptionist, who knows?

Note that the hostel is summer-only and thus closes before Oktoberfest, which is probably a good thing.

How to get there:

By bus/train: From main train station take #17 tram to Botanischer Garden stop, then walk up Franz-Schrank-Strasse to In den Kirschen; hostel is on right. Or take U-Bahn line U1 to Rotkreuzplatz stop, then change to the #12 tram to Botanischer Garden stop; walk up Franz-Schrank-Strasse to In den Kirschen.

By car: Contact hostel for directions.

Best bet for a bite:
HL Markt for picnic
supplies

Insiders' tip:
Bring earplugs

What hostellers say:
"Roll another one!"

Gestalt:
Big Top

Safety:

Hospitality:

Cleanliness:

Party index:

JUGENDHERBERGE 👍 MÜNCHEN-NEUHAUSEN (MUNICH NEUHAUSEN HOSTEL)

Wendl-Dietrich-Strasse 20,
80634 Munich
Phone: 089–131–156 or 089–164–545
Fax: 089–167–8745
E-mail: jhmuenchen@djh-bayern.de
Rates: 30–48 DM per Hostelling International member (about $15–$24 US); doubles 76 DM (about $38 US)

Jugendherberge München-Neuhausen
Munich-Neuhausen Hostel • Münich

(photo courtesy of Deutsches Jugendherbergswerk)

Credit cards: Yes
Beds: 391
Private/family rooms: Yes
Kitchen available: Yes
Season: Closed December 1–31
Office hours: Open twenty-four hours
Affiliation: Hostelling International-DJH
Regional office: Bavaria
Extras: TV room, bike rentals, bistro ($), meeting rooms, foosball, patio, garden, breakfast, luggage storage, laundry, lockers, information desk, bar, games, bike tours ($)

Must be under age twenty-seven to stay

As more and more competitors continue to enter the Munich hostelling market, things have recently improved even at the city's Hostelling International–affiliated hostels—especially at this one. Built and opened way back in 1927, between the wars, this was Hostelling International's very first city hostel and Europe's biggest until 1991. Now, minus the curfew and lockout that once made it a bad choice, it is finally starting to meet backpackers' needs. Though the furniture doesn't seem to have changed too much since, um, 1927, things are being kept in one piece and acceptably clean.

It's located 2 miles west of the central train station but reachable by public transit. Once there, you'll find the hostel compound is actually made up of several linked stone buildings with a nice garden and bar between them. Three big stone arches frame the front doors; behind, you'll find a few double rooms and mostly six-bedded dorms. However, take heed: There's one giant thirty-bed dormitory they call the "stable," with stinking socks and snorers all round; if you end up here you'll want to lock your stuff up fast. (Thankfully, lockers in the rooms are big enough for backpacks.) This huge room must be a real treat around Oktoberfest, what with the various scents of beer, sweat, urine, and other fluids wafting through the air.

Best bet for a bite:
Santa Fe

Insiders' tip:
Sheets are free here

What hostellers say:
"Getting better."

Gestalt:
Institutionalized

Safety:

Hospitality:

Cleanliness:

Party index:

There are also seventeen doubles, twenty-four quads, and thirty-six six-bedded rooms in addition to the monster dorm, if that gives you some sense of the size of this place. Bathrooms and showers are in the hallways, not in the rooms.

There are good and bad things about the place. On the down side of the ledger, rooms on the street can be noisy, and the showers are closed down early at 10:00 P.M. They have a kitchen, sure, but it comes without pots, plates, or other helpful items—you've gotta bring your own. None of the private rooms come with private bathrooms, which is too bad. Finally, it's likely to be packed with annoying school groups April through October.

On the other hand, staff is quite friendly, and they certainly offer plenty of services: You can arrange bike tours for a fee at the front desk, for example. There's a television lounge and tourist information desk. And check out the rather unusual on-premises restaurant, too—it's set in a streetcar. Yep. You heard us. Kinda cool, plus there's a patio for chilling as well. You have the option of paying for a half-board or full-board plan that includes meals, and vegetarian food can be ordered as long as you tell 'em in advance. As for party potential, this is a good place to meet people, if not exactly to rock hard. (The bar under construction at press time should help things, though.)

The hostel's located in Neuhausen, the neighborhood most commonly associated with the Schloss Nymphenburg palace, and some say it's got a snooty attitude to match. It shouldn't be too proud, though, since most of the buildings here were completely destroyed during World War II, and the ones that still stand reflect a monotonous architectural conformity. There are a few cheap restaurants around—ask the receptionist—plus an Internet cafe nearby on Nymphenburger Strasse; access is free, but you have to eat or drink to use it. Our tip? You might do best to contemplate life in the Hirschgarten, one of the nicer beer gardens in the city.

Just remember that it's always popular; you'll want to book ahead or arrive before noon to stay the night.

How to get there:

By bus/train: Take #12 or #17 streetcar and walk ¼ mile. Or, from main train station, take U-Bahn line U1 to Rotkreuzplatz Station; walk along Wendl-Dietrich-Strasse ¼ mile to hostel.

By car: Entering city, follow signs for Olympiapark, then make a right onto Nymphenburger Strasse. (If coming from Lindau, make a left.)

JUGENDHERBERGE BURG SCHWANECK (PULLACH HOSTEL)

Burgweg 4–6,

82049 Pullach (Munich)

Phone: 089–7448–6672

Fax: 089–7448–6680
Rates: 23 DM per Hostelling International member (about $12 US); doubles 63 DM (about $32 US)
Credit cards: No
Beds: 138
Private/family rooms: Yes
Kitchen available: No
Affiliation: Hostelling International-DJH
Regional office: Bavaria
Season: Closed December 22–January 6
Curfew: 11:30 P.M.
Extras: Meeting room, grill, pool table, meals ($), terrace, breakfast, bowling, sports facilities, patio

Must be under age twenty-seven to stay

If you're staying here, you're in for some amazing castle (yeah, castle) hostelling . . . but you're so distant from the action that once you check in you might never get into Munich at all—at the very least, you'll have to work to get in and out of town via the S-Bahn (commuter train) in time for the brutal curfew. If you're wanting a country break between cities, though, this is just ideal.

Situated in a park, in a real-life castle with some history to match (ask the staff about the parties that were thrown here back in the nineteenth century), it's full of four- to eight-bedded dorms. Good breakfasts are included with your bunk, which is gonna probably be more comfortable than you expected. The views are stupendous from the patio, and they've

Best bet for a bite:
Meals on-site

Insiders' tip:
Prinz for entertainment listings

What hostellers say:
"Fit for a king!"

Gestalt:
Royal flush

Safety:

Hospitality:

Cleanliness:

Party index:

decked the place out with some nice touches: bowling, some sports facilities, a game room, stuff like that.

They don't take reservations in advance, however, so you need to call from the Munich train station on the same day.

How to get there:

By bus: Contact hostel for transit details.

By car: Head south from München on Highway B11 to Pullach.

By train: From München take S-Bahn line S7 to Pullach Station, then walk along Margarethenstrasse to Heilmannstrasse; turn right on Charlottenweg and continue to hostel, about ½ mile total.

JUGENDGÄSTEHAUS THALKIRCHEN (THALKIRCHEN MUNICH GUEST HOUSE HOSTEL)

Miesingstrasse 4,
81379 Munich
Phone: 089–723–6550 or 089–723–6560
Fax: 089–724–2567
E-mail: jghmuenchen@djh-bayern.de or BineMunich@aol.com
Rates: 32.50–37.50 DM per HI member (about $16–$19 US)
Credit cards: No
Beds: 376
Private/family rooms: Yes
Kitchen available: No
Season: Open year-round
Office hours: Open twenty-four hours
Lockout: 9:30 A.M.–2:00 P.M.
Curfew: 1:00 A.M.
Affiliation: Hostelling International-DJH
Regional office: Bavaria
Extras: TV room, playground nearby, foosball, pool table, parking, luggage storage, table tennis, garden, cafeteria ($), laundry, lockers, breakfast, bike rentals, meeting rooms

Must be under age twenty-seven to stay

Far out of town and not exactly full of warm fuzzies, this should *not* be your first choice in Munich, despite its modern look—all elevated walkways and glassy rooms admitting much more light and sunshine (when there is sunshine) than most other German hostels.

But it's not enough. Dorms contain from two to fifteen beds. They've got fifty-six twin rooms—that means two single beds, not one double bed—plus fifty-five rooms with three to six beds each and then six much larger dormitories. The dorms are all segregated by sex, as is usual in an HI-affiliated joint, and to share a family room you have to be over eighteen and married. All bathrooms and showers are in the hallways, but at least breakfast is included with your bunk.

The pluses include a television lounge, game room with table tennis and a pool table, meeting room, bikes for rent, and a cafeteria serving meals and selling bag lunches. There's a locker in your dormitory room, which costs 5.00 DM (about $2.50 US) to use (and you get the money back later), then another bigger luggage room in the basement of the hostel for your big stuff; it's free. Get a key at the front desk.

Beware, however: Staff is Germanly trained, and managers have actually been known to ask for wedding certificates when couples want to share a room. (Hopefully that practice has been discontinued by now.) And, as we mentioned, it's a pain in the keister to get here. The hostel's situated in Thalkirchen, southwest of the city and some distance. Although close to the zoo, the Isar River, and woods and parks, you'll need wheels or some major public-transit time to even think about it as an option.

Given the staff's nitpicking nature, we'd skip it.

Best bet for a bite:
Cafeteria here

Insiders' tip:
Stay in town!

What hostellers say:
"Screw this."

Gestalt:
Tough as nails

Safety:

Hospitality:

Cleanliness:

Party index:

How to get there:

By bus: Take #3 streetcar to Thalkirchen stop and walk ¼ mile to hostel.

By car: Follow signs to Mittlerer Ring, then to Zoo; from Thalkirchen follow signs to hostel.

By train: From main train station take U-Bahn line U1 to Sendlinger Tor Station, then change to U-Bahn line U3 and continue to Thalkirchen Station and walk ¼ mile to hostel. Or take line U3 directly from Marienplatz toward Fürstenried West to Thalkirchen; from Thalkirchen walk ¼ mile to hostel.

BAVARIA

Würzburg

Ochsenfurt

Nürnberg

Rothnburg
ob der Tauber

Dinkelsbühl

3 The Romantic Road

Regensburg

Eichstätt

Ingolstadt

Nördlingen

Donauwörth

Augsburg

Passau 2

1

The Bavarian Alps

Bad Endorf
Prien

Strub
(Berchtesgade

Füssen

Oberammergau

Garmisch-Partenkirchen

Oberstdorf-Kornau

Mittenwald

Reutte

Page numbers follow town names

BAVARIA

Note: For Munich (the capital of Bavaria), see page 324.

Bavaria, the largest "state" in Germany, is *the* place to go when you're craving the quintessential German experience. It's got it all: castles, mountains, the best beer in the world (ok, the Brits might fight you over that one), lederhosen . . . and great hostels, too. They're well equipped, well located, and some of them even contain what are among the cheapest beds in all of Germany.

Munich is the obvious gateway, with its big airport and incredibly active train station, but in this chapter we'll focus on the *rest* of Bavaria—the part that isn't Munich. Note that it is official policy in Bavaria to exclude anyone aged twenty-seven or older from the Hostelling International hostels—with one exception: a married couple traveling with at least one child. Yes, that's discrimination. And, no, there's not a danged thing you can do about it. Normally we exclude such hostels from our books, but the overwhelming popularity of Bavaria is such that we felt it important to include these anyway. Just remember: ya can't stay if you're older than twenty-seven. Seek out an independent hostel, plead with the staff, or move along, pardner.

BAVARIAN ALPS

The Bavarian Alps are one of Germany's most interesting areas—a range of high mountains whose foothills are stuffed with historic sites, world-famous castles, and other interesting odds and ends.

It can be a little hard to get here, however; trains go to the main hub towns, from where you'll need to take one of the many local buses to see smaller areas. Due to the aforementioned castles, however, it's usually not too hard to find a bus—even from Munich—since scads of tourists are looking to see the same stuff you are. The hostels here are pretty good, too.

JUGENDHERBERGE HEMHOF 👍
BAD ENDORF (BAD ENDORF HOSTEL)

Rankhamer Weg 11,
83093 Bad Endorf
Phone: 08053–509
Fax: 08053–3292

Rates: 17.50 DM per Hostelling International member (about $9.00 US)
Credit cards: No
Beds: 40
Private/family rooms: Yes
Kitchen available: No
Season: Closed December 1–31
Affiliation: Hostelling International-DJH
Regional office: Bavaria
Extras: Grounds, volleyball, table tennis, grill, meals ($)

S 🚲

Must be under age twenty-seven to stay

Bad Endorf is a resort town, popular with German vacationer types and little-known by anyone else, so it might be a good place to get off the beaten track and relax a night. There's little else to draw you here, though.

Best bet for a bite:
Here
Insiders' tip:
Check out the castle
What hostellers say:
"Quiet town."
Gestalt:
Not Bad

Hospitality: 👍

Cleanliness: 👍

Party index: 🎉

Except maybe the hostel. Everything works as it should here, and staff is decently friendly and cool. The rooms themselves come in double, quad, eight-bedded, and a sixteen-bedded version. There's a dining room for meals, a grilling area for grillers, a game room with table tennis, and some spacious grounds where you can walk, doze, play volleyball, and the like. Too bad it's all a 2-mile hike from the station; given that bus service is pretty infrequent out here, you're probably gonna have to hoof it.

How to get there:

By bus/train: From Bad Endorf Station exit to left and head along street to Traunsteiner Strasse; turn right. Continue to Haupstrasse, making a left and coming to Lederer Bergstrasse; continue to Rankhamer Weg on left. Or take infrequent bus.

By car: Take Highway A8 from either München or Salzburg, exiting at signs for Prien.

JUGENDHERBERGE BERCHTESGADEN (BERCHTESGADEN HOSTEL)

Gebirgsjägerstrasse 52,
83489 Strub (Berchtesgaden)
Phone: 08652–943–70
Fax: 08652–943–737

Rates: 22 DM per Hostelling International member (about $11 US)
Credit cards: No
Beds: 360
Private/family rooms: Yes
Kitchen available: Yes
Season: Closed November 15–December 26
Office hours: 8:00 A.M.–noon; 5:00–10:00 P.M.
Curfew: Midnight
Affiliation: Hostelling International-DJH
Regional office: Bavaria
Extras: Disco, table tennis, foosball, grill, breakfast, laundry, meals ($)

Must be under age twenty-seven to stay

This place is unbelievably hopping for the location—near a very famous and touristy site just across the border from Austria, but otherwise quite rural. You'd have no reason to expect Party Central. Yet this hostel often *is*, for some reason.

Dorms contain four to ten beds apiece, and both the game room (with its table tennis table and other knicknacks) and the grilling area are major draws. At night the so-called "disco" here gets a workout too. The big breakfast comes with your bed (though not in it) and it's another social scene as hostellers try to load up for the entire day without getting caught by the hostel staff. Two real bonuses here are the hostel kitchen (pretty uncommon in Germany), allowing you to cook if you feel like it, and the laundry.

The town itself has one huge draw: Hitler's "Eagle's Nest," reached by bus or a stiff little uphill walk. If you're not into that (and the hordes of tourists heading there should make you think twice), you might check out the excellent national park very close at hand. Many tremendous hikes abound.

Best bet for a bite:
Edeka

Insiders' tip:
Salt mines nearby have cool tours

What hostellers say:
"Duuuuude!
The place rocks."

Gestalt:
Eagle has landed

Hospitality:

Cleanliness:

Party index:

How to get there:

By bus: From train station take #3 bus to Strub stop and then walk to hostel.

By car: Take Highway A8, exiting for Bad Reichenhall, then continue to Highway B20 to Bischofswiesen-Strub.

By train: Take train from Freilassing or Bad Reichenhall to Berchtesgaden. From Berchtesgaden Station walk 1 mile to hostel, or take #3 bus to Strub stop and then walk to hostel.

JUGENDHERBERGE FÜSSEN (FÜSSEN HOSTEL)

Mariahilferstrasse 5,

87629 Füssen

Phone: 08362–7754

Fax: 08362–2770
Rates: 21 DM per Hostelling International member (about $11 US)
Credit cards: No
Beds: 128
Private/family rooms: Yes
Kitchen available: No
Season: Closed November 15–December 26
Office hours: 7:00 A.M.–10:00 P.M.
Curfew: 10:00 P.M.
Affiliation: Hostelling International-DJH
Regional office: Bavaria
Extras: Volleyball, table tennis, foosball, grill, lockers, meals ($), breakfast, laundry, garden

Must be under age twenty-seven to stay

This quite blah-looking place gets mixed reviews from our hostel snoops, but we'll give it the thumbs-up on the strength of good location (half a mile from the station, yet not too hectic) and good management. No wonder it stays busy—and full—most of the time.

Best bet for a bite:
Plus (store)

Insiders' tip:
Good museum in town

What hostellers say:
"Good enough."

Gestalt:
Mad about you

Hospitality:

Cleanliness:

Party index:

Rooms contain two to six bunks each. There are three lounges for chilling out, plus a dining room, and they maintain a cool games room complete with table tennis and foosball tables. Outdoors, there's a grill for barbecuing and an area to play volleyball in as well. Breakfast is included, and they serve dinner in that dining room for an extra charge. One last bonus is the presence of storage lockers.

The town itself is well connected to the amazing local sights; buses run several times daily to the castles, the Weiskirche (more on that later), and over to Reutte, Austria, home to its own very good hostel. You can take a train directly to or from Munich, too.

First thing you're gonna wanna see, of course, is that "Mad Ludwig" castle that Disneyland later expropriated and somehow made into its own image. There are actually several Mad Ludwig castles around here, it turns out, and you'll need the inside skinny to know which ones get the huge crowds, and which ones are worth more of your time.

How to get there:

By bus: Take bus from Reutte to Füssen Station, then walk ½ mile along train tracks to hostel.

By car: Take Highway A7 to end of Autobahn, continuing onward to Füssen. Or take Highway B17 from Landsberg to Füssen.

By train: Direct trains from Munich. From Füssen Station exit right and walk ½ mile along tracks to hostel.

JUGENDHERBERGE GARMISCH-PARTENKIRCHEN (GARMISCH-PARTENKIRCHEN HOSTEL)

Jochstrasse 10,

82467 Garmisch-Partenkirchen

Phone: 08821–2980

Fax: 08821–58536
Rates: 21 DM per Hostelling International member (about $11 US)
Credit cards: No
Beds: 200
Private/family rooms: Yes
Kitchen available: Yes
Season: Closed November 11–December 26
Office hours: 7:00–9:00 A.M.; 5:00 P.M.–midnight
Lockout: 9:00 A.M.–3:30 P.M.
Curfew: 11:30 P.M.
Affiliation: Hostelling International-DJH
Regional office: Bavaria
Extras: Laundry, breakfast, table tennis, grill, meals ($), garden

This place isn't exactly central—you've got a good hour's walk from the station to get here—but it's certainly a good bunk placed at the base of marvelous Alpine scenery.

Dorms are triples, six-bedded rooms, or ten-bedded rooms. There's a lounge and a dining room, as you'd expect, and they pile on the extras here—stuff like a laundry (yes!), breakfast, a grilling area, and table tennis.

These two towns (Garmisch and Partenkirchen, we mean, commonly referred to by locals as GAP) have kind of a funny relationship. They don't exactly hate each other, but, well . . . they almost

Best bet for a bite:
Aldi

Insiders' tip:
Discount skiing

What hostellers say:
"Fall into the GAP."

do. Funny, isn't it? Two towns joined at the hip in the cause of Brotherly Love—or at least as a marketing ploy to help snag the 1936 Olympics—still can't stand each other seven decades later.

Anyhow, there's excellent skiing and hiking in the area, obviously. Check out the discount skiing card, which gets you three to fifteen days of discounted lift tickets in the region. The twins aren't so much sightseeing destinations for culture vultures but for those who love Alpine heights, beautiful lakes, and lots of opportunities for communing with nature. In summer you'll probably want to ascend the Zugspitz mountain.

Gestalt:
Gold medal

Hospitality:

Cleanliness:

Party index:

How to get there:

By bus/train: From station turn left to bus stop and take #3, #4, or #5 bus toward Farchant to Burgrain stop and make a right onto Jochstrasse, or walk 2½ miles to hostel.

By car: Take Highway A95 from München to Garmisch, then exit onto Highway B2, following it into the town.

NATURFREUNDHAUS GARMISCH-PARTENKIRCHEN (GARMISCH-PARTENKIRCHEN NATURE HOSTEL)

Schalmweig 21,

82467 Garmisch-Partenkirchen

Phone: 08821–4322

Rates: 20 DM per person (about $10 US)
Credit cards: No
Beds: 22
Private/family room: Yes
Kitchen available: Yes
Season: Contact hostel for current season
Office hours: Vary
Affiliation: None
Extras: Breakfast ($)

Garmisch-Partenkirchen's "other" hostel isn't in the center of town, either, but it does have several redeeming virtues: among them the low cost and the "All Ages" policy (at press time a change in this was being rumored), which can be a lifesaver down here in Bavaria.

Best bet for a bite:
HL store

Insiders' tip:
Don't try walking up
Zugspitze

There's not much to the place—a double room, which will hold you and about ten of your kids, or the huge dormitory, which resembles the Matrenzenlagers ("mattress-houses") of Switzerland. Simple and not exactly luxurious, sure, but in a resort town you just might end up here. Hey, it's a clean bunk with the option of paying for breakfast. That's it.

How to get there:

By bus: Contact hostel for transit details.

By car: Take Highway A95 from München to Garmisch, then exit onto Highway B2, following it into the town.

By train: From station go straight down Ludwigstrasse to Sonnebergstrasse and turn left; then continue 1 mile to hostel.

What hostellers say:
"Simple but fine."

Gestalt:
GAP wedge

Party index:

JUGENDHERBERGE MITTENWALD
"GANGHOFER-JUGENDHERBERGE"
(MITTENWALD HOSTEL)

Buckelwiesen 7,

82481 Mittenwald

Phone: 08823–1701

Fax: 08823–2907

Rates: 21 DM per Hostelling International member (about $11 US)

Credit cards: No

Beds: 111

Private/family rooms: Yes

Kitchen available: No

Season: Closed November 15–December 27

Affiliation: Hostelling International-DJH

Regional office: Bavaria

Extras: Grounds, volleyball, basketball, grill, table tennis, sauna, disco, winter sports programs, meals ($)

Must be under age twenty-seven to stay

You've got to make a serious effort to get here—we're talking a path through woods and hills, and that's the *only way in*—but once here you'll find it worth your while.

All the beds in this place come in double, triple, or eight-bedded rooms; there are three dining rooms and three lounges, as well. Besides running plenty of sports programs, they've outfitted the place with a sauna, disco, volleyball net, and basketball hoop. This place is good for families, and it would be good for sweeties, too—provided the sweeties in question are under the age of twenty-seven.

Best bet for a bite:
Whatever you can pack in

Insiders' tip:
Don't bring too much stuff

What hostellers say:
"Are we there yet?"

If you're a fan of the fiddle (aka the violin), this town has long been a center for guys who make violins (aka luthiers). You might want to drop by the museum behind the church for a look at some examples of the craft. Just remember: That hike in to the hostel is gonna take some effort.

Gestalt:
Smitten Mittenwald

Hospitality:

Cleanliness:

Party index:

How to get there:

By bus: Contact hostel for transit route.

By car: Take Highway A95 from München to Garmisch, then take Highway B2 to the exit for Mittenwald-Nord. Head toward Klais and continue to Schmalensee lake, then make a right and follow signs to Jugendherberge (hostel). Or contact hostel for directions.

By train: From Mittenwald Station walk 3 miles north along mountain trail toward Klais, branching off at car dealer and up around lake to hostel. Or contact hostel for directions.

JUGENDHERBERGE OBERAMMERGAU (OBERAMMERGAU HOSTEL)

Malensteinweg 10,

82487 Oberammergau

Phone: 08822–4114

Fax: 08822–1695
Rates: 21 DM per Hostelling International member (about $11 US)
Credit cards: No
Beds: 130
Private/family rooms: Yes
Kitchen available: No
Season: Closed November 15–December 26
Office hours: 8:00 A.M.–noon; 5:00–7:00 P.M.
Curfew: 10:30 P.M.
Affiliation: Hostelling International-DJH
Regional office: Bavaria
Extras: Disco, sports programs, table tennis, breakfast, meals ($)

Must be under age twenty-seven to stay

Oberammergau is a pleasant enough place, but there's really only one major reason to come—a reason that comes along once every ten years. The last time was 2000, so if you're reading this, you'll need to wait until 2010 to see the much-anticipated event. If you're still coming to the Alps anyway, though, this might be a convenient stopping-off point.

Rooms come in a variety of shapes and sizes, none of them all that remarkable, and all containing between two and eight beds apiece. They serve you breakfast with your bunk (not in it, however). There's a game room, of course—it's got table tennis, as usual in Germany—and a surprising disco in the basement, too, though it's not exactly Studio 54 or anything down there. Still, you'll be amazed at how sociable this hostel can be; it's a welcome switch from most Hostelling International joints in Germany. (It's also often full, so try to book ahead if you can.)

Now for the Great Event: Every ten years the citizens of this little town reenact a Passion Play, one of the world's most famous, as thanks for surviving a plague hundreds of years ago. You've gotta scramble to get tickets when the blessed event comes, and—as we said before—you've got until 2010 to plan. At least this time you won't have an excuse.

Best bet for a bite:
Tini's Weinstube

Insiders' tip:
Ettal monastery nearby

What hostellers say:
"Save me a seat—in ten years!"

Gestalt:
Passion dish

Hospitality:

Cleanliness:

Party index:

How to get there:

By bus: Easier by train. Contact hostel for transit details.

By car: Take Highway A95 from München to Garmisch until Autobahn ends, then pass through Oberrau and Ettal; take B23 from Schongau.

By train: From station take Raisachweg south along Ammer River; make a right at Konig-Ludwig-Strasse. Continue to Malennsteinweg, turn left and continue to hostel.

JUGENDHERBERGE OBERSTDORF-KORNAU (OBERSTDORF-KORNAU HOSTEL)

Kornau 8,

87561 Oberstdorf-Kornau

Phone: 08322–2225 or 08322–2510

Fax: 08322–80446

Rates: 23 DM per Hostelling International member (about $12 US)

Credit cards: No

Beds: 188

Private/family rooms: Yes

Kitchen available: No

Season: Closed November 15–December 27

Curfew: 10:00 P.M.

Affiliation: Hostelling International-DJH

Regional office: Bavaria

Extras: Disco, table tennis, volleyball, basketball, fields, laundry, breakfast, bar, meals ($), parking

Must be under age twenty-seven to stay

Set outside the town of Oberstdorf, this place is the usual kind of hostel with a few extras thrown in. Try a disco; a good and free breakfast; plenty of sports fields, hoops, and courts; a laundry for those sweaty socks; and a game room, for starters.

Best bet for a bite:
Haupstrasse

Insiders' tip:
Gondola nearby

What hostellers say:
"I'm goin' up."

Gestalt:
Mountain high

Hospitality:

Cleanliness:

Party index:

It's the stupendous views you come for—check out those mountains! Inside, it's nothing special. Dorm rooms contain between two and eight beds apiece, and there are two dining rooms. They rent ski equipment, though, so this place is especially good for hikers and hardbodies. Miss the bus and you'll find out just *how* hard your body is.

Oberstdorf is a nice and inexpensive alternative to the aforementioned GAP (Garmisch-Partenkirchen); you can ski affordably, and the car-free streets provide careless roaming. You'll also want to get out and explore the mountains, taking day hikes down the mountains after taking the Nebelhorn cable car up. There's also a local museum containing such oddities as the world's biggest shoe.

Try that on for size.

How to get there:

By bus/train: From Oberstdorf Station take bus toward Kleinwalsertal to Reutte stop. Or walk along Haupstrasse, turn right on Walserstrasse, and walk uphill 2 miles to hostel.

By car: Take Highway B19 toward Kleinwalsertal.

JUGENDHERBERGE PRIEN UMWELTSTUDIENPLATZ (PRIEN HOSTEL)

Carl-Braun-Strasse 66,
83209 Prien
Phone: 08051–68770
Fax: 08051–687–715
Rates: 25 DM per Hostelling International member (about $13 US)
Credit cards: No
Beds: 109
Private/family rooms: Yes
Kitchen available: No
Season: Closed December 1–January 15
Office hours: 8:00–9:00 A.M.; 5:00–10:00 P.M.
Lockout: 9:00 A.M.–1:00 P.M.
Curfew: 10:00 P.M.
Affiliation: Hostelling International-DJH

Regional office: Bavaria
Extras: Volleyball, piano, table tennis, breakfast, water sports, meals ($)

Must be under age twenty-seven to stay

Yet another adequate, unspectacular German hostel, this one at least has the good fortune to be located on the pretty Chiemsee lake halfway between Munich and Salzburg. It's an excellent stopping-off place midway between the two cities if you're city-ed out for a night—as long as you can find it between the screening trees.

Dorms have two, four, or six beds, and they've got a few single rooms as well. There are four lounges and a dining room for hangin' out. Sports-minded folks will be in luck, as the hostel maintains a volleyball court and a game room. Musicians will tinkle away on the piano (we mean play it, wiseguy), and anyone else will just concentrate on filling up at the included breakfast. Not for too long, though: They kick you out at 9:00 A.M. until late afternoon, an annoyance in a sleepy town such as this. The 10:00 P.M. curfew is also wayyyyy too early. On the other hand, the sports facilities are ace.

Most people want to take a cruise or rent a little boat to see the lake, and that's fine. If the weather isn't cooperating, though, hit the local minigolf course instead—extra points if you challenge, and defeat, the hostel staff. (No discount on your bed, though.)

Best bet for a bite:
Zur Linde
(on Fraueninsel)

Insiders' tip:
Boat rentals on lake

What hostellers say:
"Nice spot."

Gestalt:
Shake 'n' lake

Hospitality:

Cleanliness:

Party index:

How to get there:

By bus: Contact hostel for transit details.

KEY TO ICONS

Attractive natural setting

Ecologically aware hostel

Superior kitchen facilities or cafe

Offbeat or eccentric place

Superior bathroom facilities

Romantic private rooms

Comfortable beds

Editors' choice: among our very favorite hostels

A particularly good value

Wheelchair accessible

Good for business travelers

Especially well suited for families

Good for active travelers

Visual arts at hostel or nearby

Music at hostel or nearby

Great hostel for skiers

Bar or pub at hostel or nearby

By car: Take Highway A8 from München or Salzburg, exiting for Bernau and continuing to Prien am Chiemsee.

By train: From Prien Station walk beneath train tracks and follow signs 1 mile to hostel.

JUGENDGÄSTEHAUS AM GRABEN (REUTTE GUEST HOUSE HOSTEL)

Am Graben 1

A-6600 Reutte (Austria)

Phone: (from outside Austria:) 43–05672–626440

Fax: (from outside Austria:) 43–05672–626444

E-mail: jgh-hoefen@tirol.com

Rates: 160 AS per Hostelling International member (about $13 US); doubles 400 AS (about $31 US)

Beds: 51

Private/family rooms: Yes

Kitchen available: Yes

Season: January 1–November 2; December 15–31

Office hours: 8:00 A.M.–10:30 P.M.

Affiliation: Hostelling International-ÖJHV

Extras: TV, garden, table tennis, laundry, dinner ($), breakfast

A two-story building just across the (unguarded) mountain border in Austria, this is a beautiful hostel with a good dining room and good furniture—very cozy indeed in a country not always noted for homey hostels. The friendly management adds the final touch to what we consider a super place.

Best bet for a bite:
Prima

What hostellers say:
"One of the best."

Gestalt:
Reutte rooter

Hospitality:

Cleanliness:

Party index:

Rooms consist of six very good-value doubles, one triple, four quad rooms, and three larger dormitories. There are three common areas—including a TV lounge, garden, and game room—plus a useful laundry and some wonderful meals served nightly. Breakfast and sheets are included for free, too.

Located in the Ausserfern region, just across the border from south Germany, this town—say *ROY-ta* if you wanna pronounce it right—spreads out over a plain in a valley tucked between peaks. Visitors tend to hike the hills, ride a cable car up to the tippy-top of Mount Hanhnenkamm (a good Alpine flower garden here sports more than 600 kinds of flowers), or bask in the sun along the banks of the Lech River that splits the town from its "suburbs."

The best part about staying at this great hostel, though, is the proximity of two outstanding castles—both just across the border in Germany, and both well worth seeing. You've probably already heard about Neuschwanstein, the castle built by "Mad Ludwig" and later used by Walt Disney himself as the model for Sleeping Beauty's castle. But the castle where Ludwig was born, called Hohenschwangau, is close by and—to our eye—even better, if not as grand or elaborate.

You can reach both castles by a local bus service that runs from Reutte across the border to Füssen, Germany, about six times daily. Make sure you catch the last bus back to Austria, or you'll be stranded, and remember that this bus doesn't run at all on Sunday. If you'll be continuing your trip onward to anywhere in Germany, proceed from Füssen: It's much better connected than Reutte to railroad lines—just a two-hour straight shot to Munich, for instance.

How to get there:

By bus: Call hostel for transit route.
By car: Call hostel for directions.
By train: Call hostel for transit route.

PASSAU

A small Bavarian city situated picturesquely on the confluence of the Donau (the Danube), Ilz, and Inns Rivers near the Austrian border, Passau is easy to ignore as you fly through on the train. But check it out: It has an easy going Italian-like charm and spectacular sights like a baroque church, the old palace (that's where the hostel is situated), and an impressive city hall. They put on concerts during the daytime from May to October in the Stephansdom—which happens to hold the world's hugest organ—or just wander aimlessly along the rivers' edge. Either way, Passau's a good respite from the revved-up thrum of Munich.

JUGENDHERBERGE PASSAU (PASSAU HOSTEL)

Veste Oberhaus 125,
94034 Passau
Phone: 0851–493–780
Fax: 0851–493–7820
Rates: 23 DM per Hostelling International member (about $12 US)
Credit cards: No

Beds: 82
Private/family rooms: Yes
Kitchen available: No
Season: Open year-round
Office hours: 7:00 A.M.–noon; 4:00–11:30 P.M.
Curfew: 11:30 P.M.
Affiliation: Hostelling International-DJH
Regional office: Bavaria
Extras: Grill, parking, meals ($)

Must be under age twenty-seven to stay

At press time this hostel was closed for renovations and there was some question about whether it would reopen in this location or reopen in a different one. So please call ahead before making the trek—and we do mean trek—up to it.

Yeah, we said up. This place is a pain in the keister to get to, especially at night, when your already-unappealing options thin out even more. Normally you could hike a gut-busting path or take a bus here. But guess what? The buses stop running very early. No wonder they set a curfew here. Anyone who hasn't turned up by 11:30 at night probably needs a search party and helicopter rescue.

Beds here are in either four-bedded, six-bedded, or—come when they're full and you'll get this one—twelve-bedded dorms. The views of the Danube River and the city are obviously stupendous.

Right on the border with Austria, Passau isn't usually thought of as must-see territory. But its convenient position—on direct train lines to both Munich and Vienna—and wonderful Old Town, plus a load of sobering history, make it one of the more cultural places you can visit in the south of Germany.

One of the best things to do is rent a bike in town and check out the Donauradweg—the pretty riverside bike trail that runs alongside the Danube all the way to Vienna (but don't try to do *that* in one day).

Best bet for a bite:
Joe's Garage

Insiders' tip:
Tengelmann grocery store for snacks

What hostellers say:
"Let's hit the trail."

Gestalt:
Stair master

Safety:

Hospitality:

Cleanliness:

Party index:

How to get there:

By bike: From Donauradweg (bike trail), take road B12 toward Freyung, crossing over the Ilzbrücke bridge to Veste Oberhaus.

By bus: Walk to Rathausplatz and take Pendelbus to museum and walk to hostel. Or walk to Ludwigsplatz and take #1, #2, or #4 bus to Ilzbrücke stop and walk to hostel.

By car: Take Highway A3 from Regensburg to Passau, exiting at signs for Passau-Nord, then heading toward Veste Oberhaus/Ries.

By train: From Passau Station walk right along river to Luit-poldbrücke and walk uphill 2 miles to hostel. Or walk to Rathausplatz and take Pendelbus to museum and walk to hostel. Or walk to Ludwigsplatz, then take #1, #2, or #4 bus to Ilzbrücke stop.

ROMANTIC ROAD

Germany's most famous byway, without question, is the Romantic Road—yet it's actually a patchwork of roads stitched together by the German tourist office years ago as a way to promote travel to out-of-the-way villages! Never mind all that, though: Today the Road is swamped with tour buses and Sunday drivers any day of the week straining to get a glimpse of the tiny, cobbled towns.

It's also dotted with hostels. Some great ones abound, including one of the finest in the whole country. Get around by train or, better yet, local buses; one tour bus company offers a daily run from Frankfurt and Munich along the Road, and tickets are discounted with a Eurailpass.

JUGENDHERBERGE AUGSBURG (AUGSBURG HOSTEL)

Beim Pfaffenkeller 3,

86152 Augsburg

Phone: 0821–33909

Fax: 0821–151–149
Rates: 21 DM per Hostelling International member (about $11 US)
Credit cards: No
Beds: 144
Private/family rooms: Yes
Kitchen available: No
Season: Closed December 21–January 30
Office hours: 7:00–9:00 A.M.; 5:00–10:00 P.M.
Curfew: 1:00 A.M.
Affiliation: Hostelling International-DJH
Regional office: None; locally owned by Augsburg
Extras: Bar, grill, pool table, foosball table, table tennis, meeting room, TV, breakfast, courtyard, meals ($)

Must be under age twenty-seven to stay

Centrally positioned, this one's a winner despite the no-charac-ter dorms, which come with two to eight beds apiece. There's also a dining room, outdoor beer garden in a courtyard (score!), two (yes, two) television rooms—and a game room in the basement outfitted with foosball, billiards, and the ubiquitous table tennis thing. They also serve free breakfast to you in the morning.

Best bet for a bite:
Tengelmann

Insiders' tip:
Farmer's markets all week long

What hostellers say:
"Spic 'n' span."

Gestalt:
Brecht and butter

Hospitality:

Cleanliness:

Party index:

You couldn't be closer to the city center and its interesting churches, synagogues, and Fuggerei neighborhood (it's also famous as the town where playwright Bertoldt Brecht was born). This hostel also has a reputation for occasionally bending the normally strict German hostel rules about age limits and other stuff. Overall, it's well kept and tidy for a city hostel—just ignore the spare, blah decor of the rooms.

Also note, if you happen to be driving, that there's no parking at the hostel proper. You'll have to fend for yourself.

How to get there:

By bus/train: From Augsburg Station take #2 tram to Stadtwerk, then walk 1½ miles toward the big cathedral; take a right onto Inneres Pfaffen Gässchen.

By car: Take Highway A8 from Stuttgart or München, exiting at signs for Augsburg-West or Augsburg-Ost.

JUGENDHERBERGE DINKELSBÜHL (DINKELSBÜHL HOSTEL)

Koppengasse 10,
91550 Dinkelsbühl
Phone: 09851–9509

Fax: 09851–4874
Rates: 19 DM per Hostelling International member (about $10 US)
Credit cards: No
Beds: 148
Private/family rooms: Yes
Kitchen available: No
Season: Closed October 1–February 28
Office hours: 7:00–9:00 A.M.; 5:00–10:00 P.M.
Curfew: 10:00 P.M.
Affiliation: Hostelling International-DJH
Regional office: Bavaria
Extras: Pool table, foosball table, breakfast, piano, jukebox, bike tours, meals ($)

Must be under age twenty-seven to stay

You could do a lot worse than get stuck for the night in Dinkelsbühl, a stop on the Romantic Road bus from Munich north (which is free for Eurailpass holders, and as a result very hard to get a seat on). This is the real deal—an old town with crooked houses and medieval lanes that'll keep you snapping pictures till the camera battery gives out.

The hostel's in an odd building, odd for a reason—it's a kornhaus (that's German for granary) that no longer functions as breadbasket but rather as a bunk-basket. Beds here come in double rooms, quads, six-bedded dorms, and eight-bedded dorms. There's a dining room, too, in which you're served a free breakfast daily.

We've heard complaints that staff can be itchy (especially about that darned 10:00 P.M. curfew), but all in all it's a decent place and well decked-out.

The town itself oozes medieval charm from original fortifications, including eighteen towers. (Think of it as the San Gimignano of Germany. We're assuming you've read *Hostels France and Italy*, of course? Of course!) So if you're seeking Bavarian authenticity on the sometimes-Romantic Road, drop in. Begin your sight-seeing at the groovy Museum of the Third Dimension or the gothic St. Georg Münster. From spring through fall there's a free nightwatchmen's tour every night, kinda campy but fun if you're into it. If you're here in July, two key festivals take place then—Kinderzeche and a jazz festival—both cool enough to keep you around for awhile.

Best bet for a bite:
Kochlöffel

Insiders' tip:
Kinderzeche festival in mid-July

What hostellers say:
"Weird building."

Gestalt:
Towers of power

Hospitality:

Cleanliness:

Party index:

How to get there:

By bus/train: Take train to Augsburg, Donauwörth, Nürnberg, or Nördlingen, then switch to bus. From downtown walk along Baldingerstrasse away from center through walls to hostel on right.

KEY TO ICONS

Attractive natural setting

Ecologically aware hostel

Superior kitchen facilities or cafe

Offbeat or eccentric place

Superior bathroom facilities

Romantic private rooms

Comfortable beds

Editors' choice: among our very favorite hostels

A particularly good value

Wheelchair accessible

Good for business travelers

Especially well suited for families

Good for active travelers

Visual arts at hostel or nearby

Music at hostel or nearby

Great hostel for skiers

Bar or pub at hostel or nearby

By car: Take Highway A7 from Würzburg or Kempten, exiting at sign for Dinkelsbühl, then take B25 (the Romantische Stasse).

JUGENDHERBERGE DONAUWÖRTH (DONAUWÖRTH HOSTEL)

Goethestrasse 10,
86609 Donauwörth
Phone: 0906–5158
Fax: 0906–243–817
Rates: 19 DM per Hostelling International member (about $10 US)
Credit cards: No
Beds: 95
Private/family rooms: Yes
Kitchen available: No
Season: Closed December 6–January 6
Affiliation: Hostelling International-DJH
Regional office: Bavaria
Extras: Garden, foosball table, volleyball, playground, grounds, meals ($)

S

Must be under age twenty-seven to stay

Late word has it that this hostel's being fixed up, so we're going to hold off on rating it until it reopens. But here's the skinny on what *used* to be true.

Kind of overlooked, this town and hostel might make it into your travel plans if you're trying to save a buck and want to diverge from the usual touristed path. The dorm rooms contain anywhere from one to ten beds apiece, meaning you might score a single and you might get hosed with a huge room. There's a dining room, two lounges and a game area (ya know, foosball), plus some space outdoors to roam around and spike volleyballs or play with the kids or pick flowers (just kiddin') in the garden.

Best bet for a bite:
In-house grub

What hostellers say:
"Is it open yet??"

Gestalt:
Blue Danube

Party index:

The town, at the junction of the Danube and Wörnitz Rivers, is known for museums (including a puppet museum), a cathedral from the twelfth century; and a Benedictine abbey just outside town. Basically, you can suck up the whole German experience in one fell swoop here.

How to get there:

By bus: Contact hostel for transit details.

By car: Take Highway B2 from Nürnberg or Augsburg to Donauwörth Nord exit. Or take Highway E42 from Würzburgor Ulm, exiting for Dinkelsbühl and continuing on the B25 to Donauwörth.

By train: Trains run here from Würzburg, Nürnberg, Treuchtlingen, Augsburg, and München not to mention Ulm, Ingolstadt, and Regensburg. Contact hostel for transit route from Donauwörth Station.

JUGENDHERBERGE EICHSTÄTT / UMWELTSTUDIENPLATZ (EICHSTÄTT HOSTEL)

Reichenaustrasse 15,
85072 Eichstätt
Phone: 08421–980–410

Fax: 08421–980–415
E-mail: JHEichstaett@dJugendherberge-bayern.de
Rates: 25 DM per Hostelling International member (about $13 US)
Credit cards: No
Beds: 112
Private/family rooms: Yes
Kitchen available: No
Season: Closed December 1–January 31
Office hours: 8:00–9:00 A.M.; 5:00–7:00 P.M.
Lockout: 10:00 A.M.–5:00 P.M.
Curfew: 10:00 P.M.
Affiliation: Hostelling International-DJH
Regional office: Bavaria
Extras: Game room, volleyball, grill, table tennis tables, laundry, breakfast, pool table, disco, tepee, laundry, meals ($)

Must be under age twenty-seven to stay

One of the best, if not *the* best, hostels along the entire Romantic Road, this one scores points for its incredible amenities and laid-back attitude, among other things.

Rooms in this stone building range from singles to doubles to quads and up to ten-bedded rooms, all of them really nice thanks to their relative newness. Bathrooms are near the dorms but, unfortunately, not in them. Management has outfitted three lounges and two dining rooms, as well, plus a couple of dayrooms for just hanging out—which you'll need to do, since they coldly boot you out all day long! At least the views are peaceful.

They serve all three meals here and offer the use of a washer and dryer, too.

The only other drawback we can find is that school groups like to book this place up *en masse* during the school

Best bet for a bite:
Vesuvio

Insiders' tip:
Lidl (supermarket) nearby

What hostellers say:
"Great hostel, noisy kids."

Gestalt:
Jurassic park

Hospitality: 👎

Cleanliness: 👎

Party index:

🎉 🎉 🎉 🎉

year. Other than that, it's hard to find fault with this one.

If you're an outdoors type, you'll find respite from the little darlings in a huge park nearby with hiking, biking trails, and other stuff. Or hit the museum in the castle to get the lowdown on the region's first-ever hosteller—the woolly mammoth.

How to get there:

By bus: Contact hostel for transit route.

By car: Take Highway A9 from Nürnberg or München, exiting at signs for Altmühltal and following Jurahochstrasse. Or from the A9 exit at signs for Ingolstadt-Nord, then take Highway B16 and Highway B13.

By train: Trains run here from München and Treutlingen. From back of station walk uphill along Bergstrasse to Willibaldsburg.

JUGENDHERBERGE INGOLSTADT (INGOLSTADT HOSTEL)

Friedhofstr 4½,

85049 Ingolstadt

Phone: 0841–34177

Fax: 0841–910–178
Rates: 21 DM per Hostelling International member (about $11 US)
Credit cards: No
Beds: 84
Private/family rooms: Yes
Kitchen available: No
Season: Closed December 15–January 31
Affiliation: Hostelling International-DJH
Regional office: Bavaria
Office hours: 7:00 A.M.–11:30 P.M.
Curfew: 11:30 P.M.
Extras: Foosball, table tennis, breakfast, lockers, meals ($)

Must be under age twenty-seven to stay

Housed inside a former fort, this place gets our thumbs-up despite dorm rooms that really could be bigger. (But the guys who designed the fort probably didn't realize it one day would be a hostel crammed with backpackers.)

Dorms here contain anywhere from two to twelve beds; couples will have the option of staying (though you must be younger than twenty-seven unless you've got a kid). There are two dining rooms, where the staff—who seemed surprisingly cool for a German hostel when we popped in—serves free breakfast and other meals for a charge. If that's not good enough, there's also a kitchen you'll find more than adequate for whipping up budget meals. They've got a games room with table tennis and foosball, plus lockers for storing your valuable stuff. The hostel's well placed, too, near the Kreuztor gate and a neighborhood of bars and other cool hangouts.

Ingolstadt is a pretty neat little town. There's a well-preserved old town for history buffs and a small university to invigorate the cultural Szene. Among the attractions are a cool Museum of Concrete Art and a somewhat gory medical museum. (How appropriate—the real Dr. Frankenstein went to school here and did medical experiments on cadavers.)

Best bet for a bite:
Tengelmann

Insiders' tip:
Corner pub

What hostellers say:
"Really good!"

Gestalt:
Kreuz control

Hospitality:

Cleanliness:

Party index:

Yuck. Let's get back to cool stuff. Germany's megastrict beer laws were enacted here in Ingolstadt; perhaps big American brewmeisters should take a look at these and reform their heathen and unpure beer-making ways. So suck down a local brew and rejoice. And when you need a break from all this culture in such a small package, rent a bike and head up into the verdant hills ringing the town.

How to get there:

By bus/train: Direct trains run from Nürnberg and München. From train station take #10, #50, #53, or #60 bus to hostel. Or from center of city, walk west along Theresienstrasse beyond Kreuztor to hostel on right.

* *By car:* Take Highway A9 from München or Nürnberg, exiting at signs for Ingolstadt-Süd. Or, from the A9 exit for Ingolstadt/Nord onto Highway B13, then take Highway B16 to Ringstrasse.

By train: Direct trains run from Nürnberg and München. From train station take #10, #50, #53, or #60 bus to hostel. Or from center of city, walk west along Theresienstrasse beyond Kreuztor to hostel on right.

JUGENDHERBERGE NÖRDLINGEN (NÖRDLINGEN HOSTEL)

Kaiserwiese 1

86720 Nördlingen

Phone: 09081–271–816

Fax: 09081–271–816

Rates: 19 DM per Hostelling International member (about $10 US)

Credit cards: No

Beds: 104

Private/family rooms: Yes
Kitchen available: No
Season: Closed November 1–February 28
Office hours: 8:00–10:00 A.M.; 4:30–7:00 P.M.
Affiliation: Hostelling International-DJH
Regional office: Bavaria
Extras: Meals ($)

$

This isn't the hugest place in Germany, and that's a good thing—you'll get a bit more personal attention from the staff. It's not terribly luxurious, either.

You simply get what you need: a clean bed, a kitchen with a dining room, a low low price, and a lounge. Dorms contain two to twelve beds each. The town is little more than a transit hub for train and boat traffic. You'll find almost nothing to do here, and we wouldn't recommend staying in the town unless you're stuck.

Best bet for a bite:
Lidl

Insiders' tip:
Church tower is climbable

What hostellers say:
"Pretty good."

Gestalt:
Nordlingenberry

Hospitality: 👍

Cleanliness: 👍

Party index:

How to get there:

By bus: Romantic Road bus and Dinkelsbühl bus run to Nördlingen. Contact hostel for transit details.

By car: Take Highway B25 (the Romantische Strasse/Romantic Road) to Highway B29 and then Highway B466; or take the A7.

By train: From the Nördlingen Station walk ¾ mile north to hostel.

JUGENDGÄSTEHAUS NÜRNBERG 👍👍
(NÜRNBERG GUEST HOUSE HOSTEL)

Burg 2,
90403 Nürnberg
Phone: 0911–230–9360

Fax: 0911–230–93611
Rates: 30–58 DM per Hostelling International member (about $15–$29 US); doubles 70 DM (about $35 US)
Beds: 316
Private/family rooms: Yes
Kitchen available: Yes
Season: Closed December 24–26
Office hours: 7:00–1:00 A.M.
Affiliation: Hostelling International-DJH
Regional office: Bavaria

Jugendgästehaus Nürnberg
Nürnberg Guest House Hostel • Nürnberg
(photo courtesy of Deutsches Jugendherbergswerk)

Extras: Breakfast, table tennis, foosball, piano, luggage storage, information desk, TV room, meeting rooms, meals ($)

Must be under age twenty-seven to stay

Formerly part of the city castle, this hostel is an awfully long way from the action—and there is lots of action to be had here—but otherwise makes a great stop. Just make sure you're in good shape for the considerable uphill climb to get here. Also note that it's more expensive than many other hostels in Germany, although there's a reason: It's right in popular (and infamous) Nürnberg, usually spelled Nuremberg by non-Germans.

It's a beautiful, beautiful building, bombed at the end of the war but lovingly restored down to every last stone, window, and tower. Dorms here are mostly small and comfortable rooms containing two to six beds each (plus a few singles—ask if you want one, but they cost twice as much). They've got three lounges to chill in, a dining room (serving three meals a day), and a television lounge; luggage storage; a travel help desk; and other goodies like a piano.

The city itself was founded back in 1050 and—as you're no doubt aware—played a big and sad role in German history as the site of Nazi party rallies and, later, war crimes trials. Despite the notoriety, however, modern-day Nürnburg is actually a nice place to stroll and drink. Cathedrals, statues, crown jewels, fountains, underground breweries, the German National Museum and castles . . . they've got it all. For a more serious dose of the past, visit the Nazi Rally Grounds or the Court of Justice.

Best bet for a bite:
Aldi

Insiders' tip:
Eric's Bar

What hostellers say:
"Climb every mountain."

Gestalt:
No-hassle castle

Safety:

Hospitality:

Cleanliness:

Party index:

How to get there:

By bus/train: From Nürnberg Station take U-Bahn line U1 or U11 to Lorenzkirche stop, changing to #46 or #47 bus to Heilig-Geist-Spital zum Maxtor stop; walk ¼ mile to hostel. Or take #9 streetcar to Krelingstrasse. Or from Marktplatz walk ¾ mile up Baldingerstrasse and through gate; follow signs to hostel.

By car: Take Autobahn, exiting toward Nürnberg Center (Stadtzentrum), then continue north of old town.

JUGEND-HOTEL NÜRNBERG (NÜRNBERG YOUTH HOTEL HOSTEL)

Rathsburgstrasse 300,
90403 Nürnberg
Phone: 0911–521–6092

Fax: 0911–521–6954
Rates: 26–37 DM (about $13–$19 US) per person; doubles 58 DM (about $29 US)
Credit cards: No
Beds: 320
Private/family rooms: Yes
Kitchen available: Yes
Season: Open year-round
Office hours: 8:00 A.M.–10:00 P.M.

Affiliation: None
Extras: Breakfast ($), grounds

Achtung! (Attention!) The staff here speaks only German.

This place is actually more hotel than hostel, but they do have a few dorms rooms—in addition to a whole bunch of single and double rooms—and, most important, there is NO AGE LIMIT. Therefore you have a chance to stay here if you're over the old, old age of twenty-six.

Every room in the place has its own bathroom, a major plus, and the place is surrounded by quiet greenery. Don't forget the option of breakfast (it does cost extra, however). All this relative luxury, though, comes with a price—you are realllly far from downtown, even farther than the other hostel in town. This is really best for a family, someone with a car, or someone who doesn't mind switching buses for a long ride into and out of town.

How to get there:

By bus/train: From train station take U-Bahn line U2 toward Hernhütte to final stop; then change to #21 bus to Zum Zelsenkeller stop.

By car: Contact hostel for directions.

Best bet for a bite:
Bratwurst Röslein

Insiders' tip:
Great Christmas market each year

What hostellers say:
"If only they could move this place into town . . . "

Gestalt:
Far out

Safety:

Hospitality:

Cleanliness:

Party index:

JUGENDHERBERGE OCHSENFURT (OCHSENFURT HOSTEL)

Hauptstrasse 1,
97199 Ochsenfurt
Phone: 09331–2666

Fax: 09331–2696
Rates: 17.50 DM per Hostelling International member (about $9.00 US)
Credit cards: No
Beds: 30
Private/family rooms: Yes
Kitchen available: No
Season: Closed November 1–March 31
Affiliation: Hostelling International-DJH
Regional office: Bavaria

Extras: Table tennis, meals ($)

Must be under age twenty-seven to stay

A simple joint, this hostel is located in a seven-floor tower, although it doesn't take up the whole thing. There are actually only three dorm rooms; one contains six beds, one contains eight, and another one contains fourteen. The friendly English-speaking manager has recently finished renovating the shower rooms that are located outside the bedrooms, a nice addition.

The same manager also plays the chef and prepares meals when there are more than ten folks staying—so you might happen on a feast of Italian or Chinese food or even a good old German standby. Note that you might want to phone ahead when making reservations to see if they'll be serving a meal that night. Don't worry if they're not, though, because there are plenty of other cheap eats nearby.

Most fellow hostellers here seemed to be adults (or families) on bike tours; they're calmer than the German school groups who sometimes stay here during school-year weekends or holidays. There's not much to entertain you inside the hostel aside from a common room stocked with board games in German (!), but the place is smack-dab in the middle of town, so at least you won't have to rely on public transportation to move you about. (And if you have just pedaled in, you can store your bike in an on-site storage shack.)

There's little to say about the town, which is on the main train lines from Munich and Würzburg but otherwise isn't really memorable or

Best bet for a bite:
House grub

Insiders' tip:
Cyberthek for e-mail

What hostellers say:
"Nice place."

Gestalt:
Towerful

Hospitality:

Cleanliness:

Party index:

KEY TO ICONS

 Attractive natural setting

 Ecologically aware hostel

 Superior kitchen facilities or cafe

 Offbeat or eccentric place

Superior bathroom facilities

Romantic private rooms

 Comfortable beds

 Editors' choice: among our very favorite hostels

 A particularly good value

 Wheelchair accessible

Good for business travelers

 Especially well suited for families

 Good for active travelers

 Visual arts at hostel or nearby

 Music at hostel or nearby

Great hostel for skiers

 Bar or pub at hostel or nearby

notable. The neighboring tourist office will be happy to supply you with maps of trails in the area, however, so that's one thing to do.

How to get there:

By bus: Contact hostel for transit details.

By car: Drive Highway A3 from Frankfurt or Nürnberg, exiting for Randersacker, then taking Highway B13. Or take A7 from Ulm or Würzburg, exiting for Marktbreit.

By train: Direct trains run from München or Würzburg. From Ochsenfurt Station walk ½ mile to hostel.

JUGENDHERBERGE REGENSBURG KULTURSTUDIENPLATZ (REGENSBURG HOSTEL)

Wöhrdstrasse 60,

93059 Regensburg

Phone: 0941–57402

Fax: 0941–52411
Rates: 28 DM per Hostelling International member (about $14 US)
Credit cards: No
Beds: 170
Private/family rooms: Yes
Kitchen available: No
Season: Open year-round
Office hours: Open twenty-four hours
Affiliation: Hostelling International-DJH
Regional office: Bavaria
Extras: Table tennis, pool table, playground, foosball, bike rentals, breakfast, laundry, meals ($), parking

Must be under age twenty-seven to stay

This place is beautifully situated on an island right between the Danube and Regens Rivers, just north of Regensburg's interesting old town and its many restaurants, sights, and bars. It's a terrific spot from which to explore the rest of town, and you'll enjoy the hostel just as much.

Dorms contain four to eight beds each, and fifteen of these can be used as family rooms; they maintain five lounges, a kitchen and a dining room. There are tons of hosteller- and family-friendly amenities such as a laundry, a bike rental service, free breakfast, and a games room with table tennis and a pool

Best bet for a bite:
Goldene Ente

Insiders' tip:
Irish pub on Brückstrasse

What hostellers say:
"Fabulous."

Gestalt:
Regal beagle

table, among others. The only drawback? Come during school season and you're sure to see lots of kiddies on field trips. Oh, yeah, and one more—you gotta be under twenty-seven to stay here. Boo!

You can't believe how many beer cellars, beer gardens, and other great venues for eating, drinking, or people-watching there are here . . . we won't even begin to describe all the options. Ask at the hostel, or just wander around yourself looking.

Hospitality:

Cleanliness:

Party index:

How to get there:

By bus/train: From station take #3 bus to Eis-Stadion stop. Or walk Maxmilian-Strasse and cross river on the Eieserne Brücke (bridge) and take a right on Wordstrasse; total distance 1½ miles.

By car: Take Highway A3 from Nürnberg or Passau, exiting for Regensbug (Burgweinting), then follow signs toward Landshuter Strasse and Weissenburger Strasse. Or take Highway A9 or A93 from München to Regensburg, exiting at Regensburg-Pfaffenstein and following signs for Frankenstrasse.

JUGENDHERBERGE ROTHENBURG OB DER TAUBER (ROTHENBURG OB DER TAUBER HOSTEL)

Mühlacker 1,
91541 Rothenburg ob der Tauber
Phone: 09861–94160

Fax: 09861–941–620
Rates: 23 DM per Hostelling International member (about $12 US)
Credit cards: No
Beds: 184
Private/family rooms: Yes
Kitchen available: No
Season: Open year-round
Office hours: 7:00 A.M.–noon; 3:00–10:00 P.M.
Curfew: 11:30 P.M.
Affiliation: Hostelling International-DJH
Regional office: Bavaria
Extras: Meeting room, photography lab, piano, foosball, table tennis, playground, grounds, TV, VCR, disco, meals ($), breakfast, video library, luggage storage, parking, laundry

Must be under age twenty-seven to stay

If you're in a hurry to get to Germany, put down this book and don't even finish reading this entry. Why not? 'Cause this place is one of the best hostels in Germany, hands down—but you gotta be younger than twenty-seven—and darned popular, so book now. The place books months in advance, even up to a year in advance for certain times of the year.

The hostel's located inside a 500-year-old mill, yet it feels relatively modern. The rooms contain from one bed—yes, they have singles here—to twelve-bedded rooms; there are a number of family and private rooms mixed in there. The place has more built-in comforts than any other hostel in Germany: Try a small in-house disco, free breakfast, dinner for an extra charge, a kitchen, and a dining room.

Now check out the TV room, where you can borrow a video from the hostel's video library. There's a meeting room and photo lab for school groups, a music room with its own piano, a game room with a table tennis table and equipment. Staff reportedly will sometimes look the other way on Bavaria's cruel and unusual under-twenty-seven policy, too, though you didn't hear that here. Uh-uh.

Still, we can't stress this point enough: Call ahead, book ahead. Ahead. Hear us?

You won't find a quainter German town than Rothenburg—and, unfortunately, every tourist in the western world seems to have discovered it by now. You might even spy a chipper PBS travel icon in there. But ignore the throng of dewy-eyed, middle-aged white people hanging on his every word and proceed straight to the alleys and the Marktplatz. There you'll find plenty of medieval charm. Or stroll along the city walls for a better perspective on the town. The best time—or worst, depending on whether you like crowds—to experience it is during Christmas, when the seasonal market is in full swing.

Best bet for a bite:
Alt Fränkische

Insiders' tip:
Weisswurst is the local dish

What hostellers say:
"Simply the best!!"

Gestalt:
Big Tauber

Hospitality:

Cleanliness:

Party index:

How to get there:

By bus: On Romantic Road bus line; contact hostel for transit details.

By car: Take Highway B25 (the Romantische Strasse/Romantic Road) or the A7 from Würzburg or Kempten, exiting for Rothenburg. Park at Parkplatz P1.

By train: You must change trains from anywhere in Steinach. From Rothenburg Station walk ¾ mile to hostel. Or from Marktplatz walk ⅓ mile to hostel.

JUGENDGÄSTEHAUS WÜRZBURG
(WÜRZBURG GUEST HOUSE HOSTEL)

Burkarderstrasse 44,
97082 Würzburg
Phone: 0931–42590 or 42595
Fax: 0931–416–862

> **Rates:** 30 DM per Hostelling International member (about $15 US)
> **Credit cards:** No
> **Beds:** 254
> **Private/family rooms:** Yes
> **Kitchen available:** No
> **Season:** Open year-round
> **Office hours:** 8:00 A.M.–10:00 P.M.
> **Curfew:** 1:00 A.M.
> **Affiliation:** Hostelling International-DJH
> **Regional office:** Bavaria
> **Extras:** Breakfast, table tennis, foosball, cafe ($), luggage storage

Must be under age twenty-seven to stay

What a huge place; it used to be someone's villa, so you can stretch out nicely here. However, there's quite a variety of rooms. You might get a single, double, or triple room, but you also might find yourself in a room with eight beds. Or more. A *lot* more. There are fifteen family rooms here, though, as well as a kitchen, six different lounging areas, and a games room complete with the usual table tennis-foosball combo. The in-house cafe serves meals, and breakfast comes for free with your night's sleep.

Best bet for a bite:
Natur-Feinkostladen
for veggie

Insiders' tip:
Trend magazine lists
stuff to do

What hostellers say:
"You're not *supposed*
to swallow."

Gestalt:
For better or Würzburg

Hospitality:

Cleanliness:

Party index:

You can see the city from up here, which is known for several great palaces looking down upon the old town from positions high above the Main River. (You'll have to peer through the leafy trellises of the vineyards to see them, however.) This is another German university town, with many of these students cramming to be future doctors. You'll catch the youthful buzz in the wide array of cultural goings-on such as a huge disco complex and the late-May Weindorf food and wine festival. Or, in late September, show up for a smaller version of Munich's crazy Oktoberfest with excellent beer but without such massive crowds.

How to get there:

By bus/train: From Würzburg Station take #3 and #5 tram toward Heidingsfeld or Rottenbauer to Löwenbrücke stop. Follow signs downstairs across street to right to hostel on left, just after tunnel.

By car: Take Highway A3 from Frankfurt or Nürnberg, exiting at signs for Heidingsfeld. Or take Highway A7 from Hamburg or Würzburg, exiting for Estenfeld, then take Highway B19 in the direction of Stadtmitte, following signs.

BAVARIA
OTHER HOSTELS

JUGENDHERBERGE AMBERG

(Amberg Hostel)

Fronfestgasse 22,

92224 Amberg

Phone: 09621–10369

Fax: 09621–10369
Rates: 17.50 DM per HI member
(about $9.00 US)
Beds: 36
Private/family rooms: Yes
Kitchen available: No
Season: Closed December 24–
January 3
Affiliation: HI-DJH
Regional office: Bavaria
Extras: Volleyball, meals ($)
**Must be under age twenty-seven
to stay**

How to get there:

By bus: Contact hostel for transit
details.
By car: Take Highway A6 from
Nürnberg or Amberg, exiting at
signs for Amberg-West. Or take
Highway A93 from Regensburg
or Weiden, exiting for Fronsberg
and continue onto B85 to
Amberg.
By train: Direct trains run from
Nürnberg, Amberg, and Furth.
From station contact hostel for
transit details.

JUGENDHERBERGE AMORBACH

Kniebreche 4,

63916 Amorbach

Phone: 09373–1366

Fax: 09373–7140
Rates: 19 DM per HI member
(about $10 US)
Beds: 92
Private/family rooms: Yes
Kitchen available: No
Season: Closed December 1–
January 15
Affiliation: HI-DJH
Regional office: Bavaria
Extras: Grill, table tennis, disco,
meals ($)
**Must be under age twenty-seven
to stay**

How to get there:

By bus: Contact hostel for transit
route.
By car: Take Autobahn from
Würzburg through
Tauberbischofsheim and
Walldürn and Amorbach/West.
Or from Frankfurt take
Autobahn through
Aschaffenburg and Miltenberg
to Amorbach/West. Or from
Heilbronn take Autobahn
through Osterburken to
Walldürn to Amorbach/West.
By train: Direct trains run from
Frankfurt, Würzburg, and
Heilbronn. Contact hostel for
transit route.

JUGENDHERBERGE ASCHAFFENBURG

(Aschaffenburg Hostel)

Beckerstrasse 47,

63739 Aschaffenburg

Phone: 06021–930–763

Fax: 06021–970–694
Rates: 19 DM per HI member
  (about $10 US)
Beds: 110
Private/family rooms: Yes
Kitchen available: No
Season: Closed December 20–
  January 20
Affiliation: HI-DJH
Regional office: Bavaria
Extras: Table tennis, basketball,
  grill, soccer, disco, meals ($)
Must be under age twenty-seven
  to stay

How to get there:

By bus/train: Direct trains run
  from Frankfurt and Nürnberg.
  From Aschaffenburg Station
  take #5 or #41 bus to
  Schoberstrasse, then walk ½
  mile to hostel.
By car: Take Highway A3 from
  Frankfurt or Würzburg, exiting at
  signs for Ost. Follow signs in
  direction of Stadtmitte (downtown), then take Highway B8
  toward Würzburg to Kneipp-
  strasse, then Beckerstrasse.

JUGENDHERBERGE BAMBERG–WOLFSSCHLUCHT

(Bamberg Hostel)

Oberer Leinritt 70,

96049 Bamberg

Phone: 0951–56002

Fax: 0951–55211
Rates: 21 DM per HI member
  (about $11 US)
Beds: 84
Private/family rooms: Yes
Kitchen available: No
Season: Closed December 15–
  January 31
Affiliation: HI-DJH
Regional office: None; owned by
  city of Bamberg
Extras: Table tennis, grill, piano,
  gardens, meals ($)
Must be under age twenty-seven
  to stay

How to get there:

By bus/train: From Bamberg
  Station take #1 bus to ZOB
  Promenade bus station, then
  change to #18 bus and continue to Jugendherberge (hostel) stop.
By car: Take Highway A3, exiting at signs for Bamberg, then
  take Highway B505 to Pett-
  stadt exit and Highway A73 to
  Bamberg.-Süd exit. Or take
  Highway A70 from Bayreuth,
  exiting at signs for Bamberg
  Centrum, then following signs
  toward the Klinikum. Or take
  Highway B22 from Würzburg
  to Bamberg, taking Stadt-
  grenze exit.

JUGENDHERBERGE BAYERISCH EISENSTEIN

(Bayerisch Eisenstein
Hostel)

Brennesstrasse 23,

94252 Bayerisch Eisenstein

Phone: 09925–337

Fax: 09925–730
Rates: 21 DM per HI member
  (about $11 US)
Beds: 142
Private/family rooms: Yes
Kitchen available: Yes
Season: Closed November 11–
  December 26
Affiliation: HI-DJH
Regional office: Bavaria
Extras: Playground, volleyball,
  basketball, soccer, grill, table
  tennis, disco, laundry, meals ($)
**Must be under age twenty-seven
  to stay**

How to get there:

By bus: Contact hostel for transit
  route.
By car: Take Highway A3 from
  Nürnberg or Regenburg, exiting
  at signs for Deggendorf, then
  take Highway B11 through
  Regen and Zwiesel to Bayerisch
  Eisenstein.
By train: Direct trains run from
  Nürnberg and Regensburg to
  Bayerisch Eisenstein-Nord
  Station; or from München to
  Bayerisch Eisenstein-Süd
  Station. From either station
  walk 1½ miles to hostel or con-
  tact hostel for transit route.

JUGENDHERBERGE
SUDELFELD

(Bayrischzell Hostel)
Unteres Sudelfeld 9,

83735 Bayrischzell

Phone: 08023–675

Fax: 08023–274
Rates: 23 DM per HI member
  (about $12 US)

Beds: 94
Private/family rooms: Yes
Kitchen available: No
Season: Closed November 11–
  December 27
Affiliation: HI-DJH
Regional office: Bavaria
Extras: Tennis court, volleyball,
  basketball, table tennis, game
  room, meals ($)
**Must be under age twenty-seven
  to stay**

How to get there:

By bus: Contact hostel for transit
  details.
By car: Take Highway A8, exiting
  at signs for Weyarn and following signs toward Tatzelwurm. Or
  take Highway A8 to A93 in the
  direction of Innsbruck, exiting
  at signs for Brannenburg or
  Oberaudorf. Follow signs in
  direction of Bayrischzell 3 miles
  to Bayrischzell.
By train: Trains run from
  München to Bayrischzell.
  Contact hostel for further transit
  details.

UMWELTSTUDIENPLATZ/
JUGENDHERBERGE
BENEDIKTBEUERN

(Benediktbeuern Hostel)
Bahnhofstrasse 58,

83671 Benediktbeuern

Phone: 08857–9050

Fax: 08857–694–680
E-mail: dJugendherberge.
  don.bosco.schwester@iló.de
Rates: 25 DM per HI member
  (about $13 US)
Beds: 130
Private/family rooms: Yes

Kitchen available: No
Season: Closed December 15–
January 15
Affiliation: HI-DJH
Regional office: Bavaria
Extras: Grounds, table tennis,
meditation room, bike rentals,
tours, meals ($), wheelchair
access
**Must be under age twenty-seven
to stay**

How to get there:

By bus: Contact hostel for transit
details.
By car: Take Highway A95 from
München or Garmisch, exiting
at signs for for Sindelsdorf.
By train: From München take
train toward Kochel, getting off
at Benediktbeuern. Contact hostel for further transit details.

DON-BOSCO-
JUGENDHERBERGE
(Benediktbeuern Hostel)

Umweltstudienplatz

Don-Bosco-Strasse 3,

83671 Benediktbeuern

Phone: 08857–88350

Fax: 08857–88351
E-mail: lichtenstern
@don-bosco-Jugendherberge.de
Web site: www.don-bosco-
Jugendherberge.de
Rates: 25 DM per HI member
(about $13 US)
Beds: 170
Private/family rooms: Yes
Kitchen available: No
Season: Closed December 15–
January 10
Affiliation: HI-DJH
Regional office: Bavaria

Extras: Sports facility, climbing
wall, bicycles, soccer field,
grill, disco, children's play
room, nature study, parking,
meals ($)
**Must be under age twenty-seven
to stay**

How to get there:

By bus: Contact hostel for transit
details.
By car: Take Highway A95 from
München or Garmisch, exiting
at signs for Sindelsdorf.
By train: Take train from
München or Kochel to
Benediktbeuern. From
Benediktbeuern Station walk ¼
mile to hostel.

JUGENDHERBERGE
BERGEN
(Bergen Hostel)

Hochfellnstrasse 18,

83346 Bergen

Phone: 08662–48830

Fax: 08662–48838
Rates: 21 DM per HI member
(about $11 US)
Beds: 40
Private/family rooms: No
Kitchen available: No
Season: Closed November 11–
December 25
Affiliation: HI-DJH
Regional office: Bavaria
Extras: Volleyball, grill, table ten-
nis, ski rentals, sled rentals,
meals ($), parking
**Must be under age twenty-seven
to stay**

How to get there:

By bus: Contact hostel for transit
details.

By car: Take Highway A8, exiting at signs for Bergen, then take Hauptstrasse to the Esso gas station.

By train: Trains run from München and Salzburg to Bergen. From Bergen Station walk 1½ miles to hostel. Or contact hostel for transit details.

JUGENDHERBERGE BODENMAIS

(Bodenmais Hostel)

Am Kleinen Arber,

94249 Bodenmais

Phone: 09924–281

Fax: 09924–850
Rates: 23 DM per HI member (about $12 US)
Beds: 71
Private/family rooms: Yes
Kitchen available: No
Season: Closed April 20–May 20; November 11–December 26
Affiliation: HI-DJH
Regional office: Bavaria
Extras: Volleyball, soccer field, table tennis, grill, ski rental, ski trails nearby, laundry, meals ($)
Must be under age twenty-seven to stay

How to get there:

By bus: Contact hostel for transit route.

By car: Take highway to Bodenmais, then continue to Tal. From Arbersessellift cable-car station, park and take gondola to Berg, then walk ½ mile to hostel. Or contact hostel for directions.

By train: Take train to Bodenmais, then contact hostel for transit route.

JUGENDHERBERGE BURGHAUSEN

(Burghausen Hostel)

Kapuzinergasse 235,

84489 Burghausen

Phone: 08677–4187

Fax: 08677–911–318
E-mail: Jugendherbergeburghaus @aol.com
Web site: www.burghausen.de
Rates: 21 DM per HI member (about $11 US)
Beds: 110
Private/family rooms: Yes
Kitchen available: Yes
Season: Closed December 1–31
Affiliation: HI-DJH
Regional office: Bavaria
Extras: Music school, grounds, volleyball, badminton, table tennis, bike rentals, grill, gym, pottery room, wheelchair access, laundry, meals ($), parking
Must be under age twenty-seven to stay

How to get there:

By bus/train: Trains run from München and Mühldorf to Burghausen. From Burghausen Station take Citybus to Jugendherberge (hostel) stop.

By car: Take Highway A3 to Straubing, then Highway B20 to Burghausen. Or take Highways B12 and A97 from München.

JUGENDHERBERGE COBURG

(Coburg Hostel)

Parkstrasse 2,

96450 Coburg

Phone: 09561–15330

Fax: 09561–28653
Rates: 23 DM per HI member
(about $12 US)
Beds: 128
Private/family rooms: Yes
Kitchen available: No
Season: Closed December 15–
January 15
Affiliation: HI-DJH
Regional office: Bavaria
Extras: Table tennis, grill, piano,
disco, music room, game room,
meals ($)
**Must be under age twenty-seven
to stay**

How to get there:

By bus/train: From Coburg Station
take #1 bus to Ketschendorf-
Jugendherberge stop or #6 bus
to Neue Heimat stop and walk
to hostel.
By car: Take Highway A7, then
Highway A73/B4 to Coburg; or
from Hof take Highway
B173/303; or from Erfurt take
Highway B4.

JUGENDGÄSTEHAUS DACHAU

**(Dachau Guest House
Hostel)**
**Rosswachtstrasse 15,
85221 Dachau**
Phone: 08131–322–950

Fax: 08131–322–9550
E-mail: JugendgästehausDachau
@dJugendherberge-bayern.de
Rates: 33 DM per HI member
(about $17 US)
Beds: 110
Private/family rooms: Yes
Kitchen available: Yes

Season: Open year-round
Affiliation: HI-DJH
Regional office: Bavaria
Extras: Restaurant ($), wheelchair
access, parking, bar/cafeteria,
table tennis, pool table, foosball, small performance stage,
**Must be under age twenty-seven
to stay**

How to get there:

By bus/train: From München
Station take the S-Bahn or local
train to Dachau Station. Then
take #726 or #720 bus to
John-F.-Kennedy-Platz stop and
walk to hostel.
By car: Take Highway B304 from
Müchen to Karlsfeld, exiting for
Dachau/Ost, and follow signs in
direction of Dachau. Or from
Nürnberg take Highway A92 (or
from Stuttgart Highway A8),
exiting at signs for Dachau, then
take Highway B471 to Dachau.

JUGENDHERBERGE ERLANGEN

(Erlangen Hostel)
**Südl. Stadtmauerstrasse 35,
91054 Erlangen**
**Phone: 09131–862–274;
Anmeldungen:
09131–862–555**

Fax: 09131–862–119
Rates: 21 DM per HI member
(about $11 US)
Beds: 66
Private/family rooms: No
Kitchen available: No
Season: Closed December 23–
January 2
Affiliation: HI-DJH

Regional office: Bavaria

Extras: Boats, piano, TV room, meals ($)

Must be under age twenty-seven to stay

How to get there:

By bus/train: Direct trains run from Frankfurt, Würzburg, Bamberg, and Nürnberg. From Erlangen Station walk to Hugenottenplatz and take #284, #285, #286, #287, or #294 bus to Langemarckplatz stop, then walk 150 yards to hostel.

By car: Take Highway A3 from Würzburg to Nürnberg, exiting for Erlangen-West or Erlangen-Tennenlohe.

How to get there:

By bus/train: Take train to Ansbach Station or Dombühl Station, then take bus to Feuchtwangen, and walk ½ mile from center of town to hostel. Or contact hostel for transit route.

By car: Take Highway B25, Romantischen Strasse (Romantic Road), or Highway A7 from Würzburg and Kempten; exit for Feuchtwangen. Or take Highway A6 from Heilbronn or Nürnberg, exiting for Dorfgütingen. Once in Feuchtwangen follow signs toward Bechhofen.

JUGENDHERBERGE FEUCHTWANGEN

(Feuchtwangen Hostel)

Dr.-Hans-Güthlein-Weg 1, 91555 Feuchtwangen

Phone: 09852–670–990

Fax: 09852–670–9920

Rates: 21 DM per HI member (about $11 US)

Beds: 74

Private/family rooms: Yes

Kitchen available: No

Season: Closed December 20–January 2

Affiliation: HI-DJH

Regional office: Bavaria

Extras: Grounds, table tennis, grill, foosball, piano, parking, meals ($)

Must be under age twenty-seven to stay

JUGENDHERBERGE FRAUENAU

(Frauenau Hostel)

Hauptstrasse 29 a, 94258 Frauenau

Phone: 09926–735

Fax: 09926–735

Rates: 17.50 DM per HI member (about $9.00 US)

Beds: 24

Private/family rooms: No

Kitchen available: Yes

Season: Closed December 1–31

Affiliation: HI-DJH

Regional office: Bavaria

Extras: Table tennis, meals ($)

Must be under age twenty-seven to stay

How to get there:

By bus/train: Trains run from Platting or Deggendorf to Zwiesel; from train station take bus to Frauenau.

By car: Take Staatsstrasse from Zwiesel to Grafenau.

JUGENDHERBERGE FURTH IM WALD
(Furth im Wald Hostel)
Daberger Strasse 50,
93437 Furth im Wald
Phone: 09973–9254

Fax: 09973–2447
Rates: 21 DM per HI member (about $11 US)
Beds: 128
Private/family rooms: Yes
Kitchen available: No
Season: Closed November 11– December 26
Affiliation: HI-DJH
Regional office: Bavaria
Extras: Beach volleyball, table tennis, piano, bike tours, sled rental, disco, fireplace, meals ($)
Must be under age twenty-seven to stay
How to get there:
By bus/train: Trains run from Nürnberg or Prague to Furth im Wald. From Furth im Wald Station contact hostel for transit route.
By car: Take Highway B20 to Furth im Wald.

JUGENDHERBERGE GÖSSWEINSTEIN
(Gössweinstein Hostel)
Etzdorfer Strasse 6,
91327 Gössweinstein
Phone: 09242–259

Fax: 09242–7135
Rates: 21 DM per HI member (about $11 US)
Beds: 129
Private/family rooms: Yes
Kitchen available: No
Season: Closed December 1– January 15
Affiliation: HI-DJH
Regional office: Bavaria
Extras: Table tennis, volleyball, soccer field, basketball, grill, boat rentals, boat rides, meals ($)
Must be under age twenty-seven to stay
How to get there:
By bus/train: From Forchheim Station or Pegnitz Station take bus to Gössweinstein and walk ½ mile to hostel.
By car: Take Highway A3 from Frankfurt or Nürnberg, exiting at signs for Höchstadt Süd. Or take Highway A9 from München or Berlin, exiting at signs for Pegnitz/Gräfenwöhr. Or take Highway A73 from Bayreuth, exiting at signs for Forchheim-Süd.

JUGENDHERBERGE GUNZENHAUSEN
(Gunzenhausen Hostel)
Spitalstrasse 3,
91710 Gunzenhausen
Phone: 09831–67020

Fax: 09831–670–211
Rates: 23 DM per HI member (about $12 US)
Beds: 132
Private/family rooms: Yes

Kitchen available: Yes
Season: Open year-round
Affiliation: HI-DJH
Regional office: Bavaria
Extras: Table tennis, volleyball courts, playground, bike rentals, water sports nearby, meals ($), laundry, parking, wheelchair access
Must be under age twenty-seven to stay

How to get there:

By bus/train: Direct trains run from Würzburg and Nürnberg to Gunzenhausen. From Gunzenhausen Station contact hostel for transit route.

By car: Take Highway A6 from Heilbronn or Nürnberg, exiting at signs for Ansbach to Highway B13. Or from the A6 exit for Schwabach-West and take Highway B466. Gunzenhausen is at junction of routes B13 and B466.

JUGENDHERBERGE GÜNZBURG "ADOLF-KOLPING-JUGENDHERBERGE"

(Günzburg Hostel)
Schillerstrasse 12,
89312 Günzburg
Phone: 08221–34487

Fax: 08221–31390
Rates: 21 DM per HI member (about $11 US)
Beds: 34
Private/family rooms: Yes
Kitchen available: No
Season: Closed November 15–January 15

Affiliation: HI-DJH
Regional office: Bavaria
Extras: Soccer field, volleyball, basketball, table tennis, grill, canoe rides, inner tubes, bike trails, meals ($)
Must be under age twenty-seven to stay

How to get there:

By bus/train: Trains run from Stuttgart and Ulm. From Günzburg Station walk 1 mile to hostel. Or contact hostel for transit details.

By car: Take Highway A8 from Stuttgart or München, exiting for Günzburg, then stay on Highway B16 to Günzburg (2 miles). Or exit for Ulm-Leipheim, take the B10 to Günzburg (5 miles).

JUGENDHERBERGE FRAUENBERG

(Haidmühle Hostel)
Frauenberg 45,
94145 Haidmühle
Phone: 08556–467

Fax: 08556–1021
Rates: 21 DM per HI member (about $11 US)
Beds: 157
Private/family rooms: Yes
Kitchen available: No
Season: Closed November 11–December 26
Affiliation: HI-DJH
Regional office: Bavaria
Extras: Table tennis, basketball, volleyball, piano, ski trails nearby, ski storage room, disco, meals ($), laundry

Must be under age twenty-seven to stay

How to get there:

By bus/train: From Passau Station take bus to Haidmühle and walk 1 mile to hostel.

By car: Take Highway A3 to Passau. Then take Highway B12 to Abzweigung Waldkirchen, continuing to Altreichenau and 2½ miles more to Haidmühle.

JUGENDHERBERGE HARTENSTEIN

(Hartenstein Hostel)

Salzlecke 10,

91235 Hartenstein

Phone: 09152–1296

Fax: 09152–1328
Rates: 21 DM per HI member (about $11 US)
Beds: 68
Private/family rooms: No
Kitchen available: No
Season: Closed December 15–January 15
Affiliation: HI-DJH
Regional office: Bavaria
Extras: Sports fields, grill, sports facilities, volleyball, basketball, table tennis, ski rental, meals ($)
Must be under age twenty-seven to stay

How to get there:

By bus: Contact hostel for transit details.

By car: Take Highway A9 from Nürnberg or Berlin, exiting for Homersdorf or Plech.

By train: Direct trains run from Frankfurt and Würzburg to Hersbrucker or Velden. From Velden Station walk 1½ miles to hostel.

JUGENDHERBERGE HOF

(Hof Hostel)

Beethovenstrasse 44,

95032 Hof/Saale

Phone: 09281–93277

Fax: 09281–92016
Rates: 21 DM per HI member (about $11 US)
Beds: 91
Private/family rooms: Yes
Kitchen available: No
Season: Closed December 1–28
Affiliation: HI-DJH
Regional office: Bavaria
Extras: Table tennis, volleyball, grill, playground, bike trails, hiking trails, laundry, meals ($)
Must be under age twenty-seven to stay

How to get there:

By bus/train: Direct trains run from Nürnberg and Berlin to Hof. From Hof Station take #3 or #7 bus to Münsterschule stop, then walk ½ mile to hostel.

By car: Take Highway A9 from Nürnberg or Berlin, exiting at signs for Hof and following signs in direction of the Klinikum.

JUGENDHERBERGE BURG HOHENBERG

(Hohenberg an der Eger Hostel)

Auf der Burg (Postfach 24), 95691 Hohenberg an der Eger

Phone: 09233-77260

Fax: 09233-772-611
E-mail: sswhohenberg@t-online.de
Web site: www.burghohenberg.de
Rates: 21-35 DM per HI member (about $11-$18 US)
Beds: 130
Private/family rooms: Yes
Kitchen available: No
Season: Closed December 21-26
Affiliation: HI-DJH
Regional office: Bavaria
Extras: Volleyball, grill, table tennis, laundry, piano
No age limit

How to get there:
By bus/train: Take train to Schirnding. From Schirnding Station catch bus to Hohenberg.
By car: Take Highway 303 to Schirnding and then Hohenberg.

JUGENDHERBERGE KELHEIM

(Ihrlerstein Hostel)

Kornblumenweg 1, 93346 Ihrlerstein

Phone: 09441-3309

Fax: 09441-21792
Rates: 19 DM per HI member (about $10 US)
Beds: 112
Private/family rooms: Yes
Kitchen available: No
Season: Closed December 15-31
Affiliation: HI-DJH
Regional office: Bavaria
Extras: Table tennis, pool table, foosball, volleyball, meals ($), laundry, grill
Must be under age twenty-seven to stay

How to get there:
By bus/train: From Saal Station take bus to Kelheim/Wöhrplatz, getting off at Ihrlerstein stop. Walk 1½ miles to hostel.
By car: Take Highway B16 from Ingolstadt or Regensburg, exiting at signs for Kelheim; or take Highway A9/A93 from München to Regensburg, exiting at signs for Abensberg. In Kelheim head in direction of Hemau to Ihrlerstein.

JUGENDHERBERGE KEMPTEN

(Kempten Hostel)

Saarlandstrasse 1, 87437 Kempten

Phone: 0831-73663

Fax: 0831-770-381
Rates: 19 DM per HI member (about $10 US)
Beds: 82
Private/family rooms: No
Kitchen available: No
Season: Closed November 1-December 27
Affiliation: HI-DJH
Regional office: Bavaria
Extras: Playground, table tennis, volleyball, meals ($)
Must be under age twenty-seven to stay

How to get there:
By bus/train: Direct trains run from München and Ulm to Kempten. From Kempten

Station take #4 bus to hostel.
By car: Take Highway A7 from Ulm to Kempten, exiting at signs for Kempten-Leubas; or from München take Highway B12 to Berliner Platz, then head in direction of Füssen.

JUGENDHERBERGE KOCHEL

(Kochel Hostel)
Badstrasse 2,
82431 Kochel
Phone: 08851–5296

Fax: 08851–7019
Rates: 21 DM per HI member (about $11 US)
Beds: 31
Private/family rooms: No
Kitchen available: No
Season: Closed November 15– December 26
Affiliation: HI-DJH
Regional office: Bavaria
Extras: Meals ($), table tennis, rafting and kayaks nearby
Must be under age twenty-seven to stay

How to get there:

By bus: Contact hostel for transit details.
By car: Take Highway A95 from München to Garmisch, exiting for Murnau-Kochel.
By train: Direct train runs from München to Kochel. From Kochel Station walk ½ mile to hostel.

JUGENDHERBERGE KÖNIGSBERG

(Königsberg Hostel)
Schlossberg 10,
97486 Königsberg
Phone: 09525–237

Fax: 09525–8114
Rates: 19 DM per HI member (about $10 US)
Beds: 89
Private/family rooms: Yes
Kitchen available: No
Season: Closed December 15– January 7
Affiliation: HI-DJH
Regional office: Bavaria
Extras: Table tennis, grill, piano, game room, foosball, parks nearby, meals ($)
Must be under age twenty-seven to stay

How to get there:

By bus/train: Direct trains run from Würzburg, Nürnberg, and Bamberg to Hassfurt. From Hassfurt Station take bus to Königsberg.
By car: Take Highway A70, exiting for Hassfurt or exiting for Königsberg.

JUGENDHERBERGE KREUTH AM TEGERNSEE (Kreuth am Tegernsee Hostel)

Nördl. Hauptstrasse 91,
83708 Kreuth am Tegernsee
Phone: 08029–99560
Fax: 08029–995–629

Rates: 23 DM per HI member (about $12 US)
Beds: 103
Private/family rooms: Yes
Kitchen available: No
Season: Closed November 1– December 26
Affiliation: HI-DJH
Regional office: Bavaria
Extras: Table tennis, foosball, disco, meals ($), laundry
Must be under age twenty-seven to stay

How to get there:

By bus/train: Trains run from München to Tegernsee. From Tegernsee Station take bus to Kreuth-Scharling; contact hostel for transit details.

By car: Take Highway A8 from München and Salzburg, exiting for Holzkirchen, then take Highway B318 in the direction of Tegernsee. Continue through Bad Wiessee in the direction of Achensee, exiting at signs for Scharling.

JUGENDHERBERGE KRONACH
(Kronach Hostel)
Festung 1,

96317 Kronach

Phone: 09261–94412 or 09261–97312

Rates: 19 DM per HI member (about $10 US)
Beds: 106
Private/family rooms: No
Kitchen available: No
Season: Closed December 15– February 27

Affiliation: HI-DJH
Regional office: Bavaria
Extras: Sports facilites, table tennis, grill, Internet access, laundry
Must be under age twenty-seven to stay

How to get there:

By bus: Contact hostel for transit details.
By car: Contact hostel for directions.
By train: Take train from München or Berlin to Kronach. From Kronach Station walk ¾ mile to hostel.

JUGENDHERBERGE LAM
(Lam Hostel)
Jugendherbergsweg 1,

93462 Lam

Phone: 09943–1068

Fax: 09943–2936
Rates: 21 DM per HI member (about $11 US)
Beds: 130
Private/family rooms: Yes
Kitchen available: No
Season: Closed November 1– December 26
Affiliation: HI-DJH
Regional office: Bavaria
Extras: Playground, volleyball, basketball, grill, table tennis, disco, meals ($)
Must be under age twenty-seven to stay

How to get there:

By bus/train: Trains run from Nürnberg to Lam. From Lam Station walk 1 mile to hostel or take bus; contact hostel for transit details.

By car: Take highway from Nürnberg through Amberg, Cham, and Kötzting to Lam; or from München via Deggendorf, Bodenmais, and Arnbruck to Lam.

JUGENDHERBERGE LANDSHUT
(Landshut Hostel)
**Richard-Schirrmann-Weg 6,
84028 Landshut
Phone: 0871–23449**

Fax: 0871–274–947
E-mail: stadt.landshut. Jugendherberge@landshut.org.
Rates: 21–30 DM per HI member (about $11–$15 US)
Beds: 100
Private/family rooms: Yes
Kitchen available: Yes
Season: Closed December 23– January 7
Affiliation: HI-DJH
Regional office: Bavaria
Extras: Volleyball, table tennis, grill, foosball, TV room, laundry, wheelchair access, meals ($)
Must be under age twenty-seven to stay

How to get there:
By bus/train: Direct trains run from München, Nürnberg, or Regensburg. From Landshut Station walk 2 miles to hostel or take #1, #3 or #6 bus to Old Town.
By car: Take Highway B15 from Regensburg or Highway B11

from München or Highway A92 from München-Deggensdorf.

JUGENDHERBERGE WEISSENBRUNN
(Leinburg Hostel)
**Badstrasse 15,
91227 Leinburg
Phone: 09187–1529**

Fax: 09187–5920
Rates: 17.50 DM per HI member (about $9.00 US)
Beds: 60
Private/family rooms: No
Kitchen available: No
Season: Closed December 1– January 15
Affiliation: HI-DJH
Regional office: Bavaria
Extras: Table tennis, piano, meals ($)
Must be under age twenty-seven to stay

How to get there:
By bus/train: Trains run from Nürnberg to Altdorf. From Altdorf Station take bus to Weissenbrunn, then walk ¼ mile to hostel. Or from Nürnberg take S-Bahn-Anschluss.
By car: Take Highway A6 from Nürnberg or Amberg, exiting for Altdorf/Leinburg.

JUGENDHERBERGE LOHR
(Lohr Hostel)
**Brunnenwiesenweg 13,
97816 Lohr
Phone: 09352–2444**

Fax: 09352–70873
Rates: 23 DM per HI member
(about $12 US)
Beds: 94
Private/family rooms: Yes
Kitchen available: No
Season: Closed December 15–
January 31
Affiliation: HI-DJH
Regional office: Bavaria
Extras: Table tennis, disco, foos-
ball, grill, meals ($)
**Must be under age twenty-seven
to stay**
How to get there:
By bus: Contact hostel for transit
details.
By car: Take Highway A3 from
Frankfurt or Würzburg, exiting
for Rohrbrunn or
Marktheidenfeld, then take
Highway B26 or B27.
By train: Trains run from
Frankfurt and Würzburg. From
Lohr Station walk 1 mile to
hostel.

JUGENDHERBERGE
MARKTREDWITZ
(Marktredwitz Hostel)
Wunsiedler Strasse 29,
95615 Marktredwitz
Phone: 09231–81082

Fax: 09231–87346
Rates: 19 DM per HI member
(about $10 US)
Beds: 40
Private/family rooms: No
Kitchen available: No
Season: Open year-round
Affiliation: HI-DJH

Regional office: Bavaria
Extras: Table tennis, grill, walking
trails, labyrinth nearby, meals
($)
**Must be under age twenty-seven
to stay**
How to get there:
By bus: Contact hostel for transit
route.
By car: Take Highways B303,
E48, and B15 (or A93).
By train: Trains run from
München, Berlin, and Nürnberg
to Marktredwitz. From Mark-
tredwitz Station walk 1 mile to
hostel.

JUGENDHERBERGE
MAUTH
(Mauth Hostel)
Jugendherbergsstrasse 11,
94151 Mauth
Phone: 08557–289

Fax: 08557–1581
Rates: 21 DM per HI member
(about $11 US)
Beds: 96
Private/family rooms: Yes
Kitchen available: No
Season: Closed November 1–
December 26
Affiliation: HI-DJH
Regional office: Bavaria
Extras: Table tennis, disco, grill,
ski storage room, sports nearby,
laundry, meals ($)
**Must be under age twenty-seven
to stay**
How to get there:
By bus/train: Take train from
Munich to Passau. From Passau

Station take bus to Mauth.

By car: Take Highway A3 from
Deggendorf or Passau, exiting
for Hengersberg in direction of
Grafenau and Freyung. Exit at
Freyung, then continue 7 miles
to Mauth.

JUGENDHERBERGE
MEMMINGEN

(Memmingen Hostel)

Kempter Strasse 42,

87700 Memmingen

Phone: 08331–494–087

Fax: 08331–494–087
Rates: 17.50 DM per HI member
(about $9.00 US)
Beds: 60
Private/family rooms: Yes
Kitchen available: No
Season: Closed December 1–
February 28
Affiliation: HI-DJH
Regional office: Bavaria
Extras: Garden, playground, grill,
table tennis, foosball, game
room, meals ($)
**Must be under age twenty-seven
to stay**

How to get there:

By bus: Contact hostel for transit
details.
By car: Take Highway A7 from
Ulm or Kempten, exiting at
signs for Memmingen Süd or at
B18. From München take
Highway B18 (via Kreisverkehr),
exiting in the direction of
Kempten.
By train: From Memmingen
Station walk ⅓ mile to hostel.

JUGENDHERBERGE
MÜHLDORF

(Mühldorf Hostel)

Friedrich-Ludwig-Jahn-
Strasse 19,

84453 Mühldorf/Inn

Phone: 08631–7370

Fax: 08631–7437
Rates: 17.50 DM per person
(about $9.00 US)
Beds: 52
Private/family rooms: No
Kitchen available: Yes
Season: Contact hostel for current
season
Affiliation: HI-DJH
Regional office: Bavaria
Extras: Grill, table tennis, disco,
meals ($)
**Must be under age twenty-seven
to stay**

How to get there:

By bus: Contact hostel for transit
details.
By car: Take Highway B12 from
München or Passau.
By train: Trains run from
München, Passau, and
Landshut. From Mühldorf
Station walk 1 mile to hostel.

JUGENDHERBERGE
NEUREICHENAU
"ROSENBERGERGUT"

(Neureichenau Hostel)

Ortsteil Lackenhäuser 146

94089 Neureichenau

Phone: 08583–1239

Fax: 08583–1566

Rates: 19 DM per HI member (about $10 US)
Beds: 109
Private/family rooms: Yes
Kitchen available: No
Season: Closed December 15–26
Affiliation: HI-DJH
Regional office: Bavaria
Extras: Playground, volleyball, basketball, winter sports program, hikes in national park, table tennis, ski storage room, meals ($)
Must be under age twenty-seven to stay

How to get there:

By bus/train: Take train from München to Passau. From Passau Station take bus to Neureichenau.

By car: Take Highway B12 from Passau, going through Waldkirchen, Jandelsbrunn, and Lackenhäuser.

JUGENDHERBERGE WALDHÄUSER-NEUSCHÖNAU

(Neuschönau Hostel)

Umweltstudienplatz

Herbergsweg 2,

94556 Neuschönau

Phone: 08553–6000

Fax: 08553–829
Rates: 25 DM per HI member (about $13 US)
Beds: 117
Private/family rooms: Yes
Kitchen available: Yes
Season: Closed November 15–December 26
Affiliation: HI-DJH
Regional office: Bavaria
Extras: Volleyball, basketball, table tennis, grill, disco, nature study room, winter sports, meals ($), laundry
Must be under age twenty-seven to stay

How to get there:

By bus/train: From Grafenau Station take bus to Waldhäuser.

By car: Take Autobahn from Regensburg or Passau, exiting at signs for Hengersberg and continuing in direction of Schönberg, Grafenau, and St. Oswald. Go through Waldhäuser, then take Staatsstrasse from Zwiesel to Grafenau.

JUGENDHERBERGE OTTOBEUREN

(Ottobeuren Hostel)

Kaltenbrunnweg 11,

87724 Ottobeuren

Phone: 08332–368

Fax: 08332–7219
Rates: 17.50 DM per HI member (about $9.00 US)
Beds: 102
Private/family rooms: No
Kitchen available: No
Season: Closed November 30–February 28
Affiliation: HI-DJH
Regional office: Bavaria
Extras: Meals ($), volleyball, grill, table tennis
Must be under age twenty-seven to stay

How to get there:

By bus/train: From Memmingen Station take bus to Otable tennisobeuren.

By car: Take Highway A7 from Ulm or Kempten, exiting for Memmingen Süd; or take Highway A96 from München or Lindau, exiting for Erkheim and continuing to Otable tennisobeuren.

JUGENDHERBERGE POTTENSTEIN

(Pottenstein Hostel)
Jugendherbergsstrasse 20,
91278 Pottenstein
Phone: 09243–92910

Fax: 09243–929–111
Rates: 21 DM per HI member (about $11 US)
Beds: 163
Private/family rooms: Yes
Kitchen available: No
Season: Open year-round
Affiliation: HI-DJH
Regional office: Bavaria
Extras: Table tennis, volleyball, grill, piano, meals ($), wheelchair access
Must be under age twenty-seven to stay

How to get there:

By bus/train: Direct trains run from Nürnberg and Bayreuth. From Pegnitz Station take bus to Potable tennisenstein, then walk ¾ mile to hostel.
By car: Take Highway A9 from Nürnberg or Berlin, exiting for Pegnitz/Grafenwöhr, then follow B470. Or take Highway A3 from Nürnberg or Frankfurt, exiting for Höchstadt-Ost, then continue through Forchheim.

JUGENDHERBERGE ROTHENFELS

(Rothenfels Hostel)
97851 Rothenfels
Phone: 09393–99999

Fax: 09393–99997
Rates: 21 DM per HI member (about $11 US)
Beds: 168
Private/family rooms: No
Kitchen available: No
Season: Closed April 14–24; December 15–January 5
Affiliation: HI-DJH
Regional office: Bavaria
Extras: Sports facilities, piano, meals ($)
Must be under age twenty-seven to stay

How to get there:

By bus/train: From Lohr Station or Wertheim Station take #8051 bus to Rothenfels.
By car: Take Highway A3 from Frankfurt to Würzburg, exiting for Marktheidenfeld, then continue 7 miles in the direction of Lohr.

JUGENDHERBERGE SALDENBURG

(Saldenburg Hostel)
Ritter-Tuschl-Strasse 20,
94163 Saldenburg
Phone: 08504–1655

Fax: 08504–4449
Web site: http://bayerwald-info.de
Rates: 21 DM per HI member (about $11 US)

Beds: 140
Private/family rooms: Yes
Kitchen available: No
Season: Closed January 10–31;
  December 1–26
Affiliation: HI-DJH
Regional office: Bavaria
Extras: Grounds, table tennis,
  foosball, grill, volleyball, basket-
  ball, disco, piano, meals ($)
**Must be under age twenty-seven
  to stay**

How to get there:

By bus/train: Take train from
  Munich to Passau. From Passau
  Station take bus to Abzweigung
  Saldenburg stop and walk 1½
  miles to hostel.
By car: Take Highway A3 from
  Regensburg or Passau, exiting
  for Iggensbach or Garham.

JUGENDHERBERGE
SCHLIERSEE -
JOSEFSTHAL
(Schliersee Hostel)
**Josefsthaler Strasse 19,
83727 Schliersee**
Phone: 08026–97380

Fax: 08026–71610
E-mail: JugendherbergeJosefsthal
  @dJugendherberge-bayern.de
Rates: 21 DM per HI member
  (about $11 US)
Beds: 93
Private/family rooms: Yes
Kitchen available: No
Season: Closed November 1–
  December 26
Affiliation: HI-DJH
Regional office: Bavaria
Extras: Spielwiese, table tennis,

foosball, bike rentals (sometimes), laundry, meals ($)
**Must be under age twenty-seven
  to stay**

How to get there:

By bus/train: Trains run from
  München. From train station
  take bus to Josefstal or from
  Fischhausen-Neuhaus train sta-
  tion take bus to Josefstal.
By car: Take Highway A8
  München from Salzburg, exiting
  for Weyern. Go through
  Miesbach and Schliersee to
  Neuhaus, then head in the
  direction of Josefstal.

JUGENDHERBERGE
SCHWEINFURT
(Schweinfurt Hostel)
**Niederwerrner Strasse 17½,
97421 Schweinfurt**
Phone: 09721–21404

Fax: 09721–23581
E-mail: jugendherberge
  @schweinfurt.de
Rates: 21 DM per HI member
  (about $11 US)
Beds: 110
Private/family rooms: Yes
Kitchen available: No
Season: Closed December 22–
  January 8
Affiliation: HI-DJH
Regional office: Bavaria
Extras: Garden, fitness facility,
  table tennis, grill, meals ($)
**Must be under age twenty-seven
  to stay**

How to get there:

By bus: Contact hostel for transit
  details.

By car: Take Highway A7 from Kassel to Würzburg, exiting for Schweinfurt-Bamberg, or take A70 to exit for Schweinfurth-Hafen-Ost, then Highway B286.

By train: From Schweinfurt Station walk 1 mile to hostel.

JUGENDHERBERGE SPALT - WERNFELS

(Spalt Hostel)

Burgweg 7–9,

91174 Spalt

Phone: 09873–515

Fax: 09873–244
E-mail: info@cvjm-bayern.de
Web site: http://www.CVJM-Bayern.de
Rates: 23 DM per HI member (about $12 US)
Beds: 167
Private/family rooms: Yes
Kitchen available: Yes
Season: Closed December 20–27
Affiliation: HI-DJH
Regional office: Bavaria
Extras: Volleyball, meals ($), laundry, basketball, table tennis, piano,
Must be under age twenty-seven to stay

How to get there:

By bus/train: Direct trains run from Nürnberg and München to Schwabach. From Schwabach Station take bus to Wernfels.

By car: Take Highway A6 from Nürnberg or Heilbronn, exiting to Schwabach, Abenberg, Gunzenhausen, and then Wassermungenau.

JUGENDHERBERGE MAIBRUNN

(St. Englmar Hostel)

Haus-Nr. 5,

94379 St. Englmar

Phone: 09965–271

Fax: 09965–1342
Rates: 21 DM per HI member (about $11 US)
Beds: 59
Private/family rooms: No
Kitchen available: No
Season: Closed November 1–December 15
Affiliation: HI-DJH
Regional office: Bavaria
Extras: Playground, table tennis, grill, meals ($)
Must be under age twenty-seven to stay

How to get there:

By bus/train: Trains run from Regensburg and Passau. From Straubing Station take daily postbus to hostel.

By car: Take Highway A3 from Regensburg or Passau, exiting at signs for Schwarzach or Bogen. Or take Highway B85, exiting for Schwarzach.

JUGENDHERBERGE STRAUBING

(Straubing Hostel)

Friedhofstrasse 12,

94315 Straubing

Phone: 09421–80436

Fax: 09421–12094
Rates: 17.50 DM per HI member (about $9.00 US)

Beds: 57
Private/family rooms: No
Kitchen available: No
Season: Closed November 1–
March 31
Affiliation: HI-DJH
Regional office: Bavaria
Extras: Garden, table tennis,
disco, pool tables, dartboard,
foosball, grill, meals ($)
**Must be under age twenty-seven
to stay**

How to get there:

By bus: Contact hostel for transit
details.
By car: Take Highway 3 from
Regensburg or Passau, exiting
at signs for Kirchroth, then B20
or B8, exiting at signs for
Straubing.
By train: Direct trains run from
Nürnberg, Regensburg, or
Passau. From train station walk
¾ mile to hostel.

JUGENDHERBERGE TRAUNSTEIN

(Traunstein Hostel)

Trauner Strasse 22,

83278 Traunstein

Phone: 0861–4742

Fax: 0861–12382
Rates: 19 DM per HI member
(about $10 US)
Beds: 57
Private/family rooms: No
Kitchen available: No
Season: Closed December 1–
January 15
Affiliation: HI-DJH
Regional office: Bavaria
Extras: Grill, volleyball, meals ($)

**Must be under age twenty-seven
to stay**

How to get there:

By bus/train: From Traunstein
Station take bus to hostel; contact hostel for further details.
By car: Take Highway A8 from
München or Salzburg, exiting
for Siegsdorf/Traunstein and
continue to hostel.

JUGENDHERBERGE TRAUSNITZ

(Trausnitz Hostel)

Burggasse 2,

92555 Trausnitz

Phone: 09655–92150

Fax: 09655–921–531
Rates: 23 DM per HI member
(about $12 US)
Beds: 131
Private/family rooms: Yes
Kitchen available: No
Season: Open year-round
Affiliation: HI-DJH
Regional office: Bavaria
Extras: Table tennis, foosball,
badminton, basketball, pool
table, playground, disco, park-
ing, meals ($)
**Must be under age twenty-seven
to stay**

How to get there:

By bus: Contact hostel for transit
details.
By car: Take Highway A93 from
Regensburg, exiting at signs for
Pfreimd, continuing along
Staatsstrasse in direction of
Tännesberg. Continue 6 miles to
hostel.

By train: Contact hostel for transit details.

JUGENDHERBERGE URFELD/WALCHENSEE

(Walchensee Hostel)

Mitable tennisenwalder Strasse 17,

82432 Walchensee

Phone: 08851–230

Fax: 08851–1022
Rates: 23 DM per HI member (about $12 US)
Beds: 97
Private/family room: Yes
Kitchen available: No
Season: Closed November 11–December 26
Affiliation: HI-DJH
Regional office: Bavaria
Extras: Surfing, table tennis, meals ($), skiing nearby
Must be under age twenty-seven to stay

How to get there:

By bus/train: From München take train to Kochel, then change to bus and continue to Urfeld.
By car: Take Highway A95 from Münchenor Garmisch, exiting for Murnau or Kochel, then take Highway B11 in direction of Mitable tennisenwald.

JUGENDHERBERGE WALDMÜNCHEN

(Waldmünchen Hostel)

Schlosshof 1,

93449 Waldmünchen

Phone: 09972–94140

Fax: 09972–941–433
E-mail: office@jugendbil dungsstaett.org
Web site: http://www.jugend bildungsstaett.org
Rates: 23 DM per HI member (about $12 US)
Beds: 120
Private/family rooms: Yes
Kitchen available: No
Season: Open year-round
Affiliation: HI-DJH
Regional office: Bavaria
Extras: Parking, laundry, meals ($), wheelchair access, garden, volleyball, basketball, table tennis, foosball, skis
Must be under age twenty-seven to stay

How to get there:

By bus: From Schwandorf or Cham take bus to Waldmünchen; contact hostel for transit details.
By car: From the direction of München head toward Regensburg and Weiden, follow signs through Bodenwöhr, Neunburg, Rötz and Waldmünchen.
By train: From Schwandorf or Cham take train to Wald-münchen; contact hostel for transit details.

JUGENDHERBERGE WIESENTTAL-STREITBERG

(Wiesenttal Hostel)

Am Gailing 6,

91346 Wiesenttal

Phone: 09196–288

Fax: 09196–1543

Rates: 21 DM per HI member (about $11 US)
Beds: 122
Private/family rooms: Yes
Kitchen available: No
Affiliation: HI-DJH
Regional office: Bavaria
Extras: Table tennis, volleyball, basketball, grill, foosball, disco, meals ($), laundry
Must be under age twenty-seven to stay

How to get there:

By bus: Contact hostel for transit details.
By car: Take Highway A3 from Würzburg or Nürnberg, exiting at signs for Höchstadt-Süd, then take Highway B470. Or take Highway A9 from Berlin or München, exiting at signs for Pegnitz, then take Highway B470. Or take Highway A73 from Nürnberg or Bamberg, exiting at signs for Forchheim-Süd, then take Highway B470.
By train: Contact hostel for transit details.

JUGENDHERBERGE TANNENLOHE

(Windischeschenbach Hostel)
Tannenlohe 45,
92670 Windischeschenbach
Phone: 09637–1067 or 09637–267

Fax: 09637–276
Rates: 23 DM per HI member (about $12 US)
Beds: 162
Private/family rooms: Yes
Kitchen available: No

Season: Closed December 15–January 15
Affiliation: HI-DJH
Regional office: Bavaria
Extras: Saunas, grill, table tennis, fields, volleyball, meals ($), laundry, wheelchair access
Must be under age twenty-seven to stay

How to get there:

By bus: Contact hostel for transit details.
By car: Take Highway A93 from Regensburg or Weiden, exiting for Falkenberg. Or take Highway A6 from Nürnberg or Highway B22 from Bamberg or Bayreuth. Follow Highway B299 in direction of Tirschenreuth.
By train: Direct train runs from München or Nürnberg. From Wiesau Station or Reuth bei Erbendorf Station contact hostel for transit details.

JUGENDHERBERGE WIRSBERG

(Wirsberg Hostel)
Sessenreuther Strasse 31,
95339 Wirsberg
Phone: 09227–6432

Fax: 09227–902–767
Rates: 21 DM per HI member (about $11 US)
Beds: 50
Private/family rooms: Yes
Kitchen available: No
Season: Open year-round
Affiliation: HI-DJH
Regional office: Bavaria
Extras: Grill, table tennis, piano, meals ($), parking
Must be under age twenty-seven to stay

How to get there:

By bus/train: From Neuenmark/Wirsberg Station take KBS bus #8358 to Wirsberg, or walk 1½ miles to hostel.

By car: Take Highway A9 from München or Berlin, exiting at signs for Himmelkron/Bad Berneck. Head in direction of Wirsberg/Kronach.

JUGENDHERBERGE STEINEBACH

(Wörthsee Hostel)

Herbergsstrasse 10,

82237 Wörthsee

Phone: 08153–7206

Fax: 08153–89214

Rates: 17.50 DM per HI (about $9.00 US)

Beds: 30

Private/family rooms: No

Kitchen available: No

Season: Closed December 1– January 15

Affiliation: HI-DJH

Regional office: Bavaria

Extras: Meals ($), table tennis

Must be under age twenty-seven to stay

How to get there:

By bus: Contact hostel for transit details.

By car: Take Highway A96 from München or Lindau.

By train: From München take S-Bahn line S5 to Steinebach Station then walk 1 mile to hostel.

JUGENDHERBERGE WUNSIEDEL

(Wunsiedel Hostel)

Am Katharinenberg 4,

95632 Wunsiedel

Phone: 09232–1851

Fax: 09232–70629

Rates: 23 DM per HI member (about $12 US)

Beds: 112

Private/family rooms: Yes

Kitchen available: Yes

Season: Closed December 1– January 1

Affiliation: HI-DJH

Regional office: Bavaria

Extras: Table tennis, foosball, pool table, grill, skis, piano, grounds, meals ($), wheelchair access, laundry

Must be under age twenty-seven to stay

How to get there:

By bus/train: From Marktredwitz Station or Holenbrunn Station take bus and walk 100 yards to hostel.

By car: Take Highway A93 from Regensburg or München, exiting at signs for Wunsiedel. Or take Highway A9 from Berlin, Nürnberg, or München, continuing via Highway B303.

JUGENDHERBERGE ZWIESEL

(Zwiesel Hostel)

Hindenburgstrasse 26,

94227 Zwiesel

Phone: 09922–1061

Fax: 09922–60191
Rates: 21 DM per HI member
  (about $11 US)
Beds: 53
Private/family rooms: Yes
Kitchen available: No
Season: Closed November 15–
  December 26
Affiliation: HI-DJH
Regional office: Bavaria
Extras: Grill, table tennis, basket-
  ball, ski equipment, meals ($),
  parking
**Must be under age twenty-seven
  to stay**

How to get there:

By bus: Contact hostel for transit
  route.
By car: Take Highway A3 from
  Regensburg or Passau to
  Deggendorf, via Highway B11.
By train: Direct trains run from
  Nürnberg, Regensburg,
  München, and Landshut. From
  Zwiesel Station walk 1½ miles
  to hostel.

THE BEST HOSTELS
IN GERMANY

TEN OUTDOORSY HOSTELS

NINE CLASSIC GERMAN HOSTELS

EIGHT SOCIAL, PARTYIN' HOSTELS

ABOUT THE AUTHORS

Paul Karr is an award-winning writer, writing coach and author or co-author of several travel guidebooks. He contributes regularly to magazines such as *Sierra, New Age,* and *Spa,* and writes screenplays when he's not traveling. He has twice been named a writer-in-residence by the National Parks Service. You can contact him directly by e-mailing him at the following address:

Atomev@aol.com

Martha Coombs works as a translator, writer, and photographer. During the past few years she has worked on location in England, France, Italy, Canada, and the United States.